PSYCHOANALYTIC MEMOIRS

Also by Jeffrey Berman

Joseph Conrad: Writing as Rescue

The Talking Cure: Literary Representations of Psychoanalysis

Narcissism and the Novel

Diaries to an English Professor: Pain and Growth in the Classroom

Surviving Literary Suicide

Risky Writing: Self-Disclosure and Self-Transformation in the Classroom

Empathic Teaching: Education for Life

Dying to Teach: A Memoir of Love, Loss, and Learning

Cutting and the Pedagogy of Self-Disclosure (with Patricia Hatch Wallace)

Death in the Classroom: Writing about Love and Loss

Companionship in Grief: Love and Loss in the Memoirs of C.S. Lewis, John Bayley, Donald Hall, Joan Didion, and Calvin Trillin

Death Education in the Writing Classroom

Dying in Character: Memoirs on the End of Life

Confidentiality and Its Discontents: Dilemmas of Privacy in Psychotherapy (with Paul W. Mosher)

Writing Widowhood: The Landscapes of Bereavement

Writing the Talking Cure: Irvin D. Yalom and the Literature of Psychotherapy

Off the Tracks: Cautionary Tales about the Derailing of Mental Health Care (with Paul W. Mosher).

Mad Muse: The Mental Illness Memoir in a Writer's Life and Work

The Art of Caregiving in Fiction, Film, and Memoir

Norman N. Holland: The Dean of American Psychoanalytic Literary Critics

PSYCHOANALYTIC MEMOIRS

Jeffrey Berman

BLOOMSBURY ACADEMIC
LONDON • NEW YORK • OXFORD • NEW DELHI • SYDNEY

BLOOMSBURY ACADEMIC
Bloomsbury Publishing Plc
50 Bedford Square, London, WC1B 3DP, UK
1385 Broadway, New York, NY 10018, USA
29 Earlsfort Terrace, Dublin 2, Ireland

BLOOMSBURY, BLOOMSBURY ACADEMIC and the Diana logo are trademarks of
Bloomsbury Publishing Plc

First published in Great Britain 2023
Paperback edition published 2024

Copyright © Jeffrey Berman, 2023, 2024

Jeffrey Berman has asserted his right under the Copyright,
Designs and Patents Act, 1988, to be identified as Author of this work.

For legal purposes the Acknowledgements on p. ix constitute an extension
of this copyright page.

Cover design and illustration by Rebecca Heselton
Brush stroke © petekarici/ iStock. Texture © Slavica/ iStock

All rights reserved. No part of this publication may be reproduced or transmitted in any
form or by any means, electronic or mechanical, including photocopying, recording, or
any information storage or retrieval system, without prior permission in writing from the
publishers.

Bloomsbury Publishing Plc does not have any control over, or responsibility for, any thirdparty
websites referred to or in this book. All internet addresses given in this book were
correct at the time of going to press. The author and publisher regret any inconvenience
caused if addresses have changed or sites have ceased to exist, but can accept no
responsibility for any such changes.

A catalogue record for this book is available from the British Library.

Library of Congress Cataloging-in-Publication Data

Names: Berman, Jeffrey, 1945- author.
Title: Psychoanalytic memoirs / Jeffrey Berman.
Description: London ; New York : Bloomsbury Academic, 2022. |
Includes bibliographical references and index. | Summary: "The first book-length study of the
psychoanalytic memoir, this book examines key examples of the genre, including Sigmund Freud's
mistitled An Autobiographical Study, Helene Deutsch's Confrontations with Myself: An Epilogue,
Wilfred Bion's War Memoirs 1917-1919, Masud Khan's The Long Wait, Sophie Freud's
Living in the Shadow of the Freud Family, and Irvin D. Yalom and Marilyn Yalom's A Matter of
Death and Life. Offering in each chapter a brief character sketch of the memoirist, the book shows
how personal writing fits into their other work, often demonstrating the continuities and
discontinuities in an author's life as well as discussing each author's contributions to psychoanalysis,
whether positive or negative"– Provided by publisher.
Identifiers: LCCN 2022027012 | ISBN 9781350338562 (hardback) |
ISBN 9781350338609 (paperback) | ISBN 9781350338579 (ebook) |
ISBN 9781350338586 (epub) | ISBN 9781350338593
Subjects: LCSH: Psychoanalysts as authors. | Psychoanalysts–Biography–History and criticism. |
Psychoanalysis–History. | Psychoanalysis and literature.
Classification: LCC PN494.5 .B47 2022 | DDC 150.19/50922–dc23/eng/20221018
LC record available at https://lccn.loc.gov/2022027012

ISBN: HB: 978-1-3503-3856-2
PB: 978-1-3503-3860-9
ePDF: 978-1-3503-3857-9
eBook: 978-1-3503-3858-6

Typeset by Deanta Global Publishing Services, Chennai, India

To find out more about our authors and books visit www.bloomsbury.com
and sign up for our newsletters.

For Julie, as always

CONTENTS

Acknowledgments ix

INTRODUCTION 1

Chapter 1
SIGMUND FREUD: *AN AUTOBIOGRAPHICAL STUDY* 9

Chapter 2
THE WOLF-MAN: *MEMOIRS* 25

Chapter 3
HELENE DEUTSCH: *CONFRONTATIONS WITH MYSELF—AN EPILOGUE* 41

Chapter 4
WILHELM STEKEL: *AUTOBIOGRAPHY* 53

Chapter 5
C.G. JUNG: *MEMORIES, DREAMS, REFLECTIONS* 71

Chapter 6
WILFRED R. BION: *WAR MEMOIRS 1917-19* 95

Chapter 7
MARION MILNER: *ON NOT BEING ABLE TO PAINT* 109

Chapter 8
M. MASUD R. KHAN: *THE LONG WAIT* 131

Chapter 9
JEFFREY MOUSSAIEFF MASSON: *FINAL ANALYSIS* 143

Chapter 10
F. ROBERT RODMAN: *NOT DYING* 161

Chapter 11
LOUIS BREGER: *PSYCHOTHERAPY LIVES INTERSECTING* 175

Chapter 12
BRENDA WEBSTER: *THE LAST GOOD FREUDIAN* 189

Chapter 13
MADELON SPRENGNETHER: *CRYING AT THE MOVIES* — 201

Chapter 14
SOPHIE FREUD: *LIVING IN THE SHADOW OF THE FREUD FAMILY* — 215

CONCLUSION: IRVIN D. YALOM AND MARILYN YALOM—*A MATTER OF DEATH AND LIFE* — 229

Works Cited — 239
Index — 256

ACKNOWLEDGMENTS

Sections of this book first appeared in shorter and slightly different versions published as reviews in the following journals and newspapers:

W. R. Bion, *War Memoirs 1917–1919*. *Psychoanalytic Books* 9 (1998): 280–4.

Louis Breger, *Freud: Darkness in the Midst of Vision*. *American Journal of Psychotherapy* 55 (2001): 431–4.

Brenda Webster, *The Last Good Freudian*, *San Francisco Chronicle*, May 7, 2000.

Brenda Webster, *Vienna Triangle*, *San Francisco Chronicle*, January 13, 2009.

Brenda Webster, *After Auschwitz: A Love Story*, *Women's Studies* 43 (2014): 979–80.

"'One's Effort to Find a Little Truth': Ethel Schwabacher's Artistic and Psychoanalytic Odyssey." *The Psychoanalytic Review* 78 (1991): 607–27.

Madelon Sprengnether, *Mourning Freud*. *Journal of the American Psychoanalytic Association* 67 (2019): 405–10.

Sophie Freud, *Living in the Shadow of the Freud Family*. *Psychoanalytic Books* 25 (2008): 560–3.

I am grateful to Stefania Magidson for reading my chapter on Robert Rodman and for sharing with me her experience of being in analysis with him. After the death of her father, Louis Breger, his daughter Lisa Millerd kindly shared with me her impressions of reading my discussion of his work. Thanks to Madelon Sprengnether for reading my chapter on her writings.

As with my other books, I would not have been able to conduct my research without the invaluable help of the Interlibrary Loan staff at the University at Albany. Thanks to Timothy Jackson, Angela Persico, and Glen Benedict for fulfilling scores of Interlibrary Loan requests.

I am grateful to the two anonymous reviewers whose suggestions for revision strengthened the book. Thanks, as always, to my sterling editor at Bloomsbury Academic, Ben Doyle, who never lost faith in this project.

INTRODUCTION

"This is the age of the memoir," William Zinsser contends at the beginning of *Inventing the Truth* (1998). "Never have personal narratives gushed so profusely from the American soil as in the closing decade of the twentieth century. Everyone has a story to tell, and everyone is telling it" (3). Despite Zinsser's admonition, which contains more than a hint of condescension in his voice, I discovered to my surprise that there are relatively few psychoanalytic memoirs and even fewer scholarly studies of the subgenre of analysts' life writing. How odd, I thought, especially in light of Laura Marcus's observation in *Autobiography* (2018) that psychoanalysis has been an influential force in shaping twentieth-century autobiography, offering insights into identity and subjectivity. Moreover, one would think that psychoanalysts, who spend countless hours helping patients become more aware of their lives, would be interested in penning their own life stories. Of the 125 memoirs Thomas Larson lists in *The Memoir and the Memoirist* (2007), only one psychoanalytic memoir, Jung's *Memories, Dreams, Reflections*, appears. What makes the scarcity of psychoanalytic memoirs more surprising is the belief held by some literary theorists that memoirs are "little more than therapy." Sven Birkerts is sympathetic to the memoir in *The Art of Time in Memoir: Then, Again* (2008), but he concedes that the genre is symptomatic of our therapeutic self-help culture. "Were you abused, neglected, discriminated against; did you turn in your pain to pills, drink, or satanic cults? Write a memoir!" Birkerts concludes that "we cannot allow the many to wreck things for the few" (7). If the memoir betrays the national appetite for lurid confession, as Zinsser opines, reveals a shaping influence by psychoanalysis, as Marcus suggests, and encourages writing by the worried well, as Birkerts warns, does this explain psychoanalysts' reluctance to write about their own lives?

Apart from the vexed question of whether psychoanalysis is a "science," there is no doubt that psychoanalysis is an introspective art. Similarly, writing a memoir encourages introspection, the turn inward to reflect on motivation, conflicts, fears, and desires. Psychoanalysis emboldens self-disclosure, as does memoiristic writing. And psychoanalysis requires truth telling, as does the memoir, despite countless examples of fictional embellishing, as can be seen in Lauren Slater's controversial *Lying: A Metaphorical Memoir* (2000). Surely, I thought, psychoanalysts would use the writing cure to convey their passion for the talking cure. I was, alas, wrong.

A History of Psychology in Autobiography

Tellingly, unlike psychoanalysts, psychologists are not loath to write about themselves. There is, for example, the nine-volume series, *A History of Psychology in Autobiography*, which contains 120 essays by distinguished psychologists who write about their own lives. Each volume illuminates the history of psychology from its nineteenth-century origins to cognitive psychology, social psychology, and cognitive neuropsychology. The first three volumes of *A History of Psychology in Autobiography* appeared between 1930 and 1936. After a hiatus of thirty years, volumes have continued to appear, the latest, volume 9, in 2007. The editors of the series recognize, to cite the present publisher, the American Psychological Association, that "Autobiographies can provide a valuable perspective on the network of persons, publications, interpersonal relationships, and departmental politics out of which different traditions in psychology have been and are being formed" ("Preface," PsychINFO Database Record, 2007).

The history of *A History of Psychology in Autobiography* is itself interesting. A committee of eminent psychologists issued the following instructions to invited contributors, as Edwin G. Boring and Gardner Lindzey, the editors of volume 5, explained in 1967:

> The important decisions in regard to the contents of your autobiography are yours. We hope, however, that the document will devote some attention to the historical details of your life. In connection with the *facts of life*, we hope you will identify yourself with regard to such matters as place and date of birth, significant educational and professional experiences, and family. We are, of course, particularly interested in the *intellectual and professional* aspects of your life as they have influenced and been influenced by events, ideas, and persons in and out of the field of psychology. Your perception of major developments and issues within psychology during your lifetime and your relation to these events will be of special importance. We should appreciate any discussion of your *feelings, motives, and aspirations* or of significant events that would increase the reader's understanding of you and your contributions to psychology. In brief, we are interested in your intellectual life history, but at the same time we feel that it should be illuminated by as much information about your personal background and inner motives as you are ready and able to divulge. (Vol. 5, "Preface" vii)

To these questions we can add others involving therapist self-disclosure. To what extent does therapist self-disclosure facilitate patient self-disclosure? How much vulnerability is a memoirist willing to disclose to readers? Is it likely that a therapist who writes a memoir has used the same personal material, albeit in disguised form, in an earlier case study? How do therapists write about their lives without betraying the confidentiality of a patient, relative, or friend? What are the difficulties, including clinical resistances, that must be overcome for therapists to write about their lives? What are the therapeutic or countertherapeutic implications of writing a memoir? When does a memoir become a straitjacket, inhibiting an author's ability to self-disclose?

One more question. Are psychoanalytic memoirs different from those penned by other mental health professionals? Insofar as psychoanalysis may be defined, succinctly, as the study of ambivalence, and given the fact, as Freud noted wryly, that psychoanalysis brings out the worst in people, the answer to this question is likely in the affirmative.

Of the fifteen eminent men—yes, they are all men—who appear in volume 5, my favorite is Carl Rogers. Nor am I alone in appreciating Rogers. In a 2006 survey of the most influential psychotherapists, undertaken by *Psychotherapy Networker* magazine on the occasion of its twenty-fifth anniversary, respondents were asked the question, "Over the last twenty-five years, which figures have most influenced your practice?" Respondents could list up to ten people. Carl Rogers won in a landslide, as he had done a quarter of a century earlier when the magazine asked the same question. "In other words," reports Rich Simon, "the therapist who became famous for his leisurely, nondirective, open-ended, soft focus form of therapy 50 years ago remains a major role model today." Rounding out the top four on the list were Aaron Beck, the founder of cognitive therapy; Salvador Minuchin, an originator of family therapy; and Irvin Yalom, the leading existential therapist. Sigmund Freud did not make the list; Carl Jung was ranked eighth.

The single most intriguing detail we learn from Rogers's autobiography is how he discovered the secret of being a good therapist: listening attentively, and empathically, to his patients. He describes this aha! moment as a story, one that seemed to end in failure before a sudden reversal:

> I had been working with a highly intelligent mother whose boy was something of a hellion. The problem was clearly her early rejection of the boy, but over many interviews I could not help her to this insight. I drew her out, I gently pulled together the evidence she had given, trying to help her see the pattern. But we got nowhere. Finally I gave up. I told her that it seemed we had both tried, but we had failed, and that we might as well give up our contacts. She agreed. So we concluded the interview, shook hands, and she walked to the door of the office. Then she turned and asked, "Do you ever take adults for counseling here?" When I replied in the affirmative, she said, "Well then, I would like some help." She came back to the chair she had just left and began to pour out her despair about her marriage, her troubled relationship with her husband, her sense of failure and confusion, all very different from the sterile "case history" she had given before. Real therapy began then and ultimately it was highly successful—for her and for her son. (359)

We learn, additionally, about Rogers's decision to go into therapy during a time of intense personal distress. He's not afraid to reveal his vulnerability. "I have come to realize that if I can drop some of my defenses, can let myself come forth as a vulnerable person, can express some of the attitudes which feel most personal, most private, most tentative and uncertain in me, then the response from others is deep and receptive and warming" (*A History of Psychology in Autobiography*, vol. 5, 381).

Rogers was no friend of psychoanalysis. He was impressed with Otto Rank's description of his therapeutic approach but not with Rank's theories. Rogers admired the work of Erik Erikson, "a splendid person whose very appearance is therapeutic" (372). Rogers believed that although psychoanalysis as a school of thought was dead, "none but the very brave analysts mention this fact as they go on to develop theories and ways of working very remote from, or entirely opposed to, the Freudian views" (372)—a comment that has proven prescient, as we shall see.

Interestingly, many of the contributors to *A History of Psychology in Autobiography* found writing their autobiographies a "valuable experience," as the coeditors of volume 9, Gardner Lindzey and William M. Runyan, point out in the preface (ix). "Valuable" is not necessarily "therapeutic," a word that is conspicuously absent from the nine volumes, as is almost any reference to psychoanalysis. Regrettably, there is no *A History of Psychoanalysis in Autobiography*, an intriguing research project for another editor.

Patients have not been reluctant to write about their analytic experiences. There are many accounts of the talking cure, and they present conflicting views of Freud. The poet H.D. dedicates *Tribute to Freud* (1956), an account of her year in analysis in 1933, to her "blameless physician." The most curious moment in the year-long analysis occurs when Freud lays down one law: "Please, never—I mean, never at any time, in any circumstance, endeavor to defend me, if and when you hear abusive remarks made about me and my work" (86). H.D. offers only one criticism of Freud. "He said (as I remember) that women did not creatively amount to anything or amount to much, unless they had a male counterpart or a male companion from whom they drew their inspiration" (149). Contrasting H.D.'s highly idealized portrait of Freud, Joseph Wortis's *Fragment of an Analysis with Freud* (1954) presents an embattled account in which Freud comes across as aggressive, intolerant, and dogmatic. From the beginning to the end of the 1934 analysis, Wortis resents Freud's implication that psychoanalysis stood "clear and perfect, like divine revelation," and that "only those could share its secrets who enjoyed grace" (17). Wortis rejected psychoanalysis in its entirety and later became a prominent professor of psychiatry. In *My Analysis with Freud* (1977), a story of his treatment from 1921 to 1922, A. Kardiner offers a largely sympathetic account of his experience. But Kardiner, one of the founders of the New York Psychoanalytic Society, the oldest in the United States, concludes, after being an analyst for fifty-five years, that attempts to revise psychoanalytic theory were defeated by the "Keepers of the Orthodoxy" (121). *Tribute to Freud*, *Fragment of an Analysis with Freud*, and *My Analysis with Freud* could not be more different, presenting sharply different portraits of the founder of psychoanalysis.

A Note on Terminology

As I suggest in *Mad Muse: The Mental Illness Memoir in a Writer's Life and Work*, "Much ink has been spilt over the differences between autobiography, a chronological narration of one's life, and memoir, an account of only one aspect or part of one's life. The relationship between autobiography and memoir has always been complex and shifting" (11). The autobiography was considered superior in the past, as G. Thomas Couser suggests in *Memoir* (2011), but now the opposite is true. "To write memoir is to be selective," Thomas Larson observes; "to write one's autobiography is to be indiscriminate" (2). Other literary theorists make different distinctions between the two genres. The early twentieth-century German philosopher Georg Misch argued that autobiographers reveal an active relationship to the world whereas memoirists reveal a passive one, an active/passive binary that betrays differences between power and powerlessness. In her 1994 book *Auto/biographical Discourses*, Laura Marcus suggests that it is "no accident that women have tended to write 'memoirs' rather than 'autobiographies,' and that the memoir-form has been consistently belittled in autobiographical criticism" (151). Despite the distinctions between autobiography and memoir, many of the authors in my study use the terms interchangeably, as I will.

The Plan of This Book

Any study of psychoanalytic memoirs logically begins with Freud. In Chapter 1 suggest that despite his mistitled *An Autobiographical Study*, Freud objected strenuously to biographers writing about his life. Freud betrays a "hermeneutics of suspicion" toward biography and autobiography long before the expression was coined by late twentieth-century deconstructive literary theorists. An account of psychoanalytic memoirs must acknowledge Freud's hostility to biographical inquiry. Readers will decide for themselves whether the hostility is justified or betokens clinical resistance. Chapter 2 focuses on Freud's most famous patient, the "Wolf-Man." There are, in fact, four conflicting accounts of the same patient: case studies written by his two analysts, Freud and Ruth Mack Brunswick, the Wolf-Man's *Memoirs*, and a lengthy interview he gave near the end of his long life. The four accounts reveal a far more complex and contradictory portrait than readers first imagined. Chapter 3 highlights Helene Deutsch, one of the most influential early female psychoanalysts. Her memoir *Confrontations with Myself* illustrates her struggle between remaining loyal to orthodox Freudian theory while at the same time true to her instinct as a feminist pioneer. It's fascinating to see how her theoretical discussions of motherhood reveal and conceal her ambivalence toward her own parenting experiences.

The next two chapters explore two of Freud's earliest supporters who found themselves banished from his inner circle: Wilhelm Stekel and Carl Jung. Chapter 4 considers Stekel's posthumously published *Autobiography*, which evokes a far more sympathetic portrait of an analyst than the one who was pathologized by Freud and Ernest Jones simply for being a dissenter. Long before I knew anything about psychoanalysis, I came across what I thought were Stekel's words in one of my favorite twentieth-century American novels—though further research indicated an irony of which I was not aware. Chapter 5, on Carl Jung's *Memories,*

Dreams, Reflections, also published posthumously, examines a mystifying early childhood trauma. My early belief that one had to choose between Freud or Jung has changed to an appreciation of the greatness of both geniuses.

The next three explore three prominent psychoanalysts who were either born or lived in England. Chapter 6, Wilfred Bion's *War Memoirs 1917–19*, looks at his harrowing account of his experience during the First World War, one that he could never exorcise. The event haunted Bion his entire life, and he returned repeatedly to it in his clinical and fictional writings. Chapter 7, Marion Milner's *On Not Being Able to Paint*, shows how the memoir, like her other life writings, is personal without being, paradoxically, autobiographical. In Chapter 8 I show how M. Masud R. Khan's *The Long Wait* has the dubious distinction of being the most self-destructive psychoanalytic memoir, one that horrified the entire profession. One can only speculate on why the nefarious maverick Khan decided to publish a book filled with hateful and hurtful prejudice. Chapter 9 discusses another *enfant terrible*, Jeffrey Moussaieff Masson, whose memoir *Final Analysis* represents his repudiation of psychoanalysis. The vindictive apostate's sensationalistic statements about psychoanalysis generated a lawsuit that made its way to the US Supreme Court. What began as Masson's love affair with psychoanalysis went terribly wrong, and two of the world's most famous analysts, Anna Freud and Kurt Eissler, whom he had seductively courted, found themselves jilted.

Psychoanalysts seldom write memoirs about a dying spouse, and for this reason, F. Robert Rodman's *Not Dying*, the subject of Chapter 10, is noteworthy. While researching the chapter, I came across on the Amazon website a former patient who wrote about her experience reading *Not Dying*. Her response to my chapter gives us additional insights into Rodman's heartfelt story, demonstrating how an analyst's memoir may have a lifelong impact on a patient. Chapter 11, Louis Breger's *Psychotherapy Lives Intersecting*, gives us a personal insight into his lifelong experience as a clinician, showing us what worked and didn't work with his patients. My life intersected in many ways with Breger's, as can be seen in his spousal loss memoir, *The Book of Barbara*.

The final three chapters highlight memoirs written by three contemporary psychoanalytic scholars rather than clinicians. Chapter 12, on Brenda Webster's ironically titled *The Last Good Freudian*, chronicles a life spent and misspent lying on the couch. Webster, a psychoanalytic literary critic and novelist, writes with mordant humor about her experiences with the talking cure. Madelon Sprengnether's *Crying at the Movies*, the subject of Chapter 13, shows how her body began convulsing in tears in a darkened theater as she struggled to come to terms with the early loss of her father. Sprengnether is a literary critic who has written extensively on the theme of unresolved mourning in Freud, a topic that has characterized her own life. *Crying at the Movies* contains an intellectual and emotional richness that serves as a model for psychological self-discovery. I end with Sophie Freud's *Living in the Shadow of the Freud Family*, a double memoir in that she edits and annotates the life story written by her mother, Esti Freud, who was married to Freud's oldest son Martin. A retired professor of social work, Sophie Freud is a trenchant critic of psychoanalysis. The opening and closing chapters of my study thus serve as bookends, casting light on the life stories of three generations of the Freud family—and demonstrating the profound changes that have transformed psychoanalysis. In the conclusion, I discuss *A Matter of Death and Life,* by Irvin D. Yalom and Marilyn Yalom, a unique spousal loss memoir that forced the existential psychiatrist to question all of his assumptions about therapy.

Insofar as a memoir often comments on the author's other books, I offer in each chapter a brief character sketch of the memoirist, showing how personal writing fits into his or her professional work. It's instructive to see the continuities and discontinuities in an author's life, especially if the author has lived a long life. Life experience has a habit of changing theory. I also discuss each author's contributions to psychoanalysis, either positive or negative. Insofar as every interpretation reveals something about the interpreter, I remark on my changing attitude toward psychoanalysis, a subject I have studied passionately as an outsider for more than half a century.

I have not sought to be comprehensive in my study. Some excellent memoirs I mention here only fleetingly, such as Esther Menaker's *Appointment in Vienna* (1989), the story of her analytical training in the 1930s. As an aside, Menaker was the most inspiring teacher I encountered in my three years of study in the early 1980s at the National Psychological Association of Psychoanalysis (NPAP), the first nonmedical psychoanalytic institute in the country, founded by Freud's student, Theodor Reik, for whom Freud wrote *The Question of Lay Analysis* (1926). In *Norman N. Holland: The Dean of American Psychoanalytic Literary Critics* (2021), I discuss memoirs by Holland, "The Story of a Psychoanalytic Critic" (1999), and by his closest academic colleague, Murry M. Schwartz, "Psychoanalysis in My Life: An Intellectual Memoir" (2018). Other memoirs I recommend, to name only a few, include Paul Ornstein's *Looking Back* (2015), an account of his transformative encounter with Heinz Kohut, the founder of self psychology; Linda I. Meyers's *The Tell* (2018), a coming-of-age memoir about surviving her mother's suicide and learning to live with a legacy of guilt; and Susan Mailer's *In Another Place* (2019), a story about her conflicted relationship with her father, the novelist Norman Mailer, and his friendship with the psychoanalyst Robert Lindner, the author of the bestselling books *Rebel Without a Cause* and *The Fifty-Minute Hour*. My book may be the first study of psychoanalytic memoirs, but it won't be the last.

Doing Justice to Mental Life

"To do justice to the psychoanalytic conception of mental life," Maud Ellmann observes, "autobiography would have to jettison the principle of chronological development, inventing forms of narrative responsive to the dynamics of regression, deferred action, compulsive repetition, and other temporal upheavals characteristic of the primary process of the unconscious" (315). Is this one of the reasons for the scarcity of psychoanalytic memoirs: the daunting literary challenge of representing the talking cure? Few psychoanalytic memoirists can be compared to the great literary experimenters of the past century, such as James Joyce,

Virginia Woolf, Joseph Conrad, and D.H. Lawrence. Nevertheless, psychoanalytic memoirists do their best to probe the conscious and often unconscious forces that compelled them to devote their lives to the talking cure. As Ellmann remarks, psychoanalytic memoirs are often "a fragment of a great confession," to quote the title of Theodor Reik's absorbing 1949 autobiography, which itself is an allusion to the title of Goethe's autobiography. All confessional writing is dangerous whether it is based on real or imagined crimes. Memoirs are among the most personal writings, and in laying down their guard, writers expose their heightened vulnerability. Another challenge of doing justice to one's mental life is that, as Liran Razinsky points out in an essay on psychoanalysis and autobiography, "one is inspecting oneself, with the same biases, tendencies and repressions that have made certain things inaccessible to oneself in the first place" (145, n.13).

Memoiristic writing is not for the faint hearted, especially when memoirists expose their vulnerability. "Why does the act of writing generate so much anxiety?" Hilary Mantel asks in the beginning of her lacerating 2003 memoir *Giving Up the Ghost*, about her experience in 1979 when, at age twenty-seven, she was diagnosed with severe endometriosis. Surgery rendered her unable to have children, and a hormonal imbalance, worsened by medication, disrupted her life for years. After quoting Margaret Atwood's answer to the question—the written word is evidence that can be used against the writer—Mantel adds, "I used to think that autobiography was a form of weakness, and perhaps I still do. But I also think that, if you're weak, it's childish to pretend to be strong" (7). Writing is for her, as I suspect it is for most authors, psychoanalytic and otherwise, a way of writing herself into existence. She returns to this observation at the end of her memoir. "I am writing in order to take charge of the story of my childhood and my childlessness; and in order to locate myself, if not within a body, then in the narrow space between one letter and the next, between the lines where the ghosts of meaning are" (338–9). Mantel used to believe that, as a writer, she was always the smart one, the person with the last word and last laugh; but now she is ready to admit that she hasn't been smart at all—which is, paradoxically, a form of wisdom.

Most people assume that authors reveal more of their "real selves" in autobiographical than in fictional writings, but this is not always true, as three of our greatest writers realized. Ralph Waldo Emerson wrote in his journal in 1841: "Many men can write better in a mask than for themselves" (196). Nietzsche agreed in *Beyond Good and Evil*: "Every profound spirit needs a mask; nay, more, around every profound spirit there continually grows a mask, owing to the constantly false, that is to say, *superficial* interpretation of every word he utters, every step he takes, every sign of life he manifests" (426). Oscar Wilde affirmed the same truth. "Man is least himself," he quipped, "when he talks in his own person. Give him a mask, and he will tell you the truth" (389). We should not be surprised, then, that psychoanalytic memoirists, unmasked, do not convey the full truth of themselves, nor should we be puzzled, in Nietzsche's words, that to "talk much about oneself may also be a means of concealing oneself" (470).

Chapter 1

SIGMUND FREUD

An Autobiographical Study

Readers who believe that Sigmund Freud's *An Autobiographical Study* (1925) lives up to its title will be disappointed, for it contains little that is personal. There's nothing about Freud's feelings as a son, brother, husband, or father; nothing about his childhood, adolescence, or early adulthood; nothing about his interests, hobbies, or passions; nothing about his grievous losses, such as his beloved daughter Sophie's sudden death in 1920 from influenza or the death in 1923 of her orphaned four-year-old son Heinz (Heinele), Freud's favorite grandchild. *An Autobiographical Study* contains nothing, in short, about the private side of his life.

Freud cites the word *ambivalence*, coined by the Swiss psychiatrist Eugen Bleuler, but he never admits conflicting feelings toward the key figures in his professional life: Wilhelm Fliess, Josef Breuer, C.G. Jung, or his other intimate colleagues with whom he angrily broke off relations. Unlike nearly every other psychoanalytic memoirist, Freud refuses to disclose his vulnerability. Although he declares in the Postscript added in 1935 that two themes run throughout *An Autobiographical Story*, the story of his life and the history of psychoanalysis, he insists in the next sentence that "no personal experiences of mine are of any interest in comparison to my relations with that science" (*SE*, vol. 20, 71), a statement with which every student of autobiography or memoir will surely disagree.

Nevertheless, it's fascinating to read Freud's *An Autobiographical Study* for precisely what it omits, disguises, or simplifies about his life: his identification with the great heroes of the past, such as Oedipus, Moses, Alexander the Great, Hannibal, Napoleon, and Bismarck; his Jewishness; his fierce ambition; and his struggle for originality. Why was he so wary of self-disclosure in the book purportedly about the story of his life? A better title would be an *Anti-Autobiographical Study*. Erik H. Erikson observed in *Young Man Luther* (1958) that "there is always an implicit psychology behind the explicit antipsychology" (36). What is the implicit psychology, we may ask, behind Freud's *An Autobiographical Study*? Freud's other writings, including his vast correspondence, numbering over 20,000 letters, provide clues to his lifelong ambivalence toward self-disclosure.

In his late essay "Analysis Terminable and Interminable" (1937), Freud famously referred to the three "impossible professions"—government, education, and psychoanalysis (*SE*, vol. 23, 248). A fourth impossible profession for Freud was biography (and autobiography), the art of writing a subject's life. In his "Address Delivered in the Goethe House at Frankfurt," written in 1930 upon receiving the most prestigious award of his life, Freud observed that Goethe was "not only, as a poet, a great self-revealer, but also, in spite of the abundance of autobiographical records, a careful concealer" (*SE*, vol. 21, 212). Freud's characterization of Goethe is strikingly true of *himself*. To understand how Freud was a great self-revealer and careful self-concealer, we may turn briefly to *The Interpretation of Dreams*, his most autobiographical work albeit in disguised form. Harold Bloom suggests that *The Interpretation of Dreams* may be the most influential single intellectual work of the twentieth century. "Though the greatest of demystifiers, surpassing Nietzsche and Marx, Freud almost allows himself to hint that he is a secular messiah. His ultimate motive as a dream interpreter was to mask his own ambition, the mask being 'science'" (*Omens of Millennium* 108–9).

The Interpretation of Dreams

Freud's challenge in *The Interpretation of Dreams* (1900) was herculean. He recognized that the best source of dreams to analyze was his own, yet this created an immediate problem. "But if I was to report my own dreams, it inevitably followed that I should have to reveal to the public gaze more of the intimacies of my mental life than I liked, or than is normally necessary for any writer who is a man of science and not a poet" (*SE*, vol. 4, xxiii–xxiv). Freud was willing to take the risk of describing his self-analysis but not before asking his readers to put themselves in his position and treat him with indulgence. He reminds his readers in "On Dreams" (1901) that he cannot present a full interpretation of any of his dreams because he would be obliged to "betray many things which had better remain my secret." He then adds a surprising qualification: "for on my way to discovering the solution of the dream all kinds of things were revealed which I was unwilling to admit even to myself" (*SE*, vol. 5, 640).

Throughout *The Interpretation of Dreams*, Freud betrays his misgivings over self-disclosure. After citing the experimental Belgian psychologist Joseph Delboeuf's observation that psychologists are obliged to confess their own weaknesses to cast light on intractable problems, Freud reminds us that he has not presented a complete interpretation of any of his own dreams. "I have probably been wise in not putting too much faith in my readers' discretion" (*SE*, vol. 4, 105, n.2). A few pages later he dares his readers to be equally forthright. "If anyone should feel tempted to express a hasty condemnation of my reticence, I would advise him to make the experiment of being franker than I am" (*SE*, vol. 4, 121).

And yet, sixteen years before *The Interpretation of Dreams*, Freud was suspicious of self-disclosure. In an April 28, 1884, letter to his fiancée, Martha Bernays, Freud, not quite twenty-nine, boasted that he had recently destroyed all his notes, letters, and scientific writings of the past fourteen years. "As for the biographers, let them worry, we have no desire to make it too easy for them. Each one of them will be right in his opinion of 'The Development of the Hero,' and I am already looking forward to seeing them go astray" (*Letters* 141).

Freud's reference to the development of the hero is fraught with irony. The biographer Ronald C. Clark offers two shrewd comments about this passage: "first, Freud's confidence that the future would want to know about him; secondly, his obsession to wipe the slate clean, as though a future *Dozent* [university lecturer] might not wish to acknowledge, or even remember, some of the ideas he had once contemplated" (63).

One of Freud's most problematic assertions in *An Autobiographical Study* is his criticism of his future wife for impeding his fame. After describing his early life as a physician, Freud rationalizes that it was his fiancée's "fault" that he narrowly missed becoming famous in the mid-1880s, when his friend, the ophthalmologist Carl Koller, received credit for discovering the anesthetic properties of cocaine, which Freud was also experimenting with (and consuming) at the time. But why would Freud blame his future wife for this in *An Autobiographical Study*? Why blame anyone? Nor does he convince us of his magnanimity when he states on the next page that he bore his fiancée "no grudge for the interruption." A footnote tells us that in the 1924 edition, he used the words "'*mein damaliges Versäumnis*' (my omission at the time)" but changed this in the 1935 edition to "'*die damalige Störung*' (the interruption at the time)" (*SE*, vol. 20, 15, n.2), indicating the deepening of his resentment. Why didn't Freud simply say, if anything, that he came close to a serendipitous medical discovery before creating psychoanalysis?

"Unbridled Ambition"

Freud never acknowledged publicly his fierce ambition and drive for success, his "development as a hero." Many of his writings convey the impression that he was uninterested in winning fame or glory. "The trouble is I have so little ambition," he lamented to Martha on April 19, 1884 (*Letters* 105), a statement subverted by his belief that the world will not be allowed to forget his name. After achieving fame, he did not hesitate to chastise others whom he judged guilty of excessive ambition. "While I should very much like to welcome your collaboration with open arms," he reproached Georg Groddeck in a letter written on June 5, 1917, "there is one thing that bothers me: that you have evidently succeeded so little in conquering that banal ambition which hankers after originality and priority" (*Letters* 317).

Those familiar with Freud's life know that *no one* was more obsessed with originality and priority. To give only two examples of Freud's anxiety of influence, Peter L. Rudnytsky has remarked in *Reading Psychoanalysis* that Freud appropriated Groddeck's concept of the "it" (which Freud named the "id") by alleging that Groddeck borrowed the concept from Nietzsche (146). Moreover, Freud denied being influenced by Nietzsche, claiming that he didn't read the philosopher's writings, despite the fact that his library contained a complete set of Nietzsche's books, a gift from Otto Rank. (Freud once said, according to Richard Sterba, "He who wants to be original as a psychoanalyst should not have read Nietzsche"

[120].) And so it's ironic, if not disingenuous, that Freud warned Groddeck about the dangers of "unbridled ambition."

Freud repeatedly denied his own ambitions when the truth was otherwise. Examples abound of his quest for fame. In an 1873 letter to Emil Fluss—the opening letter in the 1960 volume edited by the analyst's son Ernst—the seventeen-year-old Freud advises his friend to save Freud's own letters for posterity: "I advise you as a friend, not as an interested party, to preserve them—have them bound—take good care of them—one never knows" (*Letters*, 4; Helene Deutsch cites this letter in *A Psychoanalytic Study of the Myth of Dionysus and Apollo* as an example of Freud's "dreams of immortality" [46]). Discussing in *The Interpretation of Dreams*, his pleasant surprise over being appointed an assistant professor at the University of Vienna, something he thought would not happen because of the anti-Semitic climate in that city, Freud averred that he was "not an ambitious man" (*SE*, vol. 4, 137); yet he is honest enough to admit, when interpreting one of his own dreams, how much he wanted to be a professor (*SE*, vol. 4, 271). He was also candid enough to admit receiving a reprimand, when he was seven or eight, from his father: "The boy will come to nothing," which he interprets as a "frightful blow to my ambition, for references to this scene are still constantly recurring in my dreams and are always linked with an enumeration of my achievements and successes, as though I wanted to say, 'You see, I *have* come to something'" (*SE*, vol. 4, 216).

Freud's epigraph to *The Interpretation of Dreams* is telling. "*Flectere si nequeo superos, Acheronta movebo*": "If I cannot move Heaven, I will raise Hell," from Virgil's *The Aeneid*. Freud chose a heroic epigraph because he saw himself as heroic for his discoveries. If he could not triumph, he was willing to pay the price, as he declares in *Fragment of an Analysis of a Case of Hysteria* (1905), better known as the story of Dora: "No one who, like me, conjures up the most evil of those half-tamed demons that inhabit the human breast, and seeks to wrestle with them, can expect to come through the struggle unscathed" (*SE*, vol. 7, 109). The man who disturbed the world's sleep, who called himself a "conquistador" of the unconscious, and who created a system of thought that produced, along with the Copernican and Darwinian discoveries, one of the great revolutions in history, had little need to proclaim publicly his greatness. All he needed to do, he must have thought, was to deny ambition, publicly and privately, and allow his achievements to speak for themselves. The sociologist Robert Merton concluded, after examining scores of passages in which Freud denied a concern for priority, that he exhibited a "profound interest in the question" (39). Mikkel Borch-Jacobsen and Sonu Shamdasani remark in *The Freud Files: An Inquiry into the History of Psychoanalysis* (2012) that by comparing himself to Copernicus and Darwin, Freud engages in self-canonization:

> One sees here nearly all of the key elements of the master narrative woven by Freud and his followers: the peremptory declaration of the revolutionary and epochal character of psychoanalysis, the description of the ferocious hostility and irrational "resistances" which it gave rise to, the insistence on the "moral courage" which was required to overcome them, the obliteration of rival

theories, relegated to a prehistory of the psychoanalytic science, and a lack of acknowledgement of debts and borrowings. (12)

Hero Worship

Despite disappointment over the sales of *The Interpretation of Dreams*, Freud knew that he had written a revolutionary book. "Do you suppose," he asked Fliess in a letter written on June 12, 1900, "that someday one will read on a marble tablet on this house":

> Here, on July 24, 1895,
> the secret of the dream
> revealed itself to Dr. Sigm. Freud
> (*Complete Letters of Sigmund Freud to Wilhelm Fliess* 417)

Many of Freud's early disciples saw him as a hero, as can be inferred from the title of Hanns Sachs's 1944 memoir *Freud: Master and Friend*. Sachs makes no effort to be objective:

> In a certain sense this could be called a piece of my autobiography since it concerns the personality of the man who was, and still is, a part—and certainly the most important and absorbing part—of my life. The rest of my life, whatever I may think of it, would hardly seem important to the world in general. My first opening of the *Traumdeuting* (*Interpretation of Dreams*) was the moment of destiny for me—like meeting the "femme fatale," only with a decidedly more favourable result. Up to that time I had been a young man who was supposedly studying law but not living up to the supposition—a type common enough among the middle class in Vienna at the turn of the century. When I had finished the book, I had found the one thing worthwhile for me to live for; many years later I discovered that it was the only thing I could live by. (1–2)

The man of destiny was perfect in the eyes of his disciple and, according to Sachs, Freud's wife and children. Martha Freud never wavered in her adoration of her husband: "he was a great man to her before a word of his books was written as well as afterwards" (71)—a far different impression than we receive from Freud's later biographers, who reveal that Martha regarded her husband's work as pornography. Sachs puts the best possible spin on Freud's darker qualities that others might find disturbing, such as his refusal to be reconciled with former allies who wished to restore their friendship with him, or being "strangely unmoved" by a colleague or patient's suicide: "Suicide meant to him—except in certain extreme cases—the shirking of a task, an attempt to escape in the midst of action; he felt it so strongly that his humanity was balanced by contempt" (Sachs 147).

Freud's Defensiveness

Readers of *An Autobiographical Study* cannot expect Freud to capture in a few paragraphs the complexity of his friendship with Breuer, with whom he collaborated in his first book, *Studies on Hysteria* (1895). It's misleading, however, when Freud, after describing the equivocal review the book received from the influential German neurologist Adolf von Strümpel, claimed that he was "able to laugh at the lack of comprehension which his criticism showed, but Breuer felt hurt and grew discouraged" (*SE*, vol. 20, 23). It's unlikely that Freud laughed at *any* criticism. He bristled over Breuer's increasing skepticism of psychoanalysis and felt deep ambivalence toward his former mentor and benefactor. Freud's depiction of Breuer as an intellectual coward became inscribed in the early history of psychoanalysis. Albrecht Hirschmüller points out in his 1978 biography of Breuer, translated into English in 1989, that Freud's account of his former mentor is an "interpretative reconstruction" that changed over time (131). Irvin Yalom presents us with a fascinating portrait of Breuer in his 1993 historical novel *When Nietzsche Wept*, a fictionalized but highly plausible account of mutual analysis between the physician and philosopher, each suffering from mental conflicts that undergo the talking cure. It's rare to read a story, clinical or fictional, where Freud is secondary to Breuer, but one sees in Yalom's account the latter's brilliance as a diagnostician and empathic healer.

Freud never conceded his contradictory statements about Breuer. In "On the History of the Psycho-Analytic Movement" (1914), Freud goes out of his way to praise Breuer. "[I]t was not I who had brought psycho-analysis into existence: the credit for this was due to someone else, to Josef Breuer, whose work had been done at a time when I was still a student engaged in passing my examinations (1880-1882)." Freud then mentions that colleagues believed his gratitude was hyperbolic, expressed "too extravagantly on that occasion" (*SE*, vol. 14, 7–8). Expressing gratitude, on the one hand, followed by faint/feigned praise, on the other, highlights Freud's ambivalence that he could not bring himself to confess, especially when it came to the talking cure, to which he unapologetically (and possessively) referred, in "On the History of the Psycho-Analytic Movement," as "my creation" (*SE*, vol. 14, 7). Ironically, as Louis Breger points out in his biography, effective psychotherapy is far closer to Breuer's approach than to Freud's (121).

Freud was wary of being beholden to anyone. He could not tolerate being financially indebted to Breuer, who had loaned him money, and when the latter generously offered to cancel the debt, Freud felt doubly indebted—and doubly troubled. "Recently Breuer pulled another brilliant stunt," Freud confided to Fliess on January 16, 1898. After describing in a long paragraph the details of Breuer's "deeply hurt feelings" when his younger colleague tried to pay him back, Freud concludes, "It is genuine Breuer. It is enough to make one extremely ungrateful for good deeds" (*Complete Letters of Sigmund Freud to Wilhelm Fliess* 294). Breuer was one of many people whom Freud first idealized and then later harshly devalued. "My emotional life has always insisted that I should have an intimate friend and a hated enemy," Freud disclosed in *The Interpretation of*

Dreams (*SE*, vol. 5, 483), neglecting to point out that many of his intimate friends later became hated enemies. Freud confesses in *The Psychopathology of Everyday Life* (1901) that "there is scarcely any group of ideas to which I feel so antagonistic as that of being someone's protégé." James Strachey, the editor and translator of the *Standard Edition*, notes that Freud deleted this footnote in editions published after 1924, replacing it with a less revealing one: "in my conscious life I myself was resistant to the idea of being dependent on a protector's favor" (*SE*, vol. 6, 149–50, n.2). In *Freud: Biologist of the Mind* (1979), Frank J. Sulloway makes a shrewd distinction between the coauthors of *Studies on Hysteria*. "In a word, Freud feared mediocrity and others' anticipation of his ideas more than he feared error in science, and he fully accepted the risks inherent in this particular choice of values. Breuer, on the other hand, placed exactitude and humility above all else" (87).

Splendid Isolation?

In "On the History of the Psycho-Analytic Movement," Freud refers to his early professional life as a period of "splendid isolation," a time when, "like Robinson Crusoe," he "settled down as comfortably as possible on my desert island" (*SE*, vol. 14, 22). He's quick to add, however, that it was a lonely period for him, when he toiled with single-minded devotion in a world that ignored the birth of his new creation. He repeats in *An Autobiographical Study* the same characterization of his early professional life. For the first ten years after his break with Breuer, he was "completely isolated. In Vienna I was shunned; abroad no notice was taken of me." He continues to heroicize his isolation a few pages later: "I stood alone and had to do all the work myself" (*SE*, vol. 20, 48, 55).

Upon closer examination, Freud's splendid isolation was largely an example of his heroic self-mythology. In his encyclopedic and scrupulously balanced *The Discovery of the Unconscious* (1970), the Canadian psychiatrist and medical historian Henri F. Ellenberger concludes that there is no evidence to suggest that Freud was isolated or that his early writings were either ignored or dismissed. "Contrary to the usual assertion, his publications did not meet with the icy silence or the disparaging criticism that are said to have existed. Actually the reception was mostly favorable, though at times accompanied by a mixture of surprise and puzzlement" (455). Ellenberger raises a thorny question that he doesn't attempt to pursue: "how Freud's oversensitiveness and subjective feeling of isolation could have led him to the conviction that he was rejected and ostracized, a conviction that all available documents show to have been unfounded" (468). The biographer Peter Gay, while noting that Freud was less isolated than he wanted readers to believe, offers an answer to Ellenberger's question (though oddly, Gay never mentions Ellenberger's 932-page tome): Freud was "something of an advocate and something of a storyteller, both occupations that resort to painting in strong colors and stark outlines" (140).

Creative Illness

Ellenberger's work is noteworthy for another reason. He was the first to point out the role of "creative illness" in Freud and Jung's lives:

> A creative illness succeeds a period of intense preoccupation with an idea and search for a certain truth. It is a polymorphous condition that can take the shape of depression, neurosis, psychosomatic ailments, or even psychosis. Whatever the symptoms, they are felt as painful, if not agonizing, by the subject, with alternating periods of alleviation and worsening. Throughout the illness the subject never loses the thread of his dominating preoccupation. It is often compatible with normal, professional activity and family life. (447)

Freud's letters to Fliess dramatize his creative illness, a subject he does not discuss in *An Autobiographical Study*. Without citing Ellenberger's research, George Pickering expands the concept in his 1974 book *Creative Malady*, showing the link between Freud's ill-health and creativity, including the counterintuitive observation that Freud could not write when he was feeling perfectly healthy (222).

It's instructive to point out the major difference between "On the History of the Psycho-Analytic Movement" and *An Autobiographical Study*, the latter of which was written during a time when Freud felt he would shortly succumb to oral cancer diagnosed two years earlier in 1923. James Strachey is correct in pointing out that in the earlier study, we find "Freud adopting a far more belligerent tone than in any of his other writings" (*SE*, vol. 14, 4). The statement becomes more remarkable because of Freud's often bellicose tone elsewhere. Strachey's comment about the 1925 essay is also worth recalling. "The controversies that embittered the earlier paper had now faded into insignificance and he was able to give a cool and entirely objective account of the evolution of his scientific views" (*SE*, vol. 20, 5). To which one might respond: cool, yes; entirely objective, no.

Biography, Autobiography, and Psychobiography

Freud was intrigued by biography, including psychobiography, a subgenre he created in his 1910 study, "Leonardo da Vinci and a Memory of His Childhood." Like future psychobiographers, Freud emphasized the importance of childhood experiences and psychosexual development, the parents' influence in shaping a child's behavior, and the role of the unconscious. Sometimes a psychobiographer is wrong, as Freud was, when he based his interpretation of Leonardo's life on an erroneous German translation of the Italian word *nibbio*, which means *kite*, not a *bird of prey*, as Freud asserted. From this mistranslation, Freud concluded that Leonardo revealed a childhood dream or fantasy of a vulture thrusting its tail into his mouth. Freud then constructed an elaborate psychobiographical interpretation of the role of the vulture in Leonardo's life, equating the bird with mother goddesses and virgin mothers. Despite the misreading, Freud's essay on

Leonardo remains of great interest to later psychobiographers, who continue to believe, as Freud wrote, that "there is no one so great as to be disgraced by being subject to the laws which govern both normal and pathological activity with equal cogency" (*SE*, vol. 11, 63).

Why, then, was Freud so mistrustful of the subgenre he invented? He was not mistrustful of biography in a letter to Jung written on October 17, 1909, around the time he was writing his essay on Leonardo. After declaring that psychoanalysis must "conquer the whole field of mythology," he exclaimed, "We must also take hold of biography." The "riddle" of Leonardo's character suddenly became clear to Freud; the only difficulty, he conceded to Jung, was that the historical material was so sparse that he despaired of demonstrating his conviction to others (*Freud/Jung Letters* 158).

Freud did everything he could to dissuade others from writing about his life. "That one doesn't like one's own portrait, or that one doesn't recognize oneself in it, is a general and well-known fact," he complained to Stefan Zweig in 1931, upon receiving a copy of *Mental Healers*, which contained a chapter on Freud's life (*Letters* 402). Freud was also distressed when he received a copy of Fritz Wittels's 1924 biography, *Sigmund Freud: His Personality, His Teaching and His School*. "You know my attitude to this book," he wrote sternly to Wittels, his first "unsolicited biographer," on August 15, 1924; "it has not become friendlier. I still maintain that someone who knows as little about a person as you do about me is not entitled to write a biography about that person. One waits till the person is dead, when he cannot do anything about it and fortunately no longer cares" (*Letters* 350). The biography infuriated Freud. As Michael Molnar points out in *The Diary of Sigmund Freud*, the "wealth of marginal notes and interjections in Freud's copy of this book reveal his antipathy toward the work." In one passage in Wittels's book, Freud scrawled the words "wrong," "nonsense," "no," along with several exclamation marks (Molnar 153).

Freud was opposed to biographies even when the subjects had died. "Anyone turning biographer," Freud lectured Arnold Zweig in a letter written on May 31, 1936, "commits himself to lies, to concealment, to hypocrisy, to flattery, and even to hiding his own lack of understanding, for biographical truth is not to be had, and even if it were it couldn't be used" (*Letters* 430).

It's odd that Freud's comments on biography betray all-or-nothing thinking, also called binary or dichotomous thinking, the assumption that one can either know *all* of the truth or *none* of it. Nearly always, as Freud has shown us elsewhere, the truth usually lies somewhere in the murky middle. William James, whom Freud mentions admiringly in *An Autobiographical Study*, knew this. James points out in the conclusion to his aptly titled "A Certain Blindness in Human Beings" that "neither the whole of truth, nor the whole of good, is revealed to any single observer, although each observer gains a partial superiority of insight from the peculiar position in which he stands" (149).

Freud was not the only writer who dreaded future biographers. David Remnick, in his review in *The New Yorker* of Blake Bailey's 2021 biography of Philip Roth, observes that many authors destroyed their writings to deter future biographers, including Charles Dickens, Wilkie Collins, Walt Whitman, Henry James, and Sylvia Plath. Remnick quotes Janet Malcolm's observation that a biographer resembles a burglar, "breaking into a house, rifling through certain drawers that he has good reason to think contain the jewelry and money, and triumphantly bearing his loot away" (62). Other authors, like Roth, take the opposite approach. In an effort, usually futile, to control every aspect of their life stories, the authors invite a biographer into their homes and write long statements to be read by future readers. It's easier to understand the above novelists' and poets' mistrust of biography than it is to understand Freud's, who was himself a psychobiographer.

Freud believed after writing *The Interpretation of Dreams* that he did not need to disclose more about his life. When Joseph Wortis remarked, during his analysis with Freud in the mid-1930s, that the world would like to learn more about the creator of psychoanalysis, Freud snapped, "It won't hear anything from me; I have told enough about myself in my *Traumdeutung*," adding, "If it discovers things in some other way, that is not my concern. People should interest themselves in psychoanalysis, and not in my person" (121). Freud remained unconvinced even when Wortis told him that the personal factors in scientific work are always important. It's puzzling that Freud, who never hesitated to make psychobiographical speculations, should deny the personal factors in the formation of psychoanalysis.

Surprisingly, Freud never "theorized" biographical or autobiographical writing, apart from claiming, as he does in his essay on Leonardo, that biographers are "fixated on their heroes in a quite special way," by idealizing them (*SE*, vol. 11, 30). Nor did he anticipate the Heisenberg principle: the observer cannot be separated from the observed. Or as Nietzsche observed in *Beyond Good and Evil* in 1886, "It has gradually become clear to me what every great philosophy up till now has consisted of—namely, the confession of its originator, and a species of involuntary and unconscious autobiography" (386). Nietzsche's insight applies to psychology as well as philosophy. Freud never considered that autobiography may be the most truthful writing when scrutinized in a certain way, as Mark Twain, one of Freud's favorite authors, quipped in *The Mark Twain-Howells Lectures*: "An autobiography is the truest of all books; for while it inevitably consists of extinctions of the truth, shirkings of the truth, partial revealments of the truth, with hardly an instance of plain straight truth, the remorseless truth is there, between the lines" (vol. 2, 782). Ernest Jones is correct when he states that *An Autobiographical Study* is one of the "most important source books for the student of Freud" (Jones, vol. 3, 117), but we must read this source book in the way Mark Twain suggested, between the lines, against the grain, with Freud as an unreliable narrator. Master theorist that he was, Freud never considered the ways in which the theorist's race, class, gender, and religion play a crucial role in the construction of his or her theory.

Freud's Jewishness

Freud's Jewishness played a key role in the creation of psychoanalysis. He touches upon this subject in *An Autobiographical Study*, informing us that he never felt ashamed of his descent or "race," emphasizing the positive consequence of difference: "at an early age I was made familiar with the fate of being in the Opposition and of being put under the ban of the 'compact majority.' The foundations were thus laid for a certain degree of independence of judgement" (*SE*, vol. 20, 9). He expanded upon his feelings about being Jewish in his 1926 "Address to the Society of B'nai B'rith," published posthumously in 1941, where he evokes the aspects of Judaism that attracted him despite being an unbeliever: "many obscure emotional forces, which were the more powerful the less they could be expressed in words" (*SE*, vol. 20, 274).

Beginning with David Bakan's kabbalistic speculations in *Sigmund Freud and the Jewish Mystical Tradition* (1958), scholars have commented on these obscure emotional forces, but no one has written more incisively than Sander Gilman about how Freud's deep ambivalence toward his religion became etched into his creation of psychoanalysis. A prolific psychoanalytic historian, cultural critic, and literary scholar, Gilman has authored or coauthored over ninety books, including two published in 1993: *Freud, Race, and Class* and *The Case of Sigmund Freud*. It's impossible to summarize briefly Gilman's Freudian scholarship, but in one of his most provocative insights, he suggests that the Jew in Freud's Jewish jokes becomes the woman, embodying insecurity, weakness, and passivity, the opposite of the idealized German with whom he unconsciously identifies. Freud thus ironically allies himself with the non-Jew's caricature of the Jew. In Gilman's view, Freud exorcises his insecurities as an Eastern European Jew by creating a new discipline of study, psychoanalysis, and by inventing a new language, the discourse of the unconscious, a speech he alone mastered. Yet, if Freud needed to distance himself from female lack, a subject Gilman explores in greater detail in his later books, Freud did not want to imply, as most of his contemporaries did, that sexuality was pathological. Rather, Freud asserted the opposite: sexuality was natural, normal, the opposite of degeneracy.

The Pope of Psychoanalysis

"[A] man like me cannot live without a hobbyhorse," Freud exclaimed to Fliess in a letter on May 25, 1895, "without a consuming passion, without—in Schiller's words—a tyrant" (*Complete Letters of Sigmund Freud to Wilhelm Fliess* 129). Freud's tyrant was psychology, but he could be a dictator to those who rebelled against him. In *An Autobiographical Study*, he describes Alfred Adler and C.G. Jung ("and a few besides," such as Wilhelm Stekel) as "two heretics" to whom he responded with "mild" criticism. He then lists several psychoanalysts who remained loyal to him, claiming, in his own defense, that an "intolerant man, dominated by an arrogant belief in his own infallibility, would never have been able to maintain his hold upon so large a number of intellectually eminent people" (*SE*, vol. 20, 53). The list of heretics is much longer, however, than Freud acknowledges, including two analysts of his inner circle whom he later rejected, Sándor Ferenczi and Otto Rank. "Heretics" is an apt metaphor for Freud, who remained the pope of psychoanalysis.

Freud did not simply disagree with dissenters; he pathologized them, as Borch-Jacobsen and Sonu Shamdasani have shown. A typical example: "Adler is a very decent man," Freud wrote to Jung in 1910, "but he is paranoid" (*Freud/Jung Letters* 373). If there's anything worse than a paranoid, it's a "malicious paranoid," as Freud described Adler in a letter to James Jackson Putnam in 1912. In the same letter Freud describes Jung, from whom he was not yet completely estranged, as "our friend . . . who apparently has not outgrown his own neurosis" (Hale 217).

From its inception, faithful adherents to psychoanalysis regarded Freud as the supreme authority of psychological truth, using the words, "As Freud himself said." Nancy J. Chodorow declares in *The Psychoanalytic Ear and the Sociological Eye* (2020) that no scientist believes that the contributions of Einstein, Bohr, Fermi, or Heisenberg are the last word in physics. "So it should be with psychoanalysis and its founder" (169, n.2).

"Insufficiently Analyzed"

Freud could not help believing that the psychoanalysts who disagreed with him were "insufficiently analyzed," an explanation or rationalization (the word was coined by Ernest Jones) that has continued to this day. And yet Freud also knew that one could not invoke this justification in polemical disputes, as he wrote to Ernest Jones in 1927:

> When two analysts have differing opinions on some point, one may be fully justified, in ever so many cases, in assuming that the mistaken view of one of them stems from his having been insufficiently analyzed, and he therefore allows himself to be influenced by his complexes to the detriment of science. But in practical polemics such an argument is not permissible, for it is at the disposal of each party, and does not reveal on whose side the error lies. We are generally agreed to renounce arguments of this sort and, in the case of differences of opinion, to leave resolutions to advancements in empirical knowledge. (Paskauskas 619)

Freud's excellent conclusion, however, was more honored in the breach, and his early (and later) followers showed no reluctance in accusing fellow analysts of unresolved personal conflicts to explain their "deviance" from the truth.

As we shall see, unlike Stekel and Jung (and others such as Ferenczi and Rank), who wrote about their anguish over their break from Freud, the founder of psychoanalysis never acknowledged publicly his pain over lost colleagues. This was Freud's pattern over failed friendships. In *Freud: Darkness in the Midst of Vision*, Breger quotes a letter written by Hannah Breuer about how wounded her elderly father-in-law was when, walking in Vienna, he suddenly saw Freud approaching him. Josef Breuer opened his arms instinctively to embrace his former colleague and friend, but Freud passed by, pretending not to see him (125). Freud knew how to cut his losses. Everything had to be sacrificed for the welfare of psychoanalysis. No statement Freud ever wrote contains more ironic truth, or self-fulfilling prophecy, than his observation in "On the History of the Psycho-Analytic Movement": "psychoanalysis brings out the worst in everyone" (*SE*, vol. 14, 39).

Sphinx-like

How do we finally explain Freud's lifelong antipathy to biography and autobiography? Without explicitly referring to biography as an impossible profession, the British psychoanalyst and literary critic Adam Phillips teases out the paradoxical implications of life stories in his 1999 book *Darwin's Worms*. Phillips suggests that Freud's statement to his fiancée about destroying all of his writings reveals his wish to be the Sphinx, rather than Oedipus who solved its riddle. "By getting rid of the written evidence of the past he has unburied that Sphinx again, recovered the riddle of himself, at least for posterity" (68). Freud destroyed biographical evidence to taunt his future biographers because of the desire to become the kind of person for whom biographers will compete. Freud has it both ways, Phillips continues, receiving two pleasures for the price of one: "the pleasure of reading his biographies (in the plural), and the pleasure of watching, or just secretly knowing that his biographers have gone astray" (69).

Freud's Sphinx-like character remains paradoxical, Phillips argues, given that he believed he had unlocked universal truths about human nature, solving the Sphinx's riddle with the discovery of the Oedipus complex. As further evidence of Freud's "Sphinx complex," the wish to be the "mysterious monster that asks the impossible questions" (70), Phillips contends that Freud's mistrust of biography may betray his misgivings about psychoanalysis itself. Freud uncovered the fundamental truth about people, ambivalence, which both biography and psychoanalysis confirm. In Phillips's words, "It is an insufficiently acknowledged—insufficiently enjoyed—paradox that the more Freud elaborated psychoanalytic theory the less impressed he was by the knowability of the human subject" (94), a conclusion that calls into question the perception of Freud as a child of the Enlightenment. In his 2014 biographical study *Becoming Freud*, Phillips presents us with an anti-Enlightenment radical who is first and foremost a literary Freud, an author whose books were indelibly shaped by his own reading.

Keeping and Betraying Secrets

Phillips's emphasis on Freud's Sphinx-like character reminds us that the man who sought to detect his patients' secrets, and who was often casual about betraying these confessions to others, kept many secrets from his readers. "He that has eyes to see and ears to hear," he writes in *Fragment of an Analysis of a Case of Hysteria*, "may convince himself that no mortal can keep a secret. If his lips are silent, he chatters with his finger-tips; betrayal oozes out of him at every pore" (*SE*, vol. 7, 77–8). Freud revealed his personal secrets early in his career; his lips remained silent in *An Autobiographical Study*, though this has not prevented students of psychoanalysis, myself included, from trying to pry open his lips.

In the "Postscript" to *An Autobiographical Study* added in 1935, Freud once again insists that having revealed so much about his life in *The Interpretation of Dreams* and *The Psychopathology of Everyday Life*, he has no further obligations to posterity. "I have had small thanks for it, and from my experience I cannot recommend anyone to follow my example" (*SE*, vol. 20, 73). I doubt Freud imagined that *all* of his writings would be read for their autobiographical significance, including the extent to which they represent his involuntary and unconscious confessions.

It's ironic that *The Interpretation of Dreams* is Freud's real autobiography while *An Autobiographical Study* remains one of his most opaque, defensive works, a text which, despite its title, makes the author's life disappear from the story. *An Autobiographical Study* continues to intrigue scholars, however. Jacques Derrida, who was fascinated by the ambiguous boundaries between the writer's life and work, raised a provocative question about the connection between Freud's autobiography and the construction of psychoanalytic theory: "how can an autobiographical writing, in the abyss of an unterminated self-analysis, give to a world wide institution *its* birth?" (531).

Dying in Harness

"[I]t still strikes me myself as strange," Freud observes in *Studies on Hysteria* (1895), "that the case histories I write should read like short stories and that, as one might say, they lack the serious stamp of science" (*SE*, vol. 2, 160). Freud was, regardless of what one thinks about psychoanalysis, a masterful writer. In an article published in the *New York Times Book Review* in 1986, the influential American literary critic Harold Bloom argued that "No 20th century writer—not even Proust or Joyce or Kafka—rivals Freud's position as the central imagination of our age." Bloom believed that Freud was a "fourth in the sequence of Plato, Montaigne, and Shakespeare." No fan of psychoanalysis, Bloom asserted in *The Western Canon* (1994) that Freud was far greater than his creation and would long outlive it. Freud's writing was, as Patrick J. Mahony suggests evocatively, a "distinctive kind of self-expression," a "veritable w(rites) of passage" (885). Mahony makes another notable observation: "of all his legacies his authorial powers have gone unquestioned" ("Freud's Writing" 900).

Like nearly all of his writings, *An Autobiographical Study* abounds in literary references, revealing Freud's great love for literature. He viewed creative writers as allies in the search for psychological truth. Freud's 1907 essay "Delusions and Dreams in Jensen's *Gradiva*" is the first example of psychoanalytic literary criticism. It's surprising, however, that in *An Autobiographical Study*, Freud refers to Jensen's 1902 novel as having "no particular merit in itself" (*SE*, vol. 20, 65), an uncharacteristic disparagement of literature.

No one can say that *An Autobiographical Study* reads like a short story or even an engrossing memoir. Unlike Freud's great case histories, which are captivating *stories* filled with colorful imagery, engaging dialogue, unexpected plot twists, and animated prose, *An Autobiographical Study* is written in tendentious language. Freud's goal was to offer a brief account of his life, written at a time when he thought he had only a few more months to live, not to probe the contradictions and paradoxes of his life, as he had done with his analysands' lives. The tone of *An Autobiographical Study* often has a valedictory quality, explained, in part, by his reference to a "grave illness [which] warns me of the approaching end" (*SE*, vol. 20, 55). What is genuinely heroic about Freud's life story is not his self-mythologizing but his formidable work ethic, writing to the end, enduring for the last sixteen years of his life dozens of cancer surgeries on his jaw. "I cannot face with comfort the idea of life without work," Freud wrote to Oskar Pfister in 1910; "work and the free play of the imagination are for me the same thing, I take no pleasure in anything else." Freud's one "secret prayer," the godless Jew wrote to the Swiss minister, is that he would follow the words of Macbeth: to die in harness (Meng and E. Freud, *Psychoanalysis and Faith* 35). He did.

Like his hero Goethe, Freud was a great self-revealer and a careful concealer, though he never acknowledged these contradictions in *An Autobiographical Study*. "If authors had more self-criticism," he wrote to his fiancée on October 6, 1883, "nine-tenths of them would not be authors" (*Letters* 67)—including, we might add, Freud himself, whose self-criticism with respect to the development of psychoanalysis was severely limited. Walt Whitman must have been thinking of Freud when he famously declared in *Song of Myself*, published in 1855, one year before Freud's birth, "Do I contradict myself?/ Very well then I contradict myself,/ (I am large, I contain multitudes)." Like all geniuses, Freud contained multitudes, or, to cite the words of another genius, Nietzsche, Freud was human, all too human. To read Freud's autobiography oppositionally, discovering the hidden contradictions and ambivalences in his story, his lifelong unconscious pursuit of ambition, fame, and glory, is thus, ironically, to be a true Freudian.

Chapter 2

THE WOLF-MAN

MEMOIRS

"I, who am now a Russian émigré, eighty-three years of age, and who was one of Freud's early psychoanalytic patients, known as 'The Wolf-Man,' am sitting down to write my recollections of my childhood" (4). Thus begins the most extraordinary case study in psychoanalytic history, all the more singular because of the patient's arresting pseudonym. The ghost of Sigmund Freud must have been beaming when he read the Wolf-Man's *Memoirs*, for one cannot imagine a more idealized account of psychoanalysis.

We now know that the Wolf-Man's real name was Sergei Pankejeff. Most scholars continue to refer to him by Freud's pseudonym, as I will. Born on January 6, 1887, to a wealthy land-owning St. Petersburg family, he remains Freud's most iconic case, the only patient we can follow from infancy to death in 1979 at age ninety-two. The cover of the paperback edition of *The Wolf-Man by the Wolf-Man* characterizes the *Memoirs* as the "double story of Freud's most famous case," but this is an understatement. We have several counterstories of the same patient, each with its own insights and blind spots: Freud's *From the History of an Infantile Neurosis*, written in 1914 but not published until 1918; the Wolf-Man's *Memoirs*, edited and translated by the psychoanalyst Muriel Gardiner, published in 1971; Ruth Mack Brunswick's "A Supplement to Freud's 'History of an Infantile Neurosis,'" first published in 1928 and then included in Gardiner's 1971 volume; Muriel Gardiner's impressions of her meetings and correspondence with the Wolf-Man; and the Viennese journalist Karin Obholzer's startlingly candid book *The Wolf-Man: Conversations with Freud's Patient—Sixty Years Later*, published first in German in 1980 and then in English in 1982. The bewildering story of the Wolf-Man, narrated by four different people over a period spanning nearly seven decades, has a Rashomon-like quality, offering conflicting interpretations of the same enigmatic person.

The stories are strikingly different in what they reveal and conceal. For Freud, Gardiner, Brunswick, and Anna Freud, who wrote the foreword to *The Wolf-Man by the Wolf-Man*, the case history is irrefutable proof of the validity of psychoanalytic *science*. As Anna Freud writes, "The Wolf-Man stands out among his fellow figures by virtue of the fact that he is the only one able and willing to cooperate actively in the reconstruction and follow-up of his own case" (x). Other, more dispassionate readers, however, will see a psychoanalytic ideology in the Wolf-Man's story that is far from scientific. There is little question that the Wolf-Man was convinced, as Anna Freud observed, that he would have been condemned to lifelong suffering without psychoanalysis. But the question remains: what most benefited him from his analysis with Freud? The answer, if we are to believe the Wolf-Man's conversations with Obholzer, is not what was most obvious to Freud and the orthodox psychoanalytic community.

Freud's Case Study

We begin with *From the History of an Infantile Neurosis*, described by James Strachey as the "most elaborate and no doubt the most important of all Freud's case histories" (*SE*, vol. 17, 3). Freud's first analysis began in February 1910, when the patient was twenty-three, and lasted until July 1914. The patient entered a second analysis with Freud for another four months from November 1919 to February 1920. Prior to the first analysis, the patient's health had broken down, Freud tells us, when he was eighteen as a result of a gonorrheal infection contracted from a peasant woman that left him entirely incapacitated and dependent upon others. He had visited two of the world's most renowned specialists, including the German psychiatrist Emil Kraepelin, who diagnosed him (and, years earlier, his father) as a case of "manic-depressive insanity." The patient spent several months in various sanatoria, but his psychological problems persisted, including severe obsessional neurosis and depression.

The main component of the case involved a wolf phobia that first appeared in an elaborate dream when the patient was four. The Wolf-Man dreamed that six or seven wolves were sitting on the branches of a tree. Freud determined that the wolf dream was a belated response to the boy's experience when he was one and a half years old, traumatized by witnessing several times his parents having coitus *a tergo* (from behind). The boy thus witnessed the "primal scene," the first time Freud referred to this term in his published writings. The boy's parents became the terrifying wolves in the dream that bedeviled him throughout childhood. According to Freud, witnessing the primal scene resulted in the boy's fear of castration, a central element of psychoanalytic theory.

Freud uses *Grimms' Fairy Tales*, which his patient read as a young boy, to understand the lupine dream. The patient draws a picture of a tree with wolves, which recalls the illustrations in the fairy-tale book. With Freud's help, the patient identifies two of the stories that influenced the creation of the dream: "Little Red Riding Hood" and "The Wolf and the Seven Little Goats." Regardless of the accuracy of Freud's interpretation of the Wolf-Man's recurrent nightmare, we see how the analyst envisions stories, fairy tales, and mythology, no less than dreams, as the royal road to the unconscious.

Beholding the primal scene was not the boy's only experience of sex, for when he was three, his sister, Anna, two years his senior, had "seduced him into sexual practices"—mainly by playing with his penis and telling him "incomprehensible stories," presumably of a sexual nature, about his Nanya, or nurse (*SE*, vol. 17, 20). Despite Freud's rejection of the seduction theory in 1897, which may be viewed as a turning point in the history of psychoanalysis, he never questions that his patient's recollection of his sister's seductive behavior is based on factual truth. What Freud called seduction, and what the Wolf-Man called his "sister complex," might now be called childhood sexual abuse, though others might call it siblings' sexual curiosity, healthy or otherwise. Anna committed suicide a few years later, an act Freud attributes to the beginning of dementia praecox, schizophrenia, evidence of the "neuropathic heredity" in the family (*SE*, vol. 17, 21). Freud places greater emphasis on the impact of Anna's seductive behavior than on the suicide's lifelong consequences in her brother's life.

Freud comes across in the case study as nonjudgmental and good-natured. Encouraging his patients to offer their free associations, Freud was accustomed to being the target of verbal threats, as when the Rat Man imagined rats boring their way into a captain's anus. Sometimes a patient would elicit Freud's negative countertransference, as in *Fragment of an Analysis of a Case of Hysteria*, when Dora's abrupt decision to terminate analysis results in his vindictiveness toward her: "I do not know what kind of help she wanted from me, but I promised to forgive her for having deprived me of the satisfaction of affording her a far more radical cure for her troubles" (*SE*, vol. 7, 122).

Nothing the Wolf-Man says or does offends Freud, not even when, according to Ernest Jones's biography, the patient offered during the first analytic session to have anal intercourse with Freud and then defecate on his head (vol. 2, 274), a proposal that likely would have terminated treatment with other therapists. (According to a letter Freud wrote to Ferenczi, the Wolf-Man's threat occurred *after* the first session.) Throughout the case study, Freud affirms the patient's positive qualities, promising him a complete recovery from his intestinal problems. The Wolf-Man is comfortable enough in analysis to confess his worst blasphemous thoughts, as when he says "God-swine" or "God-shit" (*SE*, vol. 17, 17). Some of Freud's most imaginative speculations appear in the case study, including the suggestion that feces represent a child's first gift to parents.

Freud's writing throughout the case study is lively and richly metaphorical. He compares the intense clinical resistance that must be overcome in a lengthy analysis to the situation of an enemy army that needs months to make its way across a stretch of territory that would ordinarily take an express train only a few hours during peacetime. The case would have lasted longer had Freud decided not to impose a time limit, the first time he did so. "Under the inexorable pressure of this fixed limit his resistance and his fixation to the illness gave way" (*SE*, vol. 17, 11). Freud criticizes his former disciples, Adler and Jung, who take temporal shortcuts that will inevitably fail.

Freud never doubts, despite the complexity of the case, that he has arrived at a true understanding. Yet one is struck by his dichotomous or binary thinking, as when he says, after discussing how the Wolf-Man's phobias are contradicted by his otherwise sober character, "either the analysis based on the neurosis in his childhood is all a piece of nonsense from start to finish, or everything took place just as I have described it above" (*SE*, vol. 17, 56). Freud's certainty of knowledge is no less striking: "It is always a strict law of dream-interpretation that an explanation must be found for every detail" (*SE*, vol. 17, 42, f.1).

Freud's case study of the Wolf-Man provoked much controversy, including sharp parody from Vladimir Nabokov, who never missed an opportunity to deride the "Viennese witch doctor," as I show in *The Talking Cure: Literary Representations of Psychoanalysis* (1985). Indeed, no novelist has waged a more relentless campaign against Freud than Nabokov. Humbert Humbert, the pedophiliac narrator of Nabokov's masterpiece, *Lolita* (1955), delights in psychiatry baiting, teasing his psychiatrists with fake primal scenes. Hints of the primal scene appear throughout Nabokov's fiction, particularly in his 1962 novel *Pale Fire*. Nabokov and Sergei Pankejeff had much in common: both were sons of aristocratic Russian families forced into exile after the Russian Revolution; their lives were characterized by profound loss and nostalgia for the past. But whereas Pankejeff spent much of his life in analysis, defining his identity as Freud's most famous patient, Nabokov devoted his entire novelistic career to mocking Freud, observing mordantly in *Lolita* that the difference between the rapist and therapist is but a matter of spacing.

Freud's affection for the Wolf-Man is obvious; by contrast, Ruth Mack Brunswick feels far less sympathy for him in her two brief analyses, the first from October 1926 to February 1927, the second two years later. Far from praising his admirable qualities, she writes about his dishonesty and hypocrisy, suggestive to her of his disturbing change in character. Seeking to undermine what she believes is the Wolf-Man's defensive idealization of Freud, betraying, in her view, his unconscious hostility, she asks him a curious question: whether he knew, socially, Freud's family? "He was obliged to admit that he had never met Freud's family, thereby badly damaging his entire case" (*The Wolf Man by the Wolf-Man* 284).

Brunswick's therapeutic strategy is to destroy the patient's "grandiose" belief that he was Freud's favorite son. Ironically, the strategy reveals her own negative countertransference: jealousy of the Wolf-Man's privileged position in the history of psychoanalysis. Analysis quickly deteriorated into a state of active enmity, as her metaphors indicate. "I remarked that his was not the only published case—this being a source of enormous pride to the patient. He countered with the statement that no other patient had been analyzed for so long a period of time: this too I was able to contradict. From a state of war we now reached a state of siege" (284–5). Although the Wolf-Man refers briefly in *Memoirs* to being "successfully analyzed" by Brunswick (125), he has nothing good to say about her in his *Conversations* with Obholzer.

Unlike Brunswick, Muriel Gardiner affirms the Wolf-Man's central position in the history of psychoanalysis. Gardiner's affection and respect for him never waver during their long albeit interrupted friendship. As a medical student studying in Vienna, Gardiner helped facilitate his analysis with Brunswick. Gardiner assisted him in the spring of 1938 with getting a passport to leave Austria for Paris, though he soon returned to Vienna, where he lived most of his life. She became a trusted friend, but she resisted becoming his unofficial psychoanalyst, as he wanted her to be. (The Wolf-Man cast Obholzer into the same role.) His constant seeking for advice and counsel from Gardiner is one sign of his obsessional thinking. Gardiner is, along with Obholzer, the best source of our understanding of the Wolf-Man's later years as well as our knowledge of the impact of writing his *Memoirs*.

"Recollections of My Childhood": Early Traumatic Losses

The Wolf-Man's *Memoirs* is divided into two parts. The opening chapters of Part 1—"Recollections of My Childhood," "Unconscious Mourning" (1905–8), and "Castles in Spain" (1908)—cover the same period that Freud writes about in his case study. Additional information about the Wolf-Man's life appears in the later chapters in Part 1: "Shifting Decisions" (1909–14); "After My Analysis" (1914–19); "Everyday Life" (1919–38); and "The Climax" (1938). Part II consists of a single chapter, "My Recollections of Sigmund Freud." The chapters were written over a period of several years, and though they appear in chronological order in his *Memoirs*, some of the later chapters were written earlier. "My Recollections of Sigmund Freud," for example, was written in 1951 and published in the *Journal of the American Psychoanalytic Association* in 1958 under the title "How I Came into Analysis with Freud." The publication delighted him.

Unlike Freud, who is mainly preoccupied with the Wolf-Man's early sexual encounters, the patient dwells on his history of traumatic loss. Suicide, not sexuality, represents the greater problem for him. He offers details about his sister's slow, agonizing death, from drinking a bottle of mercury, that are missing from Freud's case study. Nor was this the first suicide in the Wolf-Man's family. His father's sudden death at age forty-nine from an overdose of veronal was likely a suicide, as was the Wolf-Man's paternal grandmother's death. After his sister's death, the Wolf-Man became obsessed with killing himself. He is perceptive enough to recognize the contagious nature of suicide, but he cannot stop torturing himself over Anna's death. "Everything repelled me and thoughts of suicide went around in my mind the whole time without, however, my having the courage to carry them out" (25–6). Years later, after being spurned by the woman he eventually married, Therese, he swallowed a handful of sleeping pills, though he woke up the next morning without serious harm.

All of this is a prelude to the most catastrophic experience in the Wolf-Man's life, an event that seemed to confirm that history was fatally repeating itself. On March 31, 1938, long after he completed his initial four-year analysis with Freud and the four-month reanalysis with him a decade later, Therese committed suicide, through asphyxiation. It is the single defining event of his life, a tragedy he can neither understand nor work through.

Tellingly, the Wolf-Man mentions his lupine dream in *Memoirs*, along with reading *Grimms' Fairy Tales*, but there's not a word about witnessing the primal scene. Nor does he mention castration fear. Why? Either he doesn't wish to repeat the information appearing in *From the History of an Infantile Neurosis*, or, more likely, Freud's sexual interpretation of the dream had little if any relevance to the

Wolf-Man's life. It's possible to invoke "clinical resistance" to explain the Wolf-Man's omission of these details, but this is an interpretive slippery slope best avoided.

A Heroic Vision of Freud

The most salient section in *Memoirs*, the seventeen-page "My Recollections of Sigmund Freud," presents a heroic vision of the founder that is even more laudatory than Ernest Jones's saintly biography. As the Wolf-Man admits proudly, Freud called him a "piece of psychoanalysis" (150), and he defined his identity as Freud's most famous patient.

"My Recollections of Sigmund Freud" begins with the Wolf-Man's first meeting with Freud in 1910, when the Russian émigré was twenty-three. Freud was in his mid-fifties, and from his "simple but self-assured manner," the Wolf-Man concluded that he was a person of "inner serenity" (137). At no time during the two analyses did the Wolf-Man falter in his belief that Freud was a "great personality" (137). Freud always listened to the Wolf-Man with the "greatest attention," and the analysand concluded from Freud's comments that he had a "complete understanding of everything I had experienced" (138).

Freud comes across in the Wolf-Man's *Memoirs* as not only omniscient but also benevolent. He praises the Wolf-Man's intelligence, heightens his self-esteem, and validates his perceptions. When the Wolf-Man confesses to his characteristic doubts and brooding as a child, Freud responds that "only a child can think so logically," an opinion that convinces the Wolf-Man that, despite his conflicts, he is, in Freud's words, a "thinker of the first rank." The statement fills him with "no little pride" (139). The approbation enables the Wolf-Man to believe that he is less Freud's patient than a "co-worker, the younger comrade of an experienced explorer setting out to study a new, recently discovered land" (140). The Wolf-Man retains this feeling of accomplishment as Freud's collaborator. The close therapeutic alliance between the two men appears to be the single most noteworthy reason for the treatment's success. When the Wolf-Man reentered analysis at Freud's wish, to understand a "small residue of unanalyzed material" (111), Freud treated the now penniless patient at no cost. He also gave the Wolf-Man money, an act that would later be considered a boundary violation.

Perhaps the most poignant detail in the Wolf-Man's story is that he saw Freud the day after Sophie Freud Halberstadt's sudden death from the Spanish influenza on January 25, 1920, at age twenty-seven. "He was calm and composed as usual, and did not betray his pain in any way" (151). Did Freud disclose his daughter's death to the Wolf-Man, or did he learn about it in another way? We aren't sure. Two days after the death, Freud wrote a letter to the Swiss pastor Oskar Pfister about the tragedy. "I work as much as I can, and am thankful for the diversion. The loss of a child seems to be a serious, narcissistic injury; what is known as mourning will probably follow only later" (*Letters* 328). Nine years later, on what would have been his daughter's thirty-sixth birthday, Freud wrote to Ludwig Binsanger about the excruciating loss:

> Although we know that after such a loss the acute state of mourning will subside, we also know we shall remain inconsolable and will never find a substitute. No matter what may fill the gap, even if it be filled completely, it nevertheless remains something else. And actually this is how it should be. It is the only way of perpetuating that love which we do not want to relinquish. (*Letters* 386)

Freud's courage amidst adversity may have given the Wolf-Man hope to endure his own devastating losses. Freud's courage certainly contributed to the Wolf-Man's idealization of him. His description of Freud's apartment and office on Berggasse 19 evokes the serenity of a monastery. "There was always a feeling of sacred peace and quiet here" (139).

At the end of the first analysis, Freud gave the Wolf-Man an autographed copy of the published case study about him. Reading the book, the Wolf-Man must have been struck by Freud's description of him early in the analysis: "His unimpeachable intelligence was, as it were, cut off from the instinctual forces which governed his behaviour in the few relations of life that remained to him" (*Infantile Neurosis* 11). The words had a lasting impact on the Wolf-Man. He uses the same language in "My Recollections of Sigmund Freud" to describe the patients who benefit the most from psychoanalysis: "These are the persons whose unimpeachable intelligence seems to be cut off from their instinctive drives" (140). By using the psychoanalyst's language, the Wolf-Man validates the acumen of two people, Freud and himself.

If we can infer a memoirist's psychological health from his or her writing, then the Wolf-Man was firmly in control of his life as an octogenarian. His life story is consistently engaging, detailed, and well organized. He refers several times to being tormented by paralyzing doubts, self-recriminations, and uncertainties, but he limns these feelings with clarity, precision, humor, and irony. He conveys his ruminations, paradoxically, in a non-ruminative way. His language, which we read in English translation, is lucid and often graceful. Indeed, in his conversations with Obholzer, he refers to the positive reviews of *The Wolf-Man by the Wolf-Man*. One reviewer, he proudly tells Obholzer, concluded that the book reads like a Russian novel. "It's the atmosphere in which Dostoevsky's characters move." Another passage in the review suggests that "in Freud and his most sensitive patient, we have two masters of the language" (*Conversations* 227). A writer must have rare literary and psychological expertise to use language like Dostoevsky and Freud; examine ambivalence without succumbing to it; avoid both reductivism and psychobabble; and enable his readers to glimpse the nature of obsessional thinking.

The Wolf-Man: Conversations with Freud's Patient—Sixty Years Later

Four preliminary observations must be made before we comment on Karin Obholzer's *Conversations* with the Wolf-Man. First, the psychoanalytic establishment did not want the Wolf-Man to speak with her nor for the book to be published. "Dr. E., an Austrian analyst who had emigrated to the United States and was working at the Freud archive in New York" (*Conversations* 6)—surely Kurt Eissler—strenuously was opposed to the book, as was Muriel Gardiner, who sent the Wolf-Man a telegram urging him not to speak with Obholzer. Given the Wolf-Man's long friendship with Gardiner, he must have felt that contravening her wish not to speak with Obholzer was a betrayal. Eissler later withdrew his objections to the Wolf-Man's interviews with Obholzer, but Gardiner remained adamantly opposed to it, though she recommended, as did Eissler, that the Wolf-Man update his *Memoirs*. Additionally, the director of the Vienna Psychiatric Hospital, Dr. S., with whom the Wolf-Man had a weekly session, tried to dissuade him from speaking with Obholzer. All of them feared that the Wolf-Man, described by Obholzer as a "fading monument of psychoanalysis" (248), would say something that would tarnish the reputation of Freud's creation. They made a "showpiece of me," the Wolf-Man twice observes, sardonically (135, 186). He describes his *Memoirs* as a "propaganda piece for psychoanalysis" (185). He felt characteristically ambivalent about his *Conversations* but agreed reluctantly to its publication provided that it appear after his death. Significantly, Freud was opposed to the Wolf-Man writing anything about him. The Wolf-Man informed Obholzer that he wanted to write a tribute to Freud upon the analyst's sixtieth birthday. "I told Mack about it at the time and she said, 'The professor is against your writing something about him.' You see? He was against it" (165).

Second, the interviews took place between 1974 and 1979, when the Wolf-Man was approaching and reached his nineties. Old, infirm, and nearly destitute, the nonagenarian is asked questions about his analysis with Freud that he cannot always remember. Some of his statements about Freud are consistent with what other analysands have written about their own experiences, but other statements are not. For example, we can believe the Wolf-Man's comment that Freud told him not to look for contradictions when he was free associating. But can we believe that Freud sat at the head of the analytic couch, as the Wolf-Man claims he was told, because of a woman who tried to seduce him at the other end of the couch? The explanation contradicts the conventional wisdom that Freud didn't want his patients staring at him. Memory cannot always be trusted, and some of the Wolf-Man's observations cannot be corroborated.

Third, life has changed the Wolf-Man. There are both continuities and discontinuities between his existence as a young and old man. Sometimes he contradicts himself, as when he expresses anger toward Freud for advising him not to return to Russia, but then he agrees with Obholzer in the next breath that Freud's recommendation may have saved his life. Some of the Wolf-Man's assertions about his analytic experience are misleading or inaccurate, as when he claims that the "point of psychoanalysis is that one should not suppress one's drives" (130). Moments of their conversations read like a comedy of errors, as when Obholzer asks him about Ernest Jones, who had written about him in his biography. Having left his hearing aids at home, the Wolf-Man cannot hear her question and then, anticipating David Lodge's satirical novel *Deaf Sentence*, about a retired hearing-impaired linguistics professor, he starts talking about a different person. Pages later, when Obholzer repeats the question, he claims, contrary to Jones's statements, that he never corresponded with the British analyst. "I don't know," the Wolf-Man testily retorts, in response to learning about Jones's claim that the Wolf-Man wanted to defecate on Freud, "it seems to me he doesn't have all his marbles" (169).

Finally, the Wolf-Man's obsessional doubts and brooding seemed to infect Obholzer. She doesn't use the term *folie à deux*, a shared madness or delusion between two people, but she confesses that listening to the forty hours of taped conversations with the Wolf-Man, filled with unending complaints along with iterations about the meaninglessness and futility of his life, prevented her at times from working on the book. One thing is certain, she notes ruefully: she now knows what an obsessional neurosis is (11). The reader does too. However critical she (or the reader) is of Freud, she now has an inkling of Freud's challenge in treating the Wolf-Man.

Admiring the Creator, Not the Creation

As we saw, the Wolf-Man conspicuously avoids any discussion of the primal scene in *Memoirs*. Writing largely for a psychoanalytic audience, and with the enthusiastic approval of the psychoanalytic establishment, he did not want to tell them anything they didn't wish to hear. Silence was better than a lie. But he felt no such compulsions in his *Conversations* with Obholzer. He still characterizes Freud as a "genius" (25), but he says repeatedly that Freud's interpretation of the wolf dream was "terribly farfetched" (35). One page later he adds that the primal scene "is no more than a construct." He is sharply critical of other aspects of psychoanalytic theory, including castration and bisexuality. He's especially censorious of the idea that "everything is already contained in childhood" (139). During his annual visits to Vienna, Eissler tells the Wolf-Man that the reason he is afraid of a woman with whom he has had a thirty-year on-and-off again relationship, Luise, is because of the fear of castration, an interpretation the Wolf-Man rejects. His characterization of Eissler as a "fanatic of psychoanalysis" (174) would be endorsed by nearly everyone who was not an orthodox Freudian.

The Wolf-Man reserves his harshest criticism for Brunswick, who, in his opinion, always disliked him. He recalls that when he told her about his wife, who was still alive, the analyst sputtered, "What do I care about Therese? You are my patient!" (102), a statement that he found unacceptable. "You were married to a crazy woman for twenty-five years" (106), she adds. Moreover, he accuses her of inventing details about his life. Everything he suggests about Brunswick demonstrates her confrontational style of therapy.

Returning to Suicide

The Wolf-Man remains obsessed with his sister's suicide nearly seventy years after the calamity. "It is a mystery to me why my sister killed herself," he admits to

Obholzer (79). Two pages later he repeats the statement, this time more forcefully. "Now you tell me, why did my sister kill herself? What a strange thing. She had no reason," to which Obholzer can only agree: "It really is incomprehensible." The difference between confession and psychoanalysis, Freud remarks in *The Question of Lay Analysis*, is that in confession, the sinner tells what he knows, whereas in analysis the neurotic must tell more (*SE*, vol. 20, 189). One does not need to be a psychoanalyst to realize that the Wolf-Man feels a continued need to talk about the mystery of suicide. Gardiner reports that when she saw him in April 1938, his first words involved Therese's recent suicide:

> I tried to make out the words coming through his sobs and tears. At last I understood them: "My wife has killed herself. I've just come from the cemetery. Why did she do it? Why did this have to happen to me? I always have bad luck. I'm always subject to the greatest misfortunes. What shall I do, Frau Doktor? Tell me why she killed herself." (*The Wolf-Man by the Wolf-Man* 312)

During her visits with the Wolf-Man in Paris, Gardiner listened to his "tormented and tormenting question: 'Why, why, why did my wife kill herself?'" (314). Gardiner cannot answer his questions, but he felt a degree of relief in speaking his thoughts. And in writing them. He wrote about Therese's suicide in his *Memoirs*, but inexplicably Gardiner deleted some of the material, to his dismay. "I just happen to remember," he tells Obholzer immediately after mentioning his sister's (and wife's) suicide. "I had also written about it in my memoirs, but Gardiner took it out" (79), a statement he repeats on the next page.

Confession remains an essential aspect of the Wolf-Man's story, but it's noteworthy that Freud, Brunswick, and Gardiner read the Wolf-Man's confessions differently than he does. What would have happened, we wonder, if the three analysts spent more time discussing the Wolf-Man's sister's suicide and less time investigating his distant childhood sexual experiences? Most commentators on the Wolf-Man have not emphasized the impact of multiple suicides on his life. Patrick J. Mahony's 1984 book *Cries of the Wolf Man*, comprehensive in its scope and ingenious in its linguistic interpretations, scarcely mentions this event. Suicide was common a century ago, although the psychological research on it was not. "Suicidology" as a separate field did not begin in earnest until the second half of the twentieth century. Edwin S. Shneidman, who was co-director of the Los Angeles Suicide Prevention Center in 1958, established the American Association of Suicidology in 1968.

Some of Freud's analysands took their own lives, such as the psychoanalyst Victor Tausk. As we shall see in the next chapter, Wilhelm Stekel committed suicide. Freud, wracked with cancer and in intolerable pain, ended his life with physician-assisted suicide, although a better term, one endorsed by both the American Association of Suicidology and the American College of Legal Medicine, is aid-in-dying. Other early psychoanalysts who committed suicide, as Paul Roazen points out in *Freud and His Followers*, included Paul Federn, Herbert Silberer, Karin Stephen, Eugenia Sokolnicka, Tatiana Rosenthal, Karl Schrötter, Monroe

Meyer, Martin Peck, Max Kahane, and Johann Honegger. Although Ernest Jones disparaged the idea that psychoanalysis was dangerous, it's nevertheless troubling, Roazen remarks, that so many early analysts fell victim to suicide. Ruth Mack Brunswick's death was not officially deemed a suicide, Roazen reports, "but it was the product of at least half-intentional self-destruction" (435). It's likely that a prolonged discussion of Anna's suicide would have been far more helpful to the Wolf-Man, psychologically, than highly conjectural discussions of the primal scene and castration. His sister's suicide, along with his wife's, was part of his lived experience. Freud and Brunswick could have pointed out to the Wolf-Man what most clinicians now believe: suicide has nothing to do with courage or cowardice and everything to do with hopelessness.

Given the contagious nature of suicide, it's not surprising that the Wolf-Man expresses several times to Obholzer the desire to kill himself. There's nothing rhetorical about his question, which he repeats obsessively, "But what should one do, kill oneself? Should one kill oneself?" (*The Wolf-Man by the Wolf-Man* 162). What makes the question more urgent is that he has a definite suicide plan: gassing himself, as his wife had done. Concerned, Obholzer tells him that gas is now detoxified. He raises the same question in a later chapter, and Obholzer, unnerved, responds, exasperatingly, "Am I supposed to advise you to commit suicide?" (203). She doesn't, but we can understand her fear for his safety.

Ambivalence toward Literature

The Wolf-Man loved to read, and his *Memoirs* abounds in literary references, including *Grimms' Fairy Tales*, *Don Quixote*, *The Sorrows of Young Werther*, *Uncle Tom's Cabin*, the Sherlock Holmes detective novels, and *Dr. Zhivago*. The Wolf-Man and Freud had animated literary discussions. "When I told Freud of my liking for Maupassant, he remarked: 'Not bad taste'" (146). The two men loved Dostoevsky's fiction, including *The Brothers Karamazov*, their favorite novel. Analyst and analysand read literature for pleasure, the best of all reasons, but they had different agendas. Freud read literature mainly because he believed that it confirmed psychoanalytic theory. The Wolf-Man read literature because it helped him feel less alone. His identification with all three brothers in Dostoevsky's novel, Ivan, Dmitri, and Alyosha, helped him realize that the novelist could imagine a conflicted and self-tortured individual like himself. Dostoevsky's novel deepened the Wolf-Man's understanding of his own story.

Postmodernism posits a split, fragmented, or decentered self—a self that is anything but unitary. The Wolf-Man likely would agree that this rang true to his own experience. He saw himself as a split person, declaring to Obholzer that he was not neurotic but schizophrenic (223), although there is no evidence in his *Memoirs* or *Conversations* that he experienced hallucinations or heard voices, two common symptoms of the disorder. Brunswick diagnosed him as paranoid, another symptom of schizophrenia, but Gardiner, reluctant to disagree with her colleague, never saw any signs of paranoia in his behavior. Indignant over

Brunswick's diagnosis, the Wolf-Man insisted to Obholzer that he was never paranoid. There is no such thing as paranoia that comes and goes, he told her, observing that the reason he became well during his analysis with Brunswick was to prove her wrong.

The Wolf-Man was drawn to Dostoevsky because of the novelist's unsurpassed exploration of self-divided characters who live in a state of ambivalence, an existence that the Wolf-Man knew all too well. Objecting to the overuse of the word *ambivalence* by psychoanalysts (and literary critics like myself!), the Wolf-Man recommends an older, simpler, more evocative term: love-hate. "*Ambivalence* is watered down; it's a term you use when the differences are smaller. *Ambivalence* is much weaker than *hatred* and *love*" (136). In his identification with the three Karamazov brothers and with Raskolnikov in *Crime and Punishment*, the Wolf-Man could understand homicidal feelings. Immediately after declaring his wish to kill Luise, he observes that Dostoevsky knew better than Freud how one can escape ambivalence—through murder. He expresses homicidal wishes several times to Obholzer, though not as often as expressing suicidal wishes.

There is much evidence to suggest the value of bibliotherapy, the reading cure. And yet there are risks of a reader's overidentification with a fictional character, particularly if the character is suicidal, as with Goethe's Werther, who commits suicide at the end of the novel. Scores of readers committed suicide upon reading Goethe's story at the end of the eighteenth century, some of them audaciously holding a copy of Goethe's highly autobiographical novel and dressed in Werther's clothes, a dramatic example of the copycat effect. The Wolf-Man's pleasure in reading, as he describes it in his *Memoirs*, has changed to pain in his *Conversations* with Obholzer. "I am telling you, the whole thing is a nightmare," he says about Luise's many illnesses, real and imaginary. "It's the purest Dostoevski" (189). He now concludes that reading Russian literature has harmed him—mainly because novelists like Dostoevsky have glorified peasants and other downtrodden people, heightening his susceptibility to manipulative women like Luise.

Contemplating a novel about his life experiences, the Wolf-Man imagines a man, drawn into a sexually passive role, who recreates the situation in which the author found himself as a boy with his seductive sister. "It's only a step from sister Anna to servant Anna" in his proposed novel. The lesson of the story, as he explains to Obholzer, is that a "person is driven on the wrong sexual path and creates an ideal for himself according to which there must be a component of sadism on the part of the woman" (232). The Wolf-Man has spent much time thinking about how to fictionalize his life experiences. He speaks with such fervor that Obholzer has difficulty determining whether he is referring to a fictional character's story or his own. One can only imagine whether writing this highly autobiographical novel would have helped exorcise his demons. All he needed to become a novelist, perhaps, was encouragement. He was already a wordsmith, using language wryly and aphoristically, quipping, "To become famous is easy, to be famous difficult" (150). The Wolf-Man's fiction might have encouraged psychoanalysts to revise doctrinaire theory. Literary writers' insights into psychoanalysis are no less valuable than psychoanalysts' insights into literature.

Crafting fiction would have given the Wolf-Man greater freedom to write about his life than he felt while penning his *Memoirs*, which he knew had to be approved by the psychoanalytic community. Writing fiction might have released him from the straitjacket of memoir. A talented painter as well as a gifted memoirist, the Wolf-Man could have been a successful novelist, for he was always searching, as Muriel Gardiner pointed out, for the motives and meaning of behavior. Unlike Freud, he would have avoided far-fetched interpretations of his dreams and instead focused on conflicts closer to home, such as exploring the dark legacy, or illegacy, of suicide. He could have intuited reasons why the two most important people in his existence, his sister and wife, chose death over life. His characters might have had the same *idée fixes* as himself, such as staring into his nose with a mirror, but he would be using the veil of fiction to disguise himself. Just as writing his *Memoirs* "diverted" him from his obsessive worries, so might the writing of fiction have had the same salutary effect. He wouldn't be the first patient of psychoanalysis to write about verbal therapy: there is a long tradition of writers who explore in fiction and poetry their own therapeutic experiences, as I discuss in *The Talking Cure* (1985). The Wolf-Man might not have been entirely satisfied with his stories, but few writers are.

And Ambivalence toward Life Writing

In his *Memoirs*, the Wolf-Man speaks positively about his life story, as can be seen in his comments and letters to Muriel Gardiner. True, she had a vested interest in the talking cure, but she could be more open-minded about the writing cure. He was not simply telling her what she wanted to hear. The Wolf-Man expressed nothing but praise about the value of writing his *Memoirs*. Writing "My Recollections of Sigmund Freud" helped ease his depression. He was, in her words, "ecstatically happy and grateful" when she told him about the publication of the chapter. "I can now assure myself that not everything I have done has been in vain" (*The Wolf-Man by the Wolf-Man* 342). Although writing about his wife's suicide appeared initially to deepen his depression, mainly because he was forced to relive the terrifying details, he felt pleased that he rose to the challenge. After completing the *Memoirs*, he experienced, as many writers do, a feeling of emptiness, what might be called *post-artem depression*, which is why Gardiner urged him to continue writing.

Sadly, negativity darkened the ending of the Wolf-Man's life; the pleasure he felt toward writing his *Memoirs* changed to cynicism. He now felt, he told Obholzer, that writing the book was vanity. "Initially, one feels satisfaction. Then time passes and one asks oneself, what was the point of it all?" (166). This is not what Obholzer wants to hear, for she is writing her *own* book and wants to bring it to fruition. Wouldn't it have been better, he asks her, if *Memoirs* had never been published? She disagrees, stating that it has always seemed "glorious" to write a book. "It did to me too, I suppose" (228), he replies, and they leave the question unresolved.

Most readers will agree with Obholzer here. *The Wolf-Man by the Wolf-Man* and *The Wolf-Man: Conversations with Freud's Patient—Sixty Years Later* are fascinating companion pieces, bookends, illustrating the rise and fall of psychoanalysis. Obholzer's volume does not represent the death knell of psychoanalysis, as the antipsychiatry psychiatrist Thomas Szasz implies in his blurb: "A Gem of an addition to the history of what Freud has wrought. This follow-up on the famous case history of the Wolf-Man should help to lay to rest the canard that psychoanalysis is a cure." Szasz is only partly correct. What most benefited the Wolf-Man was not Freud's unconvincing interpretation of his patient's dreams but the strong bond between therapist and patient. It was their personal encounter that proved therapeutic.

Another Psychoanalytic Interpretation of the Story

"The whole psychoanalytic approach is centered around the therapist," stated Otto Rank, who began his career as one of Freud's greatest disciples and ended his career as perhaps Freud's most trenchant critic. "Relational therapy is centered around the client, his difficulties, his needs, his activities" ("Active and Passive Therapy" 260). This is the lesson of the Wolf-Man's *stories*. Freud did not understand the role of the therapist's active, empathic listening. Had Freud concentrated on his relational bond with the Wolf-Man, on the here and now of his patient's life, almost certainly the analysis would have achieved greater therapeutic success. Freud rejected Rank's insights, but Carl Rogers, America's most influential psychologist, listened carefully. The story of Rogers's momentous encounter with Rank in 1936, when he invited the former-Freudian psychoanalyst to Rochester, New York, for a three-day introduction to his new vision of psychotherapy, appears in Robert Kramer's *The Birth of Relationship Therapy* (2019). The Wolf-Man would have welcomed the book because of its emphasis on patient and therapist collaborating together as genuine *coworkers*.

The psychoanalytic commentary on the Wolf-Man is extensive and cannot be briefly summarized, but I should mention Otto Rank's intriguing interpretation of the six or seven wolves in the dream and the infuriated response it elicited from Freud. In *The Letters of Sigmund Freud and Otto Rank* (2012), the coeditors E. James Lieberman and Robert Kramer refer to a passage in the first volume of Rank's *Technik der Psychoanalyse* (1926), not yet translated into English:

> Rank speculates that the Wolf Man's dream was provoked by ambivalent feelings of separation anxiety in the analytic situation, not recalled from childhood. The psychoanalytic couch represents the child's bed, with its foot toward the window through which trees were visible. The "six or seven wolves" might be Freud's six children or the "wolfish" analytic colleagues, including Rank himself, whose photographs adorn the office wall. "I am convinced that this patient knew that Freud had six children; he is the seventh who alone is saved . . . by Freud = the mother." (259)

Rank's belief that the Wolf-Man's dream reveals he is Freud's seventh child, sitting on the "genealogical tree of psychoanalysis," is more plausible than Freud's conjecture of the primal scene. Like the Wolf-Man albeit in a different way, Rank was one of Freud's favorite surrogate sons, his closest Vienna colleague, the industrious secretary of the Vienna Psychoanalytic Society and the only person who, contributing chapters to *The Interpretation of Dreams*, had his name appear under Freud's on the title page of *The Interpretation of Dreams* for fifteen years. But Rank's interpretation of the Wolf-Man's dream went counter to everything Freud was trying to prove about infantile sexuality in his case study. Freud expressed his fury in a letter to Ferenczi. "He interprets the wolf dream of my Russian (at age four) from the analytic situation twenty years later! If that isn't an attempt at self-parody then it can have only one purpose" (*The Letters of Sigmund Freud and Otto Rank* 260). That implicit purpose, for Freud, was nothing less than patricide. Freud gave Ferenczi an ultimatum after the publication of *Technik der Psychoanalyse*: a choice between himself or his close friend Rank. Ferenczi's choice was never in doubt. A few years later, Ferenczi found himself in Rank's position, *persona non grata*.

Rank came to realize that insight therapy was less important to a patient than relational therapy. Significantly, there are no aha! moments in the *Memoirs* that might reflect the sudden revelation of life-transforming insights. Indeed, there are few "insight" words in his life story—and none with respect to his sister's and wife's suicides. The *Memoirs* is notable not because it dramatizes the process of intellectual discovery, showing us a mind that found itself, to quote the title of Clifford Beers's classic 1908 account of overcoming the ravages of mental illness, but because it demonstrates, in a Wordsworthian sense, emotion (and obsession) recollected in tranquility. The Wolf-Man is at his best in offering us a taxonomy of his wildly shifting moods, describing, for example, how his depression infected his father. The closest the Wolf-Man comes to epiphanic insight is when he cites, in Freud's words, the "breakthrough to the woman" (*Memoirs* 56, 138), suggestive of the Oedipal nature of his relationships with women. But little changes following this interpretation. Similarly, he conjures up the phenomenon of derealization—"people seemed to me like wax figures or wound-up marionettes with whom I could not establish any contact" (50)—but the problem remains.

Without any formal training as a psychotherapist, Obholzer intuitively grasps this. She listens carefully to Wolf-Man, validates most of his comments, and, unlike Brunswick, appreciates his role in the history of psychoanalysis. Admittedly, she has her own agenda—completing her book—but this does not detract from her presence in his life. She probably learned more about the Wolf-Man than she bargained for. Some of his statements to her would be worth pursuing if they had an analytic relationship, as when he says, "There's no woman with whom I get along as well as with you" (231). Three pages later he proclaims, "You completely changed my attitude toward women," which confuses her. "How so? I don't understand" (234). Notice how she reacts empathically, listening attentively and asking for more information. He starts to see her as a version of his sister and then begins to develop romantic feeling toward her, despite the fifty-six-year age difference between them. Soon he fears that she will finally abandon him, as his sister and wife did. "I always find it so difficult to leave you," he says. "It is a human experience. And at home, I'm alone once more" (148). Part of this is the developing transference relationship he feels toward her, as they both realize, but another part is the need for attachment and the existential fear of loneliness.

Obholzer visited the Wolf-Man several times at the end of his life, when he was in the Vienna Psychiatric Hospital. She found herself burdened by his slow dying. "Give me some advice!" he cries out to her, searching for a way to free himself from his lifelong ambivalence. Yet, he could still find gallows humor in his situation. "I am completely losing my mind" (249), he says, clapping his hands together in a harlequin gesture that enables them both to laugh. Although Obholzer is not with him when he dies, she reports that when she visited him in the hospital for the last time, she kissed him on his forehead and he responded by kissing her hand, as he used to do, an act she interprets as conveying his deep emotion and gratitude.

Chapter 3

HELENE DEUTSCH

CONFRONTATIONS WITH MYSELF—AN EPILOGUE

"Only after completing this autobiography did I realize that it forms a supplement to the autobiography hidden in my general work *The Psychology of Women*. That is why I have decided to call this book an epilogue." The opening sentence of Helene Deutsch's compelling 1973 autobiography, *Confrontations with Myself: An Epilogue*, tantalizingly invites readers to discover the personal parallels between her most famous theoretical book, the two-volumed *The Psychology of Women*, published between 1944 and 1945, and her artful life story. I'm unaware of any other psychoanalytic memoirist who offers this bold invitation to readers. Beginning with Freud, many psychoanalytic theorists and clinicians have written about themselves in case studies—but in disguised form. Deutsch is far more candid and open than her contemporaries. Yet, had she known that only three years after her death in 1982 at age ninety-seven, a biography would appear that highlighted the intensity of her ambivalence toward the closest people in her life, including her husband and son, it's questionable whether she would have felt sanguine about self-disclosure.

The title of Deutsch's autobiography is vivid albeit misleading. Much of her life and work was indeed filled with *Sturm und Drang*, befitting the career of a genuine pioneer, one of the "mothers of psychoanalysis" (along with Karen Horney, Anna Freud, and Melanie Klein), to quote the title of Janet Sayers's 1991 book. Deutsch takes pains to show in her autobiography that she sought and found harmonious resolutions to her conflicts. Yet we know from Paul Roazen's 1985 biography *Helene Deutsch: A Psychoanalyst's Life* that she excluded much from her life story. Nor is this surprising. No one discloses the full truth about his or her life, partly because no one sees the full truth, and partly because discretion, the better part of valor, limits the full revelation of dark truths. If we read *Confrontations with Myself* alongside Roazen's biography, we see that there were more protracted inner struggles in her exceptional life than she cared to disclose.

Beauty and Intelligence

Regarded as a Helen of Troy, beautiful and smart, Helene Deutsch was a strikingly elegant woman whose physical appearance and strength of character made a lasting impression on her analysands and students, as Marie H. Briehl, a supervising analyst at the Southern California Psychoanalytic Institute, wrote in 1965:

> My memory retains the physical image of Helene Deutsch thirty-five years ago. Her personal beauty—the classic structure of her features, the robust color of her skin, her penetrating blue eyes softened by the halo of brown hair, and the tall, rounded figure clad in attractive and fashionable silks—bespoke a graciousness that did not conceal the strength of character within. In the Slavic rhythm of her speech, her face was dramatically mobile and animated; at rest, it revealed kindliness and feminine softness. (288)

Deutsch was the first director of the Vienna Psychoanalytic Institute's training program, playing a key role in the selection of future analysts. She is best known for her concept of the "as if" personality and for her discussion of the positive implications of female narcissism. She wrote on a wide variety of topics, including pathological lying ("pseudologia phantastica") and the psychology of mistrust. She was the first female psychoanalyst to explore in detail women's psychological development. Although her writing on "female masochism" earned the near-unanimous condemnation of feminists, one is struck, as Brenda Webster observed in an essay published in 1985 in the feminist journal *Signs*, by Deutsch's "emphasis on self-confident activity, mastery, and self-esteem, whether in the young girl, the active mother, or the career woman" (570).

Deutsch spent her entire professional career helping her patients analyze themselves, but she discovered, to her amazement, that she learned more about herself from researching and writing her autobiography than she did from psychoanalysis. The writing cure, as practiced by memoirists, is often more powerful than the talking cure in accessing long-forgotten experiences. Memories loaded with guilt feelings, she observes in the introduction, "offer less resistance if they are called up in the course of autobiography as an objective historical report on oneself" (16). It's doubtful that anyone would today consider autobiography an objective historical report. Nor was she comfortable acknowledging, to herself or her readers, the *full* guilt of her feelings. But she knew that writing, like dreaming, is the royal road to the unconscious.

Deutsch's narrative strategy in *Confrontations with Myself*, as she observes in the chapter "Father," reveals her emotional bias: "the experiences are set down truthfully but the negative elements are often omitted" (40). It was easier for her to write about the past than the present. Unsurprisingly, she is more successful in showing us her ambivalence toward her parents than in conveying it toward her husband and son.

Pursuing Great Expectations

Deutsch always wanted to be a writer, even when she was young. An esteemed aunt convinced her that she had potential literary talent. Deutsch's autobiography abounds in literary references, beginning with Proust, whom she quotes in the introduction. "The memories that emerge from oblivion are more beautiful than the experiences themselves" (13). She cites many novelists, including her fellow Polish countryman, Joseph Conrad, but the novel that perhaps best foreshadows her own life story is Dickens's *Great Expectations*. Not that she was an orphan like Pip, but his hatred for his sadistic sister and surrogate mother, Mrs. Joe Gargery, and his love for his kindly but undependable brother-in-law, the blacksmith Joe, parallel Deutsch's own family dynamics. She despised her mother, who attempted, literally, to beat her into submission. She adored her father but couldn't understand why he chose not to protect her from his wife's wrath. Like Pip, Deutsch was filled with ambition and struggled to overcome the obstacles that prevented women in late nineteenth-century Poland from achieving professional success. Twice she fled from home as an adolescent, the first time when she bought two train tickets in opposite directions to confuse her pursuers. She felt vanquished both times she had to return home, but she never renounced her great expectations.

Pip struggles repeatedly between his strivings for success and his guilt feelings, a conflict that Deutsch knew all too well. Remarking that her parents wished to have a son rather than a daughter, Deutsch writes: "it is clear that before I was born my family had already stigmatized my life with vain expectations" (37). Deutsch's challenge, like Pip's, was to transform vain into great expectations.

Pip remains intensely ambivalent toward all the major characters in the novel, including the embittered Miss Havisham and her stepdaughter Estella, whom she teaches to break men's hearts, especially Pip's. Dickens could never resolve whether his autobiographical hero should permanently have his heart broken, and for this reason, *Great Expectations* has two different endings. Pip is implicated in the deaths of Mrs. Joe and Miss Havisham, a reflection of Dickens's lifelong anger toward his mother. Deutsch didn't kill her mother, though she wanted to. In time she came to see that her mother's cruel beatings were an outlet for her pent-up aggressions. "She let me feel the full force of the grudge she bore me for not being the boy she had wanted and expected" (62). Deutsch viewed her mother as the embodiment of *thwarted* or *morbid* ambition, a situation the daughter vowed would not be true of her own life.

A Puzzling Sentence

In writing about her childhood, Deutsch makes a puzzling statement upon which she never elaborates. In analysis, she traced her tendency to fantasize—which gave her the undeserved reputation of being a fallen woman—to an "actual attempt by my brother to seduce me" (54). How odd that a psychoanalyst would not explain this event in more detail. We recall the Wolf-Man's observation about his sister's efforts to seduce him, an act that had a lifelong traumatic impact on him. According to Roazen, Deutsch had on the waiting room wall in her office in the mid-1960s, when he interviewed her, an etching of Virginia Woolf, herself a victim of childhood sexual abuse by her two stepbrothers. Why did Deutsch believe that a single sentence would convey the significance of her brother's attempted seduction of her? Was it because the attempted seduction wasn't serious enough to warrant further discussion—or because it was too serious to discuss?

Deutsch writes with wry humor about her adolescent rebellion against her parents. A political activist, she became a sensation in the middle-sized Polish town of Przemýsl when, demonstrating on behalf of workers' rights, she encountered mounted police who blockaded her way. Eager for "heroic deeds," she threw herself in front of the horses. The police arrested her and notified her father. "Lock her up," he ordered which, to her disappointment, did not happen. Yet, she came to believe that social and political change, especially with respect to women's rights, would occur only if she worked *with* men rather than *against* them. Deutsch never rebelled against Freudian orthodoxy, but she wrote about motherhood with insights that eluded Freud.

To become a physician at the beginning of the twentieth century was problematic for a woman because of the restrictions placed on female education. To become a psychoanalyst who subscribed to Freud's anti-feminist theory was even more difficult for a brilliant, ambitious, and successful woman who had to accept the belief that women were in fundamental ways inferior to men.

L.

Unlike Pip, Deutsch never had in her childhood a mysterious benefactor like the criminal Magwitch, who rescues him from a grim life. Nor did Deutsch have a dark double, the evil Orlick, who haunts and hunts him throughout the story. But Deutsch had a long and fraught relationship with a man who was for years the center of her femininity. She refers to him frequently in *Confrontations with Myself* only by the initial of his surname, L., as if writing his full name is too painful or too secret. Only once does she refer to his full name: Herman Lieberman. Married and the father of two children, Lieberman was sixteen years older than Deutsch and, like her father, a prominent lawyer. He was also a champion of socialism and irrevocably committed to political and social change. Deutsch's relationship with Lieberman was a "pure" Oedipal situation, she later discovered, partly as a result of her training analysis but mainly as a result of writing her autobiography:

> Here again autobiography has given me a chance to reevaluate events by reliving them. My relationship with L. seems to me now an exact duplicate of my earlier relationship to my parents and a classic example of an Oedipal situation: the man much older than I; the older, unloved wife; and the impossibility of dissolving their marriage. I could not marry my father; I could not marry L. And therefore

I sustained the ambivalent situation, in effect a stalemate, frustrated my own desire for happiness, and nourished L's fantasies of self-sacrifice. (91)

Deutsch's belief, in agreement with Freud, that women were more masochistic than men seemed to arise from her masochistic relationship with Lieberman. She credits insight into her tortured relationship with Lieberman not from her training analysis with Freud or her later analysis with Karl Abraham but from writing her autobiography. "As I can see now, with the objectivity of an old person, the real expectations and demands of this relationship were transformed within my mind, as if by a kaleidoscope, into patterns of heroic resignation and sacrifice. It appears that in me the masochistic element was predominant, while for him it was the fantasy that had stayed with him since early youth of sacrificing himself as Christ did for the suffering of mankind" (103). In retrospect, Deutsch realized that her social idealism was a "modus vivendi" in her rebellion against the tyranny and reactionary attitudes of her hated mother. It was easier for her to give up her political activism than to reject her love for Lieberman, but she eventually ended the self-destructive relationship, although, according to Roazen, Lieberman remained the great love of her life. "Losing Lieberman was to be a central trauma of Helene's life" (*Helene Deutsch* 87). She read in the newspapers that he died in 1944 in London, where he was minister of culture in the Polish government-in-exile.

Felix Deutsch

Deutsch dedicated *Confrontations with Myself* to the memory of her husband, who died in 1964 at age seventy-nine, nine years before the publication of her autobiography. She idealizes him throughout her life story, speaking glowingly about his personal and professional talents that contributed to him being a "brilliant and outstanding physician" (108). Falling in love with Felix, she remarks, helped release her from her unhealthy love for Lieberman. The marriage, which took place in 1912, lasted for fifty-two years. There were conflicts in the beginning, she concedes, which "sometimes even threatened the harmony of our marriage." She never elaborates specifically about the nature of these conflicts except to imply that she was responsible for them. "I infected my husband with my own psychic problems and often caused him mental unrest which, fortunately, he could keep from interfering with his work" (115–16).

One must read between the lines to grasp the nature of their marital problems. "Even after the storms of erotic love were behind us, our deep love never diminished" (119). One page later she uses the same metaphor to describe her periodic discontent with their life together. "'The air was clear,' but somehow I longed for storms" (120). Roazen's biography casts light on her extramarital relationships, including with Paul Bray, her husband's closest friend. Deutsch makes what appears to be a Freudian slip—the only typographical error in the book—when she describes her intuitive insights into people. "My husband's work was to conform and strengthen this intuition" (105). Felix Deutsch's work may have been to *confirm* his wife's insight into human relationships, but he was the less original, innovative, and successful of the two, regarded by many of his contemporaries as serving to *conform* to his wife's authority.

Roazen quotes a letter that Deutsch wrote to her husband in 1923 in which she refers cryptically to the sexual problems in their marriage:

> You see, my dearest friend, my knowledge has been enriched by this insight: like a positive and a negative, our libidinous deficiencies toward each other complement each other and cause our relations to become lamed by friction *one against the other*. And this insight causes me to insist upon your psychoanalysis, since you will not come to health through my health, but rather through your own work. (*Helene Deutsch* 198)

Felix Deutsch was Freud's personal physician, and he incurred Freud's wrath by withholding the truth of the seriousness of his cancer when it was first diagnosed in 1923. In *Confrontations with Myself*, Deutsch does her best to defend her husband from criticism while at the same time acknowledging Freud's demand for the truth. Deutsch is admirably balanced in her discussion, and one could not infer from her autobiography the depth of her consternation, as Roazen suggests: "she was angry with Freud for later speaking so persistently against her husband's conduct. And at the same time she was furious with Felix for being the cause of the new distance between herself and Freud" (*Helene Deutsch* 218).

Deutsch believed, after her husband's death, that her colleague and friend Sanford Gifford, a "great admirer" of Felix, would soon publish a biography of him. "This book seems to be approaching completion," she observes hopefully near the end of *Confrontations with Myself* (206). The biography has never appeared. In his discussion of Felix Deutsch's reluctance to reveal to Freud the full truth of the seriousness of his oral cancer, Peter Gay refers to Gifford's "well-informed unpublished manuscript" as "sympathetic to Deutsch's plight, but unsentimental" (*Freud: A Life for Our Time* 770). Rita K. Teusch's "A Biographical Sketch of Felix Deutsch" was published in *American Imago* in 2017; she never explains why Gifford's various drafts of his extensive manuscripts of Felix Deutsch, one of which is over 100 pages long, have never been published.

"Alone in His Heroic Fight for Truth!"

Deutsch might have become a lawyer, like her father and Lieberman, but women were not allowed to study law in Poland or Vienna. She later tells us, as an aside, that with the help of two other suffragettes, she successfully petitioned the University of Vienna to allow women to study law, but this was after her decision to become a physician. She was one of only seven women in her class in medical school; only three completed the male-dominated program.

Deutsch first became aware of Freud when she read his interpretation of Wilhelm Jensen's novel *Gradiva* in 1907. She was immediately drawn to psychoanalytic theory. She began analysis with Freud in 1918, and he remained the center of her intellectual life. Deutsch's devotion to Freudian theory never wavered. Nor did she seek to psychoanalyze Freud through his own writings, as later scholars have done. Immediately after Freud's death, she wrote an essay in which she agreed with all of his criticisms of biographical writing:

> Most biographers—as is the habit of the majority of them—will be swayed by some more or less unconscious bias of their own: through an effort at popularization, some will falsify both work and master by superficiality; with others, fear of the truth will produce a hostile interpretation; still others—and these are the most dangerous—will be moved by an excess of adoration to present a cult in place of keeping to reality. ("Freud and His Pupils" 184)

After spelling out the dangers of an excess of biographical adoration, Deutsch proceeds to heroicize Freud as one of the great men of science. In the ten-page essay, she refers to Freud's work as "scientific" (or as "science") fifteen times; she uses the word *empirical* to characterize psychoanalysis twelve times. She accepts without qualification Freud's "splendid isolation" during the early years of psychoanalysis, a characterization that we now know was part of his self-mythologizing. The "luminous star on the dark road of a new science," Deutsch enthuses, Freud "stood alone in his heroic fight for truth!" (185). She sees Freud as working entirely within an "objective" tradition, citing a comment he made that does not appear in the *Standard Edition*: "'For a short while,' he said, 'I allowed myself to leave the sheltered bay of direct experience for speculation. I regret it greatly, for the consequences of so doing do not seem of the best'" (193). We can explain Deutsch's excess of biographical adoration by the fact that the essay was, in effect, her obituary of Freud, written while she was in mourning for her lost leader, but her hero worship never changed, as can be seen by *Confrontations with Myself*, written three decades later.

Deutsch never seriously challenged Freud's patriarchal theory, nor did she acknowledge to readers of *Confrontations with Myself* the tensions in their relationship, however minor. To give one example, Deutsch informs us that Karl Abraham, her second training analyst, told her about a letter he received from Freud who, in Deutsch's words, "spoke of me with great warmth and affection" (144). If one reads Roazen's biography, however, one comes across a strange detail. "Early in her analysis Abraham showed her a letter from Freud in which he instructed his disciple that this was a marriage that ought not to be disrupted by analysis" (*Helene Deutsch* 193). Why would Freud issue this warning to Abraham, his most trusted colleague? Because he sensed that the marriage was too precarious to be analyzed?

According to Roazen, Deutsch felt that her analysis with Abraham had been a failure. Deutsch admits in *Confrontations with Myself* that when Freud abruptly terminated her analysis because he needed the hour to allow the Wolf-Man to return to analysis, she felt rejected and suffered the first depression of her life. "It was a lesson for a future analyst" (133), she writes, putting on the best possible face. Elsewhere, she smooths over her conflicts with Freud. When, for instance, she told him that she and her family were moving to the United States in the mid-1930s because of their awareness of the growing Nazi menace, Freud, who was slow to recognize the threat, grew irritated. Roazen reports that when Deutsch sent Freud a congratulatory letter on the occasion of his eightieth birthday in May 1936, he responded with the words, "Loving but unreconciled" (*Helene Deutsch* 292), an indication of his disapproval over what he perceived to be her desertion of him.

Despite her objections to biographical criticism, Deutsch agreed to help Paul Roazen write his biography of her. In his 1993 edition of her collected psychoanalytic papers *The Therapeutic Process, the Self, and Female Psychology*, Roazen details his long relationship with her. He began interviewing her on a weekly basis in the mid-1960s when he was writing his first book *Freud: Political and Social Thought* (1968), a revision of his Harvard doctoral dissertation. Their cordial relationship became strained when Deutsch found out, from one of Anna Freud's supporters, about his next book *Brother Animal: The Story of Freud and Tausk* (1969). Highly critical of Freud's role in Tausk's suicide, *Brother Animal* displeased the orthodox psychoanalytic community. Deutsch told Roazen that she was "ambivalent" about the book; her colleagues believed that she had been "indiscreet" in confiding in him (*The Therapeutic Process* xv). Several years passed, and when Roazen found out in 1977 that her health was failing, he contacted Deutsch, and a year later she agreed to help him write his authorized biography. He interviewed her until shortly before her death, and she gave him access to her correspondence, which he quotes at length in his biography.

Anna Freud

In his 2004 reexamination of his biography, Roazen admits that Deutsch's relationship with Anna Freud was more tense than he initially thought. Roazen was surprised when he interviewed Anna Freud in London in 1965 that she seemed warm and friendly in her comments about Felix Deutsch but uninterested in learning how Helene Deutsch was doing in old age. In her 1998 biography of Anna Freud, Elizabeth Young-Bruehl dismisses *Brother Animal* as a "sloppy, superficial book," citing Anna Freud's remark: "Even though Roazen professes to have admiration for analysis itself, he is busy trying to dig up whatever negative facts about personalities he can find. This includes my father and me and what he cannot find he invents" (432–3). Anna Freud's annoyance with Roazen is understandable: he was the first to point out in print that Freud analyzed her, a fact she never disputed. Roazen's biography of Deutsch is, in my judgment, sympathetic and balanced; I have no reason to question his observations or conclusions about her.

Freud's insight that psychoanalysis brings out the worst in everyone becomes Roazen's guiding biographical principle. He exposes the hidden and not-so-hidden mistrust between Deutsch and Anna Freud, each competing with the other over being Freud's favorite daughter. Deutsch goes out of her way in *Confrontations with Myself* to speak highly of Anna Freud who, after her father's death, became the reigning monarch of psychoanalysis. In the discussion of Freud in *Confrontations with Myself*, Deutsch thanks Anna Freud for her help in "correcting mistakes of my memory in this chapter" (128, n.1). Later Deutsch praises Anna Freud as a "dedicated teacher of young children" (140). Deutsch named the farm she and her husband purchased in Wolfeboro, New Hampshire, "Babayaga," imagining it as a counterpart to Hochroterd (High Red Earth), the cottage outside Vienna to which Anna Freud and her companion, Dorothy Burlingham, retreated during summer vacations.

Roazen found nothing to document Deutsch's antagonism toward Anna Freud, but he notes that the founder of psychoanalysis wanted Deutsch to share more of the work at the Vienna Psychoanalytic Institute with his daughter:

> The ambivalent rivalry between them was of long-standing; although Anna had had no academic education, by the mid-1930s Freud had succeeded in building her up as his successor within the movement. Originally Helene had affectionately identified with Anna, viewing her as a pupil; yet she always remembered how coldly Freud had turned aside her compliments on Anna's first presentation in 1922 before the Vienna society. On Anna's part, she admired Helene and yet feared that she would never be as good. (*Helene Deutsch* 287)

Writing about Her Son

Named after Freud's oldest son, Martin Deutsch was born in Vienna in 1917 and immigrated to the United States with his parents in 1935. A wunderkind in physics and math, he enrolled in MIT and completed his bachelor's degree in two years. He spent the rest of his career as professor of physics at MIT except for the two years he served as a researcher at the top-secret Manhattan Project in Los Alamos, New Mexico—where he needed special security clearance because he was still a German subject. Acclaimed for his discovery of the short-lived atomic particle positronium, Martin Deutsch died in 2002 at age eighty-five.

Contrary to the idealized statement Freud made about the mother-son relationship in *New Introductory Lectures on Psycho-Analysis* (1933)—"A mother is only brought unlimited satisfaction by her relation to a son; this is altogether the most perfect, the most free from ambivalence of all human relationships" (*SE*, vol. 22, 133)—there was intense hostility between Deutsch and her only child. Deutsch doesn't write much about her son in *Confrontations with Myself*, but she implies that Martin was closer to his father than mother. Noting that she spent the year 1924 working in Berlin to create the Vienna Training Institute, she regretted she was separated from her seven-year-old son who "paid the heaviest price for my professional progress during this year" (162). She concedes in the same paragraph that he was "in a sense neglected by his mother." Deutsch believed that because of the demands of Paula, the nurse who cared for her son, she was forced to "abdicate" a great part of her motherhood (124). She uses the same word a few pages later when she acknowledges her conflicts over motherhood with Paula. "After all it was my silent agreement with this woman that made my professional activity possible: I could work on the condition that in effect I abdicate my role of mother in her favor" (133).

To understand the consequences of this early neglect, one must turn to Roazen's biography, which quotes Deutsch's worried letters to her husband. "Martin is more neurotic than I ever thought," she wrote upon his acceptance to MIT. "I believe he is more neurotic than he ever was. Besides murderous, hate-filled aggression against me, which even outsiders notice, he shows such strong masochistic tendencies that it fills one with fright" (*Helene Deutsch* 284). According to Roazen, Deutsch was so disturbed by her son's behavior that she bewailed, "I don't believe in analytic therapy" (*Helene Deutsch* 284).

Deutsch doesn't mention in her autobiography that one of her earliest professional articles was about Martin in thinly disguised form. Upon Freud's enthusiastic recommendation, "A Two-Year-Old Boy's First Love Comes to Grief" was published in 1919 and reprinted in 1959 and then again in 1965 in *Neuroses and Character Types*. The opening paragraph highlights the consequences of maternal absence:

> Rudi was just two when his nurse left him. Because of his mother's heavy professional schedule and because of the pressure of external events, this nurse had been a mother surrogate to little Rudi for two years. It was she who from the beginning served all his autoerotic needs; it was she who fed him, assisted him with his excretory functions, and fulfilled his wishes. Consequently, in his first object choice Rudi disregarded his mother. Indeed, the nurse well knew how to make little Rudi's object choice even more exclusive, for she did not allow anyone else to perform the tasks of love. (159)

As a result of his maternal surrogate's departure, Rudi became distraught, crying, soiling his bed, refusing food, and asking for his absent nurse. On the ninth day of separation, Rudi "returned to reality," albeit with a change. "In a sense, he had become socialized; he was more tender, and more in need of tenderness" (162). Deutsch uses Freud's libido theory to describe Rudi's changes. "In his eating habits, Rudi expressed the cannibalistic phase of his pregenital sexual development" (164). Rudi's reaction to maternal loss would today be better explained in terms of John Bowlby's attachment behavior. Deutsch always felt that her husband was more "motherly" than she was. In volume 2 of *The Psychology of Women*, she refers to the "motherliness of the husband, without whose active help that of the wife cannot function" (273).

Therapists can write about themselves in a case study with or without disguise, but it's ethically problematic to write about others, patients or relatives, without their permission. When writing *Confrontations with Myself*, Deutsch knew that some readers would realize that "Mrs. Smith" in volume 2 of *The Psychology of Women* was a case study about her own fraught relationship with her parents and siblings.

It's doubtful, however, that she wanted readers to see the autobiographical nature of "A Two-Year-Old Boy's First Love Comes to Grief." We don't know how Martin Deutsch felt about reading his case study, but I suspect that it only deepened his anger toward his mother, with whom he had a permanently strained relationship. Many parents can identify with Deutsch's conflict about being torn between family and career, a struggle that was more difficult a century ago. Deutsch was an inspiring role model for many women of her generation—and ours. But it's ironic that her research on motherhood interfered with her own experience of being a mother. "Motherhood is a tyrannical full-time emotional task," Deutsch writes at the end of *Selected Problems of Adolescence* (1967); "part-time motherhood is a compromise that hurts both masters: professional work and motherhood" (130). That she reprinted "A Two-Year-Old Boy's First Love Comes to Grief" twice, when her son reached adulthood, suggests that she had little reluctance in writing about him. In *Children of Psychiatrists and Other Psychotherapists* (1989), Thomas Maeder writes about children who are burdened by having a parent who is a psychotherapist. Having two therapist-parents, Maeder contends, himself the son of two therapists, is a double whammy.

What do grandparents and grandchildren have in common? A "common enemy," according to the Israeli psychologist Haim Ginott. I don't know whether Martin Deutsch would have agreed with this answer, but there's no question that he felt closer to his father than mother. Deutsch admits in *Confrontations with Myself* that often during Martin's childhood and youth, she thought to herself, "How glad I am that you're *his* son!" (125). She had a better relationship with her two grandsons, about whom she speaks tenderly throughout *Confrontations with Myself*, though she refers to one of them, Peter, far more often than to the other, Nicholas, implying favoritism.

Complicated Grief

Deutsch lived a long, rich, and full life. Anyone who has lost a beloved spouse can begin to understand her deep mourning after her husband died. "The loneliness of my present life and my ceaseless mourning for my husband are visibly influencing the associative course of my memories" (53). Whenever remorse invades her peace of mind, she observes near the end of her autobiography, she reminds herself that her devotion to him during his last days was her "expiation" (206). On two other occasions in *Confrontations with Myself*, she refers to this profound loss. "It becomes increasingly painful for me to write about the person whom I cannot and probably never will cease to mourn" (127). And near the end of her autobiography, she refers to her "never-ending grief" (215).

In her 1937 essay "Absence of Grief," reprinted in *Neuroses and Character Types*, Deutsch agrees with Freud that if mourning is excessive or delayed, the reason is usually not the positive ties to the lost loved one but rather the degree of persistent guilt and ambivalence. "In such cases, the reaction to death is greatly intensified, assuming a brooding, neurotically compulsive, even melancholic character" (227).

One wonders whether her never-ending grief over her husband's death arose from the same persistent guilt and ambivalence.

"Complicated grief disorder" is a twenty-first-century concept developed by psychiatrists and clinical psychologists, not psychoanalysts. Complicated grief involves, as Mardi Horowitz and her associates write, the "intensification of grief to the level where the person is overwhelmed, resorts to maladaptive behavior, or remains interminably in the state of grief without progression of the mourning process towards completion" (1157). There's no evidence in *Confrontations with Myself* or in Roazen's biography that Deutsch engaged in maladaptive behavior after her husband's death, but if we take her at her word, she could not imagine overcoming her mourning. She ends her autobiography with the ambiguous statement that she wants "nothing more than a very long sabbatical" (217), which is not exactly a death wish but rather a sense that her life is all but over. Roazen implies that Deutsch's idealization of her husband contained guilt for her failure to love him as much as he loved her. "Although while he was alive she could resent having overshadowed him, for the remaining eighteen years of her life Helene reacted by idealizing her union with Felix" (*Helene Deutsch* 327).

What shall we finally say about *Confrontations with Myself*? The autobiography raises many questions, not all of which are answered. "By the time this narrative is finished," Deutsch observes at the beginning of her life story, "I shall know whether I can recommend the writing of an autobiography to other lonely people whose lives are nearly at an end" (14). For whatever reason, she fails to return to this question at the end. *Confrontations with Myself* is more confessional than Deutsch is willing to disclose, reminding us of Oscar Wilde's paradoxical observation that sometimes talking about oneself is a means of concealing oneself. Nevertheless, one senses that despite her misgivings and regrets, and notwithstanding the wrenching compromises she was forced to make to find a balance between family and work, Helene Deutsch led a deeply rewarding life, fulfilling her great expectations.

Chapter 4

WILHELM STEKEL

AUTOBIOGRAPHY

I first became aware of Wilhelm Stekel through my closest friend and confidant, Holden Caulfield. I was a young teenager when I read J.D. Salinger's 1951 novel *The Catcher in the Rye*. Holden, lurching toward a nervous breakdown at the end of the story, hears his English teacher, Mr. Antolini, quote the words of a psychoanalyst, Wilhelm Stekel: "The mark of the immature man is that he wants to die nobly for a cause, while the mark of the mature man is that he wants to live humbly for one" (188). I didn't know any psychoanalysts at the time, and I wondered who Stekel was. Was he a mature man?

Years later, when I became enthralled with Freud, I read Ernest Jones's three-volume hagiographic biography (1953–7). Jones had nothing good to say about Stekel, who was one of Freud's earliest disciples. Of the many references to Stekel in the second and third volumes of Jones's biography, nearly all are negative. For example, when Stekel first met Freud, Jones informs us, Stekel suffered from a "troublesome neurotic complaint, the nature of which I need not mention" (Jones, vol. 2, 7). It's the only time Jones is circumspect about Stekel. Freud, who was often "remarkably indiscreet," as another biographer, Peter Gay, points out, told Jones about the "nature of Stekel's sexual perversion" (Gay 187).

In his other references, Jones takes pleasure—Schadenfreude—in citing Freud's and his own objections to Stekel. "Your critical remarks on Stekel's book are obviously true; you have hit the mark," Freud confided to Jones on November 20, 1909. "He is weak in theory and thought but he has a good flair for the meaning of the hidden and unconscious" (Jones, vol. 2, 62). Jones and Stekel competed for father-Freud's approval; the ever-loyal Jones won while the unfaithful Stekel lost and was excommunicated. Even when Jones tried to acknowledge Freud's initial approval of Stekel, the biographer was quick to add a damning comment. "Stekel had no critical powers at all, and when he once cut himself loose from the amount of discipline that common work with colleagues imposed, his intuition degenerated into wild guess work" (vol. 2, 134–5). Many years later, Jones reports, Freud referred to Stekel in the harshest words, a case of "moral insanity" (vol. 2, 137).

Freud also spoke brutally to his analysands about Stekel, as Joseph Wortis reports in *Fragments of an Analysis with Freud*. Freud became irate when Havelock Ellis recommended that Wortis enter analysis with Stekel:

> He then said some very harsh things of Stekel: a man of no scruples, with no regard for others, of the meanest ambitions, with petty ideas of grandeur ("*mit erbsengrossem Grössenwahn,*" if I remember him correctly; I am at least sure he used the word *erbsengross,* which means "the size of a pea") . . . whose behavior was such "that it was impossible to have any further relations with him." (30; ellipsis in original)

Nor have many later psychoanalytic scholars been kind to Stekel. His work was "somewhat journalistic," Paul Roazen declares condescendingly in *Freud and His Followers* (1975), "and his interest in sexuality remained quasi-pornographic; to some in the movement he seemed a dubious character with a dirty-minded interest in case material" (211).

Based on my reading of Freud and Jones, my initial opinion of Stekel and the other early psychoanalysts who were branded with the label "dissenters," such as Alfred Adler and C.G. Jung, was not positive. My attitude toward him changed, however, when I read *The Autobiography of Wilhelm Stekel: The Life Story of a Pioneering Psychoanalyst,* published posthumously in 1950, ten years after his death at age seventy-two. The *Autobiography* is unusually candid for its time, and Stekel comes across more sympathetically than Freud and Jones suggested. Stekel is far from perfect, as we shall see, and there's much that he holds back, but it's understandable that Mr. Antolini should quote Stekel's words—despite the dark irony that Stekel committed suicide, something the English teacher does *not* reveal to the self-destructive Holden.

Anticipating Problems

Stekel wrote the *Autobiography* near the end of his life, when he was suffering from diabetic gangrene of the foot and prostate difficulties. These medical problems occurred as the Nazis were annexing Austria, conquering Poland, France, and Norway, and bombing London, where Stekel took refuge after narrowly escaping from Vienna and Switzerland. Without a home or a homeland, penniless, and ill, his situation was desperate. After his death—he overdosed on aspirin—and following the wishes of his second wife, Hilda Stekel, his former analysand, Emil A. Gutheil, edited the "disorganized" manuscript. The editorial task was daunting, and Gutheil anticipated some of the book's problems:

> The student of psychoanalysis can see in Stekel's notes how many of his own complexes remained obscure to him, can detect his unresolved narcissism, his overcompensated feelings of inadequacy; will smile when he reads that the man who was a master in ferreting out other people's repressions believed that he had

hardly any himself. Then there is Stekel's failure to recognize his affect-heavy attitude toward his teacher, Freud, upon whom he tried in vain to transfer his own father-complex. (13).

Non-psychoanalytic readers will see the same problems. Stekel did not suffer from low self-esteem, and a good editor would have advised him to tone down the self-congratulatory passages, as when he conveys a stranger's greeting on a passenger ship, "Are you the well-known Stekel who wrote an excellent book on dreams?" (224), or when he describes how dogs look like their masters: "Do I sound conceited if I say that my dogs have always been extremely clever?" (268). Stekel proudly mentions that the journalist John Gunther presented him with a copy of a book with the inscription, "To the man who gave me Eyes and Wings." Gutheil's editorial note indicates that Gunther listed Stekel in an article in *Look* magazine as one of the ten most interesting people he had met; others on the list include Mahatma Gandhi, Winston Churchill, and H.G. Wells (283, n.4).

Writing for posterity, Stekel saw himself as a psychoanalytic pioneer who earned a place in history. It's jarring when he abruptly changes from first to third-person narration to revel in his own glory at the dawn of the psychoanalytic movement, as when he writes about a patient's father who had "read books by Freud and Stekel" (210), or when he describes the "difference between Freud and Stekel" (245). Fortunately, these problems do not seriously detract from his *Autobiography*. It remains a valuable record of the origins of psychoanalysis, as told by an insider-turned-outsider. Additionally, Stekel's *Autobiography* is a vibrant portrait of a man who, lacking the time, inclination, or ability to retouch the photo of his life, narrates a story of personal successes and failures that the other early psychoanalysts were unwilling to do. Stekel regarded himself as Freud's first student, and his *Autobiography* was one of the earliest by a psychoanalyst.

Inspired by Rousseau

Stekel's literary model for *Autobiography* was Jean-Jacques Rousseau's *Confessions*, one of the great landmarks of Western literature. According to Peter France, Rousseau's *Confessions* represents the "fountain head of modern writing about the self," in effect, the first example of the modern literary genre of autobiography (109). Completed in 1769 and published in French in 1782, four years after Rousseau's death at age sixty-six, the *Confessions* is startlingly frank for its time, exploring the psychological dynamics of masochism and masturbation, two subjects that were of personal and clinical interest to Stekel. Rousseau's *Confessions* demonstrates the Wordsworthian (and Freudian) idea that the child is father to the man. "It took Freud to think Rousseau's ideas," observed the Swiss literary critic and psychiatrist Jean Starobinski (qtd. in France 97).

Stekel lacked Rousseau's dazzling insights and expressive prose style, but he displays a gift for language and talent for paradox that enliven his story. Spurned by his "first love," Stekel, intuiting that suffering is sometimes a muse for art, was "happy in the unhappiness that provided the inspiration for new poems" (51). He was a prolific writer, authoring many books, including his magnum opus, the ten-volume *Disturbances of the Impulses and the Emotions*, published between 1912 and 1928. Stekel didn't have Freud's genius—few did—but he loved to write, repeating what the noted psychiatrist Krafft-Ebing said to him: "Should you ever become infected with the printer's ink, you will never recover" (104). Stekel includes in his *Autobiography* some of his poems, written in German and translated by Gutheil. The full extent of Gutheil's editing of the *Autobiography* is unknown. The English translator of the *Autobiography* is not listed, but it was probably James S. Van Teslaar, who translated many of Stekel's books.

Stekel was an accomplished musician, playing the piano, violin, and viola and performing in amateur orchestras and string quartets. He wrote songs, many of which were published and recorded. His love for poetry can be seen not only in his own poems but also in those he quotes, as when he cites Tennyson's well-known line from *In Memoriam*: "There lives more faith in honest doubt, believe me, than in half the creeds" (239)—an insight that foregrounds Stekel's honest doubt about Freudian theory.

Wild Analysis

Stekel wrote his *Autobiography* when psychoanalysis was approaching its golden age. Some of his statements strike us as either offensive or far-fetched. Like many of his contemporaries, he believed that homosexuality was pathological and could be "cured" through analysis. He goes out of his way to tell us that he did not respond to a flattering letter written to him by a member of an "international group of homosexuals" (70). Stekel maintained that homosexuality is always a factor in male impotence; homosexuality represents a "flight from womanhood," he opines in his two-volume *Impotence in the Male*, first published in German in 1920 and then in English in 1927. He traced homosexuality to what he considered universal bisexuality (vol. 2, 183). Later in the same volume he asserts that the homosexual "harbors an attitude of sadism (with hatred) toward womanhood" (vol. 2, 250). This homophobic interpretation is consistent with the view of many other early psychoanalysts. Stekel also believed that psychoanalysis could cure neurological diseases like epilepsy. He maintained, moreover, that an analyst can achieve "complete objectivity" (*Autobiography* 204).

Some of Stekel's clinical interpretations in his *Autobiography* are overly clever, almost unconscious self-parodies, performative art that undercuts his credibility. His early article "The Obligation of the Name" attempts to prove that a person's entire life and choice of career may be determined by his surname. Analyzing a patient who suffered from "morbid doubt," Stekel describes a man who had to sort and prepare for mailing a few packages out of hundreds. "I have the compulsion to count these packages again and again, and I am never sure." Stekel asks him his last name. "Sure" (131). Stekel was so enamored of his theory of the relationship between names and character traits that he listed the surnames in *Impotence in the*

Male: "I have found sadists who were called *Schneider* (cutter), *Stecher* (stabber), *Bohrer* (borer), *Fleischer* (butcher), *Metzger* (butcher), *Hacker* (chopper), *Klopfer* (beater), *Schlager* (beater), and masochists named, *Diener* (servant), *Unterberger* (Under-berger), *Freundlich* (Friendly), *Dulder* (martyr), *Trager* (carrier), and *Träger* (bearer)" (vol. 1, 322 f.14). Stekel cannot understand why Freud vetoed "The Obligation of the Name" for publication in their psychoanalytic journal, *Zentralblatt für Psychoanalyse*. Citing Jones, Peter Gay asserts that Stekel made up his case studies, including, presumably, the name of "Sure" (214), but another Freud biographer, Louis Breger, states that there is no evidence for this rumor (206).

Another problem with Stekel's *Autobiography* is the ease with which he announces psychoanalytic cures. These cures, he often adds, are "permanent." None of his case studies has the literary or psychological complexity of Freud's case studies. Nor does Stekel convince us with his postscripts, where he claims to have seen patients years later who attest to their complete therapeutic recoveries. In the chapter "A Trip to America," he criticizes authors of self-help books who promise therapeutic recovery, but too often Stekel's *Autobiography* sounds like the genre it rejects. The problem is not that bibliotherapy is ineffective; rather, we can never be sure of Stekel's reliability as a narrator of his patients' experiences.

Stekel's comments about art are more reductive than Freud's. Stekel refers to his book *Poetry and Neurosis*, which argues that "all poets are neurotics, and that poetry is an abreaction of neurosis" (124). It is a curious statement from a man who loved to write poetry himself. Stekel's interpretation of *Hamlet* strains belief. Based on the flimsiest textual evidence, Claudius calling Hamlet "my son" instead of "my nephew," Stekel proposes that Hamlet's doubts about his paternity explain his delay in following the Ghost's injunction to kill Claudius. "Had the liaison of Claudius and his mother started before he was born? In that case the killing of Claudius would be parricide" (232). Sometimes Stekel's use of Freudian terminology is clunky, as when he describes his first wife's hurtful words to him, which provoked his desire to avenge an unwarranted insult. "I wanted to forget it, but the id drove me to decisions I usually would not have made" (92).

Stekel's Early Life

The story of Stekel's life is lively and effectively narrated. He was born on March 18, 1868, in Boyan (Boiany), Bukovina, which at the time was Austrian territory. (It later became part of Romania during Stekel's lifetime, then was seized by the Soviet Union, and is now a village in western Ukraine.) Stekel's first language was Ukrainian, but he learned German, French, and English. It's surprising to hear that while he was growing up in a small village consisting of four nationalities—Romanian, Polish, Ukrainian, and German—he never encountered any anti-Semitism, a situation far different from Freud's upbringing in Freiberg, Moravia, now part of the Czech Republic, and from Deutsch's experience growing up in Poland. Stekel recounts with relish his many "misdeeds" as a youth, including visiting a house of "ill-fame" when he was fourteen, remarking that he experienced his first "sleepless night" (46) when he returned home.

The early chapters of *Autobiography* chronicle Stekel's childhood, university days, and medical training. There's little out of the ordinary in his depiction of a late nineteenth-century Eastern European Jew intent on studying medicine. In medical school he encountered an anti-Semitic incident that nearly cost him his life. In a pathology class he witnessed a burly German medical student tormenting a "little Jew." Enraged, Stekel challenged the German, who was an officer, to a duel. Between the formal challenge and the proposed date, Stekel studied the art of fencing, and both men sensibly agreed not to go ahead with the duel. Following medical school, he served in the First World War despite being a committed pacifist. Afterward, he established a thriving practice in Vienna. He published his first paper on "Coitus in Children," written independently of Freud, he is careful to note. Notwithstanding his egotism, Stekel readily acknowledges his medical mistakes, as when he failed to recognize, to his chagrin, that a young female patient's rash was a simple case of measles. Stekel married, built his medical practice, had children, hiked in the Alps, and played music. Life was good.

Others might have been content with Stekel's existence as a physician, a medical author, poet, musician, husband, and father. Not Stekel. Restless, ambitious, and driven, he found himself suffering from a mid-life crisis. He wrote a poem called "Resignation" and saw the handwriting on the wall. "I became rather pot-bellied," he confesses. "In the afternoon I played cards—in short, I was well on the way to becoming a Philistine" (100). It was at this moment in his life that he had his fateful meeting with Freud.

"The Apostle of Freud"

Many of Stekel's publications appeared in newspapers and popular magazines, and he soon learned to his great pleasure that Freud had quoted "Coitus in Children." Stekel returned the favor, writing a favorable review of *The Interpretation of Dreams* in 1902. One of the first to proclaim Freud's greatness, Stekel proudly quotes a comment made by Freud's first biographer, Fritz Wittels: "The printing machines of Europe sighed under the burden of the papers Stekel wrote on Freud." Stekel's next comment contains more truth than he realized: "I was the apostle of Freud who was my Christ!" (106).

Stekel was one of the first members of Freud's inner circle to warn that psychoanalysis was becoming a religious ideology masquerading as science. He returns to this idea later in the *Autobiography* when describing psychoanalytic congresses. "Psychotherapy was for many members like a religion, and opinions not fitting into a specific theory were excluded" (237). Stekel's criticisms of psychoanalysis never suggest a loss of faith in the talking cure but rather an awareness of Freud's theoreticism. (Despite the many times Freud quoted Charcot's statement, "Theory is good, but it doesn't prevent things from existing," he was always a theorist and rarely an empiricist.) Sometimes Stekel's comments about psychoanalysis are contradictory. He refers to verbal therapy as the "wonderful science of psychoanalysis" (200) and a few pages later as the "wonderful art of psychoanalysis" (215). Many have argued that psychoanalysis is both a science and art, like other forms of psychotherapy.

Stekel relished his early role as apostle, and Freud accepted his suggestion in 1902 to meet every Wednesday evening at Freud's home to talk about his new creation. In the beginning there were only five men at the Wednesday Psychological Society, which became the Vienna Psychoanalytic Society in 1908: Freud, Stekel, Max Kahane, Rudolf Reiter, and Alfred Adler. "There was complete harmony among the five, no dissonances," Stekel enthuses; "we were like pioneers in a newly discovered land, and Freud was the leader" (116).

Trouble soon invaded paradise, however. To begin with, Stekel rightly questioned Freud's exclusive emphasis on the sexual causation of neurosis. Stekel had other objections, such as Freud's belief that patients are cured once they understand their psychic traumas, an assumption that Stekel calls "one of the passing fallacies of the early days of psychoanalysis" (125). A. Kardiner makes the same criticism in *My Analysis with Freud*: "He thought that once you had uncovered the Oedipus complex and understood your unconscious homosexuality, that once you knew the origins and the sources of all these reactions, something would happen that would enable you to translate these insights into your current life and thereby alter it" (62–3). Stekel sometimes made the same mistakes that Freud did, such as offering interpretations that patients were not yet ready to hear, but he learned from his mistakes. The analyst must not be a "fanatic" with regard to truth, Stekel contends later in his *Autobiography* (206). His criticism was prescient, as were his other objections. "Many patients are cured because someone is interested in their cases," he remarked, a recognition of what is now considered the most salient factor in therapeutic success: a strong patient-therapist relationship. Stekel's next sentences are even more noteworthy:

> Often, it is not the method that is responsible for the success, it is the satisfaction of the patient's desire for sympathy, of his longing for interest and companionship. This fact may explain the success of different schools of psychotherapy; it shows that success can never prove a method to be "right." (151)

This passage, which most contemporary clinicians would endorse, is extraordinary in its prophetic accuracy. Stekel's recognition of the patient's need for sympathy, or what today would be called empathy, was unusual more than three-quarters of a century ago. Admittedly, Stekel doesn't always come across in his *Autobiography* as an empathically gifted therapist. He tells us, for example, that he could treat patients only if they awakened his interest, which did not always happen. Nevertheless, Stekel was honest enough to make this admission, which he then follows with a philosophical observation: "Paracelsus was right in saying, 'The only thing we doctors can give our patients is our love'" (117).

Indeed, Stekel was one of the first to recognize that the key to therapeutic success is the patient-analyst relationship. "*As a matter of fact*," he emphasizes in *Impotence in the Male*, "*it is not the method that cures, but only the physician*" (vol. 2, 301). The existential American psychiatrist Irvin D. Yalom makes the same statement in his 2005 novel, *The Schopenhauer Cure*: "*It's not ideas, nor vision, nor tools that truly matter in therapy*. If you debrief patients at the end of therapy about the process, what do they remember? *Never* the ideas—it's *always* the relationship. They rarely remember an important insight their therapist offered but generally fondly recall their personal relationship with the therapist" (62–3). Yalom repeats the statement in *Love's Executioner*, his 1989 collection of psychotherapy tales: "It's the relationship that heals, the relationship that heals, the relationship that heals— my professional rosary" (98). It was Stekel's credo too.

Stekel makes other valuable statements in his *Autobiography* about the nature of psychotherapy. Without confusing the roles of analysts and teachers, he argues that psychoanalysis is a process of reeducation. "I do not exaggerate when I say that the fate of humanity lies in the hands of teachers" (50). Although Jung's supervisor at the Burghölzli Hospital in Zurich, Switzerland, Eugen Bleuler, coined the term *ambivalence*, a word popularized by Freud, Stekel preceded both of them with the word *bipolarity*. Our affects are bipolar, he insisted: "Desire and disgust, love and hate, will-to-power and will-to-submission, are composed of negative and positive parts like the current of electricity" (*Autobiography* 132). "Bipolarity" has never made its way into English (apart from bipolar disorder, formerly called manic depression), nor have Stekel's other clinical words survived, such as *parapathy* (neurosis), *paralogia* (psychosis), and *paraphilia* (perversion). Some of Stekel's other terms are infelicitous, such as "Jew-complex" (259). Nevertheless, Stekel has many useful pragmatic suggestions, including the value of brief psychotherapy. Many contemporary psychoanalysts would agree with Stekel that Freud exaggerated the role of castration anxiety. Stekel also strikes a timely note in his observation that the "truths" of psychoanalysis "have not yet been fully proven" (204). Henri Ellenberger observes in *The Discovery of the Unconscious* that Stekel formulated a vision and technique of psychoanalysis that represented a valuable alternative to the Freudian view. "Stekel's teaching shows the aspect psychoanalysis might have taken if it had been a purely empirical, practical method without the solid foundation of a theoretical substructure" (598).

Masturbation

Freud never doubted that masturbation is psychologically damaging. He claimed, even in his early pre-psychoanalytic writings, that those who masturbate are likely to develop an anxiety neurosis. In *The Interpretation of Dreams* (1900), he maintained that the connection between masturbation and impotence is "obvious enough" (*SE*, vol. 4, 187). In "'Civilized' Sexual Morality and Modern Nervous Illness" (1908), Freud argued that masturbation and abstinence produce the same psychic problems, weakening one's character through "*indulgence*" (*SE*, vol. 9, 199; emphasis in original). Freud's fullest comment appears in "Contributions to a Discussion of Masturbation" (1912), which he first delivered to the Vienna

Psychoanalytic Society in 1910, a meeting in which Stekel also participated. Freud admitted that his attitude toward masturbation was "conservative," and then he made the following messianic statement. "But I know that I have a destiny to fulfill. I cannot escape it and I need not move towards it" (*SE*, vol. 12, 250). It is a "curious fact," states James Strachey, that, apart from Freud's belief that masturbation provoked guilt in boys and girls, almost all of his later references to masturbation are in relation to the "dread of castration" (*SE*, vol. 12, 242). Paul Roazen reports in *Meeting Freud's Family* (1993) that Freud warned his sixteen-year-old son Oliver against masturbation; Oliver was "quite upset for some time" over the warning and felt that it had created a definite barrier between father and son (180).

In his 1919 essay "'A Child Is Being Beaten': A Contribution to the Study of the Origin of Sexual Perversions," Freud links masochistic fantasies with guilt over masturbation. The essay is significant because we now know that it is a disguised case study of Freud's analysis of his own daughter Anna, who wrote about the same childhood experience in her 1922 paper "Beating Fantasies and Daydreams," which, as Louis Breger points out in his biography, she used to gain entrance to the Viennese Psychoanalytic Society (303). Most of the patients Freud describes in "A Child Is Being Beaten" paper are female, but he makes a statement about his male patients with which Stekel would have strongly identified.

> The masochist masturbator finds that he is absolutely impotent if after all he does attempt intercourse with a woman; and the man who has hitherto effected intercourse with the help of a masochistic idea or performance may suddenly make the discovery that the alliance which was so convenient for him has broken down, his genital organs so longer reacting to the masochistic stimulus. (*SE*, vol. 17, 197)

Stekel was the only one in Freud's inner circle who argued for the harmlessness of masturbation. It took courage for Stekel to insist on this. "Masturbation frees man from the social obligations of gratitude," he remarks in his *Autobiography*. "The onanist owes gratitude for his pleasure only to himself" (170). Despite Freud's insistence on the importance of sexuality, he sounded puritanical in warning against masturbation. Did Stekel have Freud in mind when he writes in his *Autobiography* that physicians show "ascetic tendencies" when they warn patients not to express their libido independently? "I see in this attitude the parents' revenge for the fact that they have been deprived of the pleasures of masturbation" (169).

It's not entirely clear what Freud meant by Stekel's "sexual perversion." Peter Gay suggests that Stekel disclosed to Freud that he suffered from psychological impotence (173). Paul Roazen argues, on the other hand, that Stekel's neurotic conflict may have simply been masturbation (*Freud and His Followers* 212). Peter L. Rudnytsky hints at this interpretation in *Reading Psychoanalysis*. Rudnytsky quotes Freud's letter to Wittels in 1924: "One day when I am no more—my discretion will also go with me to my grave—it will become manifest that Stekel's assertion about the harmlessness of masturbation is based on a lie" (149). Rudnytsky points out that Stekel, more than any other dissenter, "came to be regarded by Freud with unbridled contempt and loathing" (147). Rudnytsky perceptively notes that Freud used olfactory metaphors to describe his contempt for Stekel (148, n.14).

In his 1988 book *Winnicott*, the contemporary British psychoanalyst Adam Phillips doesn't mention Stekel, but the early Viennese analyst would doubtlessly be delighted by Phillips's discussion of the pleasures of masturbation. "The idea of developing a capacity for satisfying masturbatory experience has never, for some reason, found a place in psychoanalytic theory" (167, n.30). Phillips corrects that omission in *Monogamy*. "Masturbation is traditionally taboo not because it damages your health—it is not only safe sex, it is safe incest—or because it is against the law, but because we fear it may be the truth about sex: that sex is something we do on our own" (101). Monogamy points out the hidden truth of masturbation. "The virtue of monogamy is the ease with which it can turn sex into masturbation; the vice of monogamy is that it gives you nothing else. If two can be one too many, so can one be" (101–2). Stekel would have agreed with all of these paradoxical insights.

Insights into Freud

Stekel's *Autobiography* offers us intriguing glimpses into Freud's character. "In my mind," Freud confided to him as they hiked through the forests of Berchtesgaden, "I always construct novels, using my experiences as a psychoanalyst; my wish is to become a novelist—but not yet; perhaps in the later years of my life" (66). Freud never became a novelist—except to Freud-bashers, who accused him of fabricating fictions. Stekel captures Freud's vulnerability during a heated controversy that took place at the International Psychoanalytic Association Congress in Weimar, Germany, in 1911. Freud's decision to have Jung appointed lifetime president of the International Psychoanalytic Society provoked strong opposition from Stekel and others. Grabbing his coat as tears streamed down his cheeks, Freud cried, "They begrudge me the coat I am wearing; I don't know whether in the future I will earn my bread" (128–9). Freud, as we saw in the first chapter, revealed little of that vulnerability in *An Autobiographical Study*.

Stekel's observations of Freud confirm later biographers' conclusions. Perhaps because of his desire for originality, Freud was resistant to other's ideas. "He confessed to me once (in a 'weak' moment) that every new conception offered by others finds him resistant and unreceptive. Sometimes he required two weeks to overcome such resistance" (134). Hanns Sachs makes a similar observation in his memoir, albeit without a hint of criticism: Freud regarded psychoanalysis as his own "brain-child" and considered it as his "inviolable trust and sacred duty to keep it clear and free from all inferior alloy" (115). It was not unusual for Freud to adopt other clinicians' ideas, including Stekel's, without acknowledgment. George Makari remarks in *Revolution in Mind: The Creation of Psychoanalysis* (2008) that when opposed, Freud always used the same strategy: "he would fight bitterly to hold his ground, and then after rebuffing a foe, he would quietly incorporate those aspects of the challenge he most admired into his ever-expanding models.

The Freudian field grew fat on a host of vanquished opponents" (160). This was particularly true of Stekel. He used the term *Thanatos*, or "death instinct" before Freud did, though the latter received credit for the theory. Stekel calls himself a "practical man," unlike Freud, a "great thinker and theoretician," but Stekel was sophisticated enough to know when Freudian theory was misleading or wrong. Unlike Freud, who was often more interested in the development of his theory than in aiding individual patients—he confessed in *The Question of Lay Analysis* that from the beginning of his career he was less interested in alleviating suffering than in unlocking the riddles of the world—Stekel put the patient first, as he observes aphoristically. "While Freud asks himself what a case offers to science, I ask myself what science can offer to the case" (249).

It is not generally known even by psychoanalysts that Stekel convinced Freud of the importance of dream symbolism. Not until the fourth edition of *The Interpretation of Dreams* did Freud accept Stekel's intuitive gift of understanding sexual symbolism, but not before characterizing Stekel as a writer who "has perhaps damaged psycho-analysis as much as he has benefited it" (*SE*, vol. 5, 350).

Stekel's pride in being an early Freudian is palpable throughout his *Autobiography*. Freud dedicated a book to him, inscribing it with the words, "With best thanks to my colleague Stekel for his appreciation" (105). Stekel conveys his distress when, as a result of his increasing criticisms of orthodox psychoanalytic theory, members loyal to Freud denounced his work. Wittels turned against Stekel, criticizing him in several articles. Yet, even after his break with Freud, Stekel never failed to pay tribute to the founder. Perhaps the most poignant moment in the *Autobiography* occurs near the end when Stekel, arriving in England as a refugee, wrote a letter to Freud, another refugee living in London, expressing the wish for a reconciliation. Freud never wrote back.

Confessions of a Psychoanalyst

Stekel admits early in his *Autobiography* that his students often found him "unapproachable" (73), believing he did not care enough for them. He later returns to this criticism: "mine was indubitably a difficult temperament to get along with" (187). He's aware of this difficulty during these two moments, but elsewhere he seems blind to the problem. He cites a telling exchange with his son, Eric, a musician whom he had asked to correct mistakes of harmony and counterpoint in a new song Stekel had composed. The son delayed in offering a response, and when pressed by his father, blurted out, "Father! Please don't be angry, I couldn't find a free hour"—to which Stekel responded, "'You see, my son,' I said. 'That is the difference between you and me. I have always had this free hour'" (253). One can only imagine the son's mortification upon reading this passage in his father's *Autobiography*. Stekel never considers the possibility that his son's procrastination may have been caused by the fear of his father's criticism.

Other confessions are of a sexual nature. The woman who made Stekel feel like a "true poet," and with whom he had his first passionate relationship, had the same slanting look and the same eyes as his mother, from which he concludes that the "first love object reappears in a different disguise." Stekel then makes another revealing observation: "I kept my ideal apart from my carnal experiences" (52). He later pursues women who look the opposite of his mother, suggesting a split between sacred love, on the one hand, and profane love, on the other.

Stekel is forthright in the *Autobiography* about his relationships with women, far more candid than other psychoanalysts who wrote memoirs, such as Jones or Jung. In his brief analysis with Freud—the treatment lasted no more than eight sessions, mainly because Freud believed that his analysand had so few repressions—Stekel learns that, based on a dream, he has what Freud calls a mother fixation. "I could not believe it," Stekel tells us (108), words that don't necessarily imply that Stekel agreed with the diagnosis. Mother fixation or not, Stekel doesn't hesitate to reveal that he believed he was in love with a patient's attractive sister; he wrote a poem about her that appeared in his book *The Wise and the Fool*, of which the editor quotes two lines, intimating that the unhappy poet survived unrequited love: "Fools they that die for some dead past, in vain!/ All he once lost, the Wise man wins again" (164 n.1). Gutheil chose these lines as the epigraph for the *Autobiography*.

Immediately before the First World War, Stekel became infatuated with an aristocratic German woman who developed a "strong transference" toward him, and he "yielded" to his own countertransference. He became in the "throes of a veritable love fever" (176). The two of them, both unhappily married to other spouses, vowed to divorce and marry each other. Sadly, his inamorata decided to remain with her husband. At the height of their passion for each other, they thought about committing suicide together, a fantasy Stekel never analyzes. After the end of their relationship, he became like a "madman" in pursuing other women. "The atmosphere of war was favorable for cheap conquests" (180), he declares with brutal honesty. Ironically, the pursuer found himself pursued, and he grew weary of his conquests when his old "flames" reappeared. "They disturbed me in my work, and while I was yearning for true love, I was not always able to free myself from passing flirtations" (182). Finally, true love appeared, Hilda, who became his second wife, and he implies that he remained faithful to her for the rest of his life.

Stekel's *Autobiography* is often puzzling because of its omissions of key information. The reader doesn't know whether these omissions are deliberate or not. Stekel discloses, for example, that he divorced his first wife, Malvina Nelken, to marry his second wife, with whom he began to live shortly after the First World War. He fails to explain, however, why he didn't divorce Malvina until 1938, two years before his death. A possible explanation is that his first wife demanded an "enormous alimony" (165) to agree on a divorce, but it's unclear whether this was the main reason for the delay.

Stekel is candid about the failure of his first marriage, a subject that other memoirists might have ignored. Having married without his parents' approval, he found that he and his wife were growing apart, no longer sharing the same interests that first drew them together. Attempting to be fair, he discloses that his former wife was a "fine woman, but she had so many virtues that I, a man with many faults, must have felt inferior by comparison" (123). One sentence later, however, he remarks, betraying his resentment, that she attempted to "henpeck" him. He then observes, in the single most evocative sentence in his *Autobiography*: "One day I was no longer a man."

Case Study as Disguised Autobiography

Jaap Bos and Leendert Groenendijk demonstrate in *The Self-Marginalization of Wilhelm Stekel* that some of the analyst's information about his life in the *Autobiography* first appeared as a disguised case study in volume 1 of *Impotence in the Male*. The authors show how Stekel's discussion of a lost flute when he was a young boy appears in both books, establishing beyond a reasonable doubt that he was writing about himself in the case study.

Of the 120 case studies in the two volumes of *Impotence in the Male*, the longest and most vivid is case 52, the story of a 40-year-old physician, Dr. N.M. Ten pages long, the case study describes a man who lost a shepherd's flute when he was a young boy, a symbol for the abandonment of a pretty girl in his life. The same event and interpretation occur in the *Autobiography* (33–4).

Stekel's Dr. N.M. was sexually precocious as a three-year-old boy, frolicking in a hayloft with a girl who was a year older. "I was a wild, unruly boy," he confesses, "but by 'hook or crook' always got ahead. And for all that, masturbated where and whenever I could" (vol. 1, 119). The "little Don Juan" had his first experience of sexual intercourse when he was eleven. One day he read, to his horror, that masturbation could ruin his life by causing insanity, dementia, spinal disease, or consumption. He vowed never to masturbate again but could not keep the promise. The only cure to excessive masturbation, it turned out, was frequent sexual intercourse, and at age fourteen he visited a prostitute—Stekel's age when he visited a brothel. When the patient was eighteen, he found himself impotent for the first time, and after two years, he feared the problem was permanent. The patient was cured, though, when he had sex with a woman who declared her love for him and was "enraptured" by his piano playing. From this moment on, the patient became virile again, realizing that his disorder was purely mental. "If a similar misfortune, like that just described, befell me after that, I would always ask myself: 'What are your inner inhibitions?' And I was always able to discover the inhibition, which was usually of a moral nature" (vol. 1, 125). Stekel then breaks off the "interesting" case study of Dr. N.M., which he considers an "important *document humain*" (vol. 1, 126).

The story of Dr. N.M. is indeed the most fascinating one, both aesthetically and psychologically, in the two volumes of *Impotence in the Male*. Stekel shows rather than tells, and the writing is emotionally charged. Dr. N.M. delights in recalling the fantastic tales he narrated to his young playmates. "My phallus took a walk into a body orifice (vagina), emerged from the mouth, was wrapped around the body several times and returned to my body. My little sweetheart would laugh, and I could then do anything with her" (vol. 2, 118). Stekel uses dialogue expertly, as when an attractive chambermaid, a Wagnerian "Walküre," reprimands her impotent lover, "Why do you come to me when you are such a boob?" (vol. 2, 122). Stekel conveys in a single graphic sentence his young patient's compulsive masturbation: "My pants were always torn and my hand on the penis" (118). The patient's young male friends engaged in the same frenetic behavior, which served as a healthy physical outlet for raging hormones. Through Dr. N.M., Stekel presents us with a spirited cautionary tale about the dangers of *not* masturbating. The future Dr. N.M is a budding Alex Portnoy, and his complaints become a paean to autoeroticism.

Surely Stekel knew that he was compromising his own confidentiality when he has Dr. N.M. describe himself as a "free-thinker, a confirmed atheist, and completely amoral, *i.e.*, I aspire to the high plane of a Nietzsche who believes every person has his own morals" (vol. 1, 126). Stekel describes himself in a similar way throughout his *Autobiography*. Did Stekel consider acknowledging in his *Autobiography* that he was Dr. N.M. in *Impotence in the Male*? He knew that he was dying and that he wouldn't be around when the story of his life was published. Had Stekel made the decision to reveal that he was Dr. N.M., his *Autobiography* would have been closer to the spirit of Rousseau's *Confessions*—or perhaps to *Portnoy's Complaint*.

Nevertheless, it was daring for Stekel to write in his *Autobiography* about feeling unmanned, even if he did not elaborate. Some of Stekel's generalizations in the second volume of *Impotence in the Male* may apply to his own situation. In speaking about a patient's wife, he remarks that she "had lost the potency of her husband through her attempts to educate him, and her fault finding," a comment that appears to be true, in his opinion, of the henpecked husband whose "escapades were nothing more than acts of revenge for his humiliations" (*Impotence in the Male*, vol. 2, 60). Was Stekel speaking about himself when he stated that men "who are impotent in relation to orgasm are greatly prized by women and are considered sexual athletes" (vol. 2, 129)? It's likely that he had his own unfortunate first marriage in mind when he declared that precipitous marriages later avenge themselves.

Are Stekel's sexual confessions in *Autobiography* an example of self-awareness or self-indulgence? Christopher Lasch raises this question in *The Culture of Narcissism* (1970), and although he doesn't have Stekel in mind, his observation is relevant here: "Even the best of the confessional writers walk a fine line between self-analysis and self-indulgence" (18). Stekel was not the best confessional writer, but *Autobiography* shows how he worked through his sexual and narcissistic conflicts, achieving greater self-awareness.

Although some of Stekel's statements in *Impotence in the Male* are outdated, the book remains noteworthy for urging greater understanding of and sympathy for a problem that affects millions of men and women. He argues eloquently for equality of the sexes, something Freud never did. "The greater the freedom becomes, which prevails in the association of the sexes, the greater are the prospects of two suitable individuals coming together" (vol. 2, 287). He cites the words, *Homo sum! Nihil humani a me alienum puto!* (*Impotence in the Male*, vol. 2, 261), expecting us to understand that the statement comes from the Roman comic playwright Terence expressed 2,000 years ago: "I am human, and I think nothing human is alien to me."

Ernest Jones and Free Associations

Stekel comes across as far more human in his autobiography than his bitter antagonist, Ernest Jones, does in his life story, *Free Associations*, published posthumously in 1957. Jones began working on his autobiography in 1944 but then abandoned it to write his three-volume biography of Freud, not returning to the book until 1957, a year before his death. Edited by his son, Mervyn, who contributed an epilogue, *Free Associations* breaks off with the death of Jones's first wife, Morfydd, in 1917.

Jones remarks in the preface that he is "entirely truthful" about his "sexual and love life," adding that he would be "less than candid if I did not confess that the record is incomplete" (9). It is the truest sentence in the book. Belying its title, *Free Associations* reveals nothing about Jones's extensive history of womanizing. He emigrated to Canada in 1908 to escape a sexual scandal that had enveloped him in England. As Paul Mosher and I point out in *Off the Tracks*, before becoming a psychoanalyst, Jones was charged with assaulting two young "mentally defective girls" at a special school in London, and though he was later exonerated (after spending a night in jail), new evidence suggests his culpability (Berman and Mosher, vol. 2, 14). Jones was also accused of sexual misconduct while living in Canada. Jones refers only briefly in *Free Associations* to his common-law wife, Loe Kann (calling her only by her first name, perhaps to prevent readers from learning anything more about her), with whom he lived for seven years. Freud analyzed Loe Kann, a wealthy heiress and, at the time, a morphine addict, describing her as "extraordinarily abnormal" (Paskauskas 285). She married one of Freud's patients, Herbert Jones, whom his predecessor sardonically called "Jones II."

As Andrea Celenza has observed, Jones's pattern of seductive behavior may have been one of the reasons Freud wrote his papers on technique warning analysts to guard against the temptation of having sexual relationships with patients. In his correspondence, Freud reprimanded Jones about his "difficulties" with women. "I pity it very much," he wrote to Jones on January 14, 1912, "that you should not master such dangerous cravings" (124)—a reference that the editor of the *Freud/Jones* correspondence, R. Andrew Paskauskas, explains as Jones's "penchant for other women," including an affair with Loe Kann's maid Lina (126, n.2). "The relationship with Lina was an old affair," Jones confessed to Freud in a letter written on January 30, 1913, "and in Italy I was fully determined to break it off. But some devil of desire made me yield to the temptation" (Paskauskas 190–1). Compared to Jones's silence about his misdeeds in *Free Associations*, Stekel's openness about his sexual affairs in his autobiography was truly Rousseauvian.

Stekel's Death

Despite his painful banishment from Freud's inner circle, Stekel lived a full life, deeply fulfilled in love and work. One infers from his *Autobiography* that he had few regrets. According to Hilda Stekel, the English newspapers quoted the verdict of the inquiry following the suicide as an act committed by an "unbalanced mind" (23). Paul Roazen states, without documentation, that Stekel became "paranoid" about Nazi persecution (*Freud and His Followers* 222), but there is no evidence of this in his *Autobiography*. Stekel believed that Mussolini would protect the independence of Austria before its annexation, but "should things become worse, I had resolved to commit suicide rather than be placed in a concentration camp" (270). Things became worse, and he was not paranoid in worrying that he would be taken to and murdered in a German concentration camp, despite living in England, whose fate was far from secure in 1940. Hilda Stekel quotes a letter he wrote shortly before his suicide, on June 15, 1940: "I am passing away like a warrior. Guns and cannons are only temporary. The greatness for which England stands will put right all wrongs" (22). Hilda Stekel writes unjudgmentally about her husband's decision to end his life:

> He was a realist, and, as a physician, he was aware of the fact that with his diabetes, his prostatic disorder and his arteriosclerosis becoming more severe, his future held no joy. What he dreaded most was that he might become too helpless to end it all. When he found his time was up, he bowed out gracefully like an ancient philosopher. (23)

After her husband's death, Hilda Stekel learned from his letters that he had planned his suicide several months in advance. The subject of suicide does not appear often in his clinical writings, but in volume two of *Impotence in the Male*, he asserts, following classical Freudian theory, that "No one ever kills himself who did not first want to kill some one else" (70). One can only wonder whether this generalization was true about Stekel's suicide—or Freud's physician-assisted death, which had occurred a few months earlier. Stekel ends his *Autobiography* with the statement, "Tranquilly, I look forward to my own demise" (287), words his readers hope were true.

Stekel's *Autobiography*, Emil Gutheil writes, "should be one of the most stimulating works of our time" (284). The encomium is excessive, but Stekel succeeded in crafting a life story that offers his views on mental illness and mental health, the importance of verbal therapy, and the value of resilience amidst adversity. Despite or perhaps because of his banishment, he was able to make his own unique contribution to the early history of psychoanalysis. Stekel's life was full of conflicts and inconsistencies, like any life; perhaps that's why he was fond of quoting in many of his books the lines by the Swiss poet C.F. Meyer: "I am not a book that's filled with clever fiction;/ I am a human heart with all its contradiction" (*Autobiography* 13). Many of Stekel's colleagues, including, most conspicuously, Freud, found him insufferably vain and self-promoting, but readers of his *Autobiography* see his more attractive side.

One also senses that Stekel has mellowed over time. In his 1926 essay "On the History of the Analytical Movement," a work that parallels Freud's "On the History of the Psycho-Analytic Movement," Stekel betrays his bitterness and anger toward his former mentor, a man he calls endowed with a "pathological degree of vengefulness" (152). Stekel's own venom is conspicuously absent in his *Autobiography*, suggesting that he has come to terms with the man who spurned him. Stekel thus found himself in a long line of rejected disciples, recalling Paul Roazen's paradoxical insight in *Brother Animal* (1986): "for a man really to be like Freud meant finally for him to be original. Yet originality ended his usefulness to Freud" (48). Stekel always believed that Freud was a genius and that a dwarf, presumably like himself, standing on the head of a giant might see farther than the giant himself. When Freud heard this remark, he retorted acerbically, as Richard Sterba reports in *Reminiscences of a Viennese Psychoanalyst* (1982), "Yes, but the louse in the astronomer's hair does not see a thing" (120).

Stekel admitted that his commitment to work may have compensated for the "narrow boundaries" of his life, leaving "no room in it for anyone except myself and my beloved wife" (*Autobiography* 73). In a review published in the *American Journal of Sociology*, Bruno Bettelheim agrees with Stekel's self-characterization: "he reveals his lack of ability to make close friends, a feeling of relative unrelatedness, except toward his wife, and a degree of narcissism which seem out of line with his psychoanalytic convictions" (288). Stekel's books are no longer best-sellers, but they are worth reading. He wrote his *Autobiography* in great haste, without revision, recognizing that he didn't have much time left. One senses that he lived to work, and having completed his final book, he was ready to die. As we saw in the Introduction, not only is writing a way to write oneself into existence, as Hilary Mantel observes in *Giving Up the Ghost*, writing is also a way to write oneself *out of* existence, simultaneously leaving behind a legacy for others to read.

Stekel and Salinger—and Otto Ludwig

We can only speculate on why Salinger selected a quote from a relatively unknown psychoanalyst for Holden's story. I don't know whether Salinger read any of Stekel's writings, but Holden, like Stekel, appears to suffer from psychological impotence when he is in the presence of young women. "If you want to know the truth," he stammers, with his characteristic verbal tic, "I'm a virgin. I really am. I've had quite a few opportunities to lose my virginity and all, but I've never got around to it yet. Something always happens" (92). Like Stekel, Holden attempts to keep his love ideal apart from his carnal experiences, but he cannot. Holden remains obsessed with sex but fails to understand his ambivalence toward women. In the presence of a young prostitute, Holden freezes; in the presence of Jane Gallagher, whom he respects, he is horrified by the thought of sex. *The Catcher in the Rye* reveals a pattern of homoeroticism and homophobia. Mr. Antolini caresses Holden's head while he's asleep; suddenly waking up, Holden thinks that his former teacher is sexually molesting him. Moreover, Holden makes a number of homophobic statements and fears he's becoming homosexual, once again possibly recalling *Impotence in the Male*. Stekel's epigrammatic words about suicide offer timely insight into Holden's infatuation with death.

And yet, to my surprise, Stekel was not the author of the quoted words in *The Catcher in the Rye*. In 2013, Peter G. Beidler, who has published widely on Salinger, wrote a scholarly article showing that Stekel credited the quote to the German poet, dramatist, and fiction writer Otto Ludwig (1813–65), who first made the statement, in German, in his 1843 novella *Maria*. Stekel found the passage and used it in his 1923 book *Psychoanalysis and Suggestion Therapy*, carefully acknowledging its source. Stekel thus becomes not the originator of the quote but the link between a nineteenth-century German writer and a twentieth-century American writer.

The history of "literature and psychoanalysis" highlights a rich cross-fertilization. Creative writers such as Otto Ludwig and J.D. Salinger intuit what clinicians laboriously seek to prove. Freud knew this. Upon being hailed, on the occasion of his seventieth birthday, as the discoverer of the unconscious, Freud disclaimed the title, replying, "The Poets and Philosophers before me have discovered the Unconscious; I have discovered the scientific method with which the unconscious can be studied" (Lehrman 164). Freud might have added fiction writers to his tribute. However much Stekel disagreed with Freud, he would heartily agree with this statement. Holden Caulfield will live forever in the pages of Salinger's timeless masterpiece; and through Holden's words, future readers like myself will become exposed to an early psychoanalyst who, despite his self-inflicted death and Freud's contemptuous attitude, was a mature man.

Chapter 5

C.G. JUNG

MEMORIES, DREAMS, REFLECTIONS

I can't recall exactly when I first read C.G. Jung's memoir, *Memories, Dreams, Reflections*, published in 1963, two years after his death at age eighty-five. When I began studying psychoanalysis, in my late teens, I was in thrall to Freud and, therefore, suspicious of his bitter rival, Jung, who broke away from psychoanalysis to create analytical psychology. Having read Edward Glover's 1950 book *Freud or Jung*, a stinging polemic against the Swiss psychoanalyst, and still believing at the time in binary reasoning—either/or, black/white, dichotomous thinking—I naturally sided with Freud, a Jewish atheist, like myself, not with Jung, the Christian mystic, occultist, and parapsychologist who seemed antithetical to Enlightenment wisdom. Like a Talmudical scholar (a paradoxical simile for a godless Jew), I pored over every word in Freud's twenty-four-volume *Standard Edition*, ignoring Jung's twenty-volume *Collected Works*. Another reason to dismiss Jung, I thought, was his flirtation with Nazi ideology and belief in "Aryan psychology." I delayed rereading Jung's memoir while writing the present book, but when I finally found my old paperback copy, unopened for decades, I saw a note I had scribbled to myself on the title page: "wounded, 134." Curious, I turned to the page and stared in amazement at the following words:

> As a doctor I constantly have to ask myself what kind of message the patient is bringing me. What does he mean to me? If he means nothing, I have no point of attack. The doctor is effective only when he himself is affected. "Only the wounded physician heals." But when the doctor wears his personality like a coat of armor, he has no effect. (134)

I have long been interested in wounded healers, including wounded teacher-scholars, forgetting (or never knowing) that it was a Jungian idea. It's not clear why Jung places quotation marks around the sentence containing the words "wounded healer." Neither he nor his editor, Aniela Jaffé, provides a bibliographic citation. The term "wounded healer," according to *Wikipedia*, was created by the Dutch-born Catholic priest Henri J.M. Nouwen in his 1979 book *The Wounded Healer: Ministry in Contemporary Society*, but Jung's use predates Nouwen's by several years. Moreover, *Wikipedia*, after acknowledging that in Greek mythology the centaur Chiron was a wounded healer, refers to Anthony Stevens's 1994 biography of Jung that contains a discussion of the healer archetype. Robert C. Smith calls his 1996 book *The Wounded Jung*. The idea of a wounded physician or therapist may have inspired the sociologist Arthur W. Frank's 1995 book *The Wounded Storyteller: Body, Illness, and Ethics*, though he never cites Jung's influence. Jung's own experience as a wounded healer contributes to the importance of his memoir, both for what it reveals and conceals about his life. Like Goethe and Freud, Jung was a great self-revealer and careful self-concealer, and nowhere is this more evident than in his memoir.

"Thankless Autobiographer"

Memories, Dreams, Reflections has an unusual provenance. As Jaffé explains in the introduction, the idea for the memoir came not from Jung himself but from his German publisher, Kurt Wolff, the founder of Pantheon Books, in 1956. Jung's lifelong aversion to writing a biography was well known. Sounding like Freud, Jung was contemptuous of the genre. "I know too many autobiographies, with their self-deceptions and downright lies, and I know too much about the impossibility of self-portrayal, to want to venture on any such attempt" (viii). He later called himself a "thankless autobiographer," believing that one should live one's life without writing about it. Like Freud's *An Autobiographical Study*, Jung's *Memories, Dreams, Reflections* consists of extinctions, shirkings, and partial reveilments of the truth, and the meaning of the story must be read between the lines.

Jung agreed to the memoir only after a long period of doubt and hesitation. Jaffé became his editorial assistant, and he allotted her one afternoon a week to the project. The two began the memoir in 1957, when he was eighty-two; she would ask him questions and then jot down his replies. He soon overcame his objections to writing a memoir and found the project challenging, albeit in ways he hadn't anticipated. Using words that recall Nietzsche's *amor fati*, love of fate, Jung told Jaffé that a "book of mine is always a matter of fate. There is something unpredictable about the process of writing" (vi). The project, he added, soon became a "necessity" to him. He wrote the memoir, but at the same time the memoir wrote him, an example of the power of the unconscious to shape literary art. He stipulated, however, that the memoir be published after his death, and he spoke about it as "Aniela Jaffé's project." He did not want *Memories, Dreams, Reflections* to be included in his *Collected Works*.

Jung literally felt ill on the days he could not write. Illness did not prevent him from writing; rather, not writing produced illness. "If I neglect to do so for a single day, unpleasant physical symptoms immediately follow. As soon as I set to work they vanish and my head feels perfectly clear" (vi). Writing the memoir became a compulsion, a necessity, an early example of the writing cure.

Memories, Dreams, Reflections is 430 pages long, but despite its length, the memoir is riddled with omissions and evasions. There's hardly a word about Jung's relationship to his wife, and nothing about his relationships with other women, including Toni Wolff. She began as Jung's analysand but then became, over the next forty years, his friend, lover, and collaborator, his "second wife." He needed both women for different reasons, to the distress of his family. Smith remarks that Jung originally included a chapter in his memoir about his relationship with Wolff but then deleted it. He also deleted much about his fraught relationship with his mother, especially her mental illness. "In the original version of his autobiography," Smith points out, "Jung had included even more details of his mother's mental aberrations, but other family members, fearing these would tarnish the family image, insisted that they be removed. A crucial sentence that was omitted stated that his mother only recovered her health after his father passed away" (17–18).

Jung's Parents

The few references to Jung's mother, Emilie Preiswerk Jung (1848–1923), suggest a severely conflicted relationship. "By day she was a loving mother," Jung writes, "but at night she seemed uncanny" (50). He inherited from his mother his dual personality, which he describes as his Number 1 personality, associated with the daytime, the here and now, and his Number 2 personality, associated with the darkness, the realm of the shadowy anima and animus, Jung's terms for the unconscious countersexual images present in everyone. These two personalities existed his entire life. He regarded the dual personality not as a split or dissociated personality in the usual psychiatric sense but as the embodiment of a polarity he considered universal. Smith conjectures that Jung's ambivalence toward women arose from his experience of a dual mother (93). Jung associated his father, Paul Achilles Jung (1842–96), with reliability, powerlessness, and emotional repression. Jung never had a close relationship with his father, a pastor and scholar of Oriental languages; Jung felt that he could never speak honestly and openly with him. The son's anger and disappointment created a father-hunger that he projected onto other men, particularly Freud, nineteen years his senior, who in the end became another version of a disappointing father figure.

Part of the pleasure and exasperation of reading Jung's memoir is the depth and breadth of his knowledge, his encyclopedic mind, his knowledge of five languages, and his voracious reading of mythology, philosophy, religion, Gnosticism, and ancient literature. He was a polymath, and his scholarship is daunting to readers. Whereas a Freudian psychoanalyst traces a patient's free associations to the personal events in the patient's life, a Jungian psychoanalyst traces these associations to archetypes. A single page of *Memories, Dreams, Reflections* may contain untranslated references to several recondite texts that the reader may not have encountered, obscure publications on Chinese alchemy, such as the sixteenth-century text, *Rosarium Philosophorum*, along with Buddhist and Hindu texts. James Joyce famously said that readers who wish to understand his last novel, *Finnegans Wake*, crafted in a new language, must devote a lifetime of study. The same is true of Jung's readers.

Memories, Dreams, Reflections is unusual in that it focuses not mainly on people, events, or subjects but on the writer's inner development and transformation. The contrast between Jung's rich, evocative inner world and the nebulous outer world, is striking. We shall see the same contrast in Marion Milner's memoirs. Jung regarded the outer aspects of his life as accidental, unrelated to his inner development. He compared human life to that of a rhizome, a plant that appears above ground only in the summer but whose hidden life remain underground, invisible. "What we see is the blossom, which passes," he observes in the prologue. "The rhizome remains" (4). By implication, Jung's life story focuses on the subterranean. The more intense or disturbing his affective world, the more mystifying his language. He returns to the rhizome metaphor early in the memoir. "To this day, writing down my memories at the age of eighty-three, I have never fully unwound the tangle of my earliest memories. They are like individual shoots of a single underground rhizome, like stations on a road of unconscious development" (27). The act of writing, he suggests, is a process of cutting through the tangle. But the entanglement remains, impeding the reader's efforts to grasp the story. The opening chapter of the memoir, "First Years," an account of his early childhood, is the most hidden and, for this reason, the most intriguing.

Like Freud, who regarded himself as the disturber of the world's sleep, Jung saw himself as a modern-day Prometheus, stealing fire from the gods and willing to suffer the consequences, eternal guilt and isolation. The man who has stolen the secrets of the unconscious, he asserts in *Two Essays on Analytical Psychology* (1966), has raised himself above others and cannot return to ordinary life. "He is, as the myth says, chained to the lonely cliffs of the Caucus, forsaken of God and man" (156–6, n. 1). It is easier for Jung to write about the collective unconscious, archetypes, and myths than about specific childhood events. Throughout the seventeen-page opening chapter of *Memories, Dreams, Reflections*, Jung's vocabulary is filled with words like "secret" and "mystery," both of which appear to have something to do with two other recurrent words, "shame" and "humiliation."

"My First Conscious Trauma"

"First Years" is the most haunting and enigmatic opening chapter of any memoir or autobiography I have read. The entire chapter hints at a trauma narrative not only because it contains, as Jung admits, his "first conscious trauma" (10) but also because memory of the trauma lasted his entire life. "First Years" has a nightmarish quality that resembles *Grimms' Fairy Tales*. Part of the horror lies in a dream that may be a screen memory of an actual experience. Jung doesn't connect the disparate memories, dreams, and reflections of his early childhood; that task is left to the reader. There's always the risk, whether reading psychoanalytically or not, of overanalyzing a text, but the danger becomes greater when reading the ambiguous "First Years." I'll begin by describing the dark events and dreams in the chapter and then offer possible interpretations, referring whenever appropriate to the vast commentary on the memoir.

The chapter opens with several brief sunny memories, such as lying in a pram on a warm summer day when Jung was two or three. The mood suddenly darkens, however, when he describes fishermen finding a corpse. Around the age of three, he developed eczema, which he connects to his temporary separation from his parents who were experiencing marital tensions at the time. His mother was hospitalized for several months, presumably for mental illness. He describes falling down a staircase and another fall against a stove, resulting in a head wound. While crossing a bridge over the Rhine, he began to slide under the railing and was saved by a maid. "These things point to an unconscious suicidal urge or, it may be, to a fatal resistance to life in this world" (9), a perplexing statement he doesn't develop. It's the first, though by no means the last, time in *Memories, Dreams, Reflections* that he mentions being suicidal.

Jung next recalls having vague fears at night, remembers people drowning, and refers to men wearing long black coats and tall hats burying black boxes in graves while women wept. The thought of death reminds him of a prayer he recited every night about Jesus who "ate" chicks so that they wouldn't be devoured by Satan. The young boy had conflicting feelings toward Jesus, who could be both comforting and frightening: "little children were compared to chicks which Lord Jesus evidently 'took' reluctantly, like bitter medicine." The "sinister analogy," Jung reminds us, has "unfortunate consequences" (10)—and then he links his ruminations as a young boy to his earliest, and, we suspect, most serious trauma.

Jung was three or four years old when, sitting alone on a road in front of his house, he saw a man who was wearing a broad hat and a long black robe, "women's clothes." Overcome with fright, the boy cried out, "That is a Jesuit," mainly because he had recently heard a conversation between his Protestant pastor-father and a visiting colleague about the "nefarious activities of the Jesuits." Jung did not know who the Jesuits were, but he associated them with the word "Jesus." Terrified, the boy ran inside his house and hid in the darkest corner of the attic. Later he realized that the black figure was only a "harmless Catholic priest" (11).

The Man-Eater

Fear of Jesuits evokes the earliest dream Jung can remember, one that preoccupied him his entire life. The richly detailed dream, which occurred around the same time he saw the Jesuit, opens in a vicarage located near a meadow. Seeing a dark, stone-lined hole in the ground, the boy hesitantly descends and spies a red carpet on which rests a magnificent king's throne, as in a fairy tale. On the throne stands a tree trunk 12- to 15-feet high, nearly 2-feet thick, extending to the ceiling of a rectangular chamber. But this is no ordinary tree. The tree trunk was made of "skin and naked flesh"; on the top was a "rounded head with no face and no hair." Atop the head was a "single eye, gazing motionlessly upward." Paralyzed with fright, the young boy hears his mother calling out, "Yes, just look at him. That is the man-eater!" He then woke up, "sweating and scared to death" (12).

The dream haunted Jung for years. He was too astute a psychologist to deny the obvious phallic symbolism of the man-eater. "Only much later did I realize that what I had seen was a phallus, and it was decades before I understood that it was a ritual phallus," one that was enthroned by itself, "ithyphallically" (12). Two questions troubled him. He could not decide whether his mother meant that it was the phallus, rather than Jesus or the Jesuit, who was the man-eater, or whether, more ominously, "the dark Lord Jesus, the Jesuit, and the phallus were identical" (12). Nor could he explain from where the "anatomically correct" phallus came. Jung uses the Latin expression *orificium urethrae* as the "eye" of a penis, and a footnote refers us to a fuller discussion in his 1912 book *Symbols of Transformation*. There's nothing playful or comic about Jung's sexual dream, nothing like Stekel's colorful reference to a disembodied phallus that took a walk into a body orifice. Rather, the man-eater conjures up fear and trembling, an entry into a dreaded world that threatens the nature of existence.

For the next three pages in *Memories, Dreams, Reflections*, Jung discusses the dream, informing us that it represents a "subterranean God 'not to be named.'" The Jesuit's "disguise" cast its long shadow over Jung's Christian beliefs. For years Protestant ministers and Catholic priests scared him. The childhood dream implicated him into the "secrets of the earth," an initiation into the realm of darkness. He attaches the greatest significance to the meaning of the childhood dream. "My intellectual life had its unconscious beginnings at that time" (15).

Jung's early attitude toward Catholic churches betrayed both curiosity and fear. He recalls looking into a Catholic Church when he was six, stumbling on a step, and screaming because he had done something forbidden. "Jesuits—green curtain—secret of the man-eater. . . . So that is the Catholic Church which has to do with Jesuits. It is their fault that I stumbled and screamed" (17; ellipsis in original). For years he could neither enter a Catholic Church nor see a Catholic priest without experiencing fear.

"First Years" contains Jung's earliest memory of art. He was no older than six when his aunt took him to a Basel museum that contained stuffed animals. He describes being overwhelmed in a gallery of beautiful antiquities and then hearing her reprimand, "Disgusting boy, shut your eyes; disgusting boy, shut your eyes!" Only then did he see that the figures at which he was gazing were naked and wore fig leaves. "Such was my first encounter," he declares wryly, "with the fine arts." His aunt simmered with indignation, "as though she had been dragged through a pornographic institute" (16). Another memory emerges in "First Years," ritualistically playing with a stone, between the ages of seven and nine. He imagines the following game, an event shrouded in mystery:

"I am sitting on top of this stone and it is underneath." But the stone also could say "I" and think: "I am lying here on this slope and he is sitting on me." The question then arose: "Am I the one who is sitting on the stone, or am I the stone on which *he* is sitting?" This question always perplexed me, and I would stand up, wondering who was what now. The answer remained totally unclear, and my uncertainty was accompanied by a feeling of curious and fascinating darkness. But there was no doubt whatsoever that this stone stood in some secret relationship to me. I could sit on it for hours, fascinated by the puzzle it set me. (20)

The Little Manikin

Jung recalls another remarkable memory when he was ten. He carved on the top of a ruler a little manikin, two inches long, "with frock coat, top hat, and shiny black boots." He sawed the manikin from the ruler, placed it in a pencil case, and made a little bed for it. In the pencil case he also placed a black stone, from the Rhine, which he carried in his trouser pocket. "This was *his* stone. All this was a great secret." He then hid the manikin and the stone in the attic, an act that gave him "great satisfaction." Periodically, he would secretly climb to the attic, look at the objects, and present the manikin with scrolls written in a secret language of his own invention. He doesn't use the word, but the objects became a talisman, assuming a magical healing property. "If things became too bad I would think of my secret treasure in the attic, and that helped me regain my poise" (26). The two objects were part of an "inviolable secret" that he would never betray, like the dream of the phallus. The carved manikin event formed the climax and the conclusion of Jung's childhood, he reports near the end of the chapter. He never shared these secrets with anyone until the writing of his memoir.

The words "secret" and "secretly" appear eighteen times in "First Years," exceeded only by the twenty-four references to these words in the next chapter, "School Years," when he continues his discussion of the dream and the manikin. Many of the later chapters in *Memories, Dreams, Reflections*, by contrast, do not contain a single reference to secrets. Significantly, when he does use the word "secret" in later chapters, the context suggests secret organizations or secret customs, not the secret of the ithyphallic god dream or the hidden treasure in the attic. The dominant emotion associated with these two secrets is terror, which shattered Jung's childhood innocence. Nor could his parents help him. The dream of the ithyphallic god was Jung's first great secret, the manikin, his second.

Jung never spoke about the dream of the ithyphallic god until he was sixty-five (41). Tellingly, he rules out the possibility that the dream was a "memory-trace" (13), mainly because he cannot imagine how a young boy could have witnessed a man-eater. The image of the monstrous phallus confirmed for him the existence of the collective unconscious; the dream could not have been based, he insists, on an actual event. Like Freud, who abandoned the seduction theory because he could not believe that most of his patients were molested by trusted relatives, Jung did not believe that traumatic sexual events were common. Unlike Freud, Jung did not assert that dreams disguise meaning too disturbing for the conscious mind to understand. In a later chapter in *Memories, Dreams, Reflections*, he disagrees with Freud's interpretation of dreams. "To me," Jung writes, "dreams are a part of nature, which harbors no intentions to deceive, but expresses something as best it can" (161). Nor did he believe that incest, sexual molestation committed by a relative, was frequent. Rather, incest had a religious meaning to him, as he inferred from its appearance in nearly all cosmologies and numerous myths.

"School Years" contains a startling scatological fantasy that occurred when Jung was a student in Basel around the age of twelve. The "cathedral fantasy" involved for Jung the "most frightful of sins," the unforgivable sin against the Holy Ghost. "I saw before me the cathedral, the blue sky. God sits on His golden throne, high above the world—and from under the throne an enormous turd falls upon the sparkling new roof, shatters it, and breaks the walls of the cathedral asunder." Counterintuitively, Jung felt not horror but relief. "Instead of the expected damnation, grace had come upon me, and with it an unutterable bliss such as I had never known." He never understood why God chose to befoul the cathedral, and although he often regarded himself as a "corrupt and inferior person," he had the feeling that he was "either outlawed or elect, accursed or blessed" (39–41). The one great achievement of his early life, he remarks, was that he resisted the temptation to confide these terrible secrets to anyone.

Sexual Trauma

What shall we say about the trauma Jung describes in "First Years"? The memoir evokes a mysterious sexual crime upon which it refuses to elaborate, a paradox often associated with hidden trauma. Jung's associations linking the Jesuit wearing a black gown, the fear of entering Catholic churches, the alarming man-eater, the aunt's accusation that the boy was "disgusting" in the "pornographic institute," the sense of forbidden looking, the terrible secrecy throughout his childhood, and the crushing mood of guilt and punishment the boy experienced suggest he may have been the victim of a sexual crime committed by a priest.

Variously represented as Jesus, the man-eater, the manikin, and perhaps the stone, the priest is a figure of intense ambivalence, one of whom the boy is both frightened and protective. We can understand why it might have been impossible for Jung to disclose the nature of the trauma. The idea of a pedophilic priest was almost unspeakable more than a century ago. It was not until 1985 that the problem of child sexual abuse by Roman Catholic priests became public in the United States. The Church reluctantly acknowledged these abuses only after decades of lawsuits.

Sexual abuse helps explain the recurrent depression Jung experienced early in his life, including the feeling that he was a "corrupt and inferior person" (41), along with his suicidal ideation, which he calls the "unforgivable sin" (37). Sexual abuse helps explain his ritualistic behavior with the stone, an example of Freud's repetition-compulsion principle: the boy's efforts to convert a passive experience, lying below the stone, a personification of the priest, into an active one, lying on top of the stone. Sexual abuse also helps explain why he felt he could never disclose these terrible secrets to anyone. The "strict taboo" that surrounded the ithyphallic god dream and the carved manikin incident is common to victims of childhood sexual abuse, as are the suicidal thoughts that plagued him. "My entire youth can be understood in terms of this secret," Jung writes in the next chapter. "It induced in me an almost unbearable loneliness. My one great achievement during those years was that I resisted the temptation to talk about it with anyone" (41).

Jung considered and then rejected the possibility that the dream of the ithyphallic god had a basis in reality. "The symbolism of my childhood experiences and the violence of the imagery upset me terribly," he writes in the second chapter. "I asked myself: *Who* talks like that? Who has the impudence to exhibit a phallus so nakedly, and in a shrine? Who makes me think that God destroys His Church in this abominable manner?" (47). It was easier for Jung to interpret the dream as an example of the devil's doing than as an historical event.

Jung never explicitly acknowledges in *Memories, Dreams, Reflections* that he was the victim of sexual abuse. He admitted this, however, in a letter to Freud, on October 28, 1907, when he revealed his profound need for Freud's friendship and approval. Jung confessed that his "veneration" of Freud, which has "something of the character of a 'religious' crush," awakened his self-contempt because of its "undeniable erotic undertone." Jung's attraction to Freud exposed an old wound: "This abominable feeling comes from the fact that as a boy I was the victim of a sexual assault by a man I once worshipped" (95). The feeling still "hampers" him, complicating relationships with colleagues who have a "strong transference" to him. "*I therefore fear your confidence*," he confesses (*Freud/Jung Letters* 95; italics in original). That is all Jung says about his boyhood sexual trauma. He disclosed nothing about his *craving* for Freud's confidence and affection. Freud wrote back a few days later, remarking that a "transference on a religious basis would strike me as most disastrous; it could end only in apostasy" (98).

Freud must have realized that Jung's disclosure of being sexually assaulted by a trusted older man would, transferentially, affect Jung's relationship with Freud himself. Jung's momentous disclosure to Freud, Louis Breger suggests (224), reveals the fear that he was in danger of being sexually exploited again, this time by Freud, a fear upon which neither analyst explicitly commented.

Curiously, Freud never mentioned Jung's sexual trauma. Was it because Freud did not take seriously the trauma or because he did not want to call attention to it? Peter Gay offers a different translation of Jung's sexual confession—"as a young boy, I succumbed to a homosexual attack by a man I had formerly revered"—and then adds, "Freud, at the time still musing on his own homoerotic feelings for [his former confidant Wilhelm] Fliess, took Jung's revelation in stride" (204). Whatever the reason for Freud's silence, it's odd that the psychoanalyst who propounded a sexual theory of neurosis failed to comment on Jung's most searing self-disclosure.

Questions abound about Jung's sexual abuse. How did the experience affect his sexual life? He never mentions having sexual difficulties, as sometimes happens with adults who were sexually abused in childhood. Did he experience posttraumatic stress disorder, which sometimes accompanies sexual abuse? In his discussion of terror, he doesn't mention hyperarousal, intrusion, or constriction. Nor does Leonard Shengold's observation in *Is There Life without Mother?* (2000) about child abuse appear to be true of Jung: "The most destructive psychological effect of child abuse is the need to hold on to the abuser by identification (an unconscious becoming like him or her); this is part of a compulsion to repeat the experience of abuse—as tormentor (enhancing sadism) and as victim—(enhancing masochism)" (25). Did Jung associate the sexual abuse with his Number 2 personality? He writes about having a dual personality but not a damaged or defiled self. Did he always remember the experience or repress it? He depicts alterations in consciousness but not amnesia surrounding a traumatic event.

Few Jungian or Freudian scholars have discussed the traumatic implications of Jung's childhood sexual abuse. The Jungian analyst Anthony Stevens avoids any discussion of the incident, as does Peter Homans in his 1979 psychoanalytic study *Jung in Context*. What's striking about the 1997 edited volume *The Cambridge Companion to Jung* is that even when a contributor quotes Jung's sexual confession to Freud, as does Douglas A. Davis, he avoids any mention of the sexual abuse. In the same volume, Andrew Samuels writes about a "Jungian perspective on child sexual abuse" without mentioning a single word about Jung's own experience (3). Smith devotes only one sentence to the sexual assault: "Quite possibly the man-eater dream is linked to this childhood experience" (34). The British psychoanalyst Anthony Storr asserts that Jung was "notoriously intolerant of male homosexuals" (48), but he supplies no documentation nor offers any evidence of the origins of this prejudice.

Jung's experience of sexual abuse remains a riddle to Deirdre Bair, the author of a monumental 881-page biography published in 2003. "The identity of the man who assaulted Jung has long been a mystery, as has been the truth of what actually happened between them" (71). In Jung's later life, members of his "inner circle" claimed that they had heard him speak about this incident, but Bair implies that this was hearsay. Some of Jung's descendants have described the alleged abuser as a "distant uncle," but a footnote in Bair's biography indicates that those who volunteered this information did not want to be identified (675, n. 7). Widespread agreement exists that the "most likely suspect" was a Catholic priest who was Paul Jung's best friend while young Carl was growing up, but Bair found no evidence to corroborate this. Another possibility is that Jung was sexually assaulted by his father, but again this remains speculation, unsupported by evidence. The age at which the alleged sexual abuse occurred is also unclear. Before the age of fourteen Jung had spent time in the presence of a Catholic priest; he later described the event in a single sentence: "Nothing in the least menacing happened to me," leading Bair to conclude that "[M]any interpretations are possible, but why Jung needed to express it remains a matter of speculation" (71–2).

The most detailed information about the mysterious sexual assault appears in Alan C. Elms's 1994 book *Uncovering Lives: The Uneasy Alliance of Biography and Psychology*. During his research in the C.G. Jung Biographical Archives, Elms came across an interview given by Jolande Jacobi to the Jung oral history project:

> He [Jung] told me one day that when he was 18 years old one of the best friends of his family was also his best friend—a man of about forty to fifty. He was very proud of this friendship and had the feeling that he had . . . in this man a fatherly friend with whom he could discuss everything until one day this fatherly friend tried a homosexual approach towards him. He [Jung] was so disgusted and afraid

that he immediately broke the relationship . . . . [H]e . . . explained to me, when Freud wanted to make him his son and his successor, he had the same feeling, "No, no, no. I don't want to belong to anybody. I don't want to be embraced." (68–9; ellipses and brackets in original)

Jung's acknowledgment that this sexual assault influenced his relationship with Freud is noteworthy; but equally significant is that Jung did not generally connect a mental upheaval with a specific autobiographical event. This remains one of the essential differences between Freudian and Jungian analysts. Moreover, for a man who was sexually assaulted, he showed almost no interest in childhood trauma. He maintained that the cause of neurosis was found in the present rather than in the past. It's difficult to connect Jung's experience of sexual assault at age eighteen with his first conscious trauma, as reflected in the man-eater dream, when he was three or four. Was Jung describing one sexual trauma or several? Was he deliberately evasive in *Memories, Dreams, Reflections* or simply confused? One recalls Henry James's 1898 novella *The Turn of the Screw*, a bone-chilling story of an overwrought governess and two children who may or may not be ghosts. "The story *won't* tell," exclaims Douglas, one of the characters in the tale, "not in any literal vulgar way" (3). Jung's memoir contains mysteries that will never be solved. Our wish to read it as an early trauma and testimony narrative is both encouraged and thwarted by its many ambiguities. The only certainty is that his life story raises more questions than answers. Significantly, Jung found a way to convert the traumatic experience into a positive one. Freud's most recent biographer, Joel Whitebook, argues that the cathedral fantasy enabled Jung to reject institutionalized religion in the name of a higher counter-religion. "By transforming sin into virtue—into the will of God—Jung provided himself with a rationalization for his aggression toward his father and his Church, treated it as a privileged gift from God, and elevated himself into a superior spiritual person" (258).

Jung tells us in the last paragraph of "First Years" that while in England in 1920, he carved two figures out of wood that he later realized resembled the frightening tree from the ithyphallic dream. He placed one of the figures, reproduced on a grand scale in stone, in his garden in Küsnacht, Switzerland, on the shores of Lake Zürich. His unconscious supplied him with the name for the stone, Atmavictu, the "breath of life," a symbol of the "creative impulse" (23), a tribute, in short, to Jung's mythopoeic imagination.

Freud

Around the age of twelve Jung experienced "neurotic fainting spells." They began when he lost consciousness as a result of a fall and lasted for about six months. Jung was not the only psychoanalyst who suffered fainting spells. Freud did, too, and it's ironic that two of his fainting spells both occurred in the presence of Jung.

The chapter "Sigmund Freud" in *Memories, Dreams, Reflections* was a revelation to me, not mainly in its presentation of new information about the founder of psychoanalysis, but in its fairness, balance, and sympathy. I found myself agreeing with Jung's criticisms of Freud. Jung was writing a decade after Ernest Jones's three-volume idealized biography of Freud and years before the more objective biographies by Peter Gay and Louis Breger.

Their first meeting took place in Vienna in 1907, where they talked, according to Jung, for a marathon thirteen hours without a pause. "Freud was the first man of real importance I had encountered," he writes in *Memories, Dreams, Reflections*; "in my experience up to that time, no one else could compare with him" (149). Yet Jung could not accept Freud's monomaniacal belief—my word, not Jung's—that all neuroses arise from sexual repression. Jung recalls vividly Freud's statement to him: "My dear Jung, promise me never to abandon the sexual theory. That is the most essential thing of all. You see, we must make a dogma of it, an unshakable bulwark" (150). No contemporary psychoanalyst holds to this view, but at the time Freud's disciples adhered to the dogma as an act of faith, part of their larger conviction that psychoanalysis was a science, not an ideology or a hermeneutic. In asserting his disagreement with Freud, Jung declared his own independence. He saw Freud's sexual theory as a workable hypothesis, like other fruitful speculations, "adequate for the moment" but "not to be preserved as an article of faith for all time" (151). The same can be said, of course, about Jungian theory. To agree with Jung's criticisms of Freud is not necessarily to endorse Jungian theory: both are highly speculative and have evolved over time.

It is hard to disagree with Jung's characterization of Freud as a "tragic figure" who was a "great man, and what is more, a man in the grip of his daimon" (153). Freud saw Jung as his successor; Jung acknowledges this without adding that one of the reasons Freud chose him as the crown prince was to make psychoanalysis, considered by its (anti-Semitic) critics as the "Jewish science," acceptable to the gentile world. As Ernest Jones wrote in his biography, "Jung was to be the Joshua destined to explore the promised land of psychiatry which Freud, like Moses, was only permitted to view from afar" (vol. 2, 33).

Freud's first fainting spell occurred in 1909 when he and Jung met at Bremen, Germany, from where they departed to lecture at Clark University in Worcester, Massachusetts, where they were awarded honorary degrees. Freud fainted while Jung was talking about mummified bodies in peat-bogs in Northern Germany. D.M. Thomas uses this material in his 1981 novel *The White Hotel*, which opens with a fictionalized letter written by Sándor Ferenczi describing Freud's fainting spell. Freud's explanation for the fainting, in Jung's words, was that "all this chatter about corpses meant I had death-wishes toward him" (*Memories, Dreams, Reflections* 156). The explanation startled Jung, as it would startle anyone. Freud fainted a second time in the presence of Jung at a Psychoanalytic Congress in Munich in 1912, the last year of their friendship. Jung picked him up, carried him to the next room, and laid him on a sofa. "In his weakness he looked at me as if I were his father. Whatever other causes may have contributed to this faint—the atmosphere was very tense—the fantasy of father-murder was common to both cases" (157).

Freud's fainting spells have provoked much commentary. In the first volume of his biography, Ernest Jones reports Freud's mystifying explanation: "There is some piece of unruly homosexual feeling at the root of the matter" (Jones, vol. 1, 317). In the second volume, Jones offers Freud's later interpretation, a symptom of a hidden death wish arising from defeating an opponent (vol. 2, 146). That Freud harbored a death wish toward Jung doesn't imply that Jung reciprocated the feeling. As Louis Breger notes in his biography, "far from wishing to kill Freud, Jung was enormously attached to him and needed him as the wise and protective father he had never had" (188). A more plausible interpretation, according to Breger, connects Freud's fainting spells with early childhood losses that he associated with images of death.

Freud's conviction that his chosen successor harbored a death wish against him doomed any possibility of a personal or professional relationship between them. Another reason for the failed relationship was Freud's need to preserve his authority. During their time together in the United States, each analyzed the other's dreams, but when Jung asked Freud for further details about his private life, the latter refused, saying, "But I cannot risk my authority." Jung concluded that "Freud was placing personal authority above truth" (*Memories, Dreams, Reflections* 158). Jung was not ready to end their friendship, however. During their mutual analysis, Jung narrated to Freud a long dream about exploring a house that involved the discovery of two old human skulls. Freud asked him about the hidden identity of the two people he must have wanted dead; rather than quarreling with Freud, Jung lied, saying that the two skulls represented his newly married wife and sister-in-law.

The reader senses Jung's deep disappointment and anguish over the failed relationship, yet he remains discreet throughout the chapter. He doesn't tell us, for example, any of the dreams Freud narrated to him, unwilling to betray confidentiality. Despite Freud's loss of authority to him, "he still meant to me a superior personality" upon whom Jung projected a father figure (163). Jung never elaborates on the religious and cultural differences between them, but he captures in a single sentence the way Freud saw himself. "Like an Old Testament prophet, he undertook to overthrow false gods, to rip the veils away from a mass of dishonesties and hypocrisies, mercilessly exposing the rottenness of the contemporary psyche" (169).

The Freud/Jung Letters

Jung never suspected that his massive correspondence with Freud would be published, but it casts light on his discussion in *Memories, Dreams, Reflections*. The 650-page tome, published in 1974, chronicles the rise and fall of their friendship from 1906 to 1913. The letters are, as Leonard Shengold remarks, a "record of the relationship between two men of genius that is as fascinating and dramatic as any great novel" (200). After the end of Freud's failed relationship with his most intimate confidant, Wilhelm Fliess, Jung became Freud's most trusted friend. Shengold was one of the first analysts to point out that Freud's correspondence with Jung reflects the same need for a close male friend that can be seen in Freud's correspondence with Fliess. Freud and Jung wrote 360 letters to each other, some 1,500 words long.

William McGuire, the editor of the volume, details the long, fraught negotiations between the heirs of the two analysts that allowed the letters to be made public. It was as if two superpowers were negotiating a peace treaty after a bruising, protracted war. Jung initially believed that the letters were too personal for publication; Freud's relatives believed that he had destroyed the letters from his former ally, though the letters almost miraculously survived, perhaps an indication that Freud wished to preserve them. To guarantee impartiality, both sides agreed that there would be no critical commentary in the volume. Readers are left to draw their own conclusions about the reasons for the most infamous breakup in early twentieth-century psychoanalysis. Each side chose its own translator, wary of a linguist from the opposing side. A detailed examination of the correspondence is impossible in a few pages, but we can see how each man invested complex father-son symbolism in the relationship. Each believed, for seven years, he was understood and validated by the other; each felt, finally, betrayed and misunderstood by the other.

Freud's intellectual combativeness was apparent from the beginning of their friendship. He ends one of his earliest letters, written on January 1, 1907, with an expression he had learned as a young student: "Nemo me impune lacessit" ("No one provokes me with impunity") on which he then elaborates: "The ancients knew how inexorable a god Eros is" (*Freud/Jung Letters* 19). The god Eros was Freud's libido (sexual) theory of neurosis, which he urged Jung to accept. Three months later, Freud recommends to Jung "ruthlessness; our opponents are pachyderms, you must reckon with their thick hides" (*Freud/Jung Letters* 33).

Jung's father-hunger for Freud paralleled the older analyst's wish to adopt him as a surrogate son. Biographers have conjectured that Freud was closer to Jung than he was to his three sons. Part of Freud's attraction to Jung was that he was not Jewish. "With your strong and independent character," Freud writes on August 13, 1908, "with your Germanic blood which enables you to command the sympathies of the public more readily than I, you seem better fitted than anyone else I know to carry out this mission" (168). Jung doesn't respond to this comment or to Freud's salutations as "My dear friend and heir" (172).

A glimpse of the passionate friendship between the two men appears in Martin Freud's memoir, *Sigmund Freud: Man and Father* (1959), where he describes his family's response to Jung's presence during dinner.

> Jung on these occasions did all the talking and father with unconcealed delight did all the listening. There was little we could understand, but I know I found, as did father, his way of outlining a case most fascinating. . . . I think his most outstanding characteristics were his vitality, his liveliness, his ability to project his personality and to control those who listened to him. Jung had a commanding presence (109).

It was during this visit, according to Peter Gay, that Jung claimed to have been told of an affair between Freud and his sister-in-law Minna Bernays (202). Jung's assertion has led to enormous speculation—and sleuthing. Jung's lie to Freud about the meaning of the two skulls has led one psychoanalytic scholar, Peter L. Rudnytsky, to suggest that Jung had secret knowledge of Freud's affair with his sister-in-law, an interpretation, Rudnytsky declares tantalizingly, "that is the subject of another book" (263).

Sabina Spielrein

There is one incident in the *Freud/Jung Letters* where neither man acquitted himself well. In *The Historiography of Psychoanalysis* (2001), Paul Roazen lists many of the early analysts' boundary violations: "(1) Freud's analyzing his daughter Anna; (2) Freud's analyzing Sándor Ferenczi as well as Ferenczi's step-daughter, with whom the Hungarian analyst was in love; Freud's analyzing Ruth Mack Brunswick, her husband Mark, and her brother-in-law David; and Anna Freud's analyzing the children of her most intimate friend Dorothy Burlingham" (31). In their own defense, the early analysts were not as aware of the harmful consequences of boundary violations as were later analysts.

One of the earliest boundary violations involved Sabina Spielrein, exposing in the process Jung and Freud commiserating with each other at her own expense. Aldo Carotenuto's discovery of a cache of papers written by Spielrein, hidden in Geneva for more than sixty years, highlights a woman who was not only an early psychoanalytic pioneer but also an inspiration behind Jung's work. Carotenuto's 1982 book *A Secret Symmetry* contains Spielrein's letters written to Jung along with her letters to and from Freud. Born to Jewish parents in southern Russia in 1885, she had a mental breakdown and was admitted to the Burghölzli Hospital in 1904, where she was treated by Jung. They developed a romantic relationship that may have also been sexual. Glen O. Gabbard and Eva P. Lester discuss Jung's relationship to Spielrein in *Boundaries and Boundary Violations in Psychoanalysis* (1995), suggesting that the "tempestuous love affair" nearly wrecked his career and brought her to the edge of despair (72).

Jung wrote several letters to Freud complaining about Spielrein, and while he never admitted to having had an affair with her, his remarks are self-justifying. "She has kicked up a vile scandal solely because I denied myself the pleasure of giving her a child. I have always acted the gentleman towards her, but before the bar of my rather too sensitive conscience I nevertheless don't feel clean, and that is what hurts the most because my intentions were always honourable." Jung added that he learned much from the experience: "an unspeakable amount of marital wisdom, for until now I had a totally inadequate idea of my polygamous components despite all self-analysis" (*Freud/Jung Letters* 207). In a June 4, 1909, letter to Freud, Jung characterized Spielrein as "systematically planning my seduction" (228). Freud, to whom Spielrein had written a number of letters informing him of her situation, immediately responded to Jung by saying that he had come close to such relationships himself "a number of times and had *a narrow escape*," the last words in English. Freud added, in what may have sounded reassuring to Jung but what sounds misogynistic to us, the "way these women manage to charm us with every conceivable psychic perfection until they have attained their purpose is one of nature's greatest spectacles" (230–1). Carotenuto believes (211) that a key passage in *Memories, Dreams, Reflections,* in which Jung characterizes his encounter with his unconscious anima, refers to Spielrein:

> When I was writing down these fantasies, I once asked myself, "What am I really doing? Certainly this has nothing to do with science. But then what is it?" Whereupon a voice within me said, "It is art." I was astonished. It had never entered my head that what I was writing had any connection with art. Then I thought, "Perhaps my unconscious is forming a personality that is not me, but which is insisting on coming through to expression." I knew for a certainty that the voice had come from a woman, I recognized it as the voice of a patient, a talented psychopath who had a strong transference to me. She had become a living figure within my mind. (185)

Sabina Spielrein recovered from the affair with Jung and published many psychoanalytic papers written in three languages—German, French, and Russian—before she and her two daughters were murdered by the Nazis in Russia in 1942. In his foreword to *A Secret Symmetry,* William McGuire calls Spielrein "one of the very few who preserved a dangerous rapport with both Freud and Jung" (ix).

"The Rest Is Silence"

Discord between the two men can be seen in 1910, when Jung became the first president of the International Psychoanalytic Association. The "first months of your reign," Freud wrote reproachingly, "my dear son and successor, have not turned out brilliantly. Sometimes I have the impression that you yourself have not taken your functions seriously enough and have not yet begun to act in a manner appropriate to your new dignity" (*Freud/Jung Letters* 343). Tensions increased, and two years later, in an effort to repair their relationship, Freud wrote that he wanted a "reciprocal intimate friendship" with Jung (492), forgetting that such a relationship would require him to be as open about his inner life as Jung was about his own, something Freud had refused to do when they analyzed each other's dreams in the United States.

The stormy relationship came to an end in December 1912. Freud denied the significance of the two fainting spells in the presence of Jung, calling them a "bit of neurosis that I ought really to look into" (524). Jung countered by saying that the fainting spells were more serious and then reminded him of the time they were together at Clark University: "Our analysis, you may remember, came to a stop with your remark that you 'could not submit to analysis *without losing your authority.*' These words are engraved on my memory as a symbol of everything to come" (526).

In a furious letter written on December 18, 1912, Jung admits his ambivalence toward Freud, objects strenuously to Freud's pathologizing of his colleagues "to the level of sons and daughters who blushingly admit the existence of their faults," and then asserts his own independence and psychological health:

> You see, my dear Professor, so long as you hand out this stuff I don't give a damn for my symptomatic actions; they shrink to nothing in comparison with the formidable beam in my brother Freud's eye. I am not in the least neurotic—touch wood! I have submitted *lege artis et tout humblement* [according to the law of the profession, with complete humility] to analysis and am much the better for it. You know, of course, how far a patient gets with self-analysis; *not* out of his neurosis—just like you. If ever you should rid yourself entirely of your complexes and stop playing the father to your sons and instead of aiming continually at their weak spots took a good look at your own for a change, then I will mend my ways and at one stroke uproot the vice of being in two minds about you. (535)

Two weeks later, Jung acceded to Freud's proposal to end their relationship. No longer the crown prince of psychoanalysis, Jung bitterly cited Prince Hamlet's final words: "The rest is silence" (540).

Freud's private comments about Jung during and after the break were all negative. "Jung is crazy," Freud fumed to Karl Abraham on June 1, 1913, "but I don't really want a split; I should prefer him to leave of his own accord. Perhaps my Totem [and Taboo] book will hasten the break against my will" (Freud and Abraham 141). In a January 1, 1913, letter to James J. Putnam, Freud regretted the loss of Jung, "whom I greatly overestimated and for whom I felt considerable personal affection." Implying that Jung alone was responsible for the break, Freud lamented that theoretical differences lead inevitably to "so much wounding of justified personal feelings" (*Letters of Sigmund Freud* 299). Freud neglected to add, however, what nearly all researchers of the history of psychoanalysis have pointed out: theoretical differences compelled Freud to end relationships with nearly *everyone* who disagreed with him. The history of psychoanalysis is riddled with schisms and banishments: those who disagreed with Freud were excommunicated.

Freud wasted no time in announcing publicly his break with Jung. In "On the History of the Psycho-Analytic Movement" (1914), he calls Jung a man of "exceptional talents" but then adds, describing his decision to transfer authority to a younger man a few years earlier,

> I had no inkling at that time that in spite of all these advantages the choice was a most unfortunate one, that I had lighted upon a person who was incapable of tolerating the authority of another, but who was still less capable of wielding it himself, and whose energies were relentlessly devoted to the furtherance of his own interests. (*SE*, vol. 14, 43)

In *An Autobiographical Study* (1925), Freud criticized Jung's rejection of infantile sexuality and the Oedipus complex, adding that Jung and Alfred

Adler were "heretics" who did not finally harm psychoanalysis (*SE*, vol. 20, 53). In "Psychoanalysis: Freudian School," a brief 1926 article published in the *Encyclopedia Britannica*, Freud noted that Jung's secession and formation of analytical psychology led to a "scientifically sterile" movement (*SE*, vol. 20, 270).

Of the two, Jung was far more devastated by the end of the relationship. Jung was the kinder of the two in their public statements. Decades after the end of their friendship, Jung fulfilled an odd request—one fraught with irony—that Freud made on May 29, 1907. "In the obituary you will some day write for me, don't forget to bear witness that I was never so much as ruffled by all the opposition" (55). *Always* ruffled by the fierce opposition to psychoanalysis, Freud failed to foresee that Jung would soon become part of it. Jung wrote the obituary, "In Memory of Sigmund Freud," published in a Swiss newspaper two weeks after Freud's death. Jung begins the long obituary with a statement about Freud's heroic importance. "The cultural history of the past fifty years is inseparably bound up with the name of Sigmund Freud." At the turn of the nineteenth century, Jung continues, "it was an act of the greatest scientific courage to make anything as unpopular as dreams an object of serious discussion. What impressed us young psychiatrists most was neither the technique nor the theory, both of which seemed to us highly controversial, but the fact that anyone should have dared to investigate dreams at all." Jung offers several criticisms of Freud and then comments briefly on their relationship. "In the course of the personal friendship which bound me to Freud for many years, I was permitted a deep glimpse into the mind of this remarkable man. He was a man possessed by a daemon—a man who had been vouchsafed an overwhelming revelation that took possession of his soul and never let him go."

Unlocking the Gates

A similar daimon (the Greek word, used by Plato, evokes dark, irrational psychic forces) possessed Jung. Following the discussion of Freud, the next chapter in *Memories, Dreams, Reflections*—"Confrontation with the Unconscious"—is the most difficult to fathom, intellectually. Jung began to experience a period of inner uncertainty, a state of disorientation, and found himself being "menaced by a psychosis" (176). Now he was free, he tells us, to "unlock all the gates of the unconscious psyche" (171). The metaphor, one of many to conjure up Jung's inner journey, comes from Goethe's *Faust*, which he quotes later in the chapter: "Now let me dare to open wide the gates/ Past which men's steps have ever flinching trod" (188–9). The key-to-unlock-the-gates metaphor recalls, to readers of George Eliot's novel *Middlemarch*, the pedantic scholar Edward Casaubon, who spends his life writing a book he never completes, *The Key to All Mythologies*, which symbolizes the failure of his unfulfilled ambitions.

By contrast, the ambitious Jung never doubts his own ability to find the key to all mythologies. The key to unlocking the gates for Jung lies in the study of archetypes, best seen in myths, fairy tales, and world religions. Throughout the chapter, he uses metaphors of transformation to dramatize his symbolic death and rebirth. An advantage of writing about his breakdown in densely metaphorical and mythic language is that he avoids embarrassing personal self-disclosures. Moreover, it's easier to confess "negative emotions" (178) by writing about them as intrapsychic rather than interpersonal events.

One of Jung's dreams in "Confrontation with the Unconscious" involves his struggle with the mythic warrior "Siegfried," who represents "what the Germans want to achieve, heroically to impose their will, have their own way." Jung decides he must kill Siegfried to be released from his power. After the deed, Jung feels overwhelming compassion, as if he himself has been slain, a "sign of my secret identity with Siegfried, as well as of the grief a man feels when he is forced to sacrifice his ideal and his conscious attitudes" (180). Jung had in mind Wagner's Siegfried, the hero of the third of the four music dramas that form *Der Ring des Nibelungen*. Jung had written about Wagner's *Ring* cycle in his 1912 book *Psychology of the Unconscious*, later revised and retitled as *Symbols of Transformation*. But it's tempting to view Siegfried as Sigmund Freud, as Peter Homans observes: "Siegfried, the German, wanted to impose his own will, have his own way, just as Jung felt that Freud was imposing his own theory on Jung's innovative efforts" (78).

Jung's extraordinary erudition is apparent throughout the chapter. He returns to the dream of the ithyphallic god, recalling it with "satisfaction" (174). He immerses himself in the world of fantasies, writing about them first in *The Black Book*, a collection of six private journals penned between 1913 and 1932, and then in *The Red Book*, created around the same time, containing similar fantasies, embellished with illustrations, and written in Gothic script as if it were a medieval manuscript. Both books were published posthumously. Jung refers only briefly to the two books in *Memories, Dreams, Reflections*, remarking that he never completed his "esthetic elaboration" of his fantasies and abandoned the projects because he could not find the right language (188).

A Dangerous Experiment

The story of Jung's breakdown and recovery in *Memories, Dreams, Reflections* is a highly stylized depiction of madness. He characterizes the breakdown as a dangerous experiment with life-or-death consequences. The experiment can be viewed, psychoanalytically, as a regression which, as Paul Roazen points out in *Freud and His Followers*, serves as a positive and not merely neurotic function for Jung. Jung's belief that psychosis can be a positive experience influenced many psychotherapists and creative writers, including R.D. Laing in *The Divided Self* (1960). Jungian literary critics have pointed out Doris Lessing's indebtedness to his psychological theory. Roberta Rubenstein, for example, regarded Jung as Lessing's psychological "mentor" (9). Matthew Pike has noted how *Memories, Dreams, Reflections* provided Lessing with the images and myths suggestive of the descent into the underworld in her 1971 novel *Briefing for a Descent into Hell*. Lessing used her experience with her Jungian therapist, Toni Sussman, in *The Golden Notebook* (1962), her most convincing exploration of psychological breakdown and recovery.

Jung avoids any discussion in his memoir of the impact of his breakdown on family or friends. He doesn't ask for or receive help, therapeutic or otherwise, from anyone. The breakdown heightens rather than diminishes his febrile imagination. Some writers on the edge of the abyss, such as William Styron, become so depressed that they cannot pen a suicide note. Jung, by contrast, is flooded with words. He doesn't call what he writes in *The Black Book* or *The Red Book* "art," but he never doubts the therapeutic value of written expression. He seems to have had, during the years of his oxymoronic creative malady that lasted from 1913 to 1917, from which the insights of his new theoretical system emerged, the ability to compartmentalize, fulfilling his psychiatric and familial responsibilities in the day while journeying—and journaling—in the night. He describes the process of writing as wrestling with the angel or, in his case, with his elusive anima. "Every evening I wrote very consciously for I thought if I did not write, there would be no way for the anima to get at my fantasies. Also, by writing them out, I gave her a chance to twist them into intrigue" (186).

Given the religious differences between Freud and Jung, psychoanalysts have sought to understand the messianic imagery that characterizes the rupture of their relationship. "Jung saw himself as another reincarnated Christ," John Gedo remarks in *Portraits of the Artist* (1983), "freed from the undesirable encrustations through which his divine message had been distorted by institutional Christianity. From such a perspective, a Jewish precursor, Sigmund Freud, takes on the significance of a John the Baptist" (252). How we view the breakup of their relationship depends, to a large extent, not only on our own religious beliefs or disbeliefs but also on how we align themselves with Freudian versus Jungian approaches to psychology.

Jung never seemed to doubt that his introspective psychological journey, or "nekyia," would be a life-changing experience, like Freud's self-analysis. The nekyia resembled a descent into the psychic underworld, reminiscent of Odysseus' travels in Hades, Dante's descent into hell, or Conrad's voyage into the heart of darkness. Jung found himself transformed into a new man—and a new analytical psychologist. The story of his breakdown and recovery has a beginning (following his breakup with Freud), a middle, and an end. "The haunting was over" (191), he intones near the end of "Confrontation with the Unconscious."

In a favorable review of *Memories, Dreams, Reflections* published in the *International Journal of Psycho-Analysis* in 1964, D.W. Winnicott urged all psychoanalysts to read the memoir, particularly the first three chapters, the most autobiographical of the twelve. Winnicott marvels at Jung's self-healing from "childhood schizophrenia." Winnicott then makes a whimsical statement about both Jung and himself:

> If I want to say that Jung was mad, and that he recovered, I am doing nothing worse than I would do in saying of myself that I was sane and that through analysis and self-analysis I achieved some measure of insanity. Freud's flight to sanity could be something we psycho-analysts are trying to recover from, just

as Jungians are trying to recover from Jung's "divided self," and from the way he himself dealt with it. (450)

Winnicott found *Memories, Dreams, Reflections* so powerful that he began dreaming about the book, as he recalls in "D.W.W.'s Dream Related to Reviewing Jung" (1963). The memoir became, as David Sedgwick observes, a "catalyst for important personal healing for Winnicott, helping unify a 'dissociation' that he had suffered all his life and his personal analysis had not resolved" (543).

Storytelling and Narrative Medicine

Jung is always conscious that he is writing a story; storytelling remains at the heart of *Memories, Dreams, Reflections*:

> In many cases in psychiatry, the patient who comes to us has a story that is not told, and which as a rule no one knows of. To my mind, therapy only really begins after the investigation of that wholly personal story. It is the patient's secret, the rock against which he is shattered. If I know his secret history, I have a key to the treatment. The doctor's task is to find out how to gain that knowledge. (117)

Jung's vision of storytelling anticipates the "narrative medicine" movement in which all physicians, not only psychiatrists, seek to learn everything they can about a patient's story. Narrative medicine, as conceived by Rita Charon, a professor of medicine at Columbia University who earned a PhD in English literature, integrates the values and methods of literary study into medical practice and education. Physicians write up case study notes and share them with patients, who read and respond to them with their own reports. As Maura Spiegel and Danielle Spencer remark in a volume of essays devoted to narrative medicine, there is a shift in relational therapy "from the model of seer and seen to a bidirectional interaction where clinicians recognize themselves and their patients as subjective agents" (34). Many of Jung's statements in *Memories, Dreams, Reflections* foreshadow the narrative medicine movement and two-person psychotherapy. Doctors cannot cure patients without committing themselves personally, Jung writes. "When important matters are at stake, it makes all the difference whether the doctor sees himself as part of the drama, or cloaks himself in his authority" (*Memories, Dreams, Reflections* 133).

"Confrontation with the Unconscious" reveals the fundamental differences between Freudian and Jungian psychology. For Freud, the unconscious is a dark, fearful realm, the repository of repressed sexual and aggressive drives reflective of one's personal life. The unconscious is a much more creative realm for Jung. He distinguished between the personal unconscious, which consisted of what he called complexes, and the collective unconscious, containing inherited, universal archetypes. Both forms of the unconscious were, for Jung, realms with positive spiritual and mystical implications. Freud sought to tame and domesticate the unconscious: "where id was, there ego shall be," he expressed in one of his most famous formulations (*New Introductory Lectures on Psycho-Analysis*, vol. 22, 80). Jung, on the other hand, sought to tap into the unconscious, the source of creativity.

Later chapters in *Memories, Dreams, Reflections* describe in detail Jungian theory. All of his writings, he suggests in a striking sentence, are from thoughts and feelings that had "assailed" him (222), suggesting what the English physician George Pickering called in his 1974 book "creative malady," or what Ellenberger calls "creative illness," the belief that illness plays a dominant role in creativity. Pickering includes Freud in his study but surprisingly omits Jung. Pickering's theory of creative malady recalls Edmund Wilson's influential 1941 literary study *The Wound and the Bow*, in which the "victim of a malodorous disease which renders him abhorrent to society and periodically degrades him" is also the "master of a superhuman art which everybody has to respect and which the normal man finds he needs" (240). Creative malady returns us to Smith's vision of Jung as a wounded healer, where the motivation for creativity arises from the need to heal psychic injuries. Jung uses the wound metaphor in his memoir, referring to his father as a "sufferer stricken with an Amfortas wound, a 'fisher king' whose wound would not heal." Alluding to Wagner's opera based on the thirteenth-century epic poem by Wolfram von Eschenbach about the quest for the Holy Grail, Jung then refers to his own wound. "I as a 'dumb' Parsifal was the witness of this sickness during the years of my boyhood, and, like Parsifal, speech failed me" (215).

The final three chapters of *Memories, Dreams, Reflections*—"On Life after Death," "Late Thoughts," and "Retrospect"—outline Jung's religious and spiritual beliefs, including his description of himself as a "doctor of the soul." Some of Jung's observations are easy to accept, as when he states that the "conception people form of the hereafter is largely made up of wishful thinking and prejudices" (320). Other observations strain credibility unless one believes in the hereafter: "souls of the dead 'know' only what they knew at the moment of death, and nothing beyond that" (308). And other statements are historically controversial, as when, praising Pope Pius XII for offering a ray of religious hope (332), he remains silent about the pope's own silence during the Holocaust.

Jung's involvement with the Nazis will always remain troubling. The passing of time has done little to diminish the controversy. His attitude toward Nazi Germany was, at best, naïve and ill-informed, and, at worst, blind and opportunistic. Few can doubt that Jung was slow to recognize the menace of Hitler's deeds and words in the 1930s. (The same can be said of Freud.) Jung became a charter member of the International General Medical Society of Psychotherapy in 1928, and he was elected president from 1933, the year Hitler rose to power in Germany, until his resignation in 1940. Jung continued to believe that "Aryan psychology" was different from "Jewish psychology," not understanding that race is a poisoned concept. "Jung brought upon himself much of the opprobrium that haunted him the rest of his life," Bair concludes, "by choosing to explain—over and over again—aspects of his theory of cultural types in an era fraught with tension and peril" (462).

Freud and Jung

Unlike Freud, who regarded himself as an intellectual conquistador, seeking to show how psychoanalysis could dominate other disciplines, Jung aimed to integrate disciplinary knowledge to achieve psychic wholeness. *Memories, Dreams, Reflections* is the story of that odyssey. "Psychology has no room for judgments like 'only religious' or 'only philosophical,' despite the fact that we too often hear the charge of something's being 'only psychological'—especially from theologians," he writes in "Late Thoughts" (350). Jung embraced Western and Eastern religion and philosophy along with literature and mythology to achieve wholeness. He never abandoned the hope of achieving a unified theory of creation.

Rejecting the binary Freud or Jung with which I began this chapter, I now realize that Freud *and* Jung are two geniuses with strikingly different conceptions of psychoanalysis. Jung contributed much to psychoanalysis, as Ellenberger indicates: "He introduced the terms 'complex' and 'imago,' and he was the promoter of training analysis" (732). Jung ends *Memories, Dreams, Reflection* by affirming unknowability. "The older I have become, the less I have understood or had insight into or known about myself" (358). In my youth, I would have rejected this statement as unduly pessimistic. In my old age, I now regard Jung's words as humble and wise.

Chapter 6

WILFRED R. BION

WAR MEMOIRS 1917–19

Wilfred R. Bion penned several autobiographical works, including the trilogy *A Memoir of the Future* (1975–9), which recasts psychoanalytic speculation in semi-fictional form; *The Long Week-End, 1897–1919*, published in 1982; and the incomplete *All My Sins Remembered*, published in 1985. These books "initiated a new genre of psychoanalytic writing," as James Grotstein observes. "It was as if he had crossed a veritable Rubicon of a strongly held analytic canon that the analyst should never reveal his personal life to his patients" ("Review" 463).

Bion had crossed the Rubicon years earlier, however, with *War Memoirs 1917–19*, written in 1919, when he was a 22-year-old Oxford undergraduate, but not published until 1997, marking the centenary of his birth. *War Memoirs* takes on special importance, for it not only chronicles the early life of a major British psychoanalyst, but it also reminds us of the brutality of war—particularly the "war to end all wars." Bion remained haunted by his war experience, as his wife and editor of the volume, Francesca Bion, points out. "Bion's remarkable physical survival against heavy odds concealed the emotional injury which left scars for many years to come" (np). *War Memoirs* also contains many of the themes upon which Bion elaborated in his later clinical writings.

Wilfred Ruprecht Bion was born in India in 1897 and came to England when he was eight to attend school. A tank commander during the First World War, he was awarded the Distinguished Service Order (DSO) and the Legion of Honour from the French government. He studied medicine and psychoanalysis after the war and was associated with the Tavistock Clinic in London. One of his early analysands was Samuel Beckett, who later received the Nobel Prize for Literature. During the Second World War, Bion served as a psychiatrist in the Royal Army Medical Corps, where he treated soldiers suffering from shell shock, now called posttraumatic stress disorder. Bion was president of the British Psychoanalytical Society from 1962 to 1965 and chair of the Melanie Klein Trust. He moved to Los Angeles in 1968, intending to spend only three or four years in California, but he remained there until late August 1979, when he returned to England and died three months later at age eighty-one.

Unlike many of his fellow analysts, Bion worked mainly with psychotic patients. His concept of the "container" and the "contained," which he derived from Klein's idea of projective identification, extended object relations theory. His best-known book *Experiences in Groups and Other Papers* (1961) bears the imprint of his war experiences, particularly his concept of leaderless groups. Other concepts were more conjectural, such as "beta elements," which he called unmetabolized affective experiences, and "alpha elements," available for dreams and conscious thought.

Dense with highly abstract theory and mathematical formulas, Bion's clinical writings are difficult to read. His clinical books often use a grid (containing both vertical and horizontal axes) that he thought would shorten and simplify psychoanalysis. Many of his terms, such as valency, are taken from chemistry and redefined. Bion's clinical writings are a world apart from his personal writings, which reveal lived experience. According to Neil Altman, Bion is the "second most cited analyst in the contemporary world" (163), yet it's hard for non-Bionian initiates to receive much aesthetic pleasure or psychological clarity from his theoretical books. Even Bion himself had grave doubts late in life about his "epistemological period," the term used by Gérard Bléandonu in his 1994 biography. By contrast, *War Memoirs* is highly readable, offering us insight into Bion's younger and older selves, and displaying a literary power that becomes more impressive in his later autobiographical writings. As Paulo Cesar Sandler suggests, Bion "did for the psychoanalytic movement the same that Wordsworth did for poetry and Bertrand Russell for philosophy, namely, he replaced the pompous, rarefied 'jargonized' phraseology with real life speech" (62).

War Memoirs 1917–19

The major part of *War Memoirs* is Bion's *Diary*, which records his service in France in the Royal Tank Regiment between June 1917, upon entering battle, and January 1919, when he was demobilized. As Francesca Bion explains, her husband addressed the diary to his parents. He regretted not having written to them during the war and, upon his discharge, sought to provide them with as full an account of his experiences as possible. *Diary* is nearly two hundred pages long. The rest of *War Memoirs* consists of "Commentary," an essay written in the late 1970s in which the elderly Bion offers his impressions of rereading for the first time the diary he had written more than half a century earlier; "Amiens," a ninety-four-page essay left incomplete; and a four-page "Aftermath" written by his daughter, Parthenope Bion Talamo.

War Memoirs appeals to anyone who is interested in battle—historians, military strategists, sociologists, psychologists, and general readers. The book contains dozens of photographs and sketches of tanks, bursting shells, German pill-boxes, enemy trenches, troop movements, and anti-tank rifles. Bion's language is hauntingly evocative, as we can see in his description of a photograph of a shell-cratered road where he can still hear the "weird boom and groans" of artillery fire. "The sound was quite different from anything I know. If anything was needed to complete the horror of that place, those echoes did it; for it needed no great imagination to think of those shuddering reverberations as the wails of spirits still tortured by the memories of their misery, still lamenting the incredible folly that doomed their successors to the same fate" (93). Bion never romanticizes war nor his own service, and he shows the devastating consequences of shell shock. The Great War anticipated the isolation and dehumanization experienced by many Vietnam veterans who, like the First World War soldiers, returned home only to find their patriotic service ignored or condemned by their country.

Anticipating Hemingway

Passages of *War Memoirs* eerily anticipate Ernest Hemingway's 1929 novel *A Farewell to Arms*. Like Hemingway's semi-autobiographical protagonist, Frederic Henry, Bion enlists in the Great War out of patriotic duty but gradually becomes disillusioned and embittered. Frederic drives an ambulance for the Red Cross in Italy; Bion commands a tank on the Western Front. Both experience the absurdity of war in which "friendly fire" is all-too-common. Decorated for their heroism, they nevertheless remain unimpressed with their exploits. Both find themselves acting over the heads of their immediate superiors, who accuse them of desertion in the face of the enemy. Both conclude that there is little if any difference between the two opposing forces. Frederic deserts the war to make a "separate peace" (243)—a felicitous expression John Fowles used as the title of his 1959 novel. Bion also longs to detach himself from the war, as may be seen in his description of two "tired-looking" pigeons that he sends to the French lines. "Whether they ever took a message back or not I don't know. When I *did* release them, they looked more like making a separate peace with the enemy than anything else" (122). Both men eventually become numb from battle and indifferent to suffering. Frederic recalls a time when he placed a log swarming with ants on a fire and watched them scurry from one side to another before falling into the fire. He has the opportunity to be a "Messiah" by lifting the log from the fire but instead pours a cup of water on the log, staring as the water steamed the ants. Bion uses a related image to conjure up existential absurdity. "After all, a mouse must feel that it is one up on the playful cat when it dies without making any sport for its captor" (95). There's another grim similarity between Hemingway's fictional character and Bion. Frederic Henry finally bids farewell to the arms of war and the arms of Catherine Barkley, who dies in childbirth; Bion's first wife, Betty Jardine, died three days after childbirth in 1945.

Unlike Frederic Henry, Bion never renounces his duty. His diary is a record of commitment and survival—precarious, to be sure, but nevertheless real. The most psychologically revealing moment in Bion's diary occurs when he depicts the loss of his will to live:

> This may seem hardly possible to you. But the fact remains that life had now reached such a pitch that horrible mutilations or death could not conceivably

> be worse. I found myself looking forward to getting killed, as then, at least, one would be rid of this intolerable misery. These thoughts were uppermost with me then and excluded all others—and I think many were in the same state. After all, if you get a man and hunt him like an animal, in time he will become one. I am at a loss now to tell you of our life. Such worlds separate the ordinary human's point of view from mine at that time, that anything I can write will either be incomprehensible or will give a quite wrong impression. (94)

One is struck by the wrenching honesty of Bion's description, the sense of being pushed past his limits. He had reached a breaking point; nothing, it seemed at the time, could be worse than what he was experiencing. Despite being unable to convey the full extent of his intolerable misery, he succeeds remarkably in recreating what he felt at the time.

At the end of his first Christmas fighting in France, in 1917, Bion raises a question that he never answers: "Had everyone gone mad?" (69). He repeatedly uses expressions like "All our nerves were in an awful state" (29), "We were all in a fairly shaky mood" (36), "I never struck such a nightmare in my life" (37). He recalls a soldier who was sent home for leave, returned to battle, but was then sent home again, "still stammering" after the war ended (62). *Stammering* is a key word for Bion, often reserved for traumatized soldiers. "The stammer," Bion declares in *Cogitations* (1992), is a "repudiation of awareness, an evacuation of awareness of what is currently taking place," "incompatible with a state of self consciousness" (77). Bion's friend and fellow officer Quainton returned to England for a leave, had a breakdown while driving his car, and careened into a ditch. Another officer cynically believed Quainton (and, by implication, his friends) was a "coward," faking illness to escape from the war. Not for a moment does Bion question the reality or pain of his shell-shocked comrades.

Writing and Rewriting a Soldier's Death

The most horrifying moment in *Diary* occurs when Bion writes about a young soldier whose entire left side of his body had been torn away by a shell during the Battle of Amiens on August 8, 1918, the opening phase of the Allied offensive that led to the end of the First World War. To understand the significance of this event, we should note that Bion returns to this trauma in *The Long Week-End* and his oneiric fantasy *A Memoir of the Future*. He devotes four paragraphs in *War Memoirs* to Sweeting's dying and death.

> He kept on saying, "I'm done for, sir! I'm done for!", hoping against hope I would contradict him. This I did, telling him it was nothing—but his eyes were already glazing over, and it was clear that death was even then upon him. He kept trying to cough, but of course the wind only came out of his side. He kept asking me why he couldn't cough. (127)

Bion must have thought that his brief description in *War Memoirs* did not do justice to the full horror of the scene, mainly because he had camouflaged his feelings. Sweeting's devastating injury haunted Bion for the rest of his life: "The look in his eyes was the same as that in the eyes of a bird that has been shot—mingled fear and surprise" (127). Bion doesn't describe, however, the emotional impact of this event; instead, he ends his account of Sweeting by noting that the "sooner people realize the criminal folly of their leaders the better" (127).

Nothing in *Diary* suggests that Bion felt guilty or angry with himself over Sweeting's death, but he returns to the event in "Amiens," written in 1958. Using third person, Bion reveals that he began to vomit, "unrestrainedly, helplessly." The dying soldier gives his home address, repeating, again and again, "Write to my mother." For the first time, Bion reveals how revolted and terrified he was, shouting twice at Sweeting, "Oh, for Christ's sake shut up" (255). Anger overcomes Bion, and he seems infected—and enraged—by Sweeting's fear. Bion deftly juxtaposes the soldier's mother with his own. "Never have I known a bombardment like this, never, never—Mother, Mother, Mother—never have I known a bombardment like this, he thought. I wish he would shut up. I wish he would die. Why can't he die? Surely he can't go on living with a great hole torn in his side like that" (*War Memoirs* 256). The final reference to Sweeting in *War Memoirs* occurs near the end of "Amiens" when Bion offers his most damning statement about himself. "Well, thank God he's gone, thought Bion, filled with passionate hatred of himself for his hatred of the wounded man" (290).

In "Aftermath," Parthenope Bion Talamo suggests that the "raw material" in *War Memoirs* was carried over, "with hardly any emotional or intellectual elaboration," in his later autobiographical writings (309). We can see how this is true in *All My Sins Remembered*, where Bion uses the real name of the dying soldier, Kitching, who had a "first aid bandage slung across the gap where . . . [his] chest wall should have been; it could not render invisible his heart beating away his life" (44). Bion's use of the pseudonym Sweeting, K.M. Souter suggests, implies a "pet name for a baby or lover" (802). In *A Memoir of the Future*, the unnamed psychoanalyst describes the same soldier:

> A runner who was crouching beside me in a shell hole had his thoracic wall blown out, exposing his heart. He tried to look at the ghastly wound across which an entirely ineffectual field dressing dangled. "Mother, Mother— you'll write to my Mother, sir, won't you?" "Yes, blast you," I said. If I could believe in God I would ask him to forgive me. "Dieu me pardonnera. C'est son métier." (256)

The last two sentences, "God will pardon me. That's his job" (words attributed to the poet Heinrich Heine), prompt a character, Alice (named after the eponymous protagonist in Lewis Carroll's *Alice in Wonderland*), to respond, "I thought you were supposed to be cured of such irrational guilts." The psychoanalyst, whom we infer is Bion himself, underscores the appropriateness of guilt. "Who said they were irrational? Or that one would not sometimes see sufficiently clearly to know one was damned—rationally?" (*A Memoir of the Future* 256). Apologizing to Alice for being "rude," the psychoanalyst concedes that his words "hang across the gaping wound of my mind like a ridiculous field dressing" (256).

A few pages later in *A Memoir of the Future*, Bion offers new information about the grievously wounded soldier:

> "Sir! Sir! Sir! You'll write to my mother, sir? Won't you, sir? Won't you?" "Oh *shut up damn you*." "Why can't I cough? Sir! Why can't I cough?" "Because—blast you!—your thoracic wall has been blown off?" "I don't know enough medicine for Thoracic Wall, I'm not qualified." The gunners know how to operate on the Thoracic Wall. (290)

One senses, ironically, that the more the psychoanalyst orders the dying soldier to shut up, the more he later feels compelled to open up about the dark story through his writings. It's odd to hear a psychoanalyst condemning himself as "rationally" damned. In the final section, *A Key to A Memoir of the Future*, Bion defines "Mother" as the "appeal of a fatally wounded soldier" (638), an appeal to which Bion responds through the writing of the story.

The dying Sweeting also appears in *The Long Week-End*. Confessing that he "could not stand" Sweeting's cries, Bion begins to "whimper," suggesting loss of self-control and regression to a child-like state. What follows is one of Bion's most emotionally charged passages:

> Sweeting was trying to say something. He looked horribly anxious, almost ill. "What?" I shouted, putting my ear to his mouth to catch his reply.
> "Sir! Sir, why can't I cough?"
> What a question! What a time . . . I looked at his chest. His tunic was torn. No, it was not his tunic; the left side of his chest was missing. He tried to look. I stopped him. I found his field dressing and pretended to fix it across the gap. And then he saw, under his left arm . . . . He sank back as if relieved, then started on a new tack.
> "Mother, Mother, Mother . . ." Well, thank God for his damned mother. Now at least I could have some peace and pay attention to the shell-fire. (*The Long Week-End*, 248; ellipses in original)

Bion conveys in this extraordinary passage not only Sweeting's horror, echoed in his repeated cries for his mother, but his own as well. He provides crucial details in *The Long Week-End* that we do not see in *War Memoirs*. Sweeting's incessant cries enrage Bion, and he presents himself in the worst possible way. He begins to break down himself. "I began to vomit, but had nothing to vomit." Exhausted, he promises to notify Sweeting's mother. The next sentence is fraught with ambiguity. "And then I think he died. Or perhaps it was only me" (*The Long Week-End* 249).

The Repetition-Compulsion Principle

Bion captures in this scene the survivor guilt that is part of the legacy, or illegacy, of war. Witnessing another person's suffering almost seems worse than suffering oneself. Tellingly, Bion never mentions Freud's repetition-compulsion principle, the need to relive traumatic events in an effort to gain control over them, if only temporarily. The "instinct for mastery" (16), as Freud writes in *Beyond the Pleasure Principle* (1920), has never received much enthusiasm from British psychoanalysts, who, like Melanie Klein (and French psychoanalysts), preferred to talk about the "death instinct." Yet, the repetition-compulsion principle can help us fathom why Bion felt compelled to write repeatedly about Sweeting's death, as if he is trying to exorcise a demon. One can hardly exaggerate the lifelong significance of this traumatic event in Bion's life. The Sweeting writings give the impression of "undigested material." Bion did not seem to work through the memory to achieve a degree of resolution. Bléandonu doesn't mention Sweeting by name, referring fleetingly to a soldier who had "half his chest blasted away" (32). Meg Harris Williams, who has written many books on literature and psychoanalysis, refers to Sweeting's death several times in her reading of Bion's autobiographies, yet never in the context of Freud's repetition-compulsion principle. To my knowledge, none of the many analysts or scholars who have written about Bion has interpreted his need to return repeatedly to Sweeting as an effort to master ongoing trauma.

As a psychoanalyst, Bion surely knew of the distinction between thoughts and deeds. We are responsible only for the latter, not the former. Yet, throughout his autobiographical writings, he condemns himself for feelings that nearly everyone would experience in war. Shame suffuses Bion's autobiographical writings. Léon Wurmser, perhaps the leading psychoanalytic theorist of shame, has offered three interrelated components of the darkest of emotions: shame over the fear of disgrace; shame over being looked at with scorn, the affect of contempt; and shame over being exposed. All three aspects of shame pervade Bion's autobiographical writings. Significantly, writing is a countershame technique, allowing one's darkest feelings to surface, where they can be worked through and understood. In Hemingwayesque terms, Bion made a separate peace in his clinical monographs, but he was never far from the battleground in his autobiographical stories.

Reading about Sweeting's dying and death, I was reminded of Joseph Conrad's 1899 novella *Heart of Darkness*, where Marlow's ambivalence toward his dark double, Kurtz, "the nightmare of my choice," parallels Bion's feelings toward Sweeting. The soldier's death represents a turning point in Bion's life, a (w)rites of passage that betokened to him failure, not success. No one could have saved Sweeting's life; yet, Bion judges himself guilty of an unnamed crime and condemns himself to a lifetime of self-punishment.

Bion acknowledges toward the end of *War Memoirs* that the impartial reader would probably conclude he has been grossly unfair to some of the senior officers—and Bion then admits ruefully that he *has* been unfair. Equally important, he may have been unfair to himself. In describing himself as an imposter, he becomes an unreliable narrator. It is easier to accept his judgments of cowardly officers than it is to accept his own severe self-judgments.

Bion's symptoms of traumatic suffering point to an inexpressible secret while at the same time refusing to elaborate on it—a secret that recalls Jung's in his memoir. We see this paradox throughout Bion's autobiographical writings. British object relations theorists, unlike American ego psychologists, do not emphasize Freud's repetition-compulsion principle, but the theory helps us understand Bion's need to return to a traumatic experience that irrevocably changed his image of himself.

Confronting One's Younger Self

Bion confronts the problem of judgment more fully in the most analytic section of *War Memoirs*, the twelve-page "Commentary" that is structured as a conversation between the older writer ("Myself"), a mid-septuagenarian, and his twenty-one-year-old counterpart ("Bion"). The essay begins with the older Bion disparaging the prose style of his war diary. "Do you mind if I cut out the 'verys' and superlatives? You had a 'very' bad attack of the 'verys,' verily very virulently. They make it difficult to read." The younger Bion readily agrees with this criticism: "No, of course not. But I don't want it to appear that I was better educated than I was. I find it salutary to be reminded of these disconcerting facts that I had forgotten" (200). It's possible that Bion's harsh judgment of his war diary's literary merits is a rhetorical strategy to gain the reader's approval, but I doubt this is his primary motivation, for he is genuinely self-deprecating and guilt-ridden throughout the book. "Looking at it again," the older Bion admits dryly, "I am amazed to find I wrote like an illiterate when I had already been accepted at Queen's" (200).

Like any good storyteller, Bion knows how to create tension. He is especially successful in dramatizing the contrast between his older and younger selves. We see a generational clash between the angry, rebellious son, "Bion," and the older man, "Myself," who sternly reprimands his younger self. "Your failure to write home was reprehensible and not superficial." The son painfully agrees with this judgment. "I could not. I agree—I knew—it was reprehensible. But I could not do it" (202). We never learn why Bion was unable or unwilling to write to his parents during the war. Bion remains critical of many aspects of his life. The older man cannot forgive the sanctimoniousness of his youth, and the younger man cannot forgive the accomplishments of his adult life. Asked what he finds most upsetting about his present life, the young Bion responds, "Your success, I think. I hesitate to say it, because it sounds ungrateful. I cannot imagine what was wrong, but I never recovered from the survival of the Battle of Amiens. Most of what I do not like about you seemed to start then" (209).

One cannot predict, on the basis of *War Memoirs* alone, that Bion would become a psychoanalyst, the author of fifteen books, but there is a passage that highlights how his war experience influenced his choice of career:

> Bion: I fear I was a narrow-minded prig. I often think my fellows must have had a good deal to put up with.
> Myself: From what I remember, that is true. Indeed, from what I have learned since, I and my closest friends did not stand up to the rigours of war very well.

Bion: Of course we did not know that, though I was always afraid I would not. I think even the diary shows that as it goes on, though at Oxford I was still too ashamed to admit it. And very glad of the opportunity that Oxford gave me to be seduced into a more self-satisfied state of mind. But I never quite got rid of the sense that all was *not* well.

Myself: That ultimately drove me into psycho-analysis. (201)

Bion never discloses in "Commentary" what he learned about himself through his training analysis, though he suggests that for many years he hated the experience. One of the benefits of psychoanalysis, he implies, is the value of talking to another person and, in the process, feeling less alone. The inability to verbalize dark feelings during war, for fear of spreading alarm and despondency, produced isolation and alienation. "The loneliness was intense; I can still feel my skin drawn over the bones of my face as if it were the mask of a cadaver" (204).

Contrary to Bion's assertion in "Commentary," I never felt while reading *War Memoirs* that the young author was a narrow-minded prig. It's true that he makes sweeping condemnations of many officers, but he is always harder on himself than on his fellow officers. As he states in the aptly titled *All My Sins Remembered*, a continuation of *The Long Week-End*, despite the significance of the DSO, "I had not succeeded in believing that it was more than a cosmetic cover for my cowardice, the reality of which was never in the least doubt since I knew what it felt like to have *my* feelings" (67).

Bion's war experiences heightened his understanding of mental health and illness. One insight was his discovery of emotional contagion: gloom is as infectious as cheerfulness. Another insight was the concept of containment: the ability to hold, tolerate, and defuse unruly emotions. And another insight, the idea of alpha and beta elements, may be seen in the contrast between *War Memoirs*, filled with raw, undigested emotions, and Bion's clinical writings, which contain primitive experiences that have been metabolized into coherent thoughts.

A passage in *Experiences in Groups* (1961) suggests how Bion's experience as a tank commander helped shape his vision of psychiatry. "An officer who aspires to be the psychiatrist in charge of a rehabilitation wing must know what it is to be in a responsible position at a time when responsibility means having to face issues of life and death" (13). Bion believed that the close emotional relationship between an officer and his fellow soldiers was no less significant for psychiatrists and their patients. He also recognized the value of empathy. His bitterness over officers who deserted their troops in battle compelled him to warn psychiatrists of the "hideous blunder of thinking that patients are potential cannon-fodder" (13). In *A Memoir of the Future*, Bion suggests that a psychoanalytic session is like going into war, and when a listener protests the comparison, the psychoanalyst argues that although imminent death may not be expected, the analyst must be able to "smell" danger: "If the hair at the back of your neck becomes erect, your primitive, archaic senses indicate the presence of danger. It is your job to be curious about that danger—not cowardly, not irresponsible" (517). Anyone who is unafraid of practicing psychoanalysis, Bion adds, is either "not doing his job or is unfitted for it" (517).

"Amiens" ends with a tantalizingly incomplete sentence: "He felt that people who cracked up were merely those who did not allow the rest of the world to . . ." (308). One can only guess what the final words might have been—and why Bion did not complete the sentence. Did he believe that the answer would be a platitude? Did he mistrust whatever advice he could offer to readers? Did he plan to return to the manuscript? Parthenope Bion Talamo suggests plausibly in "Aftermath" that her father spent much of the rest of his life brooding over his war experiences. She ends with a provocative question. Did Bion become a psychoanalyst because of or despite his war experience?

Bion's comments about his own psychoanalysis in *All My Sins Remembered* are equivocal. He was "assiduous" in his training analysis with Melanie Klein. He often felt that her interpretations of him were "nonsense" but hardly worth arguing about. Without being specific, he suggests that the interpretations he ignored or failed to understand later struck him as correct. Over time, he did not become more receptive to her views but rather more aware of his disagreements with them. His touchstone for psychoanalytic accuracy was the extent to which an interpretation coincided with his own sense of what was right or wrong. In *A Memoir of the Future*, Bion elaborates upon Kleinian theory, indicating that it worked with some patients but not with others. "One of the painful, alarming features of continued experience was the fact that I had certain patients with whom I employed interpretations based on my previous experience with Melanie Klein, and though I felt that I employed them correctly and could not fault myself, none of the good results that I anticipated occurred" (559).

Like Freud, Melanie Klein demanded absolute loyalty from her followers, and when they ignored or expressed disagreement with her theories, she became incensed or distraught. The biographer Phyllis Grosskurth reports that Klein broke down after a scientific meeting in which Bion had read a paper without acknowledging her influence. "'But Mrs. Klein,' someone expostulated, 'Everyone *knows* his assumptions are based on yours!'" (427).

Despite mixed psychoanalytic results, Bion remained committed to his profession. He adds a noteworthy caveat in *A Memoir of the Future*:

> The "real psycho-analysis" to which we aspire is at best only a reaching out towards that "real-psycho-analysis." But it is "real" enough to make people aware that there is "something" beyond the feeble efforts of psycho-analyst and analysand. I think it is optimistic to suppose that we do more than scratch the surface in our struggles to achieve it. (510).

Ghosts and Ancestors

Bion's autobiographical writings suggest that he was permanently haunted by his experiences in the First World War. "I died at English Farm [where his tanks were supposed to rendezvous for battle] and I've been working through Purgatory since," the "Ghost" of the psychoanalyst confesses in *A Memoir of the Future* (422). Another voice echoes this. "Pollute old age! I had plenty to regret, plenty to mourn. I thought I would never survive the shame of having lived beyond my friends who were dead by the end of August 8th" (450). Bion unconsciously linked his comrades' deaths to that of his first wife. In *All My Sins Remembered*, Bion blames himself for her demise. "I had begged Betty to have a baby: her agreement to do so had cost her her life" (70). Why did he feel guilty over her death? "I felt I had killed her by not staying with her when her pregnancy was nearing term" (26). The two deaths, first Sweeting's and then his wife's, appear indelibly etched in his mind. "These old ghosts, they never die," he admits in *The Last Week-End*. "They don't even fade away; they preserve their youth wonderfully" (264). Others who fought in the Great War felt similarly ghost-ridden. The British author Edmund Blunden (1896–1974) wrote about his experiences in both poetry and verse. "My experiences in the First World War have haunted me all my life," he wrote shortly before his death, "and for many days I have, it seemed, lived in that world rather than this" (cited in Fussell, 280).

Robert Ehrlich links another troubling event in Bion's life to Sweeting's dying and death. In *All My Sins Remembered*, Bion recalls his failure to respond to his infant daughter who was crawling toward him, demanding his attention. Bion confesses his state of numbness at the time, his inability to move, judging himself as inept and cruel—a judgment that evokes his perceived failure to save Sweeting's life. I agree with Ehrlich's conclusion that, here and elsewhere, Bion is too harsh in his self-appraisal.

In an illuminating 1960 essay, the psychoanalyst Hans W. Loewald distinguishes between ghosts and ancestors to show how trauma, like depression, evokes the image of haunting. "Those who know ghosts tell us that they long to be released from their ghost-life and led to rest as ancestors. As ancestors they live forth in the present generation, while as ghosts they are compelled to haunt the present generation with their shadow-life" (29). In Loewaldian terms, these two deaths remained Bion's ghost.

Why write an autobiography? Bion raises this question in *All My Sins Remembered*. He has no trouble answering the question. "Because it is interesting to me to review the life I have led in the universe in which I have lived" (21). We cannot know our emotions and intentions, he continues, unless we write about them. There are certainly other reasons to write a memoir or autobiography, apart from life review. Bion's personal writings allowed him to bear witness to the most formative event in his life. Sweeting's dying request, "Write to my mother," may have inspired Bion to write to his own mother—and then, years later, to write to an expanded audience. Bion knew that there was one danger in writing, as the psychoanalyst realizes in *A Memoir of the Future*. "I know, and have reason to fear that the 'pen' into which it has entered will imprison both me and my meaning—inescapably" (477). More often than not, however, the pen leads to liberation, or, at least, relief, not imprisonment.

Writing *War Memoirs* was not an act of exorcism, but it helped Bion "give sorrow words," as Shakespeare writes in *Macbeth*: "the grief that does not speak knits up the o-er wrought heart and bids it break." Another reason for penning a memoir is what Sandra Gilbert calls "writing/righting wrong," "writing (recording) as well as seeking to right (rectify) wrong" (86), in Bion's case, documenting the horrors of war and redressing grave historical injustices. Bion would agree with Gilbert that writing/righting wrong involves both "fear and ferocity," emotions that are central to *War Memoirs*.

Bion's stylistic criticisms of *War Memoirs* highlight the urgency of clear writing, as the psychoanalyst insists in *A Memoir of the Future*. "We have to use such language as is available and it may seem that we use it in the way that it is used in social intercourse." When a character objects—"You make it sound as if psychoanalysts are all professors of English"—the psychoanalyst has an instant reply: "We are not professors of English—though no doubt we would all be the better for it if we were" (535). He pays the greatest tribute to the creative writers whose poems and plays he cites throughout his books: Virgil, Shakespeare, Milton, Keats, Shelley, and Ruskin. To give only one example of the rich allusiveness of Bion's writings, he titled part of his autobiography after Hamlet's line to Ophelia: "Nymph, in thy orisons/ Be all my sins remembered." Francesca Bion cites a statement her husband wrote for an anthology that he never completed: "I resort to the poets because they seem to me to say something in a way which is beyond my powers and yet to be in a way which I myself would choose *if* I had the capacity" (*All My Sins Remembered* 241).

Bion is one of the writers who "disturbed the universe" of our psychological landscape, as the British psychoanalyst Donald Meltzer declared. James Grotstein, who was Bion's analysand in the 1970s, would agree with Meltzer's assessment. In his 2007 book *A Beam of Intense Darkness: Wilfred Bion's Legacy to Psychoanalysis*, Grotstein argues that Melanie Klein did not adequately understand the extent of Bion's war trauma. Whether Bion himself fully realized the severity of his war trauma remains unclear.

In an article published in the *International Journal of Psychoanalysis* in 2000, Albert Mason recalls his twenty-year clinical relationship with Bion, first as his supervisee and later as a colleague. He affirms Bion's humility, courage, and "binocular" vision. "One is just as likely to be shot in the back running away from the enemy," Bion told Mason, "as one is to be killed advancing towards him" (988). The observation evokes both Bion's war experiences and his fearless pursuit of confrontations with violent emotions and thoughts. Unlike his clinical books, which appeal mainly to psychoanalysts, Bion's memoiristic writings have a much larger audience. The personal writings portray a far darker image of his life than his clinical writings.

Sometimes we come across glaring contradictions in Bion's writings. In *All My Sins Remembered*, for example, he states that just as the best poets are not made but born, the same is true of psychoanalysts. "I was made a psycho-analyst, but it soon became clear that I had not been born one" (49). In *Clinical Seminars and Other Works* (1987), he makes the opposite claim. "You can't make doctors or analysts—they have to be born" (18). Rosemary Marshall Balsam and Alan Balsam offer the best answer to the question whether psychotherapists are born or made. "Psychotherapy does not come naturally. Regardless of the accuracy of one's intuition or 'gut reactions,' not everything about psychic processes is obvious. Conceptual learning means learning ways of thinking about or ways of looking at things" (16). It's likely that Bion would agree with this observation. Bion's personal writing strikes us as highly original and profoundly moving, worthy of a *born* writer. Yet, he was always observing and learning, deepening his understanding of experience, searching for the best way to *make* himself into a therapist.

Bion believed that one does not "read" certain books—one must have an emotional experience reading them. But reading itself produces intense emotional experiences. Part of the intensity of reading *War Memoirs* lies in looking at the unvarnished truth. In his 1970 book *Attention and Interpretation*, Bion cites a statement by the great eighteenth-century man of letters, Dr. Johnson. "Whether to see life as it is, will give us much consolation, I know not; but the consolation which is drawn from truth, if any there be, is solid and durable; that which may be derived from errour must be, like its original, fallacious and fugitive" (7). Readers of *War Memoirs* experience solid and durable consolation.

Chapter 7

MARION MILNER

ON NOT BEING ABLE TO PAINT

One doesn't expect an author suspicious of self-disclosure to write autobiographically, but Marion Milner (1900–98) penned a quartet of memoirs that spanned six decades: *A Life of One's Own* (1934), *An Experiment in Leisure* (1937), *Eternity's Sunrise* (1987), and *Bothered by Alligators*, published posthumously in 2012. The quartet becomes a quintet if we include her most iconic work, *On Not Being Able to Paint* (1950), which is, paradoxically, personal without being autobiographical. "All Milner's books," Hugh Haughton observes in his new introduction to *Eternity's Sunrise*, "are *sui generis*, recording a life of her own and psychological experiments of her own devising" (xii). To understand *On Not Being Able to Paint*, it is helpful to view it in the context of other writings, all of which bespeak her lifelong self-analysis. Milner's wariness of self-disclosure remained intense throughout her life, but so did her need to write personally. She continued writing until she was in her nineties, with each book casting new light on the preceding ones. Writing became for Milner not only the best way to generate and preserve the truth of her life but also a way to remain alive to the end.

Born in London at the turn of the twentieth century, Milner, also known as Marion Blackett-Milner and "Joanna Field," the pseudonym she used for three of her first four books, studied at University College, London, where she graduated with First Class Honors in Psychology in 1924. Some of our biographical information about Milner's early relationship to psychoanalysis comes from *The Hands of the Living God* (1969), a 444-page account of her treatment of a patient named Susan, a deeply disturbed woman suffering from torturing obsessional doubts, guilt, and depression who was hospitalized following a breakdown and then received electroconvulsive therapy (E.C.T.), which failed to improve her mental health. We learn from the preface that Milner was not initially drawn to Freud when her brother presented her with a newly translated copy of *Introductory Lectures on Psycho-Analysis*. She began her career as an industrial psychologist at the Institute of Industrial Psychology in London. She married Dennis Milner in 1927, and the two traveled to Boston where she studied from 1927 to 1928 at the Harvard Business School. During this visit to the United States, she was in analysis for four months with a Jungian therapist, Irma Putnam. Returning to London, she began in 1938 a Freudian analysis with Sylvia Payne. A year later, she was accepted for training by the British Psychoanalytical Society. She was also in analysis with D.W. Winnicott, as was her husband, a lawyer who suffered (and eventually died) from severe asthma. During her Freudian training, she was supervised by Melanie Klein, whose controversial theory strongly influenced her own work.

Milner overcame her resistance to writing about the people and events in her own life only in her final memoir, *Bothered by Alligators*, written when she was a nonagenarian. In *The Hands of the Living God*, she includes the following joke that Susan told her after watching a Marx Brothers film. Susan imagines someone asking Groucho, "How do you do," to which he responds, "Isn't that a very personal question?" (366).

A Life of One's Own

Milner's passion for literature is strikingly evident in *A Life of One's Own*. The title alludes to *A Room of One's Own*, Virginia Woolf's classic feminist essay published in 1929. Based on a diary Milner began writing in 1926, *A Life of One's Own* is an account, as she notes in the preface, of a seven years' study of living. "The aim of the record was to find out what kinds of experience made me happy" (11). All of her memoirs, we can add, focus on this question, or as Joseph Conrad (whom she cites in the memoir) observes in *Lord Jim*: "How to be."

Milner wrote *A Life of One's Own* in the spirit of a "detective who, baffled by the multitude of his facts, goes over and makes a summary of the progress of his investigations in the hope of finding something he has missed" (11). The metaphor is apt, for the reader, too, becomes a detective—or psychoanalyst—who seeks to uncover clues to Milner's life that she has artfully concealed. The memoir is simultaneously a cover-up and an exposé, reflecting her ambivalence toward self-disclosure, as we can see in the following passage:

> My determination to write an account of this search had begun from the conviction that unless I wrote about it I would lose my way. Yet for years I hesitated, not knowing in what form to tell it. I shrank from the thought of a direct personal account of what happened to me, yet knew all the time that only as such could it have any value to others. . . . What helped me most was the gradually growing conviction that silence might be the privilege of the strong but it was certainly a danger to the weak. For the things I was prompted to keep silent about were nearly always the things I was ashamed of, which would have been far better aired and exposed to the cleansing winds of confession. I knew then that though my decision to write in direct personal terms would lead me on to dangerous ground, yet it was the very core of my enterprise. (30)

Although Milner had not yet begun her training analysis, we see in this paragraph her conviction that writing can be therapeutic as a countershame technique. We also see her resistance to painful and shameful self-disclosures. She could have fictionalized her life, as did early modernist writers like Joseph Conrad and Virginia Woolf, disguising herself in the figure behind the veil, yet she believed that she lacked the talent to write poems or novels. Instead, she chose the memoir, based on years of diary writing.

Milner was dismayed when she reread her diaries, which displayed to her the depths of her own self-absorption. She almost abandoned the enterprise for this reason. Over time she realized that diary writing was a way to heighten self-awareness and thus *overcome* self-absorption. Writing was a lifelong love affair for Milner, a muse that rarely failed her. Paradoxically, the writing block that temporarily bedeviled her proved to be the catalyst for her originality, emboldening her to find new techniques to release her creativity. Milner's desire for literary success can be seen in her earliest writings. "*I want to write books, to see them printed and bound*," she enthused in a diary entry (52), yet at the same time she lamented that her deepest reflections were not worth committing to paper. In an unguarded diary entry, she confessed that she envied people, mainly artists (89).

Milner's four memoirs are all based on her diary writing, yet she thought primarily in visual images, not words. It took her years to realize, as she remarks in *Eternity's Sunrise*, that "in order to write any intellectual paper it was necessary always to begin with an image, even if this did not in the end appear in the paper" (48).

Sounding like both Conrad and Woolf, Milner believed that writing was perilous, requiring the writer to plumb the depths of existence, a journey that might unexpectedly lead to a dead end. *A Life of One's Own* begins with an ambiguous passage from *Lord Jim* in which the narrator Marlow is told, by the enigmatic Stein, that one must submit oneself to the "destructive element," Conrad's metaphor of the instinctual life force that exacts its revenge on those who repress or deny its elemental power. This is what diary writing represented to Milner: immersing herself in the nethermost recesses of the hidden self, with an uncertain outcome. The process is especially challenging for a writer whose own mind was "something quite unknown" to her, as she admits in a chapter appropriately called "Exploring the Hinterland" (56). Seeking to evoke memories that occurred fifteen or twenty years earlier, when she was a young child, Milner observed, with excitement and trepidation, "I was normally only aware of the ripples on the surface of my mind, but the act of writing a thought was a plunge which at once took me into a different element where the past was intensely alive" (60). Tellingly, Milner's language is most alive—and figurative—when she describes her literary fervor. She uses two different metaphors to conjure up the miracle of literary creation:

> It was as if I were trying to catch something and the written word provided a net which for a moment entangled a shadowy form which was other than the meaning of the words. Sometimes it seemed that the act of writing was fuel on glowing embers, making flames leap up and throw light on the surrounding gloom, giving me fitful gleams of what was before unguessed at. (71)

We can see here Milner's experimentation with performative art, using richly metaphorical language to evoke lived experience. Milner's memoirs are the most performative of any in my study, capturing the beauty of language and elevating experience over theory, spontaneity over restraint, process over completion. Milner's incandescent prose illuminates both the leaping flames and the surrounding gloom. The language is also mystical: one senses that she struggles to capture a mysterious reality beyond the visible world. Freud never wrote this way, nor did any other psychoanalytic memoirist. And yet as dazzling as her prose is, Milner is unsatisfied with her "fitful gleams."

Like all but her last memoir, *A Life of One's Own* is autobiographical not in describing external events or people but in the writer's reactions to them: her states of mind and feelings, the world of subjectivity—the same type of inner affective memoir that we saw with Jung. Without telling us much about her parents or siblings, Milner remarks early in the memoir her assumption that the "only desirable way to live was a male way; I had tried to live a male life of objective understanding and achievement" (14). What does this suggest about her relationship with her mother or father? We can only guess. She later discloses that she had grown up with a hatred of having her private life exposed. "When I listened to the personal talk of others I used sometimes to go hot all over, feeling it utterly impossible that I should ever talk like that about myself. I had thought that private affairs should be dealt with privately" (138). What personal talk, we wonder, what private affairs? These and other biographical questions remain mystifying. There's no doubt, however, about Milner's uneasiness over self-disclosure. At a few points she acknowledges, almost parenthetically, being married, a comment that she curiously never develops.

A Life of One's Own offers isolated clues into Milner's private life. "I lived in a constant dread of offending," she confesses (20), without explaining the nature of her perceived offenses or identifying those she feared offending. She later returns, without clarification, to being "tongue-tied for fear of saying the wrong thing" (101). She admits to her own "inadequacy and inferiority, with all its attendant ghouls of punishment and damnation" (146). Was she a serial ax-murderer or merely human, all too human, like the rest of us? She intimates her dread of "putting things into words for fear of what might be disclosed" (183), a confession that is more than a rhetorical device to create suspense. She never tells us why she believes she is a miserable sinner.

A pre-psychoanalytic memoir, *A Life of One's Own* demonstrates why Milner excelled in psychology when she was in college. She perceptively observes that D.H. Lawrence despised the "feminine" within him, an observation that Lawrence scholars would make years later. Similarly, her reference to the "destructive element" in Conrad's life and art was prescient. It was only decades later that Conrad scholars such as myself (in *Joseph Conrad: Writing as Rescue*) wrote about his early suicide attempt, arising from spurned love, and the high incidence of suicide in his fictional stories. She casually mentions in a footnote that the growth of her understanding "follows an ascending spiral rather than a straight line" (55), an insight that is probably true of most people. She realizes that "blind thinking" is "either or thinking" (127) and implies that lucid thinking is "both/and." One of her best insights is a self-criticism. "Sometimes my hatred of some part of myself which I would not accept became a hatred of someone else, and I would say all sorts of things about that person, but anyone who was perceiving could tell that I was really speaking about myself" (128–9). The epiphany foreshadows the term *projective identification* that Melanie Klein introduced in 1946 to describe an unconscious fantasy in which parts of the self are split off and attributed to another person.

Freudianism was in the air in the 1930s when Milner wrote *A Life of One's Own*. Part of her achievement is that she was one of the first diarists to devise a method to access the unconscious self. Without referring to Freud's greatest discovery, the use of free association to evoke the unconscious, she championed "free writing" as a way to understand her "automatic self," which was different from the "deliberate self." Free writing could thus immerse her in the Conradian destructive element, exposing her to inner ghosts that she ruefully called the "taskmaster in hell" (147). These outcast thoughts, banished into the hinterland, could be summoned and, in her case, tamed. She began keeping an "opposites" notebook in which she wrote down examples of the inseparability of fears and desires. "As a result of these discoveries," she declares, "moods became more under my own control" (167). She remarks in *Eternity's Sunrise* that she kept a diary of misgivings when she studied psychoanalysis (120).

Significantly, Milner gives the greatest credit in *A Life of One's Own* to two literary writers. She reminds us, first, of E.M. Forster's remark: "How can I tell what I think till I see what I say" (151). And second, in the afterword to the 1981 edition, she cites Keats, not his well-known "Negative Capability," which she explores in her next memoir, but his oxymoronic term *diligent indolence* to express a Coleridgean willing suspension of disbelief.

A Life of One's Own is a treasure trove that contains many of the seminal ideas that Milner explored in depth in her later memoirs. We see her interest in psychic bisexuality, the masculine and feminine elements that she believed exist in each person. We see her deep interest in mysticism, her desire to merge with nature, the universe, or other people. We see her love for writing and recognition of the commonalities of the talking cure and the writing cure. We see her interest in complementary modes of vision, narrow attention and wide attention. And we see her advocacy of free writing techniques that one can use without being in psychoanalysis.

It's not often that a first book receives glowing reviews from a world-famous poet, but *A Life of One's Own* was lauded by two great poets, W.H. Auden and Stephen Spender, both of whom Milner cites in the 1981 afterward. The two British poets expressed reservations, however, about Milner's discussion of male and female aspects of personality. Milner refused to disavow the idea of bisexuality. "As for me, when I eventually became a psychoanalyst I was to be continually faced with men's fear of their own femininity, if one uses the word in the sense that Hamlet did: 'a kind of gain-giving as would perhaps trouble a woman'" (222–3).

Milner always remained an "introvert" rather than an "extrovert." What changed, however, was a new appreciation of the feminine within her. Perhaps her greatest discovery, as she points out near the end of *A Life of One's Own*, was a result of her first experience of being in psychoanalysis. "I cannot tell exactly what happened, but I certainly found it an immensely interesting experience, and it had the concrete result that before I began I had often wished that I were a man, and that after it I never had such a wish again" (201). *A Life of One's Own* is, finally, an analysis of one's own, a record of Milner's brave journey toward self-understanding and a valuable self-help book for other readers and writers.

An Experiment in Leisure

A companion piece to *A Life of One's Own*, *An Experiment in Leisure* continues Milner's odyssey of self-analysis. Written shortly before the beginning of the Second World War, *An Experiment in Leisure* was, she states ruefully, "blitzed out of print" in the 1940s raids on London. Whereas in her first memoir she focuses on free writing, now she explores its pictorial equivalent, free drawing, "doodling." The memoir is a lyrical conjuring of the past written in evocative language reminiscent at times of the stream-of-consciousness prose of Joyce's *Ulysses* and Woolf's *Mrs Dalloway*.

Little has changed in Milner's life since the publication of *A Life of One's Own*. Mysticism still intrigues her. She is less interested in reading books about birds, studying them scientifically, than in entering into the "vividness of their curious, wayward life, not study it as a thing apart" (36). Her example of mystical unity in *The Suppressed Madness of Sane Men* (1987), a title derived from an essay by the philosopher George Santayana, is more vivid. While immersed in an activity like painting, one becomes "lost in a moment of intense activity in which awareness of self and awareness of the object are somehow fused, and one emerges to separateness again to find that there is some new entity on the paper" (80). The experience foreshadows what the University of Chicago psychologist Mihaly Csikszentmihalyi calls a "flow experience," in which we lose all sense of time. Whenever she feels the "clutch of anxiety," flooded by feelings of inferiority and inadequacy, she recites the mantra "I am nothing, I know nothing, I want nothing" (*An Experiment in Leisure* 41), which leads to quietude. She first began developing this idea in *A Life of One's Own* when she would tell herself, "I want nothing" (109), which heightened her awareness of nature. She returns to Keats, embracing Negative Capability, an idea he had expressed in an 1817 letter to his brothers: "that is, when a man is capable of being in uncertainty, Mysteries, doubts, without any irritable reaching after fact and reason" (*An Experiment in Leisure* 80; Keats 261). She still struggles with asserting herself in the presence of other people, including disagreeing with others: "all my life I had been aware of the impulse to agree with people, never to stand alone, and how ashamed I had been of this, I had struggled against being a sheep" (95).

Milner remains wary of psychology books, distrustful of the remoteness of abstract thought. Though her few remarks about psychoanalysis are respectful, she finds little value in talking about "castration complexes" and "masculine protests," two theories by Freud and Alfred Adler, respectively, that do not resonate with her. And yet now she finds herself drawn to Jung, especially his belief in the power of images, and she quotes the following passage from his 1921 book *Psychological Types*:

> The image is a concentrated expression of the total psychic situation. . . . The image is equally an expression of the unconscious as of the conscious situation of the moment. The interpretation of its meaning, therefore, can proceed exclusively neither from the unconscious nor from the conscious, but only from their reciprocal relation. (*An Experiment in Leisure* 90; Milner's ellipsis)

Reading this passage proves to be a life-transforming experience for Milner, an aha! moment, enabling her to see how the interpretation of her drawings can become the royal road to the unconscious. The discovery of the power of images, first conceiving them in one's mind and then drawing them, becomes Milner's signature therapeutic technique. If she had an angry quarrel with a close relative or friend, instead of being filled with impotent rage, she would draw a figure of her feelings, such as a snake around a tree trunk. By the time she finished the drawing, the rage had disappeared. She doesn't use the psychoanalytic term *sublimation*, but that is what her art accomplishes.

Milner believed that she had invented the technique of psychoanalytic doodling, allowing something meaningful to emerge from giving total freedom of movement to her hand without conscious awareness of what she was doing. While writing *Bothered by Alligators*, she suddenly recalled that she had not invented the method. She had gone to an exhibition of paintings by a psychoanalyst, Grace Pailthorpe, who had used the same technique of doodle drawing. "Only now did I remember coming home from the exhibition and saying to myself, 'I wonder if I could do that too?'" (9).

Though Milner began her training analysis shortly after the publication of *An Experiment in Leisure*, she never explicitly explains her decision to become a psychoanalyst. She mentions the "mind's infinite capacity for deceiving itself" (44), but she is vague about her own self-deceptions. After reading the memoir, one has only a shadowy impression of her life. As Maud Ellmann suggests in her Introduction, much of the memoir is enthralling—"but it can also be exasperating; as in a real analysis, one sometimes feels that one is getting nowhere, very slowly" (11).

Like *A Life of One's Own*, *An Experiment in Leisure* is tantalizingly elusive about Milner's personal life. She makes a statement that promises to open an analytic door—"I had known that my greatest conscious desire was to bear a child" (93)—but then slams the door shut. We hardly learn anything about her husband, whom she eventually divorced, or their only child, John, born in 1932. Nor is there anything about her siblings, including her brother, Patrick Blackett, who later won the Nobel Prize in physics in 1948. She admits to her desire for the "depths of self-abasement and that in some measure I had learnt how to deal with it" (42), but she refuses to offer any details until forty pages later, when she attempts to depathologize the desire: "this need to suffer was not in its essence perverse, it was an essential part of the process of perception" (82).

Milner never writes about her mother, Caroline Frances Maynard, in *An Experiment in Leisure*, but she describes women living in a state of fusion. She cites approvingly Susan Isaacs's psychoanalytic observation that the person one hates is usually the same person one loves: "The 'bad' mother is the mother that he rages against in his fury, and wants to destroy because she cannot satisfy him in the moment of demand" (113). This is the closest Milner comes to speaking about the relationship with her own mother, a subject to which she will return in *Bothered by Alligators*.

Milner reserves the most biographically self-revealing, albeit puzzling, comment for the penultimate page. "Once in adolescence, I had written some poems and shown them to my father. He said: 'Go on writing but always tear up what you have written.' Disappointed, for I was rather proud of the poems, I did not tear them up, but also I never tried to write any more poetry" (114). Why would her father, Arthur Stuart Blackett, a stockbroker, say this? Recall Milner's statement in *A Life of One's Own* that the subjects she was silent about were those of which she was most ashamed. Did her father fear that her poetry revealed only her self-absorption and should not be shown to others? That poetry represented the feminine world of subjectivity, not his own masculine world of objectivity? Did he believe that her pride in poetry was misguided and that she needed to learn a lesson in humility? Did he equate poetry writing with weakness? If so, she seemed to harbor the same fear, for in the preceding paragraph she writes: "Someone has said: 'Those who can, do. Those who can't, teach'"—and then she adds, drolly, "Those who can't, write" (114), implying that one writes because of weakness or deficiency. She immediately counters this disturbing idea, however, as if she's talking back to her self-doubting ghost. "But even if it is true that the fact of writing about a certain activity implies that one is not very good at doing it, this does not free one from the need to write, it is not much good refusing crutches when you have broken your leg just because most people have two good feet to walk upon" (114).

Rereading *A Life of One's Own* after *An Experiment in Leisure*, we see additional evidence of Milner's vexation at her father. In a paragraph of automatic writing, she begins by recalling a troubling experience at boarding school when a classmate noticed that she had tried to conceal her "poetrybook" (it's unclear whether this is a textbook or her own poems) under her desk. She recalls making excuses to her teacher for her bad work and wonders why she had to lie, a question that evokes the following flood of words, an example of free association:

> [W]hy did I lie?—to escape something?—what?—punishment?—what sort?—hole in corner—Death?—why death?—what does death mean?—End—anger—hate—fath er—cruel—homecoming—futile—foolish—who?—me?—because stupid . . . (61)

However we interpret the father's remark in *An Experiment in Leisure*, his daughter perceived it as a hurtful criticism. If she could not respond to his rejection with words, she responded with silence. She gave up writing poetry despite the fact that her favorite writers were poets: Keats, Yeats, Eliot, and Blake, the visionary writer who most profoundly influenced her. She quotes extensively from her Nature Diary, which she began keeping when she was eleven and continued for nearly a decade. She offers no examples, however, of her early poems. That Milner waited until the end of *An Experiment in Leisure* to disclose her father's criticism of her poetry attaches greater significance to it. In short, the father's rejection of his daughter's poetry, experienced by Milner as nothing less than a rejection of herself, is the most biographically self-divulging moment in either memoir, and we shouldn't be surprised if she returns to this, albeit in disguised form, in her greatest work of self-analysis.

The Human Problem in Schools

Published immediately before the beginning of the Second World War, *The Human Problem in Schools* (1938) is a pioneering psychological study of the Girls Public Day School Trust, which consisted of twenty-five British private schools. In developing personality questionnaires, Milner was influenced by Jung's use of character types in his 1923 book *Psychological Types*, particularly the distinction between introversion and extraversion. There's nothing overtly personal in *The Human Problem in Schools*, Milner's most objective book, but one of her statements about Jung reveals an insight she was struggling to apply to her own life. "Jung says that the person who over-values intellectual thought and excludes emotions, belittling them, not liking to take them into account, is liable because of this to have feelings that remain, unknown to himself, immature, highly personal, over-sensitive, petty, suspicious and resentful" (145). In offering practical advice for improving the British educational system, Milner argues that teachers should rely less on exhorting students to apply themselves to their studies than encouraging them to share their feelings and thoughts about their lives:

> So when a child is brought to the clinic for misbehaviour she is not given what we used to call "a pi-jaw" [pious or moralizing talk], but is asked to tell her own story, and her parents and teachers are asked to tell theirs, in order that the psychologist can discover what are the forces at work; and when he has come to some conclusion as to what these are, he still seldom appeals to the child's will to control those forces, but tries to give the child opportunity for a different kind of experience. (254)

On Not Being Able to Paint

On Not Being Able to Paint remains Milner's best-known book. "She becomes in the text," writes her biographer, Emma Letley, "her own analyst and, in some senses (in that she de-codes her own marks), her own art therapist" (127). Milner opens the book with an unusual confession, her "private misgivings" about her previous book, *The Human Problem in Schools*. She characteristically doesn't specify the nature of these misgivings, but she hints at them later in her "Angry Parrot" drawing, which she interprets, among other meanings, as students being trained to parrot their teachers.

Milner wrote *On Not Being Able to Paint* mainly for teachers. A second edition appeared in 1957, with Milner's own name, a foreword by Anna Freud, and an appendix that invokes classical psychoanalytic terminology, particularly Kleinian theory. Anna Freud remarks that *On Not Being Able to Paint* is written "from the eminently practical aspect of self-observation and expression" (xix), a comment that is equally true of her own writings. Milner recalls in *The Hands of the Living God* one of her psychology professors, C.T. Spearman, telling his students that if they wanted to become good psychologists, they should never use language meaningful only to specialists (xx). Milner never forgot the excellent advice. In all of her writings, Milner's prose is mercifully free of psychobabble and tendentious language. *On Not Being Able to Paint* is never dogmatic or reductive, one of the reasons for its wide appeal.

Like Milner's first two memoirs, *On Not Being Able to Paint* celebrates artistic creativity. Milner's passion for ancient and contemporary literature is palpable. She includes poems by John Donne, Thomas Traherne, and Shelley. She cites (and slightly misquotes) Blake's insight from *The Marriage of Heaven and Hell*: "Without contraries is no progression" (74), a dialectical truth that is central to her vision of both art and psychoanalysis. She interprets her drawings as if they are poems, yielding complex and ever-shifting meaning. She refers repeatedly to one of her favorite childhood novels, *Alice's Adventures in Wonderland*. Milner realizes, like Alice, that when she wants to get somewhere, she must sometimes, counterintuitively, walk in exactly the opposite direction.

In writing about how people seek to transcend "primitive hate," Milner singles out the "lunatic, the lover and the poet," adding, dryly, "or painter" (68). She cites a remark Cézanne is reported to have made about looking at a painting: "Descend with the painter into the dim tangled roots of things, and rise again from them in colours, be steeped in the light of them" (25). She echoes the words "in the destructive element immerse," expecting us to understand the Conradian allusion. She rejects the idea of "Art for art's sake," replacing it with "Art for life's sake" (140). She affirms one of the basic functions of art, "facilitating the acceptance of both illusion and disillusion, and thus making possible a richer relation to the real world" (67). She also invokes philosophers, citing Santayana's observation, "Sanity is a madness put to good uses" (28), recalling John Dryden's often-quoted line, "Great wits are sure to madness near allied."

Writing *On Not Being Able to Paint* after she had become a psychoanalyst, Milner refers several times to her "Freudian analysis," but she never tells us why she had decided to change careers from that of industrial psychologist to analyst. Her doodle drawings reflect her ongoing analysis. One of the reasons she began analysis, she discloses, was to gain "added equipment for scientific work" (37). She never explains the other reasons for entering analysis. Despite showing the drawings to her analyst, Milner tried—and failed—not to see any personal connection between the drawings and her analysis. She finally realized, though, how the "gods" and devils" of the external world, usually embodied in the same person, had entered her drawings. Readers must infer these benign and malevolent deities from her own self-analysis. Milner's need for disguise remains strong. As long as the drawings were presented only in visual imagery, she candidly observes, "no one could even know for certain that that was what I had meant" (124).

Milner comments often on the "spiritual dangers" of artistic expression, perhaps because of the dark knowledge that confronts the artist. One thinks of T.S. Eliot's line from his 1920 poem "Gerontion": "After such knowledge, what forgiveness?" Another spiritual danger for Milner, we sense, was her lifelong fear of offending those close to her. She interprets her drawings as filled with violent anger toward authority figures. As she had done in *A Life of One's Own*, she refers to projective identification, defining it now as the "trick of trying to get away from the necessity to admit unpleasant things in oneself by putting them outside and feeling that it is others who are bad, not oneself" (40). She has no problem admitting the worst in herself as long as she doesn't implicate others in her self-accusations. Like Jung's *Memories, Dreams, Reflections*, *On Not Being Able to Paint* is unique in that it represents an extended self-analysis of an analysand's inner life without saying much, if anything, about her outer life. Most of her "free drawings," Milner admits, whether they were made in chalk, charcoal, watercolor, pen and ink, or pencil, were "unfree," mainly because they betrayed a "rigidity of line" (xxi). The free drawings had little meaning to her at the time of creation, but they turned out to be suffused with meanings that she was able to fathom with the help of psychoanalysis.

The Angry Parrot

Of the forty-nine figures that appear in *On Not Being Able to Paint*, the central image is "The Angry Parrot" drawing, which appears on the cover of the paperback edition and as the frontispiece in the reprinted 2010 edition. The drawing shows an incensed parrot, sitting on a large fiery-red egg, amidst tempestuous waves. The angry parrot is terrified that the "grey woman" in the drawing will steal the egg—despite the fact that the parrot is much larger than the woman. A sinister black pincer-like image, the "thunder cloud God," looms from above, somehow in league with the grey woman, both colluding against the angry parrot. Red, black, and green dominate the painting, but a glint of sunlight is visible in the distance. The angry parrot drawing appears in the chapter called "Disillusion and Hating," a title that offers insight into the image's meaning.

Milner knows from the beginning that she is the angry parrot. Her first interpretation is theological. The grey woman's head suggests she is "God's Anointed." The parrot recognizes that it is in a difficult position, for it needs the grey woman's protection to survive a fierce storm, but it also knows that she is an old hypocrite who cannot be trusted. "Lord knows," Milner exclaims, using a double entendre, "what is going to happen to the egg" (48). How will the parrot escape from the grey woman and the thunder cloud God? If it gives them what they demand, the parrot muses, the precious egg, then it will lose its identity. But if the parrot refuses to give up the egg, it will drown. Lest readers be misled, Milner is quick to point out that the parrot's fear of losing its egg does *not* represent the common myth that psychoanalysis robs analysands of their individuality and creativity, a conviction expressed by Rilke, who feared that if he lost his demons, he would lose his angels as well; the same suspicion of therapy appears in Peter Shaffer's play *Equus*. The opposite is true, Milner maintains. *On Not Being Able to Paint* offers unqualified praise for the psychoanalytic process, which throughout her writings heightens creativity.

Artists and psychoanalysts alike intuit the "Principle of Condensation," which Milner defines in *The Hands of the Living God* as the "fact that one symbol can have very many different meanings at the same time" (xx). The grey woman represents not only the archetypal mother, the center of the child's universe, but also, Milner informs us in one of her few explicitly biographical comments, the "famous headmistress" who had once taught her (*On Not Being Able to Paint* 111). There is no mention, however, of Milner's own mother—that revelation awaits a later memoir.

Countless psychiatric case studies exemplify the therapeutic principles of *On Not Being Able to Paint*, but Milner's insights all derive from the images of the story, allowing readers to judge for themselves the accuracy, or at least plausibility, of her conclusions. Her ability to represent and then interpret the graphic images of her feelings contributes to the uniqueness of the memoir. She always sees conflicting points of view, those of both the outer and inner worlds. Nearly all of the protagonists and antagonists in the memoir are finally located within herself.

A picture may be worth a thousand words or more, but Milner's drawings, regardless of how crudely or rigidly they are drawn, require a nuanced vocabulary to synthesize and integrate warring antinomies: self and other, subjective and objective, inner and outer, female and male. Other binaries include intuition and logic, feeling and thought, dreaming and doing, art and nature. Additional antinomies appear in *Eternity's Sunrise*: "sacred and profane," "spirit and flesh," "separate and together," "freedom and dependence" (192). Milner crafts a language of reciprocity, using words like *interchange* and *interplay*. Both psychoanalysis and art lead to change and growth, expressed in words like *transformation* and *transfiguration*.

Judged from a twenty-first-century perspective, *On Not Being Able to Paint* is noteworthy for the psychoanalytic interpretations it *avoids*. Milner never refers to the misogynistic elements of Freudian theory, including penis envy. She never suggests, as Freud did, that women have less developed and independent superegos than men. Nor does she imply that women are more masochistic or narcissistic than men. Although Milner does not quote female creative writers, she paves the way for future female psychoanalytic theorists and clinicians.

Milner expands on the meaning of the angry parrot's egg in *Eternity's Sunrise*, where she observes that it represents the "theme of the cocoon, safe place in which change can take place" (102). The egg doesn't cut one off from the world, Milner continues, "because its boundaries are flexible, it can embrace, encompass what one is attending to so that one can participate in the other's being as well as one's own" (103).

Surely one of the many meanings of the egg in the angry parrot drawing is the work of art itself, *On Not Being Able to Paint*, which Milner jealously guards and nurtures. She solves the classic dilemma for women, "brains versus babies" (82), by giving birth to a new creation, her book, which springs from the lovingly nourished egg. The painter and memoirist thus join the ranks of the lunatic, lover, and poet. By the end of the story Milner has learned to live reflectively rather than blindly, achieving a paradoxical "contemplative action" (140). The writing of the book enacts the paradox of creativity.

Winnicott's review of *On Not Being Able to Paint* in a 1951 issue of the *British Journal of Medical Psychology* conveys Milner's challenge of a central aspect of psychoanalytic orthodoxy with respect to the arts.

> Psycho-analysts are accustomed to thinking of the arts as wish-fulfilling escapes from the knowledge of this discrepancy between inner and outer, wish and reality. It may come as a bit of a shock to some of them to find a psycho-analyst drawing the conclusion, after careful study, that this wish-fulfilling illusion may be the essential basis for all true objectivity.

What appears to be illusion from the outside, Winnicott continues, is not illusion from the inside. *On Not Being Able to Paint* offers psychoanalysts a way to bring their theory "into line not only with their psychotherapy but also with their daily lives" (119). In her 1999 book *Psychoanalysis and the Scene of Reading*, Mary Jacobus refers to the importance of *On Not Being Able to Paint*, noting that Milner's idea of no boundary between oneself and another makes possible intimate conversation between readers.

The Hands of the Living God

One cannot do justice to *The Hands of the Living God* in a few words, but we can sketch briefly its relevance to Milner's first three memoirs. The dedication—"To all my teachers in psychoanalysis especially my patients"—testifies to the reciprocity in psychoanalysis (and teaching) where the analyst (and teacher) learns from patients (and students). Milner's love for literature appears in the title of her book, which comes from Hebrews 10:31. The line also appears in D.H. Lawrence's poem "Hands of God," included in *Pansies*, his final collection of poems, published in 1929, one year before his death. "Hands of God" opens with two memorable lines: "It is a fearful thing to fall into the hands of the living God. / But it is a much more fearful thing to fall out of them" (Jung quotes the first line in *Two Essays on Analytical* Psychology [235, f.6.]). Like Lawrence, Milner was more spiritual than religious: Their writings brim with Christian symbolism, particularly rebirth imagery, and they were both inclined toward darkness and mysticism. The same is true, as we saw, with Carl Jung.

The Hands of the Living God begins with lines from Auden's celebrated poem "In Memory of Sigmund Freud." Freud's injunction, in Auden's words, to be "enthusiastic over the night," illuminates Milner's case study. During Milner's sixteen-year analysis of Susan, from 1943 to 1959, the darkness of the patient's world enters the analyst's own. Milner admits the "extraordinary state of darkness, being in the dark, that she so often produces in me, more intense than any state I have experienced with other patients" (324). Notwithstanding this darkness, Milner's empathy for Susan never wavers regardless of the many temporary stalemates and impasses of the long analysis. Unlike other analysts, Milner never pretends to omniscience. She often confesses to her failures of knowledge, which sometimes took the form of hasty over-interpretations. She came to see that some of her interpretations were defenses against her failure to understand her patient. Susan, in turn, experienced these words as "presumptuous attacks on her own creative processes, attacks which only strengthened the impregnability of her psychic armour" (43). Sometimes what Milner doesn't say is as significant as what she does say. For example, she silently interprets one of Susan's dreams as "allow[ing] me to exist and thereby make possible a relationship between us of mutual recognition of and adaptation to each other's existence," certainly an affirmative interpretation regardless of its accuracy or timing. "But I did not say this" (371), Milner adds, perhaps because Susan wasn't ready to hear or accept it.

Susan begins her own doodle drawings after reading *A Life of One's Own*. "Her comment on the book was that it was so like her she felt I must have thought she had been reading it before" (38). *The Hands of the Living God* abounds in paradoxes: "change of heart can only really come when one gives up trying to change" (263); "certain kinds of mastery defeat themselves by destroying what is to be mastered" (368); "by attending to the inner sensations . . . one can get more deeply related to the outer" (379).

The Hands of the Living God contains two fleeting references (241, 359) to Susan's reaction to Dennis Milner's death in 1954, but the analyst never permits herself to elaborate on her own response to the loss. It's likely that Milner deliberated over whether to reveal this detail, but it was a noteworthy reparative moment in the analysis, and for this reason she chose to include it. Hidden in one of Susan's drawings, Milner discloses, was a "compulsive restitutive activity towards me, an idea of restoring to me-mother my lost husband through herself being that husband, in a continual fertilizing activity" (241).

Unlike many psychiatric case studies in which a patient's mental conflict is traced to a past incident, there are no epiphanic moments in *The Hands of the Living God*, no turning points that suddenly chart a new direction in the patient's life. The story affirms indeterminacy, the uncertainty principle. What matters most to Susan is not Milner's theoretical approach but her steady compassion, tolerance, and presence. As in her memoirs, the case study dramatizes the dialectical interplay between separation and togetherness. The therapeutic alliance between analyst and patient remains strong. One of Milner's therapeutic goals is to help Susan learn to integrate warring antinomies instead of using the primitive defenses of splitting and projection. Early in the story Milner mentions her contact with Zen Buddhism, as practiced in both the East and the West, and although she does not elaborate on her use of Buddhist ideas in her treatment of Susan, one can see her synthesis of psychoanalytic and Buddhist ideas. *The Hands of the Living God* anticipates by more than half a century the psychiatrist Mark Epstein's 2022 memoir *The Zen of Therapy*, in which he encourages his patients to combine insight, as gleaned in the talking cure, and emotional detachment, as gained in meditation. Invoking Winnicott and Buddha, Epstein urges kindness, which can be seen throughout *The Hands of the Living God*.

Over 150 of Susan's doodle drawings appear in *The Hands of the Living God*, and they record her slow self-integration. One drawing shows a duck with its head cut off, which Milner interprets as an image of how she felt after E.C.T. Many of the drawings convey Susan's dread that she cannot express emotions: "she must be continually on her guard, particularly, it seems, against showing pleasure" (193). Milner remains convinced that the meaning of Susan's drawings must be sought in her feelings of darkness, and the analyst is willing to accompany her into the netherworld—into the Cézannian dim tangled roots of things or the Conradian heart of darkness. One of the most moving moments of the story occurs when Milner realizes that Susan needs her to put into words feelings that Susan cannot express herself. But Susan does not want Milner to know her; rather, she wants Milner to admit that she cannot grasp the full reality of Susan's inner life.

> I came to feel sure that if I did not voice this, from time to time, then she could not avoid the feeling, though she could not express it, that I was trying to "pluck out the heart of (her) mystery" and so only playing into the very process by which she had cut herself off from her roots in darkness and indeterminacy. (255)

Notice how Milner instinctively uses a literary metaphor, embodied in Hamlet's words, to convey her meaning; many readers will immediately think of another Hamletic expression—"There are more things in heaven and earth . . . Than are dreamt of in your philosophy," which was Freud's favorite expression—to convey unknowability.

Susan's doodle drawings were therapeutic for her, just as the writing of *The Hands of the Living God* was therapeutic for Milner. Writing about madness seems itself a mad enterprise, the French psychoanalyst André Green famously remarked, but it usually leads to a positive outcome. "When colleagues get together, they agree: 'What a mad profession!' Perhaps writing is also part of the analyst's private madness. He can rid himself of it, in part, only by writing of others' private madness: that of his analysands, to whom the psychoanalyst consecrates one of the most precious parts of himself in the inter-subjective exchange of the unconscious" (16).

Eternity's Sunrise

Eternity's Sunrise—the title comes from the last line of Blake's poem "Eternity"—is a travelogue that chronicles Milner's holiday trips to Greece, Venice, Kashmir, and Israel. Written in poetic, darkly radiant prose filled with sensuous details, the memoir is a lyrical evocation of the ancient sites Milner visited. Like all memoirs, *Eternity's Sunrise* is about memory, both remembering and forgetting. Milner uses two words to characterize startling insights. She calls childhood memories "beads," emotionally charged, largely unconscious epiphanies that transport her back into the past; and she uses the term *answering activity*, which first appeared in *An Experiment in Leisure*, to describe contacting the source of knowledge. She implies that the answering activity is associated with both the creative unconscious and God. To "plug" into the answering activity is like "suddenly remembering to open a kind of little trap-door inside and finding a great expansion of spirit" (59).

Eternity's Sunrise contains hints of traumatic injuries and losses: "dealing with wounds, wounds to one's self-esteem, wounds to one's heart" (37). The deepest wound appears in the following passage addressed to an unnamed "You":

> You, my early love, who railed at my books when we met again after so many years, though it was you, nearly forty years ago, who first started me writing by making me read Montaigne; you, who had since become a Marxist, and now said it was solipsism to write like this and that I should be doing objective research, with graphs and all that, as I did once—I could not understand why you raged so—yet it was me you sent for when you were dying, sitting up in bed and looking like Don Quixote. (40)

It's obvious that by refusing to name the addressee, Milner doesn't want us to know that she is speaking about her brother, Patrick Blackett. She returns to him a few pages later in *Eternity's Sunrise*, recalling her last visit to him when he was dying of cancer in 1974. The siblings had long been estranged, in part, we suspect, because of his hurtful comments over her writing. The above passage implies that Patrick Blackett wrote "objective" science books while she wrote "subjective" solipsistic books. (Her only research-oriented book, filled with graphs, was *The Human Problem in Schools*.) Milner doesn't explicitly associate objectivity with the male world and subjectivity with the female world, but the binary recalls her father's criticism of her poetry years earlier. Milner apostrophizes her brother in a later passage in *Eternity's Sunrise*, when she conveys her grief over his death. "You, my brother, so great a power now no longer there. Now I feel the pain of that day, what I could not do, fully, at the time." To endure her heavy-heartedness, she turns inward, and downward, "deliberately going down, as low as one can, it's then that one can hold the stillness and the loss" (116).

In another notable passage in *Eternity's Sunrise*, Milner identifies looking inward as emblematic of women. "Is it perhaps easier for a woman," she asks rhetorically, "potentially to do this deliberate letting awareness go down inside away from striving after assertive action in the outer world, and just letting oneself be breathed?" (50). In the same passage she cites Lao Tze's saying: "He who, being a man, remains a woman will become a universal channel" (50). All her books, with the exception of *The Human Problem in Schools*, reflect the downward plunge inside, the affective world often ignored in objective writing.

Milner's recognition of the gender implications of "inward turning attention" (51) contributes to the importance of *Eternity's Sunrise*. To write this way, she had to defy paternal authority, the world of her father and brother, not easy to do for a woman who had difficulty speaking for herself. Virginia Woolf recognized the same problem. For women to write freely, she observes in *A Room of One's Own*, they must ignore the "perpetual admonitions of the eternal pedagogue—write this, think that" (78).

Eternity's Sunrise reveals Milner's mistrust of all "creeds," whether they convey religious, educational, or psychoanalytic orthodoxies. She was always a free thinker, not surprising for a woman who champions free writing. In one of the few moments when she reflects on her life as a psychoanalyst, she raises the question, "What heals my patients?" Her answer is characteristically modest: "Not me, I only try to clear away the blocks so that they can find the answering activity in themselves, the inner grace. And have the grace to recognise it" (114).

Bothered by Alligators

A prolific author's final book has special importance, for it often involves a summing up of a career, literally the last words of a lifetime of writing. The unusual title of Milner's posthumous memoir derives from her young son, who, talking to himself about the cleaning woman of whom he was fond, asks: "are the alligators bothering you?" The work of a nonagenarian, *Bothered by Alligators* is a fascinating gloss on Milner's books, three of which were written sixty years earlier. Margaret Walters remarks in her introduction that while sorting through Milner's papers, she came across an unsigned note written by an old friend who, after reading an early version of *Bothered by Alligators*, observed, "your writing is always personal, Marion, but this is autobiographical" (xiii).

Bothered by Alligators deepens rather than changes our understanding of Milner's previous memoirs. The autobiographical meaning of "The Angry Parrot" and related drawings is now clearer. Milner states in *Bothered by Alligators* that the reason she chose a pseudonym for her early books was because she feared upsetting some of the headmistresses with whom she worked (8). She was probably more afraid, however, of hurting her mother and father, depicted in the grey woman and thunder cloud God, respectively. Milner's use of a pseudonym has gender implications, for apart from Freud's use of a pseudonym in his case study of the Wolf-Man, she is the only memoirist in my study who disguises her own name. Men and women have different relationships to their names. "For women in our culture," the feminist literary scholars Sandra Gilbert and Susan Gubar point out, "a proper name is at best problematic; even as it 'inscribes' her into the discourse of society by designating her role as her father's daughter, her patronymic effaces her matrilineage and thus erases her own position in the discourse of the future" (24).

Milner discloses for the first time being "very angry" with her father throughout adolescence but not daring to confront him with her dark feelings (4). She also admits for the first time the many similarities between her father and husband, implying that she married Dennis Milner because "in a muddle-headed way" she thought she could help him with his "strong emotional problems" (4), a belief that proved naïve. Milner is not surprised by her resentment toward her father, but what does surprise, indeed, startle her is an insight from a new drawing she had done while writing *Bothered by Alligators*:

> in recent years it had occurred to me that my mother had, almost certainly not even admitting it to herself, a sense of depression about herself and also deep disappointment over her marriage. So had I always been unwittingly protecting her, not just from my offending, hurting with my lips, but also by agreeing implicitly with her own ways of being oblivious to her own sorrows? (186)

The disturbing insight compels Milner, in the chapter called "My Mother and Us Three Children," to recollect and reflect on a perplexing comment her father had made to her eighty years earlier: "I thought you were your mother's child" (218). She cannot help asking herself whether she had spent her entire life trying to ignore her mother's pain, perhaps because of the lack of distance from her. The possibility plunges her into gloom, overwhelmed by doubts about the value of writing *Bothered by Alligators*. The gloom unleashes a torrent of memories, and the chapter ends with a new revelation, being born into a family "where my mother and father were secretly, even half unknown to themselves, battling with disillusion about their marriage, she desperately wanting him to be a hero, he very much aware of not being one" (224).

Bothered by Alligators belies Freud's conviction in the existence of psychological bedrock. Milner never reaches a final interpretation of her own life. No single revelation explains the mystery of character. She ruminates over her distant childhood, entertaining one interpretation after another about her relationships with her parents in an effort toward reaching elusive final truths. She intuits Nietzsche's observation that every interpretation reveals something about the interpreter. Analyzing her son's childhood stories and drawings, she has a sudden epiphany: "No, it's his images analysing me, helping me to find out what had been left out of my own couch analysis" (145). Characteristically, she attributes the insight to her son, not to herself.

Refusing to write anything about her husband in her early memoirs, Milner discloses for the first time that part of her disillusionment with him was for his "many infidelities" (174). Interestingly, she had expressed this fear early in her marriage when she wrote in a 1929 personal notebook that she could imagine being "too old to find anyone else and then he may find some young attractive girl and I will curse the wasted years" (Letley 24). It's revealing that Milner wrote about this fear in her private notebooks; it's also revealing that she never destroyed these writings.

In *Bothered by Alligators*, Milner interprets her drawing of "Mrs Punch" in *On Not Being Able to Paint* as symbolizing not only her anger toward her husband's mother for his marital betrayals but also self-anger: "this horrible Mrs Punch was a hidden part of me, since I could feel in my swinging arms a certain capacity for arrogant ruthlessness, but which could also seem funny in its assumption of queenly absolute power" (176).

One of the most intriguing chapters in *Bothered by Alligators*, "Being in Analysis with D.W. Winnicott," recalls her unusual relationship with the pediatrician-turned-analyst. While her patient Susan was living with Winnicott and his then-wife, Alice, from whom he would soon be divorced, he was analyzing Milner at her home, which was halfway between his house in Hampstead and his office in central London. To complicate further Winnicott's boundary violations, he paid for Susan's analysis with Milner. As the biographer F. Robert Rodman points out, although Winnicott was careful early in his career to avoid boundary transgressions, he began to cross boundaries "in a reckless fashion, finding his freedom in the process, but making mistakes as well" (136). One day Winnicott "accidentally" left a little crucifix behind after a session with Milner at her home. She failed to ask him at the time the significance of the apparent Freudian slip, but then she came across a note she had written afterward in which he cryptically said that he would not have forgotten the crucifix had she been another analysand, perhaps a hint, she surmises, that she had a secretly depressed mother, as he had. Winnicott comes across in the chapter as a humane analyst who nevertheless failed to provide Milner with the help she needed. She doesn't disagree with his statement that she was a "casualty of analysis" (235), partly because it wasn't long enough.

Rodman offers insight into Milner's character. "Within the British [Psychoanalytical] Society, Marion Milner was closest in temperament and talent to Winnicott. Her far-ranging visual imagination was always put in the service of those intellectual attributes that made her thinking so original and articulate" (137). Rodman illuminates Milner's relationship with Winnicott, including Masud Khan's statement that she was jealous that Winnicott had married his second wife, Clare, instead of herself. Additionally, Milner believed that Winnicott never encouraged her to analyze her inner aggression. To Rodman, Milner was Winnicott's "only intellectual and imaginative peer" in the British Psychoanalytical Society (139). When Rodman was in the early stages of researching his biography, Clare Winnicott asked him if there was anyone he would like to meet. "I thought immediately of Marion Milner, whose *On Not Being Able to Paint* was just the sort of quirky psychoanalytic book that continued to give pleasure and knowledge with repeated rereadings" (137).

Vintage Milner, *Bothered by Alligators* shows both the similarities and differences between her early and late life. Recalling her lifelong fear of offending others and speaking up for herself, she notes that recently she gained the courage to tell a friend to "shut up": "it did not give offence or break the relationship, and she did shut up" (250).

Appreciating Milner

Milner's writings have inspired many people, including creative writers, psychoanalysts, art therapists, religious studies professors, and feminists. Naomi Rader Dragstedt suggests that Milner's books, based on personal writing, emboldened readers to turn to diary writing as a "poor person's psychoanalysis" (426). A chapter in the 2000 volume *Art, Creativity, Living*, edited by Leslie Caldwell, contains several appreciations of Milner's work. The psychoanalyst Harold Stewart knew Milner from when he was a student. "Marion's description of the physical bases of inner emptiness was very pertinent to me, particularly as there is little in the literature on inner emptiness" (136). Val Richards, the former assistant director of the Squiggle Foundation, which is devoted to the study and promotion of Winnicott's work, remarked on Milner's greater interest in "meaning" than in fact or theory (140). The art therapist Martina Thompson was impressed by the acute vision of Milner, who was the honorary president of the British Association of Art Therapists from the late 1970s to her death. "Her perusal of Blake's drawings for the Book of Job made her see things that I doubt any art historian ever noticed; for instance, that at the beginning Job's face is the same as God's. It gave rise to a wonderful piece of writing, 'The Sense in Nonsense,' where she paralleled Blake's perceptions with those of psychoanalysis" (144).

Kelley A. Raab argues in a 2000 issue of *American Imago* that Milner's interest in the relationship among creativity, transcendence, and the unconscious has valuable implications for religious studies. "Her emphasis on the body offers encouragement for an immanent theology, one that focuses on body and nature. Also, by giving unconscious creativity a feminine connotation, Milner's work suggests feminine symbols for deity" (213). In an article appearing in the *American Journal of Psychoanalysis* in 2012, Marilyn Charles observed, after reading the Routledge reissue of Milner's collected writings, that in a field in which the "female perspective has in many ways remained a 'dark continent' [a reference to Freud's bafflement over female psychology], Milner's recounts of her own personal journey are both illuminating and vitalizing" (287).

What is perhaps most inspiring about *Bothered by Alligators*, an end-of-life memoir that I had not read when I penned *Dying in Character* (2012), is that Milner wrote it at the end of her life. Though she was nearly blind, her mind was still active; her curiosity about life, her own and others, never waned. An assistant who had worked with her on the memoir received a telephone message from her, the night before her death, announcing her wish to see him the next day. "On the day she died I was due to work for her and arrived at the house to find that she had died an hour or so earlier sitting up in bed working on the manuscript" (269). Margaret Walters speculates that Milner wrote the book "to stave off death" (xxi). Milner died in character, endlessly thinking and rethinking her life.

For a person who feared that she could not stand up to others, who could not find her own voice, and who was often tongue-tied, Marion Milner was remarkably successful in narrating her life story. She was never a parrot, angry or otherwise. A fascinating postscript in *The Suppressed Madness of Sane Men* bespeaks Milner's desire to remain an independent thinker. Despite the fact that her copies of Freud's *The Future of an Illusion* and Anna Freud's *The Ego and the Mechanisms of Defense* are full of her own pencil annotations, Milner found that she had left out both books in her bibliographical references. Why? "I can only see these omissions as symptomatic of the constant struggle both to use the 'parents' insights and at the same time to be sensitive to my own experience, to see with my own eyes" (297). Concluding his review of *The Suppressed Madness of Sane Men*, Gilbert J. Rose praises the book as "open minded yet questioning, down-to-earth yet unafraid of mysticism"—like Milner herself. "One feels after reading this book that one not only has learned a great deal, but from a person one would wish to know" (131).

Milner remained true to her convictions, plumbing the depths for the best and worst of existence, summoning her own angels and demons. She had made peace with the taskmaster in hell, and she had learned how to immerse herself in the destructive element without drowning. She used Freudian and Kleinian theory judiciously, but she was no one's disciple. She stopped attending Klein's seminars because she could not accept Klein's belief that envy was inborn. Milner never denied her own envy of artists, but without knowing it, she became one herself.

Chapter 8

M. MASUD R. KHAN

The Long Wait

It is unprecedented in the history of psychoanalysis—a century-old period fraught with bizarre, untoward events—for an eminent analyst to write a book, published shortly before his death, containing repugnant anti-Semitic and homophobic rants. One can easily imagine a person impulsively making a derogatory remark, perhaps under the strain of mental illness or alcohol, which he or she later regrets. But writing a book, by contrast, is a long, slow, deliberate process that involves not only careful revision but also evaluation by outside reviewers along with copy editing by another reader. Many people usually read a manuscript before it is published, and authors become alerted to potentially problematic statements. How can an experienced writer not know that his hateful words will mortify readers? Can a writer who has authored books on hidden and private selves not be in control of his own dark self? How can an analyst who has helped suicidal patients be blinded by his own self-destructiveness? These questions confront every reader of Masud Khan's *The Long Wait and Other Psychoanalytic Narratives*.

"Transgression," Khan informs us in the foreword, was the original title of *The Long Wait*, published in 1988, one year before his death at age sixty-four. (The book appeared in Great Britain under the title *When Spring Comes: Awakenings in Clinical Psychoanalysis*.) "Transgression" would have been a more accurate title, not because of the dominant theme of "awakening," as he naively intended, but because of the book's cruel caricature of a Jewish patient, "Mr. Luis," in chapter 4, "A Dismaying Homosexual." As its subtitle suggests, *The Long Wait* is not a memoir but rather a series of psychoanalytic case studies, some of which occurred decades earlier. The book returns repeatedly to Khan's privileged life in what is now Pakistan, where he was born, and in London, where he lived in "self-elected exile." Khan reveals much about his own life, and he uses his patients to convey his tarnished reputation in the analytic world.

Khan was born in 1924 in Jhelum in the north of Punjab province that later became Pakistan. He was the youngest of nine living sons raised by a wealthy septuagenarian father who had several wives, the fourth of whom was Khan's mother, who was only seventeen when he was born. He did his undergraduate and graduate training at the University of Punjab, focusing on English literature and psychology. Fluent in seven languages, he wrote his master's thesis on James Joyce's *Ulysses*. Khan's literary training is palpable in his publications, and he was sought out by those who were themselves imaginative and literary. He was the training analyst of two of the world's leading contemporary psychoanalysts, Christopher Bollas and Adam Phillips. Khan's own training analyst was Winnicott, with whom he was in treatment from 1951 until 1966. Khan edited Winnicott's writings from 1949 to Winnicott's death in 1971. Khan was close to Anna Freud, who greatly admired his intellect. He was married twice: his first wife, Jane Shore, was a dancer; his second wife, Svetlana Beriosova, was a ballerina. Both marriages ended in divorce. In her 2006 biography *False Self: The Life of Masud Khan*, Linda Hopkins observes that Erik Erikson, the most influential twentieth-century American psychoanalyst, proclaimed that "The future of analysis belongs to Khan" (xxii). That future never came.

The Literary Khan

In his first three books—*The Privacy of the Self* (1974), *Alienation in Perversions* (1979), and *Hidden Selves* (1983)—Khan offers keen insights into psychoanalysis as a humanistic and hermeneutic enterprise. He was one of the first analysts to recognize the power of Marion Milner's *The Hands of the Living God*, calling it in *The Privacy of the Self* the "only extensive and candid clinical account of the treatment and cure of a gravely ill and mad person that we possess in psychoanalysis" (96). (Milner gratefully acknowledges Khan's help in the second edition of *On Not Being Able to Paint*.) He recognizes that literature cannot be judged by the same standards as science. "By the year 2027 we cannot say, or it would be imbecile to do so, that any man alive could understand Shakespearian experience better than Shakespeare. Whereas any decent eighteen-year-old student of physics in that year will know now more physics than Newton" (120). He reveals an intriguing paradox of psychoanalysis: "very few illnesses in a person are difficult to handle and cure. What, however, is most difficult to resolve and cure is the patient's practice of self-cure" (97).

Alienation in Perversions abounds in paradoxes, as when Khan observes that "Only the genius finds what he is not looking for, the rest of us have to be content with re-discovering the discovered for ourselves" (13). He quotes Andre Gide quoting Oscar Wilde's statement that there are two kinds of artists: those who bring answers and others who raise questions (18). Khan's most absorbing case studies succeed in raising destabilizing questions. He bids farewell to a patient by quoting lines by Rilke: "Love consists in this/ that two Solitudes protect and / touch and greet each other" (218). In the chapter "Pornography, Rage and Subversion," he observes that despite celebrated writers' statements to the contrary, "no one can really claim any virtues for the style of Sade" (*Alienation in Perversions* 221).

In *Hidden Selves*, Khan cites a passage from T.S. Eliot's 1950 play *The Cocktail Party* to a patient who appreciates the playwright's insight that, in Eliot's words, one requires "the kind of faith that issues from despair" (78). Khan refers to James

Joyce's nearly unreadable novel *Finnegans Wake*, quoting the line "Let us pry" to show the Freudian effort to probe the unconscious. Khan also refers to Jung's *Memories, Dreams, Reflections*, pointing out that the "secret can provide a space in which the threatened ongoing life of a child can be sustained intact" (107). In all three books, Khan quotes effortlessly scores of literary writers, showing how their words illuminate the clinical process. Khan speaks affectionately and respectfully of his patients. When an analysand asks him whether he has read all of the books in his consulting room, he responds, "cultured persons do not read books, they live with them" (*Hidden Selves* 90). Cultured people also see plays: according to Hopkins, Khan saw twenty-seven consecutive performances of *King Lear* (28).

"The Old Fox"

The Long Wait is most memoiristic in chapter 2, "When Spring Comes." Ostensibly about a teenager, Veronique, who had stopped eating, the chapter offers a lively portrait of Khan's complex relationship with Winnicott, the "old fox [who] had premeditated everything," including manipulating him into driving twenty miles each way to visit the young patient. The case study describes a time in late 1969 when Winnicott was in failing health, having suffered three severe heart attacks. The elegiacal chapter is the most moving and lyrical one in the book.

Khan succeeds in conveying the deep affection, even love between the two men. One can see their devotion to each other. Winnicott comes to life here in a way that he doesn't in any of the biographies written about him. The chapter reads less like a clinical case study than a Jamesian short story; Khan appears as a person on whom nothing is lost, particularly the cultural differences between the two men. He tells us, for example, that he didn't like visiting Winnicott in the evening because it "ruptured his private living" (39). The two men are always bantering and jibing with each other: their repartee sparkles. Khan conveys Winnicott's clinical acumen and child-like humor, his kindness and peevishness. Khan always treats Winnicott with ceremonial respect, but he is unafraid to suggest that his mentor is haunted by ghosts:

> "You know, D.W.W., you do have one thing in common with Freud, and he had *it* common with Prince Hamlet . . ." "What thing?" he always asked impatiently. "You, Freud and Hamlet could live happily in an egg-shell, but that each of you have had bad dreams." (48; ellipsis in original)

Khan's gift for characterization, dialogue, and narration is striking. Winnicott tells Khan that he will like Veronique, whose aristocratic background resembles Khan's. As Khan prepares to depart in his car, Winnicott urges him, with his usual irony, to go dressed as he is: "Your riding boots and cravat would give Veronique more confidence in you than anything you could say at first" (29). Details like these heighten Khan's power as a storyteller.

Throughout the chapter Khan implies a master-servant relationship, not merely because of the way in which they addressed each other: as "Khan" and "D.W.W." Although Khan was Winnicott's analysand, mentee, and amanuensis, they inhabited vastly different cultures. "I was never any part of his social and family life, nor he of mine" (27). Winnicott comes across as a strict taskmaster who dispenses praise with indirect criticism: "Thank you for almost never letting me down" (36). Khan knows his place, but he can't resist expressing "barbaric outrage" when Winnicott sips a glass of diluted malt whisky. Khan often finds himself "fuming at" Winnicott. Khan sees many similarities between his father and Winnicott: "Each of them was brutally demanding, without realizing it, of the few others they respected and/or had affection for" (50). One can only wonder whether Khan revealed this in his analysis with Winnicott. Clinicians have speculated on what may have gone wrong with Winnicott's analysis of Khan. James B. McCarthy hypothesizes that both men's conflicted relationships with their fathers may have led them to avoid any analysis of their feelings of aggression and disillusionment with each other. Whatever the reason, Khan doesn't discuss his analysis with Winnicott. The purpose of writing the chapter, he asserts at the end, was to share with his readers his "joyous experiences, so very strict too, of 'working with' D.W.W. on living cases" (47). The joy, however, conceals animosity not only toward Winnicott but also toward middle-class British culture from which Khan feels excluded.

Had *The Long Wait* consisted of chapters like "When Spring Comes," the book would have made a notable contribution to psychoanalysis. In many of the other chapters, however, Khan comes across as imperious and grandiose. Everything he says about himself highlights his aristocratic background—though there is no evidence to suggest that he had a noble lineage. He describes his father, Raja Fazaldad Khan, as having left him "very large estates and immense wealth" (63) to pursue his studies. Khan's most extended description of himself contains more than a hint of self-conceit:

> I am tall, handsome, a good polo and squash player. Fit. Only forty-one. Very rich. Noble born. Delightfully married to a very famous artist. Live in a style of my own making. Am a Muslim from Pakistan. My roots are sunk deep and spread wide across three cultures, from the Punjab of Northern India, Rajput Indian and Shia Persian. (91)

Being wealthy was imperative for Khan. How else do we explain the fact that he informs us of his fabulous wealth on *five* separate occasions in *The Long Wait*? When Khan doesn't explicitly comment on his wealth, his patients do. Khan's patients sometimes function as choral characters in a Greek tragedy, providing us with details about his personal and professional life. One patient repeats an analyst's statement that Khan lives in a "very luxurious and expensively furnished flat" (144). Another patient repeats a lover's statement that Khan lives in a "gilded monastic cage" filled with thousands of books and expensive art (178). Luis describes Khan to a friend as "This Monsieur in London, he is a prince and well-known as an analyst" (89). A few pages later Luis is awestruck by Khan's consulting office. "Everyone and everything around you is beautiful, just beautiful ... including your houseboy.... And these Braques and Giacomettis on the wall. Just beautiful" (93; ellipses in original). Khan warns Luis to stop the excessive praise, adding, ominously, "I am your last chance. Protect me from yourself" (93), a cautionary warning that is no less true about Khan himself.

Khan's publisher allowed him to be his own editor of *The Long Wait*, according to Linda Hopkins, and while it's not apparent that he was "demented" when he wrote the book, as she suggests (106), his anger, prejudice, and grandiosity are evident. Hopkins reports that Khan's close friend Robert Stoller believed that reading *The Long Wait* was a "most interesting experience—interesting in the way it is interesting to watch a kamikaze pilot in his final plunge" (366).

Despite his fabled wealth and aristocratic claims, Khan could not stop feeling as an outsider in British society. "Why do these foreigners ape us?" Winnicott abruptly asks Khan, to which the latter gives a compelling answer. "These foreigners, D.W.W.? I am one too, and I don't ape. The trouble is, you English, D.W.W., don't like foreigners conforming to your ways." Winnicott doesn't have a satisfactory answer other than ambiguously replying, "No! No! That is not democratic" (40). Khan then reminds us, in a comment tinged with sarcasm, that every culture "has its hypocrisies but those of the British are admirably arranged" (46).

Khan's Anti-Semitism

One would think (or at least hope) that an outsider might identify or sympathize with another outsider, but history shows that persecuted or marginalized minorities rarely support each other. The two psychoanalytic explanations are identification with the aggressor, a defense mechanism popularized by Anna Freud; and projective identification, theorized by Melanie Klein, in which one projects unacceptable aspects of the self onto others, with whom one then identifies. Or to repeat Marion Milner's words from *A Life of One's Own*, projective identification is the "trick of trying to get away from the necessity to admit unpleasant things in oneself by putting them outside and feeling that it is others who are bad, not oneself" (40). The non-psychoanalytic explanation is that the oppressed becomes the oppressor. In Chapter 3, "Empty Chairs, Vast Spaces," Khan reveals his decision in 1974, shortly before he turned fifty, to create a new psychoanalytic approach to clinical work, one that will free himself of the "rigid Yiddish shackles of the so-called psychoanalysis." Lest he be misunderstood, he elaborates:

> I say "Yiddish" because psychoanalysis, for better and worse, is not only Judaic in its inherited traditions, but also Yiddish and Jewish. The three are quite distinct in my experience. Even though only two Jewesses played an important role in my education (Melanie Klein for a short while, and Anna Freud mutatively and for much longer), the impact of the Judaic-Yiddish-Jewish bias of psychoanalysis was neither small nor slight on me. If it undoubtedly nurtured me, it has also cramped my personal and ethnic styles. (62)

Despite the reference to "better and worse," Khan implies only the latter, not the former. Who were the Jewish analysts who cramped his style? He has nothing critical to say about Melanie Klein or Anna Freud. One can only wonder how and why he was cramped; he offers no concrete evidence to support his assertion. He vows now that he is nearly fifty to be his own person—in effect, revealing for the first time his hidden self, a decision that would prove calamitous.

The catastrophe occurs in the notorious chapter 4 of *The Long Wait*, when he unleashes a torrent of anti-Semitic and homophobic abuse on Mikhail Luis, who was born in a Jewish ghetto in Chicago, the son of poor Russian émigrés:

> I have little use and less praise for self-made Jews who pretend to be artists, writers or dancers. Actors seem to manage it better in America for some reason. I have met all types everywhere. Even in Moscow. The yids certainly know how to climb up. My profession is no exception. Yes, I can rise above that. You would not be the first Jew I would be treating. As to class: well, there is no *class* in America, so I cannot hold that as a negative indication in your case. Poofs, especially the gilded ageing ones, do fill me with instant disgust and disdain. I have met lots of you. All are the same in the Homo International Jetset. Isn't that what you call it? (90–1)

It would be facetious to ask whether Khan hated all Jews or only those who were self-made. If the latter, did he hate everyone, including fellow Pakistanis who succeeded through their own efforts? Why single out Jews? Surely he must have known that although a disproportionate number of analysts are Jewish, reminding us of Freud's fear that psychoanalysis would be known as the Jewish science, British society has never looked favorably on its Jewish citizens. Why would Khan later describe himself as an "Aryan" to Luis in light of the Holocaust? Indeed, he orders Luis not to fret: "like the rest of your species, you will survive and continue to harass others, and lament, and bewail yourselves. Remarkable how Yiddish/Jewish you are" (93). That Luis is a self-hating Jew who compares himself to a cobra seems to give Khan permission to spew forth his own venomous feelings about Jews.

Significantly, Khan's anti-Semitism is absent in his three other books. He never uses the words "Jew" or "Jewish" in *The Privacy of the Self* or *Alienation in Perversions*. Only one reference appears in *Hidden Selves*, when he describes Freud as an "ambitious and talented Jewish youth in the Hapsburg Vienna" (31).

Tellingly, Khan has nothing ill to say about Luis's partner, Dave, a Texas writer who is not Jewish. "Dave is safer in his person wrapped neatly round my Mongol Muslim little finger," Khan avers, "than he ever has been, these many years, wrapped round, and into as well, your dirty Jewish arse" (94). The two men, analyst and analysand, then glare at each other, each radiating contempt for the other.

Khan titles chapter 4 "A Dismaying Homosexual," but a more accurate title would be "A Dismaying Jew," though admittedly that would be redundant because *all* Jews are dismaying to him. The chapter is racist as well as homophobic and anti-Semitic. What is the link among racism, homophobia, and anti-Semitism? The three prejudices demonize the other, the outsider. Khan, too, was an outsider, a Pakistani Muslim living in Anglican England. By projecting his hateful feelings about himself onto others, he could "fit into" a society different from his own. Nowhere is Khan aware of his pathologizing of difference, his ugly stereotyping of others.

Khan's anti-Semitism was well known. In his 1996 book *Omens of Millennium*, the literary critic Harold Bloom observes that when he was thirty-five, he found himself feeling wretched, and for almost a year he was "immersed in acute melancholia." Unable to teach, he followed his Yale psychiatrist's suggestion and went abroad. Depressed in London for a year, Bloom went, again at his Yale psychiatrist's recommendation, to an eminent Pakistani psychoanalyst. "An instant hatred sprang up between the London analyst and me, so that I refused to see him again after three visits" (24–5). Bloom reveals the identity of the analyst in a letter to Linda Hopkins.

> Khan loathed me at first sight and let me know it, and I rapidly reciprocated, though I believe that generally I am amiable enough. All that I truly recall is that he attacked me for being unkempt (I still am), told me innumerable times that he was much more intelligent than I was, and seemed to have read my earlier books. What I remember most vividly is that I walked out half-way through the third session because his abusiveness became overtly anti-Semitic. (Hopkins 129)

Paul Roazen interviewed Khan in 1965 and found him "extraordinarily difficult: the word arrogance does not begin to cover the imperiousness of his manner" ("Review of *The Long Wait*" 19). Roazen, who was Jewish, found Khan's anti-Semitism "mild" compared with his other prejudices: Khan's "Francophilic convictions" struck Roazen as no less eccentric than his feelings about Jews (20).

"Hatred is so addictive," Khan states about the two-and-a-half-year analysis with Luis, adding, "A strange therapeutic alliance" (94). Strange indeed! It's difficult to believe Khan's claim that his words shock Luis out of his narcissistic self-absorption, helping him regain control over his life. Luis becomes, according to Khan, a "tamed, not timid, person," one who reaches his "creative core" (99). "Deep down you care about me," Luis affirms. "You always have. A very strange man you are, Mr Masud" (105). Khan's claim of having discovered a "mutual way of relating, trusting and working together" (99) strains belief.

I've come across only one psychoanalytic clinician, Candace Orcutt, who attempts to justify Khan's outrageous behavior toward Luis. "Khan's intervention is not an expression of bias, but rather the deliberate application of a new analytic technique" (491)—a technique that she believes helps the patient deal with otherwise unmanageable aggression. Rarely, however, does an analyst's vicious attack of a patient have a therapeutic effect. This is not to imply that a patient's anger cannot be beneficial. Harold Bloom states in *Omens of Millennium* that his fury over Khan was "therapeutic and partly dislodged me from my dark night of the soul" (25). Hopkins quotes a 2003 letter Bloom wrote to Robert Rodman elaborating on the Yale English professor's cathartic anger toward Khan. "When

I returned to Yale, I called upon Dr. Lidz [Bloom's psychiatrist] and asked why he had sent me to a madman, to which Lidz replied, 'Well, Harold, by your own account, your anger helped cure your depression!'" (436, n. 26).

How would Winnicott have responded to Khan's anti-Semitism? We can't be sure, but in his interview with Peter Rudnytsky in *Psychoanalytic Conversations* (2000), Charles Rycroft recalls Winnicott shaking his hand vigorously at a meeting of the British Psychoanalytical Society and asking, "Dr. Livingstone, I presume?," which Rycroft interpreted as an "anti-Semitic joke." As Rycroft explains, he and Winnicott were among the few gentiles in the British society. "The Society after the war was predominantly Jewish. It wasn't exactly a problem not to be, but you had to be careful. I think that was what he meant. It was a relief to meet a blonde Gentile in the woods. He was quite capable of making jokes, and some of them were arguably in slightly bad taste" (72). Hopkins cites a comment by Clare Winnicott that shows how the "English" and the "Jewish" seemed to be mutually exclusive categories. "[DWW] was very, very, very, very, very non-Jewish indeed. Very English, actually" (369).

What was in slightly bad taste for a gentile could be deeply offensive to a Jew. In *Loathsome Jews and Engulfing Women* (1993), Andrea Freud Loewenstein, Freud's great-granddaughter, agrees with what the American literary critic Leslie Fiedler decried as the "mild-as-milk, matter-of-fact anti-Semitism" that he found everywhere in England (3). British Jews, Loewenstein observes, "were resented for their refusal to assimilate while being virtually prevented from doing so" (7). T.S. Eliot, whose writings Khan cites, created in his poems personae who voice anti-Semitic statements. In his 1933 *After Strange Gods*, Eliot observes that the British population should be homogeneous; "where two or more cultures exist in the same place they are likely either to be fiercely self-conscious or both to become adulterate. What is still more important is unity of religious background; and reasons of race and religion combine to make any large number of free-thinking Jews undesirable" (20).

Boundary Violations

Khan seethes with indignation when his patient Aisha informs him of a comment made by "Dr X," who was at the time Anna Freud's "blue-eyed boy." Dr. X asks her whether Khan is an aristocrat, and when she answers in the affirmative—"he is much more. He is beyond class-status!"—he warns her that Khan takes liberties with his patients. "He said you were taken off training," Aisha informs Khan, "because of an affair with some patient. It is not done to mix with one's patients. But Khan makes his own rules" (179–80). It's likely that Dr. X was Jeffrey Masson, whose 1984 book *The Assault on Truth: Freud's Suppression of the Seduction Theory* appeared shortly before *The Long Wait*. Khan responds dryly to his readers about Dr. X. "By reviling me he only diminishes himself. No, it is not possible for him to diminish himself. There is no room for shrinkage left in him" (181). Shrinkage, ironically, turned out to be both men's fate in the psychoanalytic community.

None of the boundary violations in *The Long Wait* is as serious as those that were later reported by Khan's former analysands. In an article appearing in the *London Review of Books* in 2001, the Cambridge economics professor Wynne Godley recalled going into analysis in his early thirties with Khan, to whom he had been referred by Winnicott. Godley's analysis was a disaster. Khan intruded himself into every aspect of Godley's life, savagely criticizing Godley's British culture, talking about his own social life in London and New York, answering telephone calls during sessions, disclosing confidential information about other patients, and even recommending that the happily married Godley meet another Khan patient, "Marian." Godley, Khan, and Marian then started "meeting à trois." Khan showered Godley with expensive gifts and invited him to his home, where the analyst's wife, Svetlana Beriosova, played hostess. On one occasion, Khan and his wife had a violent fight and both passed out drunk. Khan began showing up uninvited at Godley's home. Worst of all, Khan attacked Godley's pregnant wife. "The perception that, at the level of reality, Khan had made an attempt on the life of our unborn only child was painful beyond anything I can convey." That was the end of analysis.

Godley told Robert S. Boynton in a 2003 interview in *Boston Review* that Khan discouraged him throughout the seven-year analysis from recounting anything about his childhood or past because everything of *real* significance was taking place between the two men in their sessions. "Of course this gave him a license to interfere actively, judgmentally, and with extraordinary cruelty in every aspect of my daily life." Godley emphasizes at the conclusion of his own article, enigmatically titled "Saving Masud Khan," that his devastating criticisms of Khan should not be interpreted as an attack on psychoanalysis, for which he has great respect. "I could not have gained the insight to write this piece, nor could I have recovered from the experiences I have described, if they had not at last been undone at the hands of a skilful, patient and selfless American analyst."

Khan could not have been entirely shocked that *The Long Wait* would destroy what little was left of his reputation. There are hints throughout the book that he disregards at his peril. "I am afraid they will harm you when I am gone" (40), Winnicott prophetically warns him. Responding to a psychiatrist who had called him a "maverick" among analysts, Khan admits that he is famous but not popular among his colleagues. He confesses near the end of the book, after having put Aisha through an "ordeal of total stress," that most if not all of his colleagues would conclude that he had behaved in an "outrageously haughty way" (195). Khan doesn't need to defend himself to his colleagues, he adds, though he promises an explanation to his readers. But nothing, of course, can fully explain or justify a book like *The Long Wait*.

There are partial explanations, mitigating factors, including illness, physical and mental. Khan twice refers in *The Long Wait* to being ill from cancer, the first time in the 1970s when one of his lungs was removed, the second time in the late 1980s when he had a laryngectomy. It took more than two years to recover from eleven cancer surgeries; during this time, he was unable to work or speak normally. Linda Hopkins suggests that Khan may have suffered from undiagnosed manic depression along with alcoholism. Illness can change people, bringing out the best or worst in them.

Psychoanalytic clinicians and scholars have offered various reasons for Khan's "manic tirades" against the Jewish patient in *The Long Wait*, to use Gladys Branly Guarton's term (308). One of the key issues in Khan's problematic behavior toward Luis is unanalyzed aggression, which was probably both a cause and effect of his expulsion from the British Psychoanalytical Society. Khan's aggression also expressed itself in the "scurrilous" public remarks he made about his deceased mentor, D.W.W., in the late 1977s. "At a professional meeting, he stood up and announced that Winnicott had been impotent throughout his life," Linda Hopkins reports. "His British colleagues were surprised and pained as they witnessed a favorite son attacking the father" (306).

Evaluating Masud Khan

The critical reviews of *The Long Wait* were predictably scathing. In her *New York Times Review*, Janet Malcolm observed that Khan's repudiation of psychoanalysis "seems to derive purely from his feeling that he—an extremely rich Pakistani prince—has sojourned too long among the 'nobody Jews' and 'Jewesses' of British psychoanalytic society, and that it is time he reverted to the snobbery, arrogance and anti-Semitism that are his birthright." Malcolm concludes her review with a memorable sentence. "As we read Mr. Khan's wild book, we may thank our lucky stars that in the blind lottery from which we draw our therapists we are more apt to draw a nebbish Rabbi Small than a dashing Prince Masud." In *The Jew's Body* (1991), Sander Gilman views Khan's anti-Semitism not as a "personal idiosyncrasy" but as a response to the "racial" belief that the Jew is biologically inferior (112). In a review published in the *American Journal of Psychotherapy*, Martin Grotjahn attempts to be charitable to a psychoanalyst who had done good work during his early career. "Read this book as unbridled fiction written by somebody who has taken his wish seriously to make an impossible profession possible—at least for himself, and for him alone" (140).

Masud Khan has become part of his profession's dark lore. A disguised portrait appears in Christopher Bollas's 2006 novella *Mayhem*, where Khan is given an absurd name:

> Mish Mash's unusual intimacy with his patients had occasioned widespread interest, although it was not so unusual for analysts to have sexual relations with their analysands. There was also a certain curiosity about his other "boundary violations." He and one patient, for example, had bunked off and visited bookshops, rather than engage in an analytical relation.... The real fascination with Mish Mash, however, was down to the fact that he had been in analysis with Dr Wool [a reference to Winnicott]—a treatment of which there existed no clinical records at all—and the clone analysts believed this gave them a golden

opportunity, in a series of essays and books, to attribute Mish Mash's violations to failures in the analysis. (64–5)

Bollas satirizes Mish Mash in *Mayhem*, but he was deeply saddened by Khan's behavior near the end of his life. Khan was Bollas's training analyst from 1973 to 1976, and the young analysand learned much from him, as did Adam Phillips, who in his 1988 book *Winnicott* singles out Khan (and Bollas) "from whom I learnt versions of psychoanalysis that were inspiring and intelligible" (Acknowledgments).

Robert Rodman describes Khan as the "most disgraceful individual ever associated with the British Society, notwithstanding his good mind and services as editor of the International Psychoanalytic Library, as well as his books and his editing tasks on behalf of Donald Winnicott" (Rodman, *Winnicott* 205). Rodman quotes a letter he received from Madeleine Davis shortly after Khan's death that offers a hidden meaning of the title of his first book. "[T]his is what is meant by Masud Khan's phrase 'the privacy of the self'—something which M.K. sought after all his life, and therefore, and especially, *knew* about, though he himself couldn't find it" (213). The title of Khan's last book *The Long Wait* suggests that he never found what he was looking for, or, if he did, it turned out to be Kurtz's dying words in Conrad's *Heart of Darkness*: "The horror! The horror!"

But perhaps one shouldn't end on such a grim note. In an eloquent obituary appearing in *The Guardian* on June 26, 1989, Bollas admits that *The Long Wait* is a "sordid joke book of sorts that burlesqued his earlier thoughtful and profound works." Bollas never defends the book, but he concludes the obituary with a compassionate sentence that may help us to forgive those who, having spent many years committed to helping others, die out of character: "if mental illness can be forgiven, and time's passing often does so, then the literary works of one of the most gifted psychoanalytic writers of this century may yet survive his tragically driven effort to dismantle himself before his death."

Chapter 9

JEFFREY MOUSSAIEFF MASSON

FINAL ANALYSIS

"Please don't analyze my motivation," Jeffrey Moussaieff Masson beseeches Anna Freud near the end of his 1990 memoir *Final Analysis: The Making and Unmaking of a Psychoanalyst* (179). Determined to tell the truth of his loss of faith in psychoanalysis, Masson maintains that he portrays accurately the corruption, falseness, and insularity of a profession he once wildly idealized. He readily acknowledges his earlier ignorance, naivete, and blindness but not any darker conflicts, such as wounded grandiosity. Masson sees psychoanalysis as a cult filled with "intellectual lemmings" (192). The entire profession is morally bankrupt, "sterile," as he concluded in his incendiary lecture to the Western New England Psychoanalytic Society in 1981. The lecture was followed by equally inflammatory comments Masson expressed to Ralph Blumenthal, who wrote about him in two articles published in the *New York Times* in August 1981.

Narrative reliability—or unreliability—becomes a key question in *Final Analysis*, the same problem we saw in Khan's *The Long Wait*. Some of Masson's criticisms are prescient, including the observation, confirmed by Douglas Kirsner, that psychoanalytic institutes often have a stultifying educational atmosphere. But Masson's other criticisms are at best half-truths. Readers cannot determine from the memoir alone the accuracy of his devastating portrait of his training analyst at the Toronto Psychoanalytic Institute, Irvine Schiffer—a cruel, vulgar, bombastic, and vindictive man, according to Masson, who must surely rank as one of the most egomaniacal therapists in any nonfictional account of the talking cure. Why does Masson believe that Schiffer is representative of nearly all analysts? With few exceptions, the other psychoanalysts who appear in *Final Analysis* are similarly petty, duplicitous, and greedy. Those who aren't, such as Anna Freud and Kurt Eissler, seem brainwashed by their loyalty to the founder of psychoanalysis.

Final Analysis claims to be a tell-all memoir about Masson's acceptance by and then irrevocable banishment from the psychoanalytic community. Before his sudden fall from grace, the modern-day Humpty Dumpty was "in demand everywhere in analytic circles" (124), a celebrity who loved every moment of his fifteen minutes of fame. But there's much about which the former professor of Sanskrit turned psychoanalyst remains silent. Why does Masson, who succeeded in entering the inner circle of psychoanalysis, becoming the projects director of the Sigmund Freud Archives and a director of the Sigmund Freud Copyrights, regard complex historical and psychological truths as either/or binaries? Why does he take an all-or-nothing approach to a discipline that is constantly evolving in its understanding and treatment of mental disorders? And how trustworthy are Masson's characterizations of those whom he skewers in his memoir, including his analyst?

The infamous prehistory of *Final Analysis* complicates our understanding of the memoir. Janet Malcolm's sensationalistic *In the Freud Archives* (1984), based on her two lengthy articles, "Trouble in the Archives," which first appeared in *The New Yorker* in December 1983, used extensive quotations that she claimed were Masson's exact words during their interviews. Masson sued Malcolm for libel, and the decade-long highly publicized case, which has been compared to the interminable *Jarnydce v. Jarndyce* court case in Dickens's *Bleak House*, reached the Supreme Court.

As Masson's subtitle suggests, we must understand the making of the psychoanalyst before we can grasp his unmaking. There is a special irony in the word *making*, for it implies a person *on the make*, one who is aggressively in pursuit of fame, glory, and, in Masson's case, sexual as well as intellectual conquest. Like his former-hero Freud, Masson was determined to be a conquistador, the disturber of the world's sleep. In rejecting Freud's "moral cowardice" for abandoning the seduction theory, which he held between 1895 and 1897, the belief that many of his female patients were sexually abused in childhood, Masson was determined to follow his conscience regardless of the consequences, a decision that led to apostasy and excommunication.

Complete Letters of Sigmund Freud to Wilhelm Fliess

The publication of *The Complete Letters of Sigmund Freud to Wilhelm Fliess, 1887–1904* by Harvard University Press in 1985 was a landmark in psychoanalytic scholarship. The earlier abridged edition, *The Origins of Psycho-Analysis*, published in German in 1950 and then in English in 1954, contained only 168 letters, presented in full or in part. Masson persuaded a reluctant Anna Freud to include 133 previously unpublished letters in his authoritative edition, which he edited and translated. "It is a hazardous undertaking to edit a work of this magnitude, which is likely to change the image of a great man," Masson writes in the Preface, mythologizing the heroism of his project. "Still, I think most readers will agree that a more human, more likable Sigmund Freud emerges from this complete version of his letters to Fliess" (ix). Few can dispute Masson's claim that Freud's letters to his closest confidant are the most noteworthy documents in the early history of psychoanalysis. Gifted in languages, Masson learned German to read Freud's writings in the original.

The story of Anna Freud's regret over the publication of the unabridged letters to Fliess appears in Elisabeth Young-Bruehl's 1988 biography. Masson's "personal charm and his enthusiasm for the edition," Young-Bruehl reports, overcame Anna Freud's objections to the new edition, despite her annoyance with his "rambunctious and greedy behavior" in her father's library. Anna Freud regarded as "unnecessary and grandiose," in her biographer's words, Masson's initial proposal to publish a three-volume edition of the letters, the first volume containing Freud's letters and notes, the second containing auxiliary documents, and the third containing Masson's speculations. This information never appears in *Final Analysis*. "For my part," Anna Freud lamented to Eissler, "I could only say one thing: that I am deeply sorry that I ever agreed to the publication of the unabridged Fliess letters" (*Anna Freud: A Biography* 436–7).

The Assault on Truth

The Complete Letters of Sigmund Freud to Wilhelm Fliess betrays none of Masson's backstage maneuverings to secure the approval of Anna Freud and Kurt Eissler, the "pope of orthodox psychoanalysis," that made possible the volume's publication. Nor does the edition allude to the bitter controversy surrounding Masson's most contentious book, *The Assault on Truth: Freud's Suppression of the Seduction Theory*, published one year earlier. Indeed, in the acknowledgments Masson expressed his thanks to Anna Freud and Kurt Eissler, "gratitude" which they must have felt was bitterly ironic.

Masson asserted that Freud's rejection of the seduction theory was a fatal mistake for both psychoanalysis and psychiatry. But as Sander Gilman asserts, "No credence can be given to any view, such as that of Jeffrey Masson, which attempts to isolate reality from fantasy. Freud himself never denied the possibility of actual seduction. What he stressed was the ubiquitousness of fantasies of seduction" (57).

Masson could have chosen a less sweeping claim. Based on the newly discovered letters to Fliess, Masson might have plausibly argued that Freud had misgivings over his rejection of historical reality for psychological reality. Freud could not be blamed for failing to know at the turn of the twentieth century the startling incidence of child sexual abuse, which no one at the time had suspected. Had Masson reasserted what scholars, clinicians, and feminists became aware of only in the late 1960s and 1970s, namely, that Freud should have trusted, as he originally did for a few years, what his female patients told him, then Masson would have offered a healthy corrective to the belief that stories of incest and sexual abuse are merely wishful fantasies.

Nor did Freud's rejection of the seduction theory imply moral cowardice, as Masson charges. "As long as he held to the seduction theory, Freud was alone" (136). But Freud clung steadily to other unpopular beliefs, such as the importance of infantile sexuality, the universality of the Oedipus complex, and the ubiquity of penis envy. In his late book *Moses and Monotheism* (1939), Freud deprived fellow Jews of the man whom they revered as their greatest leader. "To deprive a people of the man whom they take pride in as the greatest of their sons is not a thing to be gladly or carelessly undertaken, least of all by someone who is himself one of them" (*SE*, Vol. 23, 7). Masson states repeatedly that Freud did not have the courage of his convictions, but courage (or cowardice) had little to do with his continual revision of psychoanalytic theory.

A Dark Science

Masson wasted little time in condemning *all* psychoanalysis, psychiatry, and clinical psychology regardless of their theoretical orientations. In 1986, he published *A Dark Science: Women, Sexuality and Psychiatry in the Nineteenth Century*, a book of readings that he selected and translated from French and German medical journals that appeared from 1865 through 1900. Catherine A. MacKinnon's statement in the Preface heralds the book's extremist approach. "Behind psychotherapy's guise of treatment, just as surely as beneath pornography's protestations of liberation, lies the sexual sadism that is at the core of misogyny, here in its medical form" (xi). From this moment on, Masson identifies himself with the anti-psychiatry movement, though tellingly, he rejects two of its leading figures, R.D. Laing and Thomas Szasz, because they don't go sufficiently far in their criticisms. "Neither Laing nor Szasz struck me as radical enough" (18).

As an example of child sexual abuse, Masson cites in *A Dark Science* the scandalous McMartin case. He rejects the possibility that the phenomenon was merely an example of mass hysteria, one that might lead to the false conviction of innocent citizens. But Masson doesn't give us any of the details of the event, which began when a mother in Los Angeles telephoned the police to report that her two-year-old son was sexually victimized because she noticed a spot of blood on his anus. The boy's teacher was arrested, and prosecutors determined, as a result of the use of highly suggestive and manipulative interviewing techniques, that over 350 children were victims of sexual abuse by teachers at the school. The McMartin case proved to be the longest and most costly criminal trial in American history, but it resulted in not a single conviction. The spot of blood that triggered the case turned out to be the result of the boy's anal itching.

The cognitive psychologist Elizabeth Loftus has shown, in a series of elegant experiments focused on being lost in a shopping mall, that it is easy to create false memories in children. As many as a third of the people in Loftus's experiments recalled childhood experiences that never happened. As Alison Winter observes in *Memory* (2012), although Loftus's critics have accused her of inflating her results, some replications of her original experiments have shown higher rates of memory reconstruction than she found. Nor does Masson point out that the discredited "recovered memories" movement in the 1980s and 1990s was caused, in large part, by therapists who planted false memories in their patients. One should not conclude from these examples that child sexual abuse is not widespread; rather, these and countless other examples suggest that it is sometimes impossible to separate fantasy from reality. And sometimes it is hard to distinguish between narrative truth and historical truth, as Donald J. Spence has argued.

Against Therapy

Masson prides himself on being a trouble maker, as Dorothy Rowe admits cheerfully in her Foreword to his next book, *Against Therapy* (1988). "Every one of his books has been written to create trouble" (7), a statement with which both his admirers and critics can entirely agree.

Masson cannot escape the sharp criticisms he received after the publication of *The Assault on Truth*, as he caustically admits in the Preface to *Against Therapy*: "wherever I lectured, even in France, Italy, Spain, and Holland, the discussions focused on my physical appearance, my clothing, my motivation in researching child abuse, my relationship with my father, my mother, my analyst, Anna Freud, and others" (26). He contends that he no longer feels bitterness as a result of his psychoanalytic excommunication, yet his dismissive generalizations indicate otherwise: "the very *idea* of psychotherapy is wrong" (24). Some of his criticisms are accurate: Freud's insensitivity toward Dora in *Fragment of an Analysis of a Case of Hysteria*, Jung's flirtation with Nazi ideology, John Rosen's sadistic treatment of his patients, and D. Ewen Cameron's frightening experimentation with human depatterning at McGill University in Montreal, Canada. *Against Therapy* abounds in cautionary tales of the misuse of mental health treatments, a thesis that Paul Mosher and I explore in detail in our two-volume study *Off the Tracks: Cautionary Tales about the Derailing of Mental Health Care* (2019).

There are, sadly, countless stories of malevolent therapists, but even so-called benevolent ones, such as Carl Rogers, evoke Masson's censure, mainly because they pretend to be empathic and understanding when they may be silently judgmental. "It is in the nature of therapy to distort another person's reality" (247). The generalization admits to no exceptions. Therapists may struggle to be honest, Masson insists, but therapy is always a fraud. Psychiatry is not concerned with cure, Dorothy Rowe writes in her Foreword, but only with power (10). Nor is there a need for psychotherapy, Masson argues, because mental illness doesn't exist.

We may agree with Masson's claim at the beginning of *Against Therapy* that one should be "skeptical of anybody who profits from another person's suffering" (39), but by the end we realize that he is opposed to psychotherapists being paid for their services simply because money promotes self-interest. The criticism can be applied to *every* profession. Masson is, paradoxically, as the novelist D.M. Thomas said admiringly in his blurb on the back cover of *Against Therapy*, a "guru against gurus," but the darker meaning of the comment is Masson's belief that he alone has seen the light. "There is no point in studying therapy," he concludes (286, n. 1), a pronouncement that prepares us for *Final Analysis*.

Final Analysis

"I was a gossip," Masson admits in *Final Analysis*. "I still am" (64). *Final Analysis* teems with gossip, much of it malicious. Masson uses pseudonyms for many of the analysts, with the result that the memoir reads like a roman à clef. Masson loves not only gossip but also secrets, his own and others, which he doesn't hesitate to betray. In reporting his conversations with Anna Freud, Masson cannot help telling us that "[r]umors abounded concerning her sexual life" (158). Losing Eissler's friendship was painful, yet Masson makes his former mentor sound pathetic and whining, as when Eissler asks: "Has anybody ever done as much for you as I have? And is this how you repay me?" (201). Some of Masson's attacking statements are inadvertently funny, as when he writes about the "fist time" (160) he met the anti-Semitic British psychoanalyst Masud Khan who admitted to sleeping with his own patients. The apparent Freudian slip aptly conveys Masson's pugilistic feelings toward Khan.

The most stunning sections of *Final Analysis* focus on Masson's vexed relationship with Schiffer, who was still alive when the memoir was published. Acknowledging that he reconstructed conversations with his analyst, Masson reassures us that the quoted dialogue in *Final Analysis* was based on the notes he wrote immediately after each session. Schiffer regarded himself as a classical psychoanalyst, but far from remaining a blank screen, as Freud recommended but never practiced himself, Schiffer freely speaks his mind, according to Masson, hurling insult after insult, as he does during the first session, on September 12, 1971. Ordered to express his free associations, Masson confesses, using a Yiddish word—both analyst and analysand are Jewish—that he was disappointed with the appearance of the analyst's office, which contains furniture that looks like "Woolworth schlock":

> I paused, expecting him to wait for me to continue. He didn't. "Listen—this is my office. I furnish it any way I please. You don't like it? Leave. As for the 'tacky' furniture—fuck you, my mother died recently, and these were her things. I am proud to have them here." (25)

Given Schiffer's foul temper, which gets only worse, why did Masson remain in analysis with him for five years, five days a week, each session being a lesson in humility—and humiliation? Declaring that he alone makes and breaks the analytic rules, Schiffer arrives late to almost every session, missing sometimes as much as forty-five minutes of each fifty-minute session, yet charging his analysand the full fee. "I'm your only analytic friend," Schiffer huffs, "you are your worst analytic enemy" (35). The first statement is unverifiable, the second undeniably correct.

The two chapters in *Final Analysis* that dramatize Masson's tempestuous relationship with Schiffer are "The Worm of Analysis" and "The Worm Turns." The worm turns out to be a viper: No one escapes Schiffer's venomous stings in the memoir. He calls Masson a liar for pointing out he was late for nearly the entire analytic session, implies that Masson lacks the courage to understand the truth about himself, betrays confidentiality about his other patients, trashes his analytic colleagues, asserts paranoidly that his patients will betray him (which is true, according to *Final Analysis*, confirming his realistic fear), and, in violation of all analytic rules, suggests that he, Masson, and Masson's parents have lunch together at a restaurant. Schiffer has a talent for aiming at the jugular, in Masson's words, his "narcissistic weak spot" (35).

"There is only one analyst who could handle you," Masson's psychiatrist tells him early in *Final Analysis*: "Irvine Schiffer" (21). These are magic words for Masson, who believes that he deserves only the best. Yet when Masson tries to read Schiffer's publications, he can find almost nothing. This was true in 1971, when Masson began his training analysis with Schiffer, but the Toronto analyst wrote two books published later in the decade: *Charisma: A Psychoanalytic Look at Mass Society* (1973), and *The Trauma of Time: A Psychoanalytic Investigation* (1978). In *The Analysand's Tale* (2007) Robert Morley examines the patient-therapist relationship in *Final Analysis* but without reference to Schiffer's two books, both of which give us insight into his character. *Charisma* and *The Trauma of Time* do not confirm the portrait seen in *Final Analysis*, but they are consistent with some of Masson's observations.

Schiffer was in his sixties when the thirty-year-old Masson began seeing him. Schiffer's credentials were impeccable. Trained as a neurologist in Boston, he was the president of the Toronto Psychoanalytic Institute, a faculty member of the Canadian Institute of Psychoanalysis, and both a research professor of political economy and an associate professor of psychiatry at the University of Toronto. Masson was impressed that Schiffer's training analyst was Felix Deutsch, who had been Freud's personal physician. In being analyzed by Schiffer, Masson imagined that he had a direct link to Freud.

Schiffer doesn't describe how his office looked in the 1970s, but he mentions, ruefully, how it appeared at the beginning of his career, when he had "some of the affectations of the novitiate, including an office appointed with a suitable aura of Freudianism, including an analytic couch that was carefully upholstered with fabric reminiscent of the early Freudian circle" (*The Trauma of Time* 20)—an office that Masson presumably would not have identified as Woolworth schlock. Schiffer admits to some of his human failings, especially when he was beginning his career, such as his "defensive cocksureness that commonly stamps the younger therapist" (20). If we are to believe *Final Analysis*, Schiffer had not outgrown his audacious overconfidence and grandiosity.

According to Masson, sarcasm was Schiffer's favorite mode of attack. Based on Schiffer's two books, there is some truth in this statement. He was fond of saying, in Masson's words, that "in many marriages farting was the only mode of communication" (*Final Analysis* 78). The joke appears, in slightly more clinical language, in *The Trauma of Time*: "In courtship the sound of flatus is a matter to be handled with shy reserve; after the honeymoon is over, it is often the only mode of communication" (127). Schiffer's fondness for scatological humor is palpable throughout *Charisma*. After offering several examples of what he calls "bowel language," he observes that psychotherapists highlight the primal scene and the primal scream, but "surely someone could make a case for the primal poop" (128). Some men use women as "merely toilet bowls" (71). Schiffer's profanity-laced speech in *Final Analysis* appears in *Charisma* when he writes about Scotland's national identity. "What happens if you remove the bagpipes and the kilts from the

'Ladies from Hell'—do you really annihilate the fighting capacities of a Highland regiment? What happens if you take the 'f' out of 'fuck'"? (126).

Some readers may find Schiffer's eccentric humor funny, but others—including most past and present psychotherapy patients—will be troubled by his remarks about the therapist's boredom. Few may be surprised to learn that therapists sometimes become bored by their patients, but I'm unaware of any analyst who confesses to feel trapped by patients who are, in Schiffer's words, classic bores:

> I have discovered that those patients who made the "honor role [sic]" as all-time bores are indelibly etched in my memory. I can almost relive the boredom just thinking about some of their analytic sessions . . . the feeling of going under, the prodromal claustrophobia . . . the tug from consciousness . . . the apprehension of the patient's catching me snoring . . . the painful muscles and the gurglings of the stomach . . . then the panic . . . strange thoughts of my doing something unprofessional, like crying out in torment, or simply turning resignedly (and secretively) to the *Daily News* (respected analysts have admitted to acting on the latter fantasy)! (*The Trauma of Time* 79; ellipses in original)

Schiffer must have thought that he was being honest and entertaining in this passage, but didn't he worry that patients would be alarmed by this confession—even if most readers of the now defunct International Universities Press were analysts like himself? How could he not sense that patients who read this statement would fear that they, too, would make this notorious honor-roll of all-time bores? Can an analyst be so blind to his own countertransference? Based on this comment alone, one can believe Masson when Schiffer exclaims to him, "Yours is the one hour in the day that brings me pleasure" (*Final Analysis* 64)—sadistic pleasure.

Several of Masson's accusations of Schiffer's analytic transgressions seem possible on the basis of *Charisma* and *The Trauma of Time*, including Schiffer's reference to patients who invariably come late for therapy sessions. "I, too," he confesses in the latter, "as you may have guessed, am rarely on time for anything" (66). Schiffer doesn't disclose inviting patients and their parents to lunch, but he admits in *The Trauma of Time* to socializing with former analysands (103). He offers a novel explanation for this boundary violation: the wish to convert a passive situation, silently listening to a patient, into an active one, becoming the storyteller himself. When Masson informs Schiffer that he and his wife are writing a paper titled "The Navel of Neurosis: Trauma, Memory, and Denial"—a paper presented to the San Francisco Psychoanalytic Institute in 1976—Schiffer shrilly denounces him as a thief, shouting, "That's my paper" (*Final Analysis* 83). Schiffer then demands to be listed as one of the paper's coauthors—which Masson refuses to do. Masson's accusation becomes more credible when we read Schiffer's observation in *The Trauma of Time*, where he refers to the compulsion "not only to collect other people's views, but to jealously claim them as one's own" (67–8).

Schiffer doesn't confess to plagiarism, but his statement in *Charisma* about loving and being loved—"It seems we cannot love ourselves without being loved by another and we cannot love another without being loved by ourselves" (164)—

is suspiciously close to Freud's observation in "On Narcissism" (1914): "in the last resort we must begin to love in order not to fall ill, and we are bound to fall ill if, in consequence of frustration, we are unable to love" (*SE*, vol. 14, 85).

Schiffer's most brutal insult in *Final Analysis* occurs when he tells Masson that his wife, Terri, is not beautiful. "In fact, she looks like a horse's ass" (73). Schiffer then deepens the disparagement by combining the most misogynistic element of psychoanalytic theory, penis envy, with his own chauvinistic view of women:

> "By the way, your wife's intelligence is not natural. In fact, I find it disgusting. Because I know what it is really all about. And so does every other normal woman. Normal women don't want to be with your wife. They can't stand her. And you know why? Because they can tell that she is using her brain like a penis. Her mind is so developed because she is so filled with penis envy. She is so desperate for a penis that she has created one in her head. Her brain. Her huge brain is nothing but a substitute for her desire for a huge penis. Your wife has a cock for a brain, Masson, and you're getting fucked." He chortled in delight. (75)

The remark raises two disturbing problems. First, did Schiffer make this statement? We cannot be sure, but in *The Trauma of Time* he defends Freud's theory of female sexuality and offers a dim view of feminism. "Many of the female members of this 'enlightened society' behave as if Freud had once hit them in the crotch with an axe" (222)—a comment that Masson quotes in *Final Analysis* (77). One can imagine Schiffer chortling in delight over this description. In *Charisma*, he calls the birth control pill the psychological equivalent to "hormonal plastic surgery on the vital organs of the individual who uses this chemical," adding that the sexually alienated find themselves "'making love to the pill' like fornicating with an effigy or a knothole in a fence" (137–8).

Second, if Schiffer made this vile assertion, why does Masson repeat it in *Final Analysis*? Didn't he realize that his wife, from whom he was divorced when *Final Analysis* appeared, would likely be mortified? Masson states in the Preface that he was uncertain whether he had the right to invade the privacy of those who were close to him, but he rationalizes his decision with the claim that there was no other way to write truthfully. And yet the pursuit of truth does not require repeating vicious statements that are bound to hurt loved ones. Masson informs us in the Preface that his parents and ex-wife read *Final Analysis* in manuscript and didn't ask him to delete any passages, but it's hard to believe that the publication of the book did not distress them.

Masson convinced himself that he was writing truthfully and courageously about his life, but readers of *Final Analysis* may think otherwise. He comes across, here and elsewhere in his memoir, as a writer intent on settling scores—motivation of which he seems unaware. Wounded by others, he strikes back. Revenge appears to be a key motive behind his storytelling. Discretion may not always be the better part of valor, but the art of self-disclosure lies in knowing what to include and exclude from a story.

Patients can write about their therapists, but the latter cannot write about the former unless patients waive confidentiality. Masson signed a waiver allowing Schiffer to give his side of the story, which appeared in Philip Marchand's article in the *Toronto Star* in 1993. The seventy-six-year-old psychoanalyst vigorously denied all of Masson's charges except for two, admitting that he was occasionally late to sessions and used "salty language," once calling his patient a "goddamn f_____ liar." The rest of *Final Analysis* was a distortion, in Schiffer's view. "I know Masson better than Masson knows himself." Marchand's readers don't know whom to believe, though Schiffer's response to the journalist's question—"But why would Masson invent such stories?"—is surely curious:

> "I wish I had the freedom to tell you why he's doing this," Schiffer says. "But if I told you it would detract from my own book. Because I think I'm going to have a bestseller, by the way." The book Schiffer is working on, from what I can gather, is on the psychology of pathological deceit.

Apart from the fact that Schiffer never wrote the book, or at least never had it published, one can only conclude from this statement that he was as grandiloquent as Masson, each competing with the other over who was the more popular writer. Ironically, Schiffer's contempt for his own profession matched Masson's. "As a group, we stink to high heaven," Schiffer confided to Marchand. "Quote me. Let's face it, we all come into the specialty having some kind of mental axe to grind. We all obviously had some kind of psychological hang-ups." I don't know whether Schiffer rued these words, but his statements to the journalist appear as reckless and reductive as his patient's in *Final Analysis*. In a 1993 article in *New York* magazine, Dinitia Smith refers to a public debate on the Canadian television program *Fifth Estate* (which I have not been able to locate) in which Schiffer turned to Masson and opined, "Let's put it this way. You would mount any woman that moved" (40). Each man engaged in the character assassination of the other.

Narcissistic Personality Disorder

"I never did get a diagnosis from Schiffer that related to me," Masson says, noncommittedly, "but I suppose he thought I was suffering from a narcissistic personality disorder" (41), an example, we cannot help thinking, of the pot calling the kettle black. Of the two, Schiffer appears the more narcissistic in *Final Analysis*, particularly when he shouts repeatedly, "You have to be more like me" (39). Schiffer's narcissism may eclipse Masson's, but *Final Analysis* is itself a highly narcissistic memoir, self-referential, self-serving, and self-righteous.

It's always risky to engage in armchair diagnosis, but there is much evidence in *Final Analysis* to suggest that Masson exhibits the symptoms of narcissistic personality disorder as defined in the *Diagnostic and Statistical Manual of Mental Disorders* (*DSM-IV-TR*): (1) a grandiose sense of self-importance, (2) a preoccupation with fantasies of unlimited success, (3) a belief in being special, understood only by other high-status people, (4) a need for excessive admiration, (5) a sense of entitlement, (6) an interpersonal exploitativeness, (7) a lack of empathy, (8) an envy of others, (9) and an arrogant, haughty behavior toward others. Five or more of the above symptoms must be present for a diagnosis of narcissistic personality disorder; in Masson's case, *all* nine are present.

The most striking of these symptoms in *Final Analysis* is grandiosity. Most scholars would like to believe that their scholarship will contribute to the world's knowledge and benefit humankind, but Masson remains convinced that he alone sees the truth—and that *Final Analysis* will expose psychoanalysis as nothing more than a cult or a hoax. *Final Analysis* will thus be the death knell of the talking cure. To change metaphors, he believes that he alone has discovered that the wellspring of psychoanalysis is empty. The other striking symptom in *Final Analysis* is lack of empathy. There is never a moment in his account of working with patients when Masson feels any compassion for their suffering. "So much of what I said came from my head, not from my heart" (147). A female patient accuses Masson of not feeling "any genuine empathy, even sympathy" (146), a judgment with which he never disagrees. Additionally, Masson's all-or-nothing temperament suggests an essential dynamic of "borderline" patients. All of his idealizations—particularly of the academic and psychoanalytic worlds—end in virulent devaluations. He feels, for example, "complete contempt for lesser minds who criticized Freud without having any of his gifts" (121), which is to say, he feels disdain for nearly everyone. He ultimately rejects Freud, too.

Ironically, although Masson feels only contempt for the two leading psychoanalytic theorists, Heinz Kohut and Otto Kernberg, rejecting the former as a "total narcissist," "awful beyond words" (131), and the latter as a man who "writes horribly, and far too much" (120), their insights cast much light on the psychological dynamics of *Final Analysis*. Kernberg's description of pathological narcissism appears especially true of Masson's story:

> These patients present an unusual degree of self-reference in their interactions with other people, a great need to be loved and admired by others, and a curious apparent contradiction between a very inflated concept of themselves and an inordinate need for tribute from others. Their emotional life is shallow. They experience little empathy for the feeling of others, they obtain very little enjoyment from life other than from the tributes they receive from others or from their own grandiose fantasies, and they feel restless and bored when external glitter wears off and no new sources feed their self-regard. (227)

"Have you been faithful to your wife?" (5). Masson opens *Final Analysis* with this blunt question, which a training and supervising analyst with the Toronto Psychoanalytic Institute asked him during an interview. The question strikes Masson—and us—as inappropriate and would now be illegal if asked of a job candidate in the United States. Married only for a brief period of time when he applied for psychoanalytic training, Masson admits that he was already struggling with "monogamy," a word he prefers to "faithful." He never answers the question, but he cannot avoid it entirely in the memoir, though he does his best to sugarcoat the truth.

Whatever word we use to describe Masson's behavior—his struggle with monogamy or his lack of faithfulness—the issue comes up repeatedly in his analysis. Schiffer uses a harsher word to describe his analysand's sexual behavior. The most striking presenting symptom of Masson's pathology, according to Schiffer, is his "promiscuity." Masson doesn't disagree, but he remains uncertain whether to pathologize the problem. Sometimes he characterizes his behavior, euphemistically, as revealing his "insatiable love for women"; he found his "common humanity" in sexuality" (37). Yet he also acknowledges the compulsive nature of his sexual behavior. "I had to do it over and over" (37). He cannot see an attractive woman without trying to pick her up. "Not only was this bad for Terri and for our marriage, it was also bad for me" (73).

Masson enters analysis with the hope that it will free him from his promiscuous urges. The problem remains, however, even after he terminates analysis and becomes a psychoanalyst himself. Nowhere does Masson refer to himself as suffering from a "Don Juan" complex, male hypersexuality, yet he never believes, even at the end of his analysis, that he is free from his promiscuous urges, a word that he sometimes uses without quotation marks (76). To soften the word, and thus the confession, he places this urge within other more acceptable ones. "I longed for adventure, sexual, intellectual, or even emotional" (76).

Schiffer conjectures that Masson's problem, or character disorder, arose from having a father who was himself a womanizer. Masson begrudgingly admits this in the following paragraph, implying a problem without a solution:

> "I suppose my difficulty around fidelity has to do with wanting to imitate my father," I would say. "He was never faithful, and claims that his father hadn't been either. It's in our blood, he says. There is nothing in life as wonderful as a beautiful woman, and when you see such a woman, it is only natural to want to go to bed with her. If this is a disease, then I will be sick for the rest of my life, just as he is. There is nothing for it. Marital deception is the only decent thing to do. I must have lovers as he had (he called them mistresses) and never let my wife know. But I want very much to get away from this model." (38)

Schiffer has much to say in *Charisma* about the "charismatic sexual mystique," and we can only wonder whether he was thinking of analysands like Masson:

> The image says, "I'm really not all that sure of myself . . . please, I need your help. . . . I'm as unproven as a virgin . . . winner though I am, I'm just a shy guy when it comes to sex!" How can we hold in regard such a figure of fumbling stupidity, especially now that we've arrived at an era of a full sexual enlightenment? (43-4; ellipses in original)

My Father's Guru

Masson's 1992 book *My Father's Guru* contains intriguing biographical information about the possible sources of his promiscuity, details that are only hinted at or ignored in *Final Analysis*. Of particular importance is Masson's paternal grandfather, Henri, who changed the family name from Moussaieff to Masson. "I was told that he seduced every girl and woman around him whether they were eight or fifty-eight. Nor did he exempt his own family" (6). A "menacing aura of sexuality" surrounded Henri Masson, we learn a few pages later. "He openly lusted after his daughters and was not opposed to using his own sons for his sexual pleasures either" (20). It is a startling accusation. Masson doesn't mention these details in *Final Analysis*, but almost certainly they figured into his analysis with Schiffer. One can only guess how Henri Masson's behavior affected both his son and grandson. Masson remarks cryptically in *My Father's Guru* how his paternal relatives were "oversexed" (104), adding that sexuality was his father's "demon" (109). And apparently his own as well.

Masson remains silent in *Final Analysis* about his mother's role in his promiscuity, but he offers a few clues in *My Father's Guru*. He recalls how his entire family would bathe together regularly, though he cannot recollect anything sexual about it. "Even as an adolescent I can remember bathing with my mother, possibly until I was sixteen. The family was considered special and therefore exempt from ordinary rules" (63). These details do not appear in *Final Analysis*, though they may help to explain his voracious desire for women. Noting the sexually charged atmosphere of his family life and that sexuality and purification were "fused in a dance of denial," he observes that his mother insisted that he and his sister take enemas given by her until he was an adolescent. "My sister flatly said no. I went along" (64). He also tells us in *My Father's Guru* about being sexually aroused, as an eight-year-old boy, by a seductive aspiring actress named Martha who lived with his family (and who had sex with his father). He cannot recall explicitly what happened with Martha, though he now would consider it "unmistakably sexual exploitation" (42). He admits to becoming obsessed with sex when he was in college. "I saw it everywhere. I wanted it. I thought about it all the time. No woman seemed safe from my predations. I look back at it with horror. I had absolutely no understanding of what I was doing" (152).

Memoirists are not required to disclose intimate facts like these, but it's puzzling that Masson fails to include this information in *Final Analysis*. He was, after all, a psychoanalyst who was trying to understand his problematic sexual behavior. Was he too embarrassed to include these details in *Final Analysis* or saving the material for his next book? What other noteworthy details does he exclude from *Final Analysis*? Ironically, Masson refers to himself in the Introduction to *My Father's Guru* as "destined to become a debunker" (xv), having demythologized psychoanalysis, but his experience with Martha reveals the challenge of separating reality from fantasy, the same problem Freud confronted with his seduction theory. According to Philip Marchand, Masson's parents gave their "cautious approval" to their son's assertions in *My Father's Guru*, though his mother maintained that his comments about Martha were "absolutely not true." His father denied that he was a womanizer.

Masson was engaged, briefly, to Catharine MacKinnon, the American radical feminist and legal scholar who was among the first to argue that pornography is a civil rights violation. Was it under MacKinnon's influence that Masson became, for a time, a feminist? In a brief sentence that contradicts nearly everything he tells us about his sex life in *Final Analysis*, he states in *The Assault on Truth* that seduction "is a form of hatred, not love" (149). What would have happened, we wonder, if Schiffer made the same observation?

Janet Malcolm

Confidentiality prevented Schiffer from writing about Masson's promiscuity, but Janet Malcolm had no such restriction. *In the Freud Archives* contains one of the most damning portraits of a libidinous psychoanalyst. Had Masson read Malcolm's *Psychoanalysis: The Impossible Profession* (1981), published three years before *In the Freud Archives*, he might have declined her request for an interview. But given his hunger for fame, Masson figured that the attention was worth the risk. One suspects that he preferred negative attention to no attention.

In her acknowledgments in the 1981 book, Malcolm, the daughter of a psychiatrist, expresses gratitude to "Aaron Green," the forty-six-year-old Manhattan psychoanalyst whom she interviewed, for being a "remarkable and lovable man who opened his mind and heart to me and gave this book its life." Notwithstanding these laudatory words, the graduate of the New York Psychoanalytic Institute comes across as abrasive, snobbish, self-absorbed, insecure, envious, and narrow-minded. Malcolm has the ability to elicit her biographical subject's dangerous disclosures and then watch as he is hoist by his own petard. Many of her questions to Green are disingenuous, as when she expresses surprise about analysts who are "supposed to be wiser and more reflective than the rest of us." Her feigned innocence succeeds in evoking Green's self-flagellating confessions. On another occasion, Malcolm admits that she resented always listening to Green and never talking about himself, which prompts the following reply: "'There it is,' Aaron said, with an ironic gesture of his hand" (114). He proceeds to vent his professional frustrations and disappointments—albeit not to the extent of listing his honor-roll of classic bores, as Schiffer does.

Masson's promiscuity is perhaps the single most striking detail in Malcolm's exposé. "I knew there was something wrong," he recklessly confides to her, "I'd slept with close to a thousand women by the time I got to Toronto" (*In the Freud Archives* 39). But it's Masson's grandiosity that is most startling. In her November 1982 interview with Masson, which he gave while he was writing *The Assault on Truth*, he boasts that "when my book comes out there is not a patient in analysis who will not go to his analyst with the book in hand and say, 'Why didn't you tell me this? What the hell is going on? I want an explanation'" (*In the Freud Archives* 14). *The Assault on Truth*, he continues breathlessly a few pages later, will be "dynamite" to the psychoanalytic community. "They sensed that I could single-handedly bring down the whole business—and, let's face it, there's a lot of money in that business" (35). Sounding almost like Schiffer, whom he refers to as "Dr. V.," Masson dismisses all psychoanalysts as "terribly dull people," adding that if he had met Freud, "I would have found him dull, too, after a while" (42).

Malcolm's portrait accentuates Masson's egotism and overweening arrogance, his penchant for extravagant hyperbole, his narcissistic longing for success, and his betrayal of those who formerly befriended him. She cites the psychoanalyst Leonard Shengold's characterization of Masson as someone who "seemed to be courting the favor of anyone who could do anything for him" (83). At the end of *In the Freud Archives*, Malcolm quotes one of the few women who did *not* sleep with Masson, Wendy O'Flaherty, a professor of divinity at the University of Chicago and a fellow Sanskrit scholar: "He's full of self-hate of a very complicated kind" (157). Masson cites O'Flaherty in *My Father's Guru*, misspelling her maiden name and failing to mention her belief that he is a sexual predator.

After quoting Masson's self-excoriating words, Malcolm makes sure that we know his state of mind while uttering them, as when he predicts the impact of *The Assault on Truth*. "'Wait till it reaches the best-seller list, and watch how the analysts will crawl,' he crowed" (162). Masson misses Malcolm's barbed irony, as when she tells him, "You have, as they say, decathected from analysis," which occasions Masson's naïve reply, "I was a fool then" (160), not realizing that he should use the present tense.

Malcolm never acknowledges how she had ingratiated herself with Masson to extract his confessions. As Robert S. Boynton reported in *The Village Voice* in 1994, she interviewed Masson first in Berkeley, where he was living at the time, and then in her townhouse in New York City, where he and his girlfriend stayed with her for four days. Before her first article appeared in *The New Yorker*, she sent him a letter with the words, "I think you'll love it."

He didn't. Instead, Masson filed a $13 million lawsuit in California against Malcolm and *The New Yorker*, alleging that she had fabricated five quotations, including, most notoriously, his statement calling himself an "intellectual gigolo" (*In the Freud Archives* 38). The first trial ended in deadlock because the jury could not agree on damages. The case then went to the Court of Appeals, which ruled in favor of Malcolm with one judge dissenting. Masson appealed, and the US Supreme Court agreed to hear the case. In 1991, Justice Anthony Kennedy delivered the opinion of the Court, which concluded that there was enough evidence to support a finding of deliberate and reckless falsification. Kennedy's opinion contains excerpts from Malcolm's more than forty hours of taped interviews that do not appear in her book, including the following revealing exchange:

Masson: ". . . analysis stands or falls with me now."
Malcolm: "Well that's a very grandiose thing to say"
Masson: "Yeah, but it's got nothing to do with me. It's got to do with the things I discovered."

The lawsuit was then retried in the federal district court. The case ended in 1994 when the jury concluded that although one of the quoted passages was defamatory, Malcolm did not act with a reckless disregard of the truth. David Margolick observed wryly in the *New York Times* that the Masson-Malcolm lawsuit took the same length of time, ten years, that it took Freud to formulate the basics of psychoanalytic theory.

Subsequently, Malcolm elevated the journalist's bad faith into both a personal credo and a universal truth. The opening paragraph of *The Journalist and the Murderer* (1990) reveals Malcolm's belief that the journalist is a confidence man, "preying on people's vanity, ignorance, or loneliness, gaining their trust and betraying them without remorse" (3). Malcolm was not directly referring to Masson, but readers will see how her relationship with him forms the subtext of *The Journalist and the Murderer*. Betrayal remains central to Malcolm's notion of journalistic ethics. Masson and Malcolm became the *enfants terribles* of their respective professions, psychoanalysis, and journalism.

As Boynton perceptively notes, although Masson never refers to Malcolm in either *Final Analysis* or *My Father's Guru*, her ghostly presence appears in both memoirs as he tries to justify the accuracy of his memory. In the same way, Masson is a spectral presence, a revenant, in Malcolm's *The Journalist and the Murderer*. She never refers to Masson by name in the two *New Yorker* articles in which *The Journalist and the Murderer* originally appeared, but he shows up in the book's Afterword. Echoing Flaubert's "*Madame Bovary, c'est moi*," Malcolm proclaims, "*Masson, c'est moi*" (149). Malcolm died in 2021 at age eighty-six. In her *New York Times* obituary, Katharine Q. Seelye cites Robert S. Boynton's warning in 1992: "Don't ever eat in front of Janet Malcolm; or show her your apartment; or cut tomatoes while she watches. In fact, it probably isn't a good idea even to grant her an interview, as your every unflattering gesture and nervous tic will be recorded eventually with devastating precision."

Masson's early faith in psychoanalysis proved to be an abysmal failure, he concedes early in *Final Analysis*, despite (or perhaps because of) his unreasonable expectations. "To paraphrase Rilke," he sadly admits, "I was sure that psychoanalysis would be the pickax that would free the seas frozen from within" (12). No matter that it was Kafka, not Rilke, who expressed this idea. The factual error, however, exposes the unreliability of Masson's memory, once again calling into question the accuracy of his story. There are other factual errors, as when he refers to "Ralph [instead of Wilfred] Bion" (118).

Final Analysis might be more aptly titled "Partial Analysis" for Masson never confronts the reasons behind his assault of psychoanalysis. How can he claim to understand Freud's motivation when he fails to understand his own? As the psychiatrist James S. Gordon points out in a review of *Final Analysis* in *The Washington Post*, unexamined narcissism pervades the second half of the book. Michael Sacks ends his review of *Final Analysis* by saying that Masson deserves the courtesy of being heard even though he doesn't grant this courtesy to others. And Sophie Freud concludes in a review of *Final Analysis*, *Against Therapy*, and *The Assault on Truth* that although she agrees with many of Masson's criticisms of psychoanalysis, she finds his indignation unconvincing, perhaps because she remains unconvinced of the authenticity of his emotions.

Final Analysis is Masson's psychoanalytic swan song. He has turned his back on his former profession without any regret, as he announces in *Slipping into Paradise*

(2004), an account of his new life in his adopted home, New Zealand. "The vast number of psychoanalytic books published each year add zero to the sum of knowledge. They are a waste of paper and should never have been published" (31). Including, apparently, his own.

Masson remains a prolific author. His popular 1995 book *When Elephants Weep* explores the emotions of our fellow species. A poor Menschenkenner, judge of character, Masson appears to understand animals better than people. An ardent animal rights advocate, he has moved in an entirely different direction from his background or training, reinventing himself, like Gatsby, searching for the green light of success. *The Assault on Truth* never made it to the *New York Times* bestselling list, but his new books have. Fitzgerald famously said that there are no second acts in American lives, but Masson has disproved the novelist's words. The apostasy-prone Masson has finally found his true calling, and, as he hoped at the beginning of his career, he is now in demand everywhere.

Chapter 10

F. ROBERT RODMAN
NOT DYING

I've come across this book while googling Dr. Rodman's name. He had been my psychoanalyst for almost five years in the mid '90s. Prior to reading it, I had known almost nothing about him beyond the transference that happens in the context of therapist-patient exchanges. Yet, what I discovered confirmed the private man behind the therapist role: a man of great intelligence and integrity, of great devotion and strength who has the ability to explore a complex, agonizing life situation with courage, complexity, humanity and inner poetry.

Stefania Magidson

I found the above comment while I was ordering on Amazon a copy of Robert Rodman's *Not Dying: A Psychoanalyst's Memoir of His Wife's Death*, published in 1977. My reaction to the story is the same as Magidson's, the founder and president of the Blue Heron Foundation, a nonprofit organization dedicated to helping abandoned Romanian children. Despite its title, *Not Dying* is a profound study of dying and death. Gripping from beginning to end, the memoir offers a piercing taxonomy of grief. Rodman writes with brutal honesty about a time in his life that forced him to challenge all of his beliefs, including the value of life itself. It was highly unusual in the 1970s for a psychoanalyst to write about caregiving and personal loss—it *still* is unusual. That the memoirist was an intensely private man, uncomfortable with public self-disclosure, makes the memoir more remarkable. Writing about disaster reveals, as Maurice Blanchot observes, the "limits of writing" because disaster "de-scribes" (7). Nowhere is this better seen than in a spousal loss memoir, which requires the memoirist to express the inexpressible.

Born in Boston in 1934, Rodman graduated from Harvard and Boston University Medical School and then moved to California, where he became a psychiatric resident at UCLA and completed his training at the Los Angeles Psychoanalytic Institute. Throughout his career, he had a private practice in Beverly Hills. He died in 2004 from a cerebral hemorrhage following heart surgery. Rodman is perhaps best known for *The Spontaneous Gesture*, a volume of D.W. Winnicott's letters, published in 1987, and for his acclaimed biography, *Winnicott:*

Life and Work (2003), which, according to Brett Kahr, who had written an earlier biography of the British analyst, took nearly twenty years to complete. Rodman also authored *Keeping Hope Alive: On Becoming a Psychoanalyst* (1986), a book that, strangely enough, fails to mention any of the events that he wrote about in *Not Dying*, another example, as we shall see, of his fierce privacy.

Rodman met his Swedish-born wife, Maria, two years his junior, in California in the early 1960s. Within a few years they married and had two daughters, Ingrid and Simone, to whom *Not Dying* is dedicated. (One of the reasons Rodman chose to remain alive after his wife's death was to care for their children.) When Maria was thirty-eight, she began suffering from abdominal pain, and in March 1974, she had a double hysterectomy. The pathologist determined at the time that she did not have cancer, but when her discomfort continued after surgery, developing into a persistent cough, the pathologist reexamined the same slides and admitted that he had made a mistake. Only near the end of the story, when her physician felt a large mass in her upper abdomen, do we learn that the cancer probably originated in her stomach and then had quickly spread to her ovaries and lungs. It's unclear whether an accurate early diagnosis would have prevented Maria's death, but the misdiagnosis only confirmed Rodman's strong anti-physician bias. Rodman did not suffer fools gladly, and one of the surprises in the story is how combative and argumentative he was to other physicians who, in his judgment, often lack expertise or humanity. "We had tried to find good doctors," he tells us early in the story, "and we had come up with technicians or careless slobs" (40), a judgment that rarely changes. Only a few physicians earn his gratitude.

We learn on the first page of the memoir that having moved to California from Boston, Rodman missed the "vast range of moods" associated with the Northeast. He's referring to the absence of seasons in southern California, but throughout the story he captures the vast range of emotional moods associated with dying and death, for both the caregiver and care-receiver. Cancer fills him with dread; a year-and-a-half earlier, his sister-in-law had died of pancreatic cancer.

Not Dying is wrenching to read, and it must have been no less wrenching to write. Curiously, Rodman explores nearly every aspect of dying and death except the motivation behind writing a book on the subject. The memoir chronicles his stygian odyssey when he was in the prime of life, happily married, with two young children, and fulfilled in his career, to a time, in less than a year, when he feels devastated and bereft. Menace lurks throughout the memoir, and *Not Dying* is scarier to read than the most frightening Gothic horror. Writing about the death of one's spouse feels like writhing. Readers are bound to be moved deeply by Rodman's story, especially if they have similarly lost a loved one to cancer. (In writing this chapter, I kept typing *On Dying*.)

Rodman tortures himself for emotions that he cannot help feeling despite a successful training analysis that one might have expected would be helpful in dealing with the terrifying experience. He judges himself guilty of a litany of crimes including selfishness, self-pity, and self-absorption—in short, guilty of being a human being. He fears that he has somehow caused his wife's cancer. He finds himself preoccupied with suicidal thoughts and fantasies, imagining himself holding a gun to his head and firing when he cannot endure more suffering. Rodman's guilt increases because he doesn't immediately tell Maria that she has cancer. When asked by her physician whether she would want to know that she has a life-threatening illness, she responds, "I don't know," an ambiguity that only increases Rodman's dilemma of when and how to tell her.

Rodman discovers Ivan Ilych's epiphanic insight in Tolstoy's iconic story of human mortality: the truth is painful, but concealing the truth is more painful. Withholding the truth from Maria calls into question Rodman's integrity as both husband and physician. Maria's physician finally informs her of the truth, but Rodman's daughters, nine and eleven, aren't told that their mother has cancer until shortly before her death. Cancer may not be as stigmatized now as it was a half century ago, but readers can understand Rodman's conundrum. (A century ago, it was routine for doctors not to tell their patients they were dying.) If it's difficult for a physician to express this truth, how much more challenging is it for a non-physician?

Hearing the dire truth of her situation on July 10, 1974, Maria responds simply and eloquently, "I want to live" (106), at which point Rodman begins to weep. His attitude toward crying changes in the story. In the beginning, perhaps as result of his professional training, he associates tears with weakness, immaturity, and selfishness, but he learns to view crying as a natural and healthy response to loss. He continues to doubt, however, the sincerity of his tears. Desiring emotional purity, crying for Maria's sake alone rather than for his own as well, he has trouble recognizing that self and other are inextricably related. How can we separate selfishness from selflessness in a world where ambivalence is the norm?

Ten days after learning her diagnosis, Maria and her family fly to Sweden to be with her relatives. She is never well enough to return home. Desperate for any treatment, conventional or otherwise, they fly to Hannover, Germany, where they meet with a fast-talking physician, more of a salesman than a healer, who prescribes a bewildering potpourri of vitamins and supplements. This is in addition to the two different chemotherapies prescribed by her American oncologist, one of which is 5-FU, which Rodman calls sardonically "5-Fuck You." Nothing helps, though, and as Maria grows weaker, her husband becomes more disabled by guilt.

Survivor Guilt

Throughout *Not Dying*, Rodman flagellates himself with survivor guilt. Popularized in the 1960s, the term describes a person who feels guilty surviving a tragic event where others have perished. Survivor guilt has both psychological and existential implications. Freud theorized in "Mourning and Melancholia" (1917) that aggression becomes internalized during both bereavement and depression. The idea of murderous feelings turned against the self may be seen in a revealing exchange of letters between Ernest Jones and Freud in late 1928, a time when both men had suffered grievous losses, Jones, the death of a young daughter, Freud, the deaths of his daughter Sophie and her son Heinz, the latter loss prompting Freud to declare that he became "tired of life permanently" (Paskauskas 643). Jones suggests that the withdrawal from a dying person is tantamount to murder. "We know in this connection the guilt that often follows, the searchings of heart, self-reproach and other more indirect consequences of guilt." Jones can now see this clearly, he adds, because his attitude toward his daughter was a "purer, non-ambivalent love" than in any other of his experiences. According to this view, mourning the dead involves not only betrayal but symbolic murder, resulting in overwhelming guilt that impedes the mourning process. Freud largely agrees, wondering why the withdrawal of libido is so painful:

> I envisaged that, in each individual case, one then has the choice of dying oneself or of acknowledging the death of the loved one, which again comes very close to your expression that one kills this person. I should not like to link guilt feelings with mourning; I believe that this appears only when ambivalence or some hostility was actually present. But here too I have not got the last word or a definitive insight. (Paskauskas 651–3)

Rodman's survivor guilt over his wife's impending death is complicated by growing up with a chronically depressed mother. His early childhood was dominated by the shadow of his brother, who died of peritonitis at the age of three, a few months before Rodman was conceived. "I had been inordinately cherished and protected but at the same time suffused with the contradictory sense that I alone was not enough to cure my mother's depression" (26). Consequently, Rodman became a "model child" for his mother, but behind his compliance was a "mixture of resentment and weakness" (23), feelings that return decades later during his wife's illness. Oddly, in his discussion of his childhood in *Keeping Hope Alive*, Rodman describes his brother's death occurring not a few months *before* his conception but *during* her pregnancy (16). The conflicting information may be a simple act of misremembering—the two books were published nine years apart. Nevertheless, if the details in *Not Dying* are accurate, Rodman was deliberately conceived as a "replacement child" or a "substitute child," terms first used by Albert C. Cain and Barbara S. Cain in 1964 to describe a child conceived shortly after parents have lost another child. Vincent van Gogh, Salvador Dali, and F. Scott Fitzgerald are famous examples of replacement children. Parents' guilt and grief over the lost child may interfere with their parenting of the new child—who may feel unable to lift one or both parents' depression. Rodman never uses the words "replacement child" or "substitute child," but he acknowledges the intense ambivalence of a child who is burdened by the task of cheering up a depressed mother still preoccupied with a lost child. Maria's depression over terminal cancer reawakens his feelings over his mother's chronic depression throughout his childhood.

Rodman's psychoanalytic training allows him to understand how the present often repeats the past. He offers one example of how a seemingly innocent gesture may have disturbing consequences. While he was visiting a patient years earlier who was hospitalized for treatment of bladder cancer, she asked him for a kiss. Feeling "blackmailed," he kisses her on the forehead and then analyzes four of his subsequent dreams that all involved a link to his early childhood, when he would kiss his mother in an effort to cheer her up. "I had cured myself of a neurotic symptom through the psychoanalysis of dreams" (28). The insight that his sadness over Maria's illness is a repetition of his feelings toward his mother does not produce much relief. Indeed, neither his medical nor psychoanalytic training does much to improve his spirits.

The Impact of a Therapist's Illness on His Patients

Maria's illness has a far-reaching impact on Rodman's practice of psychoanalysis. The three chapters that describe this change are among the most fascinating in the memoir, particularly to mental health professionals, some of whom have commented on *Not Dying*—though none in detail.

Only one patient terminated treatment. The patient, an actor with "multiple perversions," appeared gleeful when Rodman informed him that Maria's illness required him to miss several sessions. Both analyst and analysand seemed to be reversing roles, and the latter, who decided to leave for another therapist, responded "like a carnivorous animal" (67). The other patients reacted more positively, albeit in different ways. Rodman does his best to describe how therapy changed, and we trust, narratively, his inferences of their reactions. We cannot be certain, however, that he is correctly interpreting his patients' reactions. He offers us one detailed "typical moment," conveying both his patient's and his own dialogue. It is the only time in the story where we may find ourselves analyzing the analyst, and for this reason the imagined dialogue deserves close scrutiny:

> Patient enters office, somewhat disheveled, silent, fearful. She has a marked Southern drawl. "Dr. Rodman, I'm afraid I can't talk to you very well. I'm sure you don't want to be here right now, what with whatever's going on in your life." Silence. "You're angry with me. I can see it. But I can't help it." Tears. Blowing her nose. "Maybe I should quit and find somebody else. Would you like me to quit?"
> Me: "I think you're feeling more and more like an intruder right now. You think that I'm furious that you would enter my life when I seem so preoccupied with personal matters. If you stay, you're afraid I'm going to destroy you with my remarks. Therefore you can't talk to me very much. You're throwing yourself on my mercy, hoping for a little kindness at least."
> Patient: "You don't like me, do you? The way you say things like that! What do you want from me?" (She's an inhibited woman of twenty-six, terrified of a lonely life, always secretive, never fulfilled. I have represented hope, mixed with terror.) (72–3)

Rodman's imagined dialogue between his patient and himself bespeaks his vision of not only psychoanalysis but also human nature. Later in *Not Dying*, he characterizes the broad spectrum of psychoanalysis, ranging from the pessimistic belief that human nature is fundamentally envious and destructive to the optimistic belief that human nature is well-meaning and good. He doesn't name analysts, but presumably the former, the "far right" view, represents Melanie Klein and her followers, while the latter, the "far left" view, represents Heinz Kohut and self psychology. Rodman places himself in the "great Freudian middle ground, with its breadth and its capacity for change" (193).

In his imagined dialogue, Rodman appears to take a Kleinian view of nature. He admits that he reacts "with frustration" to his patient's words, trying to restrain his feeling that she is "wallowing in ambiguous mixtures of truth and untruth." Her masochism, he points out, evokes his corresponding sadism. He believes that she wants him to assault her, to destroy her, like an angry, voracious child; she is, moreover, horrified by her repressed wish for such an outcome. His words, he adds, invariably support her accusations (73).

Even if Rodman is correct in his interpretation of his patient, what would have happened if he had spoken differently to her, the way a Kohutian analyst might speak? We can only conjecture because he doesn't return to her. What if he expressed a different truth? Suppose he conveyed the kindness and reassurance for which she was obviously looking? Rodman believed, as he observes in his biography of Winnicott, that Kohut "gave short shrift to the aggressive element intrinsic to mental life" (110). Nevertheless, Rodman could have said truthfully, as Irvin Yalom, immediately following his wife's death, tells his patient in *A Matter of Death and Life* that he was happy to be with her during this punishing time, grateful for the opportunity to continue working with her. Work can be a lifeline in a time of stress, and therapists often experience therapeutic relief themselves while working with patients. Rodman would not need to tell her that he was a wounded healer, to use Jung's term, but he could say that helping his patients is a way of helping himself.

Rodman is more empathic with his other patients. One woman, he admits, became a "sort of therapist" for him, and he changed his approach, becoming more open and candid, "entering a new territory" (77). She was the only patient to whom he told the truth of what was going on in his life. For the first time he functioned in a "bilaterally truthful atmosphere" (78). Showing his human side was helpful to her, and each became grateful for the other's sympathy and understanding. Rodman wrote *Not Dying* before "two-person psychology" became acceptable in psychoanalysis, and though he worries that his self-disclosures would not be classified as "psychoanalysis in the strictest sense" (75), I suspect that many contemporary analysts would approve of his new approach, viewing him as innovative and pioneering.

Therapist self-disclosure is now more popular than it was half a century ago. Although there is not an abundance of research literature on the impact of an analyst's loss on patients, the articles published in professional journals often cite, approvingly, *Not Dying*. Most of these therapists write personally about their own losses, offering clinical vignettes examining the impact of careful self-disclosures on their patients. In a 1981 article published in *Psychiatry*, Frances Givelber and Bennett Simon acknowledge the difficulties of practicing psychotherapy after a loss but affirm the value of self-disclosure on their patients. In a 1985 article published in *Modern Psychoanalysis*, Rhoda Shapiro identifies with Rodman's experience, though she does not disclose to her patients the recent death of her mother. "My self-involvement, along with the feelings induced by the patient's rage, had produced a negative narcissistic countertransference resistance" (36). Why, after sympathizing with Rodman's approach, does Shapiro continue to remain silent about her loss? In a 2011 article appearing in *The Psychoanalytic Quarterly*, Michelle Flax agrees with Rodman that an analyst's personal loss affects therapy. She discloses only a few details of her daughter's brain tumor and subsequent seizures to her patient, Sue. To deal with her own trauma, Flax brings her young dog, Billie, to her analytic office. Noting that dogs have a long history of being in the consulting room, beginning with Freud and his succession of chows, Flax discusses how she is comforted by Billie's presence. Allowing Sue to walk Billie has a positive impact, signifying a reciprocity of caring. Writing a professional article enables Flax to understand her own mourning process: "Indeed, the writing of this paper has been an important factor in my reworking painful aspects of this period—the writing being itself a holding process" (331).

Rodman never confronts directly his need to write, but this remains one of the major questions in therapist memoirs, in general, and in *Not Dying*, in particular. Why write such an excruciating story? There are several reasons. Rodman pens several long letters to his brother, Saul, and his friend, Oliver, describing his fraught emotions. He may have anticipated that these letters would become an essential part of the story, a record of how he was feeling day to day. Writing captures details that might otherwise be forgotten. Writing heightens Rodman's connection to the outside world, helping him remain attached to life amidst the onslaught of death. "I find that I am fearful of leaving the typewriter, of returning to that awful stalking aloneness" (87). Oliver reminds him in a letter that he "*must* disburden" himself (84), which suggests another reason to write; expressing the inexpressible is part of both the talking cure and the writing cure. Writing is not only a form of venting but also purging, as in Rodman's expression, a "terrible urge to get it over with, write it off" (111). Freud made a similar observation about writing, as Joan Riviere reports. "He said: 'Write it, write it, put it down in black and white; that's the way to deal with it; you get it out of your system'" (146).

Rodman offers other reasons to write. Seeing his own words on the page enables him to accept the unacceptable. "I am beginning to commend her into the arms of death," he confesses to Oliver, "and I can hardly believe that I can write this" (90). Writing has an unexpected benefit, lifting his mood, like alcohol (which he finds himself consuming to excess), but without any of the harmful consequences of alcohol abuse. "[I]n the writing of the letter there is the same mania as is provided by alcohol, the same illusion of contact, of ability to verbalize, of being able to type, of being able to function"—the illusion of completeness (93). The illusion is real, not imaginary, an illusion that makes possible the future. Writing is Rodman's weapon against hopelessness. There's only one moment when he hints that Maria resented his writing: "my letter writing drew me away into other relationships from which she was excluded" (107).

One doesn't usually identify aesthetic motivation behind the need to write about dying and death, but this is part of the somber pleasure of writing—including authoring a spousal loss memoir like *Not Dying*. Rodman raises a seemingly trivial question that may be more noteworthy than he realizes. In typing a sentence filled with hyphens—clinging to an "all-but-vanished hope"—he asks, "how can I be concerned with punctuation when my wife is dying of cancer?" (83). The answer lies in the satisfaction of crafting powerful prose. Rodman is a fine stylist, and many of his sentences are arresting, as when he describes his wife near the end of her life: "She was shrinking back to her origins" (185). Or when he characterizes himself as "adrift on a raft breaking up in mid-ocean, radioless, parched, nearly ready for the sharks" (103). He avoids platitudes and psychologisms, and he wisely refuses to give us pat explanations of his story, as when he observes that "everyone has felt they have been taught a lesson, the nature of which is obscure" (182). It was a lesson he felt sharing with his readers after Maria's death. "It was a glorious comfort," he observes in the epilogue to the paperback edition of *Not Dying*, "to concentrate each day on writing."

Rodman is a reader as well as a writer, and his literary references bespeak his identification with fictional characters, as when, trying to find the office of a cancer specialist, he feels like a Dostoevsky character, "setting out to correct the innumerable deficiencies in his life against the backdrop of the State, hopelessly pitted against its iron will and the natural rhythms of human life" (61). His efforts to compartmentalize his life, sealing off his grief, remind him of Marianne Moore's poetry, where her use of brackets, like a picture frame, resembles the brackets of a therapy session. He reads poetry for its power to comfort and console, allowing him to feel whole again. He appends at the end of the memoir five of his own poems, memorializing the first year's passage of his wife's death, along with a poem written by his daughter Ingrid. *Not Dying* begins with a poem by the Mexican poet and Nobel Laureate Octavio Paz that includes the lines "Saying is a paring way, / A pruning of the tree of the dead," a startling image that captures Rodman's devotion to elegiac art.

In the end, what most helps Rodman is the kindness of relatives and friends. He uses simple but forceful language, unburdened by theory, to convey the meaning of his experience, as when he cites his brother's observation that "one should not be afraid to live" (37), which also means that one should not be afraid to die. Maria gifts him with the hope for a future of which she will no longer be a part, telling him, "Why should you be unhappy, when I'm not?" (199). After Maria's death, he is comforted by her doctor's words: "Your wife is the bravest woman I have ever known, and you have done everything a man could do" (201). Maria's brother puts it this way: "Don't you know it's the same for everyone" (202).

Rodman asks an urgent question near the end of *Not Dying*, underscoring it for emphasis: "*How much contradiction could I stand?*" (194). How could he live with love and hate, past and present, life and death, desire and fear, without blinding or destroying himself? He might have cited F. Scott Fitzgerald's observation in *The Crack-Up*: "The test of a first-rate intelligence is the ability to hold two opposed ideas in the mind at the same time, and still retain the ability to function" (69).

Rodman passes the test. Perhaps the most cataclysmic moment in the memoir occurs when Rodman realizes that his attitude toward death has changed. "The horrible paradox was that while death was what was most feared, once it became an inevitability, it also became something I wanted to hurry to its work, so that it could go away" (107). The insight deepens his guilt while simultaneously providing much-needed relief.

Rodman never mentions his deceased wife in *Keeping Hope Alive*, but there is one passage in which he seems to be thinking about her. A former patient dying of cancer, Lisa returns to therapy, wearing a wig to conceal the baldness resulting from chemotherapy. Rodman was wary, he remarks to us cryptically, without being specific, of the "influence of experiences of loss" in his own life on the work of helping his patient. He never shares with Lisa any information about his wife's death, but in what turns out to be their last therapy session together, he was "stricken by the inevitability of this fine young woman's early death." While still observing analytic rules, he feels closer to her, more attuned to her feelings. She asks him, apparently for the first time, to call her by her first name, and as she leaves, he says, "I'll see you next week, Lisa" (134), a way, presumably, to keep hope alive for both of them.

Why doesn't Rodman remark, in *Keeping Hope Alive* or his subsequent publications, on the impact of his wife's death on his practice of psychoanalysis? We can only speculate. He may have felt that he had nothing to add to his comments in *Not Dying*. Perhaps he did not wish to revisit the bleakest time in his life. He dedicated *Keeping Hope Alive* to his new spouse, Katherine, and he may have felt that it would be a betrayal of their relationship by talking about his deceased first wife. One can infer this fear of betrayal from a disturbing question he raises in *Not Dying* at the thought of remarriage. "Would she not be reluctant to sit at the table or sleep in the house when her obvious competitor and standard would be in everyone's mind?" (134). At the end of his foreword to *Keeping Hope Alive*, Robert Coles mentions fleetingly the death of Rodman's "much loved young wife" (xix)—it's likely that Rodman felt nothing more was necessary to say.

Winnicott

Rodman's recognition of the significance of hope may have led him to write a biography of D.W. Winnicott, whom he regarded as the most influential psychoanalyst since Freud. "He cherishes hope as the fuel by which life may advance, the opposite of depression and discouragement, the antidote to loneliness" (*Winnicott* 244). Rodman extols Winnicott's many contributions to psychoanalysis, but he doesn't hesitate to criticize him for his faults, including his serious boundary violations, his grandiose belief that he was the best person to analyze certain patients, and his ethical lapses. Rodman's biography, Martha Nussbaum wrote in a glowing review in *The New Republic*, is "as balanced and insightful a portrait of the genesis of Winnicott's ideas as we are likely to have" (35). Many of Rodman's statements about Winnicott are true of Rodman himself. Both present themselves as real people, aiming to convey their "true self"; and both reveal a balance between the real and unreal aspects of life: the influence of people and the environment, on the one hand, and the dark, demonic elements of fantasy, on the other. Rodman's observation that Winnicott's fear of destructiveness originated from early contact with a depressed mother may also have been true of himself. Rodman uses two Winnicottian ideas in *Not Dying*: the "holding environment," the belief that the analyst, like the mother, can hold or maintain a patient's turbulent emotions during regression; and the "transitional object," such as a baby blanket, which represents the space between self and (m)other. Like Winnicott, Rodman was critical of Melanie Klein and her disciples for the "arrogant attitude that implied a privileged access to the truth" (*Winnicott* 382, n.11). Not surprisingly, the Kleinian analyst M. Nasir Ilahi concluded in a review published in the *Journal of the American Psychoanalytic Association* that Rodman's biography "includes important misunderstandings and misinterpretations" (316).

Rodman notes in his biography that his professional life changed in 1969 upon receiving a four-page letter from Winnicott in response to a paper, "Accidental Technical Lapses as Therapy," he mailed the British analyst. "I was thirty-four years old and knew next to nothing, and yet he took me seriously" (*Winnicott* 346). The observation highlights the value of encouragement and validation. Midway through the biography, Rodman refers to a book-length manuscript he wrote at the beginning of his career about working with a particularly disturbed (and disturbing) patient (238); a footnote reveals that Rodman's manuscript, called *The Cure*, was never published (406)—perhaps suggesting, given the title, that the cure may not have been genuine or long-lasting.

Rodman's Training Analyst

Rodman never discloses the name of his training analyst in *Not Dying*, but he devotes a page-and-a-half chapter to expressing indebtedness to him. "One's former analyst is a ghostly figure who has subsided into the darkness from which he mysteriously emerged in the beginning" (54). Rodman summarizes in a single sentence the five-year training analysis: he had "listened to my berating of my wife when I was deeply dissatisfied, my contrition when such episodes were resolved, and had seen me through to a more balanced understanding of my life and of all life" (55). Tellingly, Rodman never reveals any criticisms of his wife or their marriage together in the memoir. One can only assume that he felt it inappropriate to recall these criticisms in a spousal loss memoir. He never idealizes his marriage with Maria, but based on this single sentence about his training analysis, one suspects that he omitted much about their life together. Rodman never hesitates to characterize himself in the worst possible way in *Not Dying*, but he may have felt that *showing* (rather than merely telling) how he berated his wife would cast her in an unsympathetic way.

Overwhelmed by grief over his wife's terminal diagnosis, Rodman visits his former training analyst one more time, pouring out his heart. Rodman captures in two terse sentences their brief talk: "This was no longer analysis. It was two people looking into the void." He conveys his former analyst's humanity and empathy. "The tears he shed, so unexpected, so deeply moving, led me toward relief." Rodman ends the chapter by expressing deep gratitude toward the man who became a "faithful ally and a friend" (55). There is never the suggestion that Rodman needs to return to his training analyst; he struggles with an existential crisis that cannot be resolved through further analysis. Freud famously ends *Studies on Hysteria* with the observation that "much will be gained if we succeed in transforming your hysterical misery into common unhappiness" (*SE*, vol. 2, 305). Nothing could cure Rodman's common unhappiness.

Who was Rodman's training analyst? Was he Leo Rangell, I wondered, whose help Rodman acknowledges at the beginning of his Winnicott biography? "Foremost among those who have helped me to understand the mind, and to revise that understanding in the light of growing knowledge, is Dr. Leo Rangell, my friend and mentor of 37 years" (xi). Rodman provides us with enough information here to allow us to infer that their relationship began in the mid-1960s, when he was in psychoanalytic training. A clinical professor of psychiatry at UCLA, Rangell (1913–2011) was one of the most prominent American psychoanalysts, twice president of the International Psychoanalytic Association and the American Psychoanalytic Association. He received the title "Honorary President" in 1997. Rodman was coeditor (along with Harold P. Blum and Edward W. Weinshel) of *The Psychoanalytic Core: Essays in Honor of Leo Rangell, M.D.* (1989). In his contribution to the festschrift, Rodman compares Rangell to that of an "Old Testament prophet" (22)—the same words he uses to describe his analyst in *Not Dying*: the "Ur-father, a sort of Old Testament God" (54). In *My Life in Theory*, published in 2004, when he was ninety-one, Rangell defines himself not as a "contemporary Freudian" but as a "developed Freudian," that is, "one who has retained the enduring insights and formulations of an evolving general psychoanalytic theory and added such new ones as he thinks have earned inclusion" (304). It's likely that Rodman would have characterized himself in the same way.

Regardless of when authors die, their last publication often illuminates their earlier writings. Rodman's final publication, "Architecture and the True Self," began as a talk given at a conference in April 2003; he died while it was in the process of publication. He mentions a patient, a novelist widely admired, who never stops worrying about the possibility that he might appear to be foolish as a result of his writings. I don't know whether Rodman had the same fear, which is common among writers, particularly when writing about something as personal as the loss of a spouse. Throughout the article Rodman writes about the conflict between being alone and being in the state of relatedness—a conflict seen throughout *Not Dying*. The only personal detail he discloses in his final publication is that he has been living in the same house for thirty-two years, emphasizing his need for "continuity and persistence" (64). That Rodman lived in the same house, located in Beverly Glen, a neighborhood in the Santa Monica Mountains region of Los Angeles, with his second wife as he had lived in with his first wife, affirms his need for continuity and persistence, two qualities that inform all of his writings.

Not Dying may not appeal to all readers, but it remains a riveting account of love, loss, and *recovery*. It joins other, more famous spousal loss memoirs that I discuss in *Companionship in Grief: Love and Loss in the Memoirs of C.S. Lewis, John Bayley, Donald Hall, Joan Didion, and Calvin Trillin* (2010) and in *Writing Widowhood: The Landscapes of Bereavement* (2015). The neurologist Oliver Sacks, who was a close friend of Rodman and his second wife, observed that Rodman turned his anguish into art, which only the best writers can do.

The used copy of *Not Dying* that I ordered on Amazon turned out to have been "withdrawn" from the Blackwell Public Library in Blackwell, Oklahoma. I noticed that the book had been charged out eleven times, beginning in 1977, when *Not Dying* was published, and ending in 1990. Was that why the book was deemed no longer valuable? For whatever reason, the patrons of Blackwell Library stopped reading the book. That's a shame. There's nothing dated about the memoir, nothing that will be superseded by a newer memoir on the same subject. One can only imagine how Rodman's patients might have felt reading the memoir.

Stefania Magidson

Almost certainly, they would have agreed with Stefania Magidson that *Not Dying* is worth reading. As she wrote at the end of her Amazon review, she felt "deep gratitude of having had the chance, for so many years, to have the undivided attention and help of someone of such great caliber, great intellect and humanity. I carry it inside my heart as a humbling and life-affirming gift."

After completing a draft of this chapter, I sent an email to Stefania Magidson asking if she would read my discussion of *Not Dying*. To my delight, she agreed. She alerted me to her 2017 book *Searching for the White Magician* that contains the following disguised account of her analysis with Rodman:

> Between 1993 and 1998 I had the welcome opportunity to be analyzed, three times a week, by a very respected psychiatrist in the Los Angeles area. Harvard educated with extensive experience in his specialty, Dr. R's method was deeply rooted in the works of Sigmund Freud, Otto Rank and Donald Winnicott, yet blended with his classic psychoanalytic methods, there was an incredibly warm and humanistic leitmotif punctuating his approach. I must confess we often clashed heads with regards to my "spiritual" filter of the world (the term "spiritual" in itself I believe irritated him) and his rather conventional way of filtering "reality." We did however find common ground, our own private Switzerland that bridged spirituality and clinical psychology, in analyzing dreams and the subconscious. And I do remember well my feelings toward him, beyond the semantics which transpired between us: he was a man of intentions immaculate and clear, determined to deeply understand my thinking process and all that was a misidentification, a judgment, an "untruth," resolute in his approach to help me heal and liberate myself. (20–1)

I wasn't surprised by the reference to "clashed heads": Rodman never expresses any religious or spiritual faith in *Not Dying*. In *Keeping Hope Alive*, he likens hysterical symptoms to the presence of "primitive, religiously enforced conscience, such as one finds in fundamentalist groups" (166). In a later email to me, Stefania Magidson commented on one of Rodman's final remarks to her:

> I remember when there was a mutual decision for our sessions to end—a somewhat organic end to an arc of deep exploration. On the very last day, at the end, there was a moment of self-disclosure before saying our good-byes. "I am a father of 4 children," he said, perhaps intuiting there might have been father-daughter thoughts/projections/transference over the years. Even that brief discovery, so late in our collaboration (because I did see it as a collaboration, he as the guide/enabler to my healing and freedom, and me as the seeker on the path to knowing myself, to stepping closer to self-realization), gave me a lot to think about afterwards. Things along the lines of "how can he have a busy practice, write a book (he had confessed over the years—the only other confession—that he was working on the biography of Winnicott), read voraciously AND be active and responsible in the lives of four children?" I was happy he hadn't told me about his family before. Based on some personal wiring and predispositions, especially back then, I would have started to worry about his well-being: if he was getting enough sleep, if he needed support, if I deserved his time, patience, undivided attention and expertise—the irreplaceable and invaluable experience. My own father had not given me that. How can I expect a "stranger" to bestow upon me this gift (does he have the time to give the same to his children?) even if he was paid.
>
> While reading your chapter, the thought of the possibility of being Dr. Rodman's client during the time when he was impacted by his first spouse's untimely and heart-wrenching death and being told about it, is unbearable. I think I would have had strong reactions of either wanting to jump in and rescue/counsel/care for him or leave so he could fully concentrate on what was unfolding in his life; it would have been unbearable for me to allow myself to have attention and focus from him. I would (I think) have been overcome by much too much worry about his own condition and would have found it unbearable to continue. To this day, I often continue to position myself in the role of the giver, the rescuer, the person who is often asked for help.
>
> I do remember Dr. Rodman's observations about how I continuously monitored his states during our sessions, how I was cautious and tenuous (I learned that word from him!), how I didn't want to take too much space or to bother/aggravate him (always worried about what time it was, didn't want to go over a single minute, didn't want to stress him or make him late for his next patient).
>
> As I reflect the many things I find important and beneficial about therapy for me to this day, the one hour and private universe when someone is fully concentrated on me and puts their issues aside, is the highest of gifts and the most healing and nourishing experience.

Although Rodman discusses in his memoir the impact of disclosing his wife's dying and death on his patients, did he wonder how his patients would respond to his *own* death? Here is Stefania Magidson's reaction, a fitting conclusion, I believe, to this chapter:

> The day I found out Dr. Rodman passed away occurred maybe 6-7 years ago. I was driving home and had an impulse to call him out of the blue. It had been more than 10 years since I had last seen him and I wanted to come in for a session. I wanted to perhaps, in so many ways, say, "Look, my life worked out. The family is thriving, I started a foundation, I continued to grow, I'm stronger now, I've overcome many of struggles." I wanted to show him that I did well, in small part, also because sometimes he seemed suspicious of my overly enthusiastic, positive nature (most of the times authentic but sometimes an automatic reflex of not wanting to be a burden and adopting the "fake it until you make it" attitude). I found myself even rehearsing what I was going to say.
>
> I dialed his number. It had been disconnected. I thought perhaps he had moved his office. Started searching on the internet. Nothing at first. And then, his obituary. I was stunned. He was still young! It was too soon to part. I had erroneously assumed, based on anecdotal observations, that psychoanalysts, people who devote their lives to deep thinking, to academia, to mysticism, live well in their '90s. I burst into tears and cried torrents on and off for several hours. SO UNLIKE ME! I'm so not a crier. What was it? More transference than I ever imagined? Maybe it was GRATITUDE and thanks for HAVING BEEN SEEN. Nobody has given me that kind of undivided attention, observant, invaluable feedback and consistency. As he said in one of his books, there is no price that can be placed on such an offering, such an experience—it is like a work of art.
>
> The undivided, unconditional positive attention bestowed on me by Dr. Rodman was something I had not received enough growing up and had unconsciously yearned for it for many years. This alone, coming from someone kind, intelligent and artful in his skill, was the most healing gift that I could have ever received. No wonder I was sobbing. I was saying Good-Bye and Thank You.

Chapter 11

LOUIS BREGER

PSYCHOTHERAPY LIVES INTERSECTING

Louis Breger's *Psychotherapy Lives Intersecting*, published in 2012, is valuable for two reasons. First, it is the only study of which I'm aware that offers a long-term follow-up of psychotherapy patients in which they speak in their own voices about the effectiveness (or ineffectiveness) of their therapy experiences with him. The patients in his book, Breger wryly admits, are his coauthors. Second, although it is not a memoir; Breger's study focuses on his own life as a psychodynamic therapist, disclosing fraught life events, such as his conflicted relationships with his parents and a divorce after many years of marriage, two experiences that analysts rarely bare in public. The title is apt, for Breger shows us how his life intersects his patients' lives, usually positively but sometimes negatively. To appreciate Breger's achievement in *Psychotherapy Lives Intersecting*, we can see how it evolves from his earlier psychoanalytic and literary studies—and how it precedes a memoir he never imagined writing.

Louis Breger (1935–2020) was not exactly a maverick, but he challenged conventional psychoanalytic wisdom. Growing up in Los Angeles, he received his undergraduate education at Cornell (which he was able to afford for only one year) and UCLA. In 1961, he received his PhD in clinical psychology from Ohio State University. After teaching at the University of Oregon, the University of California Medical School in San Francisco, and UC Berkeley, he was appointed a professor in the Humanities and Social Science Division at the California Institute of Technology in Pasadena in 1970, where he taught until his retirement in 1994. In the mid-1970s, he became a "research candidate" at the Southern California Psychoanalytic Institute. It was not until years later, when four psychologists filed a class-action antitrust suit, that the American Psychoanalytic Association reluctantly allowed non-physicians to become members. Breger graduated from the Southern California Psychoanalytic Institute in 1979, receiving the Franz Alexander Essay Award and the Distinguished Teaching Award. In the 1980s, unhappy with the orthodoxy and authoritarian control of the psychoanalytic establishment, Breger was instrumental in the creation of the Institute of Contemporary Psychoanalysis (ICP), a non-hierarchical training institute of which he became the founding president from 1990 to 1993.

Breger long insisted that if psychoanalysis is to survive, it must be open and candid about the limitations of classical Freudian theory. He was one of the first therapists to recognize that it is not the psychoanalyst's particular training or theoretical approach that is most important but rather the quality of the patient-analyst relationship. Freud was a genius, Breger points out repeatedly, but he was blinded by many prejudices that contemporary analysts must acknowledge, lest they repeat past mistakes.

Dostoevsky: The Author as Psychoanalyst

From its inception, psychoanalysis has been wedded to literature—a marriage distinctly unequal and patriarchal, where for more than half a century the analyst dominated the literary writer. Literature was used mainly to confirm psychoanalytic theory; few realized that literature can help us revise psychoanalysis. As Adam Phillips observes ruefully in *Side Effects* (2006), "[T]he psychoanalysts never seem to say: psychoanalysis led me to believe that X was the case, but then I read, say, *Pride and Prejudice*, and realized the error of my ways" (47).

Freud believed that *The Brothers Karamazov* was the "most magnificent novel" of all time, but he detested Dostoevsky as a person. Freud makes several problematic statements in his 1928 essay "Dostoevsky and Parricide." He begins by declaring, "Before the problem of the creative artist analysis must, alas, lay down its arms" (*SE*, vol. 21, 177). Disregarding his own advice, he then proceeds to attack Dostoevsky the man and his work, reducing his fiction to pathology. Freud makes a number of inaccurate or unsubstantiated charges against Dostoevsky, accusing him, for example, on the basis of fictional confessions, of sexually assaulting a young girl. "Dostoevsky threw away the chance of becoming a teacher and liberator of humanity and made himself one with their gaolers. The future of human civilization will have little to thank him for" (*SE*, vol. 21, 177). After characterizing Dostoevsky as crude, masochistic, sadistic, and self-pitying, Freud admitted his own intolerance: "my patience with pathological natures is exhausted in analysis" (*SE*, vol. 21, 196).

The subtitle of Breger's study of Dostoevsky, *The Author as Psychoanalyst*, is a welcome correction to Freudian reductiveness. Unlike Freud, Breger's admiration for Dostoevsky is boundless. First published in 1989, eleven years before his Freud biography, Breger's study defines an approach that does justice to Dostoevsky's aesthetic and psychological achievements. Whereas Freud emphasizes Dostoevsky's patricidal feelings, Breger focuses on the novelist's maternal ambivalence, which he projected onto his female characters. Breger shows how Dostoevsky's writing held in check his depression and warded off suicidal feelings. "His overriding identity was that of a writer: this is what held everything, what prevented complete disorder" (*SE*, vol. 21, 11). Dostoevsky's literary self-analysis, Breger contends, was at least as momentous as Freud's psychological self-analysis. Dostoevsky survived severe traumas—including facing a mock-execution—that would have crushed a lesser soul. He lived to write as much as he wrote to live: literature was the center of his existence, as was his identification with great writers.

Breger discusses a number of noteworthy parallels between Dostoevsky and Freud. Great writers have more in common with analysts than with patients. Both Dostoevsky and Freud were destined to become unsurpassed explorers of the unconscious. Both viewed the deaths of their fathers as turning points in their own lives. Both were riven by guilt, anxiety, and fear that they were able to analyze and later use to understand fictional and real characters. And both recognized that psychology is a knife that cuts both ways, reminding us to use psychological approaches to literature or life cautiously, lest we murder to dissect.

Freud: Darkness in the Midst of Vision

Writing *Dostoevsky: The Psychoanalyst as Author* turned out to be a warm-up for writing *Freud: Darkness in the Midst of Vision*, published in 2000. Why another biography of Freud? Surely this must be one of the first questions raised by students of the talking cure, especially those familiar with the many biographies that had already been published. Freud's life is one of the most documented of the twentieth century, and he has been deified and demonized so often that one wonders what else can be said about him. Apart from his profound influence on psychology, psychiatry, social work, literature, history, cinema, and popular culture, Freud has been the object of fascination for countless scholars. To analyze the analyst has proven irresistible, particularly since Freud disapproved of any attempt other than his own to present his life story.

The historiography of Freudian biography is itself worthy of a book-length study. The first biography was Fritz Wittels's *Sigmund Freud: His Personality, His Teaching, and His School* (1924), which provoked its subject's wrath. A decade later, Wittels concluded that he treated Freud too harshly in the biography and issued a recantation. "I have, in the ten years that have elapsed since the appearance of the book changed my opinion considerably concerning psychoanalysis and its founder, and therefore can no longer stand sponsor for the errors and misrepresentations which I have come to recognize as such" ("Revision of a Biography" 361). Wittels then wrote a substantially different biography, published in 1931 as *Freud and His Time*. In *Becoming Freud* (2014), Adam Phillips slyly observes that "we may want another biography of someone but we don't want another biography by the same biographer" (16).

Ernest Jones waited until Freud was dead before publishing his three-volume biography, but it's marred by Jones's hero worship and his biased, vitriolic comments about those who "deviated" from orthodox theory. The biographies written by other psychoanalysts, such as Max Schur's *Freud: Living and Dying* (1972), offer a portrait largely in accordance with the one that Freud perpetuates in his own writings. Biographies written by non-psychoanalysts, such as Ronald W. Clark's *Freud: The Man and the Cause* (1980) and Peter Gay's bestselling *Freud: A Life for Our Time* (1988), offer more balanced portraits, but they fail to evaluate classic psychoanalytic theory from the perspective of contemporary psychological research.

Louis Breger's *Freud: Darkness in the Midst of Vision* remains the most thoughtful, nuanced, and comprehensive biography to date, a book that appeals to scholars, clinicians, and the general public. Breger writes with the imaginative sympathy of a novelist, the acute insight of a clinician, and the skeptical questioning of a research psychologist. He is not afraid to pay eloquent tribute to Freud for his many pioneering discoveries, such as his recognition of the importance of childhood experience in shaping adult life and his theory of transference and countertransference. Yet, Breger doesn't hesitate to criticize Freud for his overemphasis of sexuality and his devaluation of women. Breger presents us with a Freud who remains one of the intellectual giants of the twentieth century—his immortality will be assured despite all attempts to pronounce his creation dead, as the leading Freud-basher of our time, Frederic Crews, seeks to do in his 2017 biography. Breger offers a Freud who was not only seriously flawed as a human being but who unconsciously transmuted these weaknesses into a theory that he then claimed was universal for all people. Breger demythologizes and deconstructs Freud, showing how the real person was far different from the public persona.

There are no earth-shattering historical or biographical revelations in Breger's biography, nothing that will radically change our conception of the man or his work. It is not likely that new sensationalistic discoveries will emerge. What is new—and controversial—is Breger's attempt to analyze Freud in terms of a traumatic childhood that left a legacy of fear, insecurity, and depression. The calamities began before Sigmund's birth when his father Jacob's first wife died, followed shortly thereafter by his second wife's death. Sigmund was the firstborn child of Jacob's third wife Amalia, but soon afterward she gave birth to another son, Julius, who died about six months later from an intestinal infection. Julius was named after Amalia's brother, who died when he was twenty. Breger conjectures that as a result of these premature deaths, it is likely that Sigmund grew up with a depressed, inattentive mother and that following the births of six more children, he may not have received sufficient maternal love and mirroring, since Amalia's attention was now elsewhere. Another serious loss came when the family nursemaid, a notable mother surrogate in the absence of Amalia, was arrested for theft and disappeared from the children's lives. All of these losses produced, according to Breger, long-lasting fear associated with maternal absence. Breger maintains that the fear of maternal loss provoked too much anxiety for Freud to confront in his self-analysis. Instead, he created a more comforting explanation, the Oedipal story, which allowed him to conclude that the central psychological issue in a son's life is sexual desire for the mother and competition with the father.

Whether Freud's childhood was as traumatic as Breger claims is open to question. One does not usually think of Freud in this way, especially since traumatic events may be seen in nearly everyone's early life. What is beyond question, however, is Breger's persuasiveness in describing the many serious conflicts, losses, and tensions that troubled Freud's life. Disappointments in his weak, ineffectual father, whom Breger fittingly compares to Willy Loman, the embattled father in Arthur Miller's *Death of a Salesman*, compelled Freud to identify with powerful men in history and literature: Moses, Oedipus, Hannibal, Alexander the Great, Napoleon, and Oliver Cromwell. He hungered for paternal love and sought out strong patriarchal figures, but he ruthlessly turned against them when they no longer supplied him with the approval he craved. This was the nature of his relationships with Josef Breuer and Wilhelm Fliess. Freud continued this pattern with his disciples, including Carl Jung, Otto Rank, and Sándor Ferenczi, from whom he demanded unwavering support. There was no middle ground for Freud: you were either a friend if you accepted his theory in its entirety or an enemy if you questioned even one aspect of it. "Freud's adversarial stance, present from the beginning of the movement, foreshadowed the great tragedy of psychoanalysis" (193). Breger adds that although political machinations and personal assaults exist in every profession, "in no other field—the sciences, medicine, the social sciences—are such attacks a part of the theory itself" (207).

Apart from its insights into the strengths and weaknesses of psychoanalytic theory, Breger's biography debunks several popular myths, such as Freud's period of "splendid isolation." Contrary to Freud's claims, *The Interpretation of Dreams* was generally well received by the scientific community. We see fascinating glimpses into Freud's personal life. The man who asserted that sexuality was the supreme driving force in human life and who passionately courted in his letters his fiancée, Martha Bernays, quickly lost sexual interest in her when she became his wife. Their long marriage was passionless. It was Fliess, not Martha, who was "the great love of Freud's adult life" (152). Freud dominated his wife but never talked back to his overbearing mother, who often made his stomach churn. Surprisingly, Freud did not attend his mother's funeral, perhaps because he felt more relief than sadness from her passing at age ninety-five.

Freud was admired by his family but remained emotionally unavailable to them. He was not the enlightened parent whom one might have expected. For example, he never explained sexuality to his children, delegating this subject to the family physician. He warned his son Oliver (named after Oliver Cromwell) not to masturbate, an admonition that upset the boy. Freud didn't want his sons to become physicians or analysts for fear they would compete with him. He never attended the weddings of his three sons, and he disapproved of his youngest child Anna's suitors because he wanted her to remain devoted exclusively to him, which she was. Indeed, he fondly called his daughter his "faithful Anna-Antigone"; she became his most perfect disciple.

After two decades, Breger's *Freud* remains timely. In *Becoming Freud*, Adam Phillips's cites Breger's biography (along with Peter Gay's) several times. Phillips, who delights in paradoxes, goes further than Breger in accentuating Freud's overheated relationship with Fliess. "Freud invented psychoanalysis mostly out of conversations with men but through the treatment mostly of women." Psychoanalysis is thus, Phillips writes hyperbolically, a "homosexual artifact" (4). Although Phillips sees Freud as an anti-Enlightenment figure—"the most dogmatic thing about Freud as a writer is his skepticism" (12)—he agrees with

Breger that the profession of psychoanalysis has much to do with Freud's traumatic childhood.

There are a few omissions in Breger's biography. There are no references to Sander Gilman's groundbreaking books, such as *Freud, Race, and Gender*, which demonstrates the extent to which Freud internalized the prevailing images of racial difference in fin-de-siècle Vienna, which he then unconsciously incorporated into the construction of psychoanalytic theory. Nor does Breger refer to Yosef Yerushalmi, whose book *Freud's Moses* explores the Jewish influences on his work. These omissions, however, do not detract from the biography. In casting light on Freud's life and work, Breger demonstrates not only his subject's extraordinary achievement but his own as well.

Breger admits in the biography's "Background and Sources" that he was still under the spell of the psychoanalyst when he wrote *Freud's Unfinished Journey: Conventional and Critical Experiences* (1981). "That is, I still believed that the wrong turns in psychoanalysis could be explained by the frequently cited cultural and historical factors" (376). *Freud's Unfinished Journey* is the beginning of Breger's psychoanalytic journey, and while the book is thoughtful, it does not break new ground in understanding the "most inventive and insightful psychological genius of the century" (127). Breger slowly realized that much of psychoanalytic theory was flawed, unsupported or, in many cases, contradicted by contemporary research.

A Dream of Undying Fame

After completing *Freud: Darkness in the Midst of Vision*, Breger published another biographical work with a revealing subtitle: *A Dream of Undying Fame: How Freud Betrayed His Mentor and Invented Psychoanalysis* (2009). For older readers such as myself who initially formed a harsh judgment of Breuer based on Freud's disparaging comments in "On the History of the Psycho-Analytic Movement" (1914) and Jones's even more rancorous remarks in his biography, it is a revelation to discover Breuer's enduring positive contributions to psychotherapy. Breger suggests that Breuer's therapeutic ideas—the singularity of the patient-analyst relationship, the crucial value of empathy, the role of trauma, and the significance of real as opposed to fantasized experience—are much closer to contemporary psychodynamic therapy than Freud's ideas. Freud was an unreliable narrator when speaking of his older colleague, who was one of the most distinguished physicians in Vienna. Freud came to resent the man who befriended him in many ways and who helped launch his psychoanalytic career. Breger shows convincingly how Breuer deserves far more credit for inventing the talking cure than Freud or his disciples admitted.

In a glowing review in the *Irish Times*, the distinguished novelist John Banville hailed *A Dream of Undying Fame* as a "scrupulously even-handed, elegantly written and, in the end, sad and frightening account of the overweening ambition that was the fatal flaw of a great man. Unreconstructed Freudians, if there are still any about, may deplore Breger's book, but the rest of us owe him a debt."

Psychotherapy Lives Intersecting

Breger continues to give examples of Freud's mistaken theoretical assumptions in *Psychotherapy Lives Intersecting*, a book written after his retirement. Breger came to realize that Freud's dream theory was incorrect. Dreams are not primarily wish fulfillments, driven by the pleasure principle, but efforts to master anxiety and conflict. Nor is there anything *universal* about the Oedipus complex, which Freud maintained was psychological bedrock. Breger observes in *Psychotherapy Lives Intersecting* that none of the thirty-one patients described in his book suffered from an Oedipus complex. Freud never put into practice the clinical techniques he insisted others must follow, such as analytic neutrality. "The doctor should be opaque to his patients and, like a mirror, should show them nothing but what is shown to him" ("Recommendations," *SE*, vol. 12, 118). Freud was never merely a mirror or a blank screen to his patients. Neither Freud nor his followers recognized the significance of attachment theory, which helps to explain the psychoanalytic community's cool response to John Bowlby, whose landmark work on attachment, separation, and loss Breger finds indispensable to his own life and clinical practice. Throughout *Psychotherapy Lives Intersecting*, Breger casts a skeptical light on Freud's theoretical imperialism, which reveals more about the man than about enduring psychological truths.

It's always easier to criticize others than oneself. *Psychotherapy Lives Intersecting* is captivating precisely because of Breger's willingness to disclose the most wrenching details of his own life, beginning with his ambivalence toward his parents: an intelligent but deeply impaired mother and a self-defeating father. His mother suffered from clinical depression, made six suicide attempts, and, when he was twenty-five, was hospitalized and received electric shock therapy. Agreeing with Freud that suicide is often internalized aggression initially directed toward another person, Breger implies that his mother's suicide attempts were motivated to hurt his father whom she expected to rescue her from death. "She would overdose on sleeping pills in the early morning hours so that, when he woke up, he would find her slipping away and have to rush her to the emergency room. She made five such attempts while he was still alive, the last after he retired and was enjoying the one thing he most loved: playing his violin in an amateur chamber music group" (48). One can only imagine how devastating these suicide attempts were to her husband and son. To make matters worse, both parents felt diminished by their son's academic success. Breger's father indirectly committed suicide by running around at full speed on a tennis court, against his cardiologist's advice, until he finally collapsed from a fatal heart attack.

As an aside, Breger notes that his mother, who struggled throughout her life with depression and suicidal ideation, lived to her late eighties. When he visited her for the last time in a nursing home, as she lay curled in bed, comatose, he said,

"It's your son, Lou," to which she responded, "I have another son?" He answered, "Yes, you have two sons, Ivan and me." The words brought an immediate reply: she rose to a sitting position, stating, "Ivan and I," eliciting Breger's droll comment to us: "And these were her last words to me, correcting my grammar (and getting it wrong)" (54). Breger's grammar is generally impeccable, but his mother might have pointed out a few errors, including the following: "it was natural that I was drawn to Freud, who[m] I first read as an undergraduate" (55).

Breger felt secure within his family during early childhood, but he sought to distance himself from his parents' problems as he grew older. Regarding his sensitivity as both a blessing and a curse, he developed "emotional over-control" (49), a characteristic that persisted throughout his life. He found himself identifying with iconic masculine heroes like the Lone Ranger and Gary Cooper in *High Noon*. Like many people, he became a psychotherapist to work through his own conflicts as well as to help others. He never doubts that psychotherapy was his true calling. Interestingly, years after he became established in his profession, Breger began chatting with a group of psychoanalyst colleagues and discovered that all six of them had depressed mothers. "It was clear that this had much to do with our choice to become therapists" (55).

Breger's most formidable challenge in *Psychotherapy Lives Intersecting*, I suspect, was writing about the collapse of his thirty-year marriage. His first wife was still alive when he wrote the book, and it must have been particularly hard to describe the divorce without violating her privacy or that of his three children. The divorce, which occurred in 1987, was the single most harrowing experience of his mid-adult life. The one redeeming aspect of the ordeal, he adds, was that it helped him understand his patients who were going through their own marital crises. Breger devotes only a few sentences to the divorce, careful not to mention his ex-wife's or children's names, but he tells us about the divorce's reverberations on those few patients who later found out about it. "Josh" assumed that it must have been another "Lou Breger" whose marriage ended in divorce. The patient's mistaken assumption, Breger explains, was an effort to maintain an idealized view of the therapist.

Breger remarried, and his second wife, Barbara Gale Breger, became his soul mate and writing companion. He warmly acknowledges her help in several of his books. She helped select the subtitle for the Dostoevsky study, which he dedicated to her. She also selected the subtitle for the 2000 Freud biography. Her feminism deepened his sensitivity to his female patients. Using research skills honed from being a doctoral student in history at UCLA, she was the primary author of the chapter on the First World War and coauthor of the chapter "Trauma Revisited," a subject about which she had personal knowledge. Reviewers singled out these two chapters for special praise. Barbara was also the inspiration, as we shall see, of a later memoir.

Is it more difficult to write about one's strengths or weaknesses? "As a rule," Freud wrote to Marie Bonaparte in 1926, "when I am attacked I can defend myself; but when I am praised, I am helpless" (*Letters* 368). Writing about strengths exposes one's vanity and narcissism; writing about weaknesses exposes one's vulnerability. Sometimes a weakness may also be a strength. Breger mentions being a "workaholic" (51), though it's never clear whether this was problematic or not. He doesn't disagree that emotional over-control and workaholism imply, for most people, negative qualities, but the positive side is "steadiness, reliability, and unflappability" (75), qualities that are abundant in his writings. Breger comes across as emotionally honest and open, a nonjudgmental, empathic listener. In Nancy Chodorow's terms, Breger is the kind of analyst who listens *to* his patients rather than listening *for* confirmation of his own theories. He acknowledges, nonetheless, that given his family history of suicide, he struggled to work with certain patients, such as those with borderline personality disorder, who often threaten to kill themselves.

Breger values insight, but it is not the most salient factor in therapeutic success. He cites a 2004 study by Rebecca Curtis and her associates, "What 75 Psychoanalysts Found Helpful and Hurtful in Their Own Analyses." The coauthors concluded that genuineness and openness were the most important personal qualities. The Socratic (and Freudian) belief that knowledge is power does not always translate into therapeutic success. "Items related to interpretation, although significant, were not among those most highly correlated" with overall psychological change (Curtis et al. 194). From patients' perspectives, an insightful interpretation is experienced as the "analyst really 'getting' or understanding them, which can have a greater impact than the unearthing of unconscious material" (*Psychotherapy Lives Intersecting* 87). Irvin D. Yalom makes a similar observation in *Existential Psychotherapy* (1980).

> The search for understanding provides a context for the formation of the therapist-patient relationship; it is the glue that binds patient and therapist together; it keeps them occupied in a mutually satisfying task (The patient is gratified by having his or her inner world scrutinized with such thoroughness; the therapist is charmed by the intellectual challenge); and all the while the *real* agent of change, the therapeutic relationship, is silently germinating. (340)

Does this mean, Yalom muses, that non-psychological interpretations may be effective in psychotherapy? Yes, he admits, and then explains why, invoking evidence from cross-cultural psychiatric research, where only magical or religious explanations are acceptable. "If an astrological or a shamanistic or a magical explanation enhances one's sense of mastery, and leads to inner, personal change, then it is valid (keeping in mind the proviso that it must be consonant with one's frame of reference)" (344). Breger would agree.

Accordingly, there are relatively few eureka or "aha!" moments in *Psychotherapy Lives Intersecting*. Most of Breger's discoveries are the result of gradual revelations that are based on his patients' experiences or his own. He always invokes research that is constantly changing. It took him years before he stopped idealizing Freud, and then he rightly resisted going to the opposite extreme by devaluing Freud. Breger understands that psychological truth usually lies in the murky middle.

Breger's Patients

Studying Freud's patients has long been a growth industry, but psychoanalysts have been reluctant to have their patients write about their own therapeutic experiences. The reasons are obvious. Most therapists are not research psychologists, trained to create, administer, and evaluate questionnaires. They may not have the time, patience, motivation—or courage—to undertake an ambitious research project. Patients may not feel inclined to discuss what worked and didn't work in their therapy. Therapists may be understandably reluctant to call into question doctrinal practices. Many therapists are skeptical of the value of psychotherapy research outcomes. Even if patients have completed treatment, they may worry that evaluations of their therapists may preclude the possibility of continuing treatment with the same person. Professors who write about their own students must receive, in addition to their students' approval, permission from their university's Institutional Review Board, which oversees all human research. Receiving IRB permission is a lengthy process, and while psychotherapists may not need institutional permission, they are still bound by ethical and legal concerns that may discourage human research.

Breger contacted former patients only after his retirement, when he had the time to reflect on his long career. He chose patients whom he saw mainly in the preceding thirty years, when he was more experienced than at the beginning of his career. He admits that his research data may be skewed because those who felt that their therapy was unhelpful may have been less likely to respond to his questionnaires. Quotations from his patients that appear in his book, he informs us, are uncensored, apart from editing out repetitions and changing certain details to preserve confidentiality. He then added an extra precaution, one essential, based on my own experience of writing about students. To avoid any surprises, Breger showed his patients his written accounts of them, which included his memories of therapy and their own, allowing them to modify or add to what he had written. He also allowed them to choose their own pseudonyms. The result was a genuine collaborative process that reflects his egalitarian vision of therapy.

Several key words recur frequently in the patients' positive psychotherapy stories. One word is *validation*: Breger's patients felt he understood and accepted them. Another word is *nonjudgmental*: he listened carefully to them, empathized, and suspended criticism. Still another word is *human*. Reading *Psychotherapy Lives Intersecting*, one is reminded of Harry Stack Sullivan's credo, "we are all much more simply human than otherwise." And another word is *grateful*: they appreciated his devotion to them, which they reciprocated.

Patients' criticisms of Breger are no less revealing. Although Alejandro, who saw Breger four times a week for four years, believed that the therapist saved his life, he was angry when Breger said to him, during the first session, "It's clear you're neurotic." Anger turned to fury when Breger disclosed that he was a friend of a person about whom Alexandro spoke. Oliver was annoyed at Breger's "stop nagging me" attitude during one session "I nailed you on that tone, accusing you of irritation with your wife that did not belong to me. Your reply was simply, 'you're right.' Done" (79). Another patient felt manipulated by Breger's exaggerated sense of responsibility and guilt. Early in his career, patients didn't appreciate what he now jokingly refers to as his "pathological modesty" (111).

Many patients referred to Breger's emotional connection to them. Ralph was moved when Breger uncharacteristically choked up, teary and distressed, during his last therapy session, a memory that Breger did not himself recall. Ralph remembered another experience when, eight years after his therapy ended, he accidentally met Breger in another city when they were visiting a man in the hospital who was Breger's former student and Ralph's current professor. "When my professor asked how we knew each other, I was very surprised and rather anxious, but Lou rather spontaneously said I was 'an old friend,' and that was that" (10).

It would be fascinating to know how many of Breger's patients read *Psychotherapy Lives Intersecting*. How did they feel reading their own therapy comments along with those of his other patients? How did they feel reading about aspects of Breger's personal life of which they were unaware? I can imagine that reading the entire book was itself an eye-opening, therapeutic experience. It's possible that some patients may have regarded themselves as "less special" than others, whose psychotherapy stories may have been longer and livelier. My sense, though, is that all of them felt special about appearing in their therapist's book. Some of them may have defined their identity as Breger's patient, as did Freud's patients, such as the Wolf-Man.

Breger doesn't report any boundary violations, but some of his actions would be condemned by orthodox Freudians, such as when, in response to hearing a patient talk about a rare happy childhood event in which he was given some cookies, Breger handed him a plate of chocolate chip cookies and said, "My wife baked these for you" (35). Giving cookies was not a usual part of therapy, Breger later tells us; in fact, this was the only time he did this. But he is not afraid to share these details with readers. He and his wife attended former patients' weddings and their children's bar mitzvahs.

Breger advocates therapist self-disclosure but only under certain conditions. "I have found that patients typically do not want to know that much about me early in their therapy, but, as the years progress, many of them find such information important" (x). Curtis and her associates offer a qualified endorsement of therapist self-disclosure. Therapists' disclosures of their feelings about patients, in other words, therapists' countertransference, are significantly correlated with positive change, whereas therapists' disclosures of aspects of their personal lives are not (198). Freud's "fundamental rule" of psychoanalysis was to insist that patients reveal everything they were thinking, thus making possible free association. Breger has a new fundamental rule: "whatever one does as a therapist must be for the patient's needs and not one's own" (81).

As Robert A. Carrere observes in his enthusiastic review, readers of *Psychotherapy Lives Intersecting* will benefit from Breger's "ruthless authenticity and candor." The book is invaluable, Carrere continues, for both beginning and experienced psychotherapists—and, I might add, for anyone interested in the talking cure. Carrere's only criticism is that Breger does not always explore his patients' negative transference, resulting in psychoanalysis, in Freud's sardonic words, as an impossible profession. Joseph Schachter has no reservations in his discussion appearing in *Contemporary Psychoanalysis*, partly because his views of treatment are similar to Breger's. Reading *Psychotherapy Lives Intersecting* was a "heart-warming experience" for Schachter, and he found himself a "tad sad" when he reached the end (421).

The Book of Barbara

Breger's final book, *The Book of Barbara: Love and Grief: A Psychotherapist's Journey*, published in 2015, a year after his wife's death, casts further light on his earlier books, including his emphasis on the long-lasting impact of trauma and criticisms of Freudian analysts who blame the victim.

Breger knew Barbara Gale at two different points in his life: as teenagers, when they dated briefly, and when they remet in 1986. She was forty-nine and he was fifty-one. Both were struggling with unhappy marriages. Her early rejection of him reinforced his feelings of inferiority. He was astonished upon learning when they were reacquainted that she had been attracted to him as a teenager but terrified of having a sexual relationship. She had been molested in her childhood by a drunken uncle who had penetrated her with his finger. Her mother and aunt came upon the event and forced him to stop, but their silence and cover-up compounded her confusion and amplified her guilt. Her grandfather, with whom she was especially close, also molested her. The thought of sexuality awakened her traumatic memories, compelling her to cry out in horror to Breger when their relationship began to develop in the mid-1980s, "Don't kill me!" (37, 99).

Did Breger's sensitivity to the lingering effects of trauma, which became the ruling thesis of *Freud: Darkness in the Midst of Vision*, arise in part from his understanding of Barbara's traumatic past? Was his dismay over silent or judgmental analysts heightened by Barbara's fraught therapy experiences? He could not discuss these questions in his Freud biography, but they are prominent topics in *The Book of Barbara*. What made the trauma worse was that when Barbara went into analysis with a classical Freudian, "Ernie," he claimed, in Breger's words, that "she must have really wanted the sex, found her uncle attractive, and was probably flirtatious and provocative with him, none of which was true" (98). One can only imagine her rage—and Breger's. Years later, after she had left analysis, Ernie came on to her sexually at a neighborhood party. Nor was treatment with a second analyst helpful. After she began dating Breger in the 1980s, Barbara began effective treatment with a Santa Monica psychiatrist, Carl Utsinger.

Married to Breger for twenty-seven years, Barbara died in 2014, at age seventy-six, after a long battle with ovarian cancer. Breger began writing about her soon after her death. Several passages in *The Book of Barbara* deepen our understanding of *Psychotherapy Lives Intersecting*. His "driven nature" is apparent. "If there was ever a person who didn't stop and smell the flowers, it was me" (119). His anguished decision to divorce his first wife compelled him to return to psychotherapy. Ruth

Aaron, a marriage and family therapist who had been one of his supervisors during his earlier analytic training, convinced him that he was making the right decision. "Ruth had to tell me over and over that I was entitled to have a life of my own. Barbara also understood me better than I did myself, despite all my training and practice as a psychoanalyst and psychotherapist" (18). Therapists rarely admit their post-analysis conflicts in self-disclosing writings.

Breger's collaborative vision of therapy reflects a similar view of collaborative writing. He acknowledges Barbara's role in his last four books. She selected literary epigrams for each chapter. My favorite is the Mark Twain passage from *Pudd'nhead Wilson* that Breger uses for the chapter affirming Barbara's love for dogs: "If you pick up a starving dog and make him prosperous, he will not bite you. This is the principal difference between a dog and a man" (21). Believing that Barbara was the coauthor of *Freud: Darkness in the Midst of Vision*, Breger couldn't convince the publisher, Wiley, to add her name. In Barbara's words, the publisher played a legal card: "I did not sign the original contract and therefore could not be a co-author. Lou was distraught" (95). Belated recognition appears in *The Book of Barbara*.

Like his other major works, *The Book of Barbara* is a relationship-centered memoir, using accounts written by Barbara's sons, friends, and acquaintances (including a statement by Carl Utsinger) to tell her story. She was not famous or well known, but she had a transformative impact on those who knew her best. Breger doesn't idealize her. She did not suffer fools gladly. She had little patience for arrogant, egotistical people. Nor could she forgive those who betrayed her. "Once an asshole, always an asshole" (106).

A secular Jew, Breger turned to writing to honor his wife's memory. The same was true for Robert Rodman. Writing became for both men a solemn and sacred death ritual, a method to memorialize their wives and bring them back to life, verbally, as only a writer can, for readers who never had the pleasure of knowing them. Breger dreaded writing the final chapter, simply called "Death," but he never doubted the value of penning a memoir. Writing became a flow experience, a way to immerse himself in her absent presence and overcome, temporarily, her loss. "[T]he most helpful thing I have found to do is write this book, which fills the empty hours and keeps me involved with her in a once-removed way" (133). Writing was at the center of Breger's identity; as with Dostoevsky, writing held everything together, preventing complete disorder.

Intersecting with Breger's Life

My own life intersected with Breger's through reading and writing. As a result of my review of *Freud: Darkness in the Midst of Vision* published in the *American Journal of Psychotherapy* in 2001, we began an email correspondence that lasted until shortly before his death. He had sent me the manuscript of *A Dream of Undying Fame*, for which I was happy to write a blurb. We corresponded often after Barbara's death. We had much in common. He had read my 2007 memoir *Dying to Teach: A Memoir of Love, Loss, and Learning*, which I had written about my first wife, also named Barbara, who died from pancreatic cancer on April 5, 2004, at age fifty-seven. Barbara Breger and Barbara Berman grew up near each other in Brooklyn, New York, a decade apart. Both were smart, beautiful, down-to-earth, and devoted to their children. They both loved dogs who were at the center of their lives.

Breger was initially unsure whether he could write a memoir about their life together, fearing that he would be reimmersing himself in pain, but the words came quickly. He sent me a draft of the manuscript along with a note. "Writing this is how I am dealing with the grief for now: keeping my mind focused on her life for the 74-and-a-half years before cancer destroyed her. Am I in a state of denial? Of course. We each deal with these horrors in our own ways." He appreciated Shakespeare's line from *Much Ado About Nothing* that serves as the epigram for the last chapter of *The Book of Barbara*: "Everyone can master a grief but he that has it." He might have also used lines from *Macbeth*: "Give sorrow words"; "the grief that does not speak knits up the o-er wrought heart and bids it break." Breger wrote eloquently about a wide range of topics in literature and life, including sorrow. His psychoanalytic and memoiristic writings affirm the healing nature of both the talking cure and the writing cure.

After Breger's death, I sent a copy of this chapter to his daughter Lisa Millerd. She sent me the following comment about her impressions of my discussion:

> I had a chance to read the chapter. As the oldest of three siblings growing up with dad, my perspective of what is captured in the text is rooted in how our family dynamic and specifically how our relationship developed over time. Some of his own personal observations, recounted in the chapter, ring true regarding family matters as these were the "stories" told about his parents and his memories. Our relationship with our parents shapes us and we had our mother who was much more of a presence while dad was building his career. The relationship I had with my father morphed over time. My memories are he was fairly engaged when I was a young child. Being the oldest may have given me a privileged place in our family structure too. Later on, he and I struggled to figure out a new dance when my parents divorced and he remarried. After Barbara died, he returned to LA and it was easier to find a place in his life again as well as to encourage him to participate in ours.

> I would say my dad was a complex person who was very hard to read and knowing his choice of professions, this made sense in my head. He was much more comfortable with highly intellectual adults or when he was immersed in books (both reading and writing them). Overall, I think your chapter captures dad's essence as he would have wanted the world to see him. It would have been important to him that others know he changed his views over time and had a deep love for his second wife.

Chapter 12

BRENDA WEBSTER

THE LAST GOOD FREUDIAN

"I was born and brought up to be in psychoanalysis and, as a result, much of my adult life was spent on the couch" (1). Thus begins Brenda Webster's 2000 memoir *The Last Good Freudian*, a riveting account of her lifelong affair with an ideology that became for her and countless others a philosophy of life, a religious faith, and finally an addiction. The title doubtlessly refers to the memoirist, but it's even truer of her mother, whose haunting shadow appears in most of Brenda Webster's fictional writings as well, including her novels *Sins of the Mothers* (1993) and *Paradise Farm* (1999).

Brenda Webster's family was involved with Freudianism from the early 1920s, when it first achieved popularity, to its "golden days" in the 1950s, and continuing through the 1980s, when it became increasingly rigid and hostile to new ideas. Webster was born in 1936 in New York City. Her father, Wolf Schwabacher, was an entertainment lawyer whose friends and clients included Dorothy Parker, Erskine Caldwell, and Lillian Hellman. He had a bohemian side: he was engaged eight times and once jumped up naked from under a table at a Marx Brothers party.

Ethel Schwabacher

The problematic figure in Webster's life was her mother, who dominates the pages of *The Last Good Freudian*. Born in 1903 to a Southern Jewish father and a New York Jewish convert to Christian Science, Ethel Kremer was raised with her older brother in a privileged setting that encouraged her creative talents. One of her first cousins was the Pulitzer Prize–winning objectivist poet George Oppen (1908–84). She is best known as an abstract expressionist painter whose dazzling canvases are in the permanent collection of the Whitney, Guggenheim, Metropolitan, and San Francisco Museums. She studied with the great surrealist painter Arshile Gorky, who was then unknown to the art world. After he hanged himself in 1948, she wrote the first critical biography of him in 1957 that helped establish his reputation. In the 1950s and 1960s, she exhibited her paintings at the famed Betty Parsons Gallery in New York City, but she lost favor with the avant-garde critics when she began to paint narratives with traditional mythological themes. Prominent in the civil rights movement, she was an early feminist, interested in the growth of a female aesthetic. She died in 1984.

Ethel Kremer was in her twenties when her brother began to experience severe psychiatric problems that resulted in hospitalization and cut short a promising career as an inventor and mathematician. While seeking treatment for him, she decided to enter therapy herself and underwent a brief analysis in New York. The analysis collapsed when she fell in love with her physician, who abruptly terminated treatment upon realizing he could not handle the troublesome transference love. Experiencing the termination as abandonment, Ethel went into mourning, attempted suicide, and renounced her promising career as a sculptress. Traveling to Vienna, she entered into a two-and-a-half-year analysis with Helene Deutsch, a disciple of Freud and one of the leading theorists of female development. There is some evidence, as I suggested in a 1991 article in *The Psychoanalytic Review*, that Ethel may have been the patient Deutsch describes in the "Hysterical Fate Neurosis" case study that appears in her 1965 book *Neurosis and Character Types*. The case study was originally published in 1930, which was around the time Schwabacher was completing her analysis in Vienna.

In evaluating Schwabacher's treatment in Vienna, the art historian Mona Hadler concludes that she "found in her many hours with Deutsch, not a successful fruition of analysis, but an encouragement to pursue her creative life" (3). Although feminists criticize Deutsch for her emphasis on female masochism, she analyzed the self-defeating elements of Schwabacher's personality and encouraged her patient to overcome feelings of inferiority and inhibition. Similarly, although Deutsch's belief in female narcissism has been widely disparaged, she recognized that narcissism could be used creatively, supporting Schwabacher's efforts to find fulfillment in love and work.

Returning to New York City, Ethel Kremer married Wolf Schwabacher in 1935, and they had a daughter and a son. The happy marriage lasted until her husband's sudden death from a heart attack in 1951 at age fifty-three. Devastated by the loss, she reentered analysis, this time with a training and supervising analyst of the New York Psychoanalytic Institute, Marianne Kris, who was one of Marilyn Monroe's analysts. Despite efforts to resist breakdown, Schwabacher became increasingly suicidal and in 1952 took an overdose of sleeping pills. The suicide attempt, like the previous one in the 1920s, seemed to be motivated by feelings of abandonment. Upon her return from the hospital, she resumed six-day-a-week analysis with Kris. The therapy lasted for nearly thirty years, until the analyst's death in 1980.

Analysis Terminable and Interminable

Schwabacher's treatment with Kris must have seemed, to analysand and analyst alike, an enactment of Freud's 1937 essay "Analysis Terminable and Interminable," wherein he calls psychoanalysis an "impossible profession" (*SE*, vol. 23, 248). We can glimpse her impossible analysis in *Hungry for Light* (1983), her journal from

1967 to 1980, the last thirteen years of her working life. The volume, coedited by Brenda Webster and Judith Emlyn Johnson, is a treasure trove of art, literary, and mythic criticism; biographical reminiscences; and meditations on old age. *Hungry for Light* recalls Virginia Woolf's journals in its masterful descriptions of the growth and education of a major twentieth-century female artist. Like Woolf, Schwabacher suffered throughout her adult life from dangerously low self-esteem, depression, and periodic breakdowns. She attempted suicide several times, and nearly succeeded. What emerges from her biography, however, is not primarily illness but art's capacity to triumph over suffering.

Based on *Hungry for Light*, Schwabacher felt a powerful need to fuse with a maternal surrogate. Significantly, her two major analysts were women. Marianne Kris's husband was Ernst Kris, the distinguished art historian, psychoanalyst, and author of *Psychoanalytic Explorations in Art* (1952). Schwabacher may have felt, with justification, that Marianne Kris was the perfect analyst for an artist.

In trying to reconstruct Schwabacher's analysis with Kris, we encounter a problem. We have the patient's but not the analyst's point of view. According to Anton Kris (personal communication, April 20, 1989), his mother's clinical notes on her patients were systematically destroyed immediately after her death. We cannot assume that the patient's understanding of her analyst's intentions is entirely reliable. It goes without saying that no narrator is completely reliable. As I discuss in *The Talking Cure* (1985), there is never a complete story of what transpires in psychoanalysis. Consequently, the inferences we draw from Schwabacher's written account of her analysis with Kris cannot be verified.

On the basis of *Hungry for Light*, Kris's therapeutic strategy consisted mainly of encouraging Schwabacher to discover the origins of her terrifying separation anxiety. Kris's approach is an example of what Erik H. Erikson calls in *Gandhi's Truth* (1969) *originology*, the "habitual effort to find the 'causes' of a man's whole development in his childhood conflicts" (98). Kris hoped that by locating the precise traumatic events of her childhood, Schwabacher would realize that her need for artistic recognition originated from a fundamental lack of parental love. The analyst focused on the distant past, believing that anxieties in the here and now were repetitions of ancient childhood injuries. Kris assumed that there was a central traumatic loss, a precipitating cause of Schwabacher's illness. Once the patient located the key unlocking the mysterious past, she would be released from her demons.

Schwabacher tried many keys to unlock the past and, with her analyst's guidance, she worked diligently to open all doors. Analysis led her back further into her dim childhood. Just when she retrieved one obscure memory, another one floated tantalizingly past her. It took her years to reach repressed Oedipal memories and additional years to reach deeper pre-Oedipal memories. She became an archaeologist of the mind, forever chipping away at the surface to locate the precious bedrock of psychic strata. By working collaboratively, analyst and analysand sought to reach the core feelings and fantasies, the heart of darkness.

Schwabacher used *Hungry for Light* as an extension of her psychoanalysis. The introspective journal reveals what she thought was the major reason for her suicide attempts. Writing in September 1979, shortly before another effort to end her life, she observes, using third person,

> Let us say that suicide was the expression of a deep anger against the woman who left her—whether the nurse or whoever—also a deep anger at the woman who returned briefly to comfort her and left again, so that this leaving of a loved person was perhaps the most terrible thing that could happen to this child. It awakened the feeling of being alone and of not being able to face this aloneness, or to fill it with thoughts, though she was full of thoughts, capable, full of talent, able to create. But these early experiences were so devastating that the hate aroused was greater than anything else and had to be expressed. (223–4)

Schwabacher reveals around the same time the challenge of being a female artist in a patriarchal culture. "Being a woman is so negative a factor that it obliterates all else," she laments. "Is it true that a woman is not capable of creating anything but children? She must suffer the 'as-though-this-were-true' consequences" (222).

As she advanced into old age, Schwabacher developed several illnesses, including arthritis, which eventually forced her to give up painting and writing. Unable to hold a pen, she had to dictate parts of the journal into a tape recorder. She also suffered from arteriosclerosis. These ailments produced physical and psychological symptoms, such as pain in her hands and diarrhea from her medication, that were interpreted, psychoanalytically, as displaced aggression, originating, Kris conjectured, from an early childhood event. Recurring throughout the journal are marginal notes such as "pain in hand = anger," in which Schwabacher tried to locate a psychological basis for her ailments.

Whether or not Kris believed that Schwabacher's physical symptoms were a psychological expression of repressed hostility, their relationship eventually reached a stalemate. If, as seems likely, Schwabacher's arthritic pain had mainly a physical basis, then the attempt to psychoanalyze its meaning would be fruitless. Moreover, the exclusive attention paid to early childhood conflicts ignored adult problems, particularly the realistic existential fears of old age, illness, and death. Schwabacher's analysis seems to have created, or at least contributed to, a dependency that she could not overcome. In fairness to Kris, she made several efforts to terminate treatment, but they were perceived by Schwabacher as abandonment. Long-term psychoanalysis may be a necessity in some cases, but, as Sophie Freud has written in "Passion as a Mental Health Hazard," for some people, the intensity of psychoanalysis may produce a lifelong dependency. Even Deutsch gradually became skeptical of prolonged therapy, as Paul Roazen notes in *Freud and His Followers* (1975). "She was disappointed in psychoanalysis as therapy since it too often seemed to serve regressive needs in patients" (473). For three decades, Schwabacher and Kris analyzed childhood traumas, only to reach no firm conclusion about what did or did not occur in the past.

What would have happened if Kris had chosen a different therapeutic strategy, one that reinforced the patient's struggle to achieve artistic recognition?

Schwabacher raises this question in one of her most perceptive entries, written on October 3, 1979:

> Can it even be that I am angry with Dr. K. that she too did not emphasize my ability to a sufficient extent but was more intent on finding out about certain psychic difficulties of childhood, my relationship to my mother, my father, my brother and that she did not sufficiently help me to overcome the more urgent, immediate need of winning recognition, of venting anger, perhaps first, of freeing myself in that way and then be able to go forward? Do I resent this? Do I have some great anger toward her that is holding me back at this point? (*Hungry for Light* 226)

The Illegacy of Suicide

Schwabacher examined the motives behind her suicide attempts but not their effect on her family. As we saw with the Wolf-Man, suicide is both a personal and interpersonal act that usually has a lasting impact on suicide survivors, a term that refers to relatives and friends of people who terminate their own lives. Webster begins the chapter in *The Last Good Freudian* that discusses her mother's 1952 suicide attempt with a statement by Edwin Shneidman: "The suicidal person leaves his psychological skeleton in the survivor's closet" (59). Suicide survivors often experience, as Edward J. Dunne and Karen Dunne-Maxim point out, marked distortions in time, emotional estrangement from others, a sense of foreboding, a pessimistic outlook on life, and a heightened vulnerability to suicidal thinking. Webster experienced some of these symptoms herself, as we can see in her efforts to rouse her mother from an overdose of sleeping pills following Wolf Schwabacher's death. The rescue scene "unrolls like a film in slow motion," Webster writes:

> I was watching, but somehow I was disassociated from the men in helmets and black rubber boots who came through the front door, one of them incongruously holding an ax, and rushed down the hall to the bedroom. A few minutes later they came out with Mother strapped to a stretcher.
>
> I had been one girl when I went into the room and another by the time the firemen came to take my mother to the hospital. What she had done made a breach of trust between us that never healed. (*The Last Good Freudian* 61)

Unsurprisingly, suicide is a central event in many of Webster's books. She first wrote about her mother's history of suicide attempts in the largely autobiographical debut novel aptly called *Sins of the Mothers*. Connie, the sixteen-year-old protagonist, is horrified when she stands next to her mother's inert body. "She'd heard a rough rasping snore that sent shudders through her. A death rattle was what she thought." After screaming for the family's cook and then dialing the police, Connie watches helplessly as time almost stops:

Because she didn't know what else to do, she kept shaking her mother's arm and begging her to open her eyes. Then she saw the empty bottle of Seconal lying on the floor with the cap off and her stomach lurched. She felt sick. Like throwing up. She stood by her mother's bed in her plaid tartan skirt and knee socks and looked at her watch. Surely an hour must have passed but it was only five minutes. Why did her mother do this? Connie's father had died in June. If she'd done it then, Connie might have understood. But almost a whole year later? Just when she'd seemed to be getting less depressed? (87)

Suicide appears in *Paradise Farm*, Webster's fictional account of her mother's journey from inexperienced art student to visionary painter. Lara, whose life parallels Ethel Schwabacher's, gazes in horror as her psychologically troubled brother, John, jumps to his death from a water tower. Planning John's funeral, Lara finds herself thinking of Antigone, who also had to bury a brother. "Could Antigone have been relieved that her brother was dead?" (220), a question that remains unanswered.

Suicide again shows up in Webster's 2014 novel *Auschwitz: A Love Story*. Renzo, an aging Italian filmmaker who is struggling with Alzheimer's disease, cannot stop ruminating over his mother's suicide when he was eight:

"I need you," I heard myself saying to my mother. How could you do this when I was so young? How could you force me to witness you with your bruised eyelids like wilted violets shutting you away from me? I had forgotten until now that one fearful moment when I touched the oxygen tube, so angry that I was tempted to pull off all the wires. (83)

Webster quotes in the novel Shneidman's observation, gives us a list of twentieth-century artist suicides (including Virginia Woolf, Anne Sexton, and Primo Levi), and recalls Renzo's failure to mourn his mother's death. "I was angry; very, very angry. So angry that I killed you off" (127).

Given a deceased father and a depressed, suicidal mother, it's not surprising that Brenda Webster entered therapy. Unlike her mother, who never rebelled against a life nearly entirely in psychoanalysis, Webster did, albeit not in the beginning. She entered analysis when she began experiencing problems at age fourteen. She was, as she ruefully tells us in her memoir, "the perfect Freudian child" (13): bright, obedient, and passive. Psychoanalysis satisfied her mother's hunger for meaning, and for many years analysis satisfied her own need as well, until she began to rebel. Webster's three psychoanalysts in *The Last Good Freudian*, all European-born who immigrated to the United States, continued the family pattern of submission to analytic authority.

The first of Webster's three psychoanalysts, Berta Bornstein (1899–1971) was born in what is now Kraków, Poland, practiced in Berlin, and came to the United States shortly before the Second World War. According to Simone Valantin, Bornstein "brought innovative techniques to child psychoanalysis. She emphasized the precocity of children and so was able to reduce the time required to win their confidence." According to Webster, however, Bornstein appeared to be straight out of *Grimms' Fairy Tales*, a scary-looking woman with a large red birthmark on her face. Bornstein was recommended to Webster by Muriel Gardiner, a psychoanalyst, close family acquaintance, friend of the Wolf-Man, and the model for Julia in Lillian Hellman's autobiographical *Pentimento*.

Bornstein insisted that the young teenager lie on the couch and free associate. Therapy sessions with her inspires Webster's biting sarcasm. "All I could think of was how ugly her birthmark was and whether her husband, if she had one, could possibly sleep with her. When I wasn't thinking that, I would compulsively imagine sucking a penis" (55). Bornstein, whose German-inflected English Webster satirizes in lines like "She knows you like ze penis" (57), encouraged her patient, who was still a virgin, to be fitted with a diaphragm. "The fact that my sexuality was being managed by my shrink only made me feel more like a baby" (56). In retrospect, Bornstein should have helped the confused teenager talk about her conflicted feelings toward a mother who relied on analysts, not experience or common sense, for parenting advice.

Webster uses caricature to depict Bertha Bornstein, but she portrays her four-year treatment with her next analyst, Kurt Eissler (1908–99), with more affection. Eissler was at the center of the psychoanalytic establishment, indeed, the creator of the Sigmund Freud Archives. "If Freud was King Arthur," Webster quips, "Eissler was Launcelot, a quixotic but fiercely loyal defender of the faith" (82). Eissler was a controversial figure, partly because of his decision, opposed vigorously by psychoanalytic researchers, to restrict scholarly access to the Freud Archives, and partly because of his disastrous selection of Jeffrey Moussaieff Masson to succeed him as head of the Archives. The would-be disciple then turned against Freud, accusing him of intellectual cowardice for abandoning his "seduction theory" of neurosis. Webster accurately conveys the highly publicized battle between Eissler and Masson.

Eissler considered his treatment of Webster, which began in 1956, as "palliative therapy," designed to help her until she was old enough to leave home. He comes across as concerned for her welfare but trapped in a Freudian straitjacket. Eissler was fascinated by artistic genius, but he subscribed to the then-prevailing psychoanalytic belief that women should not compete with men in the workplace. Nor could a woman be a genius, in his view. "If Mother had been a man, Eissler would have endorsed her passion for her art, but she was a woman. He had clear ideas about how women should feel and behave, and Mother didn't fit them. For one thing, women should care first about their children. For another thing, there could be no feminine genius" (85).

The question, in Eissler's view, was whether Webster had the ability to be the wife of a genius. One can imagine her consternation. How could she convince him that genius does not reside in phallic power? That women were not innately masochistic, passive, or envious? That they did not have a less independent superego than men, as Freud opined? Eissler took her ideas seriously, excited about her undergraduate essay on *King Lear*, but he wouldn't budge on his patriarchal views. In a revealing exchange, Eissler and Webster disagreed over Cordelia's refusal to tell her father what he wanted to hear. Eissler was impressed by Cordelia's honesty, but Webster was annoyed by Cordelia's infuriating bluntness. Both positions are understandable and equally valid, but Webster's therapy was less a dialogue than a monologue, with an authoritarian teacher instructing a resistant student. Ironically, Eissler was Webster's father surrogate, and she was thrust into the position of Cordelia, reluctant to play the role of obedient daughter.

Seeing the humor of her obsessive sexual thoughts in analysis, Webster describes one moment when, after she complained about the noise outside her apartment, the courtly Eissler stood up and handed her a pair of earplugs. "His fly was about level with my face and I remember associating the round wax earplugs with the view of his testicles I'd see if I unzipped it. I would have died rather than say this to him" (83). Died, perhaps, as an analysand, but not as a memoirist. Webster knows that everything is grist for the writer's mill.

Webster held much back from Eissler, but she is unsparingly candid and forthcoming to her readers. She is not afraid to change her mind in her search for the truth. Occasionally, she makes statements like "This may not be fair" (56), but she has the ability to see multiple perspectives. She maintains narrative distance from her younger self, showing us the process of self-education with sentences such as "None of this was clear to me then" (84).

There is nothing affectionate or endearing in the portrait of Webster's next analyst. Anna Maenchen (1902–91) was born in Lithuania, grew up in Russia, studied at the University of Vienna, and was analyzed by Anna Freud. Maenchen came to the United States in 1939, where she became a member of the San Francisco Psychoanalytic Institute. Webster was married and a graduate student at UC Berkeley when she began seeing the old-guard Freudian who had been recommended by Eissler. Webster limns her many battles with the narrow-minded Maenchen, who not only subscribed to Freud's infamous belief in penis envy but also discouraged her from ending a painful marriage to a man who failed to appreciate her desire to become a writer.

Of the three analysts, Maenchen comes across as the most mean-spirited. "Do you really want to be an intellectual?" (115) she asked when Webster expressed interest in graduate school and scholarly writing. In a word, she saw Webster as *envious*: envious of male power, envious of her brother and husband, envious of her artist-mother. The analyst saw her in the worst possible light. "If I offered my brother a piece of toast, she would suggest that I secretly wanted him to choke" (116). The wonder is not that the analysis was so disastrous but that Webster remained in it for so long. About the only perceptive remark Maenchen makes is when Webster decides to terminate treatment. "You are glad that I am letting you go," she hisses, "because you see me as your superego and you want to be free to follow your impulses" (157). The relationship between the two of them was stormy from the beginning and never improved. Webster saw Maenchen on-and-off again for several years, and each time the patient begrudgingly returned to treatment, she felt like a "battered wife who can't stay away from her abusive husband" (171). Ironically, Maenchen emphasizes in one of her professional articles the importance of the "therapeutic alliance," something she never achieved with Webster.

Webster implies in *The Last Good Freudian* that the early female psychoanalysts viewed themselves as honorary men. She states this explicitly in a 2003 interview with Jack Foley, suggesting in the same interview that her mother's paintings reveal an emerging female consciousness that countered the idea of female lack. The paintings reveal a shift in identification from Orpheus to Eurydice. "Eurydice had been just a pale shade in her early paintings. In her later paintings Eurydice became a more defined figure and Orpheus became more blurry" (659). The same is true about Webster's writings, which reveal a strengthening female identification.

For a time, Webster considered formal psychoanalytic training. Her description of applying to the San Francisco Psychoanalytic Institute is laced with humor. Asked by an interviewer whether she thought her literary work would change the field, she replied truthfully, "No," adding to us parenthetically, "Did I really look like a megalomaniac?" Her reply did not impress the interviewer. "'Oh,' he said, 'then you're just going on with the same old thing?'" (137). Her application was turned down.

The Last Good Freudian offers a witty critique of orthodox psychoanalysis without engaging in Freud-bashing (although one of her graduate school mentors was Frederick Crews). Webster includes sympathetic portraits of psychoanalysts in the memoir, such as Muriel Gardiner, who appears in *Paradise Farm*. Webster is also supportive of a marriage counselor who, despite being classically trained, believed that it was less important for her to analyze past obsessions than to concentrate on the present and future. Unlike her previous analysts (and Freud), Dr. Berg was a Menschenkenner, a good judge of character. "With Berg I discovered that I learned more about myself by writing stories than I had in years of therapy" (180).

Paradoxically, despite the ironic title of her memoir, Webster remains a good Freudian throughout the memoir, for even as she rejects her dark muse, psychoanalysis, as a therapy, she embraces it as an interpretive and hermeneutic tool. Psychoanalysis sharpened Webster's attentiveness to the inner world, allowing her to recognize the ironies, ambiguities, and contradictions of human thought and behavior. Psychoanalysis called attention to Oedipal and pre-Oedipal themes that she found useful in interpreting literature. She put her fraught analytic experience to good use in her first book *Yeats: A Psychoanalytic Study* (1972), a revision of her Berkeley doctoral dissertation. Interestingly, if not guilefully, she acknowledges both Eissler and Maenchen for her "increased awareness of certain problems and their possible solutions" (vii), a statement that betrays none of the caustic satire found in her memoir.

Webster uses psychoanalytic theory deftly throughout her Yeats book. Several of her observations about Yeats are self-revealing, as when she remarks that relationships with women involved two dangers for Yeats: "he identified with women in their weakness (as he had evidently done with his despondent mother) and this same weakness aroused his sadism" (52). Another characterization of Yeats the poet is true of Webster the memoirist and novelist: "The poet is not merely the passive recipient of vision, but actively incorporates and digests the raw material of experience, including desire and its objects, and re-creates them in his verse. In the process of making the experience manageable for artistic purposes, he also gains control over it" (60). Central to American ego psychology, which Webster learned from her reading of Freud if not from her own analysis, was the repetition-compulsion principle, the role of repeating traumatic experience for the purpose of mastery. "Yeats's purgatorial process is comparable in important ways to the reexperiencing of past events and relationships in psychoanalysis. In both cases remembering or reliving past events serves the ultimate purpose of arriving at self-knowledge and freedom from compulsion" (186). Webster uses psychoanalytic theory skillfully in her other academic study, *Blake's Prophetic Psychology* (1983), where she suggests that the poet's contradictions and misogyny arise from the conflict between incestuous desire and guilt.

The best therapy for Webster turned out to be writing. She affirms throughout *The Last Good Freudian* the passion of artistic creation, including the psychological benefits of writing. Writing kept her sane and focused in a way that analysis could not do. She cites D.H. Lawrence's insight, "One sheds one's sickness in books" (76), a line that appears in his *Letters* (volume 2, 90). Lawrence's statement is true for Webster herself. Writing fiction proved to be a lifeline: Recreating herself in fiction enabled her to recreate herself in life. Experimenting with different voices, characters, and states of mind, she made necessary revisions first in art and then in life. Webster is a fearless writer. *The Last Good Freudian* is a highly self-disclosing memoir; she bares family secrets that other memoirists might have avoided. She is generally respectful of her children's privacy, though she hints at a strained relationship with her older daughter. "We struggled for the millionth time over my faults as a mother during her adolescence" (192). Significantly, Webster tells us about these struggles in a single sentence rather than showing them to us.

Psychotherapy stories or memoirs are usually confessional with or without absolution or resolution at the end. Some readers find the talking cure tedious or self-indulgent. Lisa Jennifer Selzman complained in her *New York Times* review of *The Last Good Freudian* that too often Webster blames others for her circumstances. By contrast, *Kirkus Reviews* calls *The Last Good Freudian* "whinefree." Revealingly, Webster's criticism of others is exceeded by her self-criticism. She never engages in scapegoating. Her portraits of psychoanalysts, relatives, and acquaintances are satirical, but they do not strain belief. She accepts responsibility for her dependence on psychoanalysis and for the years wasted lying on the couch. By the story's end she has become a Berkeley-based recovering Freudian and an independent scholar, free from imprisoning ideology and ready to muddle through life on her own—a daughter of whom her mother would have been proud.

The Last Good Freudian ends with an Epilogue, written in the present tense in 1997, in which Webster updates us on her life. Having divorced her first husband, Richard Webster, a UC Berkeley professor of history, and married her second and present husband, Ira Lapidus, a UC Berkeley professor of Middle Eastern and Islamic history, she is fulfilled for the first time in both love and work. As Jennifer Money remarks in her review of *The Last Good Freudian*, the Epilogue shows an author who "lives in the present and has made peace with her past and in doing so, has laid aggressive claim to her independence and her voice, as both a writer and a woman" (666).

Vienna Triangle

The Last Good Freudian is not Webster's only account of the talking cure. In 1985, she published an illuminating scholarly article on Helene Deutsch in which she argued that the pioneering analyst deserves a new look. Without disclosing that her mother had been treated by Deutsch, Webster affirms the analyst's positive contributions to psychoanalysis and feminism: her emphasis on self-confident activity, mastery, and self-esteem.

In her 2009 novel *Vienna Triangle*, Webster imagines life among the inner circles of Freud's disciples, especially the Hungarian-born Victor Tausk, whose tragic suicide in 1919 continues to generate controversy among Freud's critics and defenders. Paul Roazen's *Brother Animal* (1969) criticizes Freud's treatment of his disciple; the ever-loyal Eissler responded with his own book, *Victor Tausk's Suicide* (1983), exonerating Freud from blame.

The novel's sympathetic heroine, Kate Berg, is a twenty-eight-year-old graduate student in psychology at Columbia who is writing her dissertation on the early female psychoanalysts. As the story opens in the turbulent late 1960s, she meets an elderly Polish woman, Helene Rosenbach, who turns out to be Helene Deutsch. While conducting her research, Kate makes an astonishing discovery, which she shares with Deutsch: Kate's mysterious grandfather, about whom her mother never talks, was Tausk. Part of the novel's achievement is that Kate's research into the early history of psychoanalysis parallels her deepening understanding of her own origins. Kate searches for the complex motives behind Tausk's suicide, partly because she is still trying to come to terms with her brother's suicide. Kate travels far outside her comfort zone in researching the past, and like Webster herself, she is an inveterate teller of secrets.

No less than Kate, Webster has done her homework in researching the vexed history of psychoanalysis. Relying on several primary sources, she creates compelling portraits of Deutsch, Tausk, and Lou Andreas-Salomé. We learn a great deal about the unstable Tausk, who had a love-hate relationship with Freud. We also learn much about Lou Andreas-Salomé, who was infatuated not only with Freud but also with Nietzsche and Rilke. Tausk's diary, which Kate stumbles upon, seems so authentic that we may forget it is entirely fictional. The triangle in the title refers to the tangled Oedipal tensions in the novel. Webster's characters are flawed human beings, which is why we care about them. Kate's observation about the early Freudians reflects Webster's interminably long psychoanalysis: "Being smart in the head doesn't mean they have emotional understanding" (14). Or as Kate's mother observes, "I'd wager that the mind doctors are just as blind as anyone else and maybe more dangerous because they claim superior wisdom" (15).

Webster favors those characters who grow and learn from experience, who revise earlier interpretations, and who develop compassion and humility, such as Deutsch, who states, "the older I get, the less I think I know, really know" (31). Older and wiser, Deutsch speaks in an authorial voice when she tells Kate that she must not be too harsh about the founder of psychoanalysis. "It's hard to feel now the power Freud had over his group—some might even say the power of life or death" (202). Deutsch speaks for her creator when she observes that "I believe in 'insight' less and less" (51)—and when she recognizes that writing is sometimes the best way to deal with grief.

Webster's analysts might not appreciate her acidic portraits of them in *The Last Good Freudian* and *Vienna Triangle*, but most readers will admire her honesty, insight, courage, and humor. She avoids psychobabble and lit-crit jargon to which so many devotees of psychoanalysis and literature succumb. *The Last Good Freudian* remains a cautionary tale, reminding us that the underexamined—or overexamined—life is not worth living. Psychoanalysis continues to change and develop, aided by inside and outside critiques, such as Webster's fictional and nonfictional writings. In the final analysis, the storyteller turns out to be a good Freudian.

Chapter 13

MADELON SPRENGNETHER

CRYING AT THE MOVIES

Feminism has taught us that the personal is political, and psychoanalytic feminism has taught us that the personal shapes our work, including our scholarship. Psychoanalytic literary criticism often contains hidden personal agendas or motives that may become apparent not at the beginning of a scholar's career but only in retrospect. Nowhere is this more strikingly true than with Madelon Sprengnether. Memoirist, poet, and feminist psychoanalytic literary critic, she is Regents Professor Emerita of English at the University of Minnesota and a graduate of the New Directions Program in Psychoanalytic Thinking in Washington, DC.

Sprengnether's early interest in psychoanalysis appears in her essay "Enforcing Oedipus: Freud and Dora," published in the 1985 volume *The (M)other Tongue*, which she coedited with Shirley Nelson Garner and Claire Kahane. Sprengnether shows how Freud's problematic 1905 case study *Fragment of an Analysis of a Case of Hysteria* betrays a power struggle between Freud and his young female patient. "Against her silence, his simulated conversations sound awkward, a manic insistence on the power of *his* voice to create her reality" (70). Sprengnether's influential *The Spectral Mother: Freud, Feminism, and Psychoanalysis* (1990) demonstrates her growing interest in why and how Freud's theorizing of the Oedipus complex obscured a deeper trauma that he failed to consider: the pre-Oedipal stage of human development. Freud's inability to theorize early development reveals his fear, in Sprengnether's view, of a spectral mother.

Crying at the Movies

This haunting appears in Sprengnether's riveting 2002 memoir *Crying at the Movies*. There is, alas, no mourning-after pill, but her film memoir reveals how grief can catalyze art. As a result of suppressed mourning, Sprengnether found herself unable to speak or write about grief. Writing *Crying at the Movies* highlighted the blindnesses that had sabotaged her two marriages. Studying her grief turned out to be liberating, producing a psychoanalytic memoir that heightens our understanding of love, loss, and recovery. Additionally, writing about her early childhood loss prepared her for writing *Mourning Freud*, her acclaimed 2018 study of the multiple childhood losses in Freud's own life.

In the notes to *Crying at the Movies*, Sprengnether credits Judith Lewis Herman's 1992 book *Trauma and Recovery*. "The psychological distress symptoms of traumatized people," Herman writes in the introduction, "simultaneously call attention to the existence of an unspeakable secret and deflect attention from it" (1). This is precisely Sprengnether's situation in her memoir. Another observation by Herman pertains to Sprengnether's situation. "Traumatic events are extraordinary, not because they occur rarely, but rather because they overwhelm the ordinary human adaptations to life" (33).

Sprengnether's deceased father may not have been "spectral," which she defines as a "ghost, a phantom, any object of fear or dread" (*The Spectral Mother* 5), but his death was harrowing enough to require in later life an effort to free herself from its spell. The opening paragraph of *Crying at the Movies* defines her dilemma. "I have no memory of my father's drowning when I was nine years old. I was present at the scene—along with my mother and two brothers—and I can remember things that happened immediately before and after, but I don't recall anything related to the actual moment of his disappearance" (5). Because of traumatic amnesia, the fragments of the story emerge like "shrapnel" (67), evoking piercing pain associated with sudden loss.

Sprengnether's challenge in *Crying at the Movies* is to link filmic free associations to the gradual unearthing of buried paternal sorrow. The memoir's double narrative proceeds chronologically, with each discussion of a different film carrying her further along in the process of self-analysis. *Crying at the Movies* is an early example of viewer-response criticism, anticipating Norman N. Holland's *Meeting Movies*, published in 2006. Both film memoirs affirm the Socratic and Freudian ideas of knowledge as power. Both explore, psychoanalytically, the film reviewer's free associations. And both memoirs provide an intimate glimpse into the memoirists' inner lives. Holland's memoir, however, doesn't interrogate a single, overwhelming traumatic event. Nor does Holland write about experiencing emotional breakdowns while watching films, as Sprengnether does.

Why does a film have the power to unleash a torrent of emotions when a poem or a novel, no less aesthetically or psychologically complex, does not? Sprengnether never directly raises this question, although she discusses the power of the film (theater) experience. Holland offers an answer in *A Sharper Focus*, an online resource created near the end of his life that features his essays on over 200 films. It is more convenient to watch a film on a DVD or streamed to television or an iPad, but there is a loss of intensity. Seeing a film in a palatial theater of the past, Holland suggests, one is part of a large audience. "You turn over part of your mental functioning—your defenses—to that collective mentality." The result is a loss of control, a loosening of psychological defenses, that intensifies the viewing experience, connecting us to emotions we may have repressed. The hyperrealism of watching a film on a large screen circumvents our usual defenses. Because the theater and the projectionist control the viewing, Holland adds, the film rules. "You have to give yourself to it or leave." For this reason, Holland continues, nothing substitutes for the theatrical experience. Sprengnether experienced this loss of emotional control in the movie theater, a loss that compelled her to look deeply at her own mental functioning.

Sprengnether's father drowned in the Mississippi River during a family outing on Labor Day weekend in 1951 while rescuing his older son, who had been swept away by a current. He was only forty-two, in the prime of life. Sprengnether suffered a double bereavement, for afterward her mother became emotionally unavailable to her three children. Talking about her father's death was taboo, literally, unspeakable—and unwritable. The bereft daughter, tongue-tied, escaped into the world of fiction, where she began to read obsessively tales of orphans and sick or dying girls—*Heidi*, *Little Women*, *The Secret Garden*, *Bleak House*, and *Jane Eyre*. The motive behind such reading was counterphobic. Sprengnether didn't cry when tragedy struck in real life, but she did when watching films, which provided a safe, anonymous outlet for suppressed emotions. In Kafka's words, viewing a film can be, like reading a book, the ax for the frozen sea within us.

There was nothing safe, however, about Sprengnether's convulsions while watching in 1969 the classic film *Pather Panchali* by the Indian film director Satyajit Ray. This experience, when she was twenty-six, turned out to be the first of two cataclysms that befell her in the liminal space of a movie theater. Six months pregnant, she couldn't stop crying. Ashamed that she was making a spectacle of herself, she continued to weep when she and her husband arrived home. What was it about the film that triggered a paroxysm of emotion?

The Satisfactions of Reading

Part of the satisfaction of reading Sprengnether's memoir is to see what she discovers specifically about herself from each film. Watching Ray's film revealed an agonizing truth: love inevitably ends in loss. The mother's ravaged face in *Pather Panchali* following her daughter's death reminds Sprengnether of her own silent mother, unable to talk about her deceased husband. The birth of Sprengnether's daughter in 1969 only heightened the fear of loss. Reading Sprengnether's memoir, one is reminded of Faulkner's wry observation: "The past is never dead. It's not even past." Shining a light on the past spotlights the present and points a way to the future.

Another satisfaction in reading *Crying at the Movies* is Sprengnether's candor in writing about painful and shameful events. She travels far outside her comfort zone in disclosing experiences about which other memoirists remain silent. She never minimizes or rationalizes her role in the failure of her two marriages. Her first marriage, which lasted a decade, collapsed when she fell in love with another man. In retrospect, she realized that she had never been in love with her first husband. She was unprepared for the fury she experienced when her lover rejected her. The pattern was repeated years later when she betrayed her second husband by having an affair with another man. She accepts responsibility for these actions. Noting the compulsive and tormenting elements of these extramarital relationships, she remarks that they were repetitions of the devastating rupture in her life, the loss of her father. "Each time my lover left, it felt like a death to me—to which I reacted with all the pent-up feelings I had had as a child. I cried, I raged, I went into a temporary downward spiral of depression" (78). Writing about depression does not magically release one from its grip, but writing is a form of problem solving, allowing one to imagine a more positive state of mind.

Crying at the Movies precedes by three years Joan Didion's legendary grief memoir *The Year of Magical Thinking*, which chronicles the sudden death of her writer-husband John Gregory Dunne. Like *The Year of Magical Thinking*, *Crying at the Movies* offers an iconography of grief. Again like Didion, Sprengnether explores the ways in which a mourner cannot fathom the reality of loss. Magical thinking is related to Freud's concept of the omnipotence of thought, the belief that one's thoughts can change external reality. But magical thinking and the omnipotence of thought do not entirely capture Sprengnether's (and Didion's) terror and shock arising from a loved one's death. Withdrawing into inner reality, Sprengnether sought to sever her connection to the past, to her fraught emotional world, a decision that proved to be a devil's bargain. The tortuous way back to real life, she discovered, was through the reel world.

The other films in Sprengnether's memoir mark different stages in the growth of her self-understanding. The six-year-old Sally in Michael Lesser's film *House of Cards* wonders where her deceased father has gone, a question that allows Sprengnether to point out that reality and fantasy are inseparable in early life. Unlike Sally, whose psychologist helps release her from the wish to join her father in death, Sprengnether did not have early psychological intervention. Seeing *House of Cards* helped her comprehend the magnitude of her loss. The first time she saw Andrei Tarkovsky's science fiction film *Solaris*, in 1977, she could not remember the denouement, where the central character is reconciled with his long lost mother and emotionally distant father. Unable at the time to imagine coming to terms with her lost father and emotionally distant mother, Sprengnether ruefully notes that she had forgotten the scenes in *Solaris* that did not personally speak to her. Watching the film seventeen years later, she can imagine the resolution of grief.

Viewing Jane Campion's *The Piano*, Sprengnether thought that her life was settled as a result of her remarriage. Unprepared for the film's violence and eroticism, she found herself identifying with the mute Ada. The film enables Sprengnether to explore her anger toward her stepfather who, she tells us in a later chapter, committed suicide, overwhelming her with guilt because she had wished for his death—an example of the omnipotence of thought. Sprengnether had first written about her stepfather in *Rivers, Stories, Houses, Dreams*, her 1983 collection of personal essays. Unable to cry for her stepfather, a figurehead father whom she had never accepted, she felt that she was "owned by death," "set apart like Cain" (39).

Sprengnether viewed Peter Weir's *Fearless*, a film about the aftermath of an airplane crash, around the time she had fallen and fractured her arm, producing a hairline crack that later struck her as an apt metaphor of a deep fissure in herself.

Watching *Fearless* in her mid-fifties, she experienced her second convulsive reaction. The order of her life came apart with a fury that felt like a Greek tragedy. Her second marriage suddenly cracked open, splitting her life apart. Seeing *The Cement Garden*, a film directed by Andrew Birken based on Ian McEwen's novel, Sprengnether was fascinated by its depiction of brother-sister incest, a subject she fearlessly writes about in her own life. Her older brother was the closest she could get to her beloved father, whom she had idealized in her grief. Without having read Freud at the time, she knew that losing her father made all love feel forbidden and incestuous.

Sprengnether was familiar with C.S. Lewis's memoir *A Grief Observed* and Richard Attenborough's film based on it, *Shadowlands*. She had much in common with Lewis, who had lost a parent in childhood at the same age. *A Grief Observed* and *Shadowlands* raise disturbing questions, including how to avoid raging at God for the loss of a loved one. "Anger breeds anger," she remarks, "like the escalating violence of a hurricane" (162). Unlike Lewis, whose loss of his wife, Joy Davidman Gresham, from cancer heightened his religious faith, Sprengnether did not experience a spiritual epiphany, but she slowly let go of her anger, learning to live with—and write about—grief. The final film discussed, Krzysztov Kieslowski's *Blue*, contains a character, Julie, who has suffered a grievous loss, resulting in inner deadness. "In the less than three hours it took me to view this film, I could see my journey whole. Julie's path from numbness to mourning paralleled my own glacially slow progress through grief" (183–4). Like Julie, she needed to reinvent herself, a process facilitated through writing.

The last chapter in *Crying at the Movies*, "Shadow Love," focuses on her mother's death in 1998 at age eighty-two. Noting that her mother never approved of her daughter's decisions, Sprengnether writes poignantly about attending to her most intimate needs at an annual Thanksgiving visit. "We've come full circle" (215), her mother dryly observes when her fifty-five-year-old daughter cleans her after a bout of diarrhea. The memoirist doesn't sentimentalize her mother's death or imply that there was a final repair in their conflicted relationship. She shows, however, that planning her mother's funeral helps her come to terms with the finality of loss.

Sprengnether and Sylvia Plath

Crying at the Movies abounds in discussions of literature as well as film. There are many references, some brief, others extended, to St. Augustine, the seventeenth-century playwright John Ford, Shakespeare, Henry James, Gerard Manley Hopkins, and Louise Glück. There's one author, not mentioned in the memoir, whose life and art uncannily intersect with Sprengnether's: Sylvia Plath. Both daughters lost their fathers at a young age—Plath was eight when her father died in 1940. Both interpreted their fathers' deaths as acts of abandonment. Both mythologize their fathers into larger-than-life figures. Sprengnether doesn't portray her father as a monstrous Nazi-like figure, "Herr Doktor," as Plath does in her poem "Lady

Lazarus," but she idealizes him and searches for father substitutes in her love relationships.

Both Sprengnether and Plath were prevented by their mothers from attending their fathers' funerals. Both believed that the failure to work through grief led to psychological difficulties. Both read Freud's "Mourning and Melancholia" to understand the dynamics of bereavement and depression. Both daughters later visited their fathers' graves and felt a degree of closure. "I had a great yearning, lately, to pay my father back for all the years of neglect, and start tending his grave," Esther Greenwood confesses in the semi-autobiographical novel *The Bell Jar*, published posthumously in the United States in 1963. "I had always been my father's favorite, and it seemed fitting I should take on a mourning my mother had never bothered with" (186). Both wrote about encountering an internalized dark double who embodied rage. The evil alter ego in *The Bell Jar* is Joan Gilling, "the beaming double of my old best self, specifically designed to follow and torment me" (231). Sprengnether characterizes the unnamed subjugated self in *Crying at the Movies* as an *"enfant terrible"* (76), a netherworldly figure whose passionate demands made a shambles of her first marriage.

Suicide dominates Plath's late poems and novel. "Dying / Is an art like everything else," the speaker admits in "Lady Lazarus," "I do it exceptionally well." In her poem "Daddy," Plath's speaker writes about an early suicide attempt as an effort to be reunited with her father in death—to "get back, back, back to you." Suicide similarly preoccupies Sprengnether in *Crying at the Movies*. She writes about a woman she met in college, Anne, a "kindred soul" (46) who later may have taken her own life. Sprengnether mentions the poet John Berryman's suicide, remarking that they both lived in the same neighborhood near the University of Minnesota campus. While watching *House of Cards*, she wonders whether she wanted to die to rejoin her father in death. Acknowledging her intellectual attraction to suicide, Sprengnether finds herself dwelling on filmic characters who end their own lives, such as Hari in *Solaris*.

Both Plath and Sprengnether enter into psychoanalysis to understand their grief, anger, and depression. Both writers acknowledge the help of psychotherapists. In *Letters Home*, Plath refers to "Dr. B.," Dr. Ruth Beuscher, the psychiatrist who treated her in the late 1950s. In her acknowledgments at the end of *Crying at the Movies*, Sprengnether expresses gratitude to Dr. Ilse Jawetz, "whose calm presence and wise counsel have sustained me for more years than either she or I imagined would be necessary" (244). Sprengnether doesn't reveal that she was in therapy with Jawetz, but this detail appears in Sprengnether's 2015 memoir *Great River Road*, where she singles out the San Francisco psychoanalyst who helped "guide me through the disruption of my second marriage into the next phase of life" (np).

Father-hunger pervades Plath's and Sprengnether's writings. Both were fascinated by Shakespeare's *The Tempest*, with its subject of shipwreck, drowning, transformation, and rebirth. Plath's poem "Full Fathom Five" refers to Ariel's Song in *The Tempest*; Sprengnether cites the same song in *Crying at the Movies* (and in *Great River Road*), and then adds that, contrary to Shakespeare's play, she felt no such transformation in her own life. There's another eerie parallel between the two writers. Plath cites in her *Journals* her mother's dream of finding her husband floating "face down and bloated" in the ocean (268–9). Sprengnether describes her father's body, after floating in the Mississippi River for two days, as "bloated and gaseous," physically repulsive (226).

Both Plath and Sprengnether discovered the healing power of literary expression. "If writing is not an outlet, what is?" Plath asks rhetorically in her *Journals* (292). She later remarks that "Writing is my health" (327). Like Plath, Sprengnether began keeping a journal, and, through an adopted persona, started to connect the emotions associated with paternal loss to their traumatic source. The process of writing, she realizes, not only alters her relationship to the past but also brings into existence a new revised self.

Unlike Plath, who asphyxiated herself at age thirty, at the height of her creativity, Sprengnether rejected suicide, what she alliteratively limns as the "siren call of surcease" (52). Another difference lies in the vexed mother-daughter relationships. Plath struggled against a symbiotic fusion with her mother, a relationship lacking in boundaries. Sprengnether had the opposite problem, trying to connect with an emotionally detached mother. Still another difference lies in the way the two writers imagine confronting their dark doubles. Plath dispenses with Joan Gilling at the end of *The Bell Jar* by having her kill herself. There is no reconciliation or integration between the warring selves in Plath's world. She imagined only two solutions to the problem of mental illness, suicide or rebirth, neither of which represents a realistic understanding of the therapeutic process.

By contrast, Sprengnether searches for self-integration. "There ought to be a word in our vocabulary for the opposite of 'exorcism,' for the process of welcoming back a self one has tried to disown or expel" (*Crying at the Movies* 75). Plath thrusts her readers into the position of the "peanut-crunching crowd," as the speaker sardonically exclaims in "Lady Lazarus," who voyeuristically partakes of the poet's suffering. Sprengnether makes no such demands on her readers. Whereas Plath relies on the primitive defense mechanisms of projective identification and splitting in her poems and novel, Sprengnether works through her lifelong tendency toward intellectualization. She is also careful not to romanticize suicide. Unnerved by her daughter's statement that some people do not want to live, Sprengnether responds, simply, truthfully, and protectively "But most people *do* want to live, just the same" (52).

Crying at the Movies leaves us with an epiphanic insight. "The lesson of crying is metamorphosis" (207). She *shows* us the process of transformation. Emotional truths are often more significant than intellectual ones. *Crying at the Movies* has an affective richness that affirms the power of feelings, a power conveyed by Sprengnether's vivid metaphorical language. To give one example, witness how she describes her body's convulsions while she gazed at the mother's contorted face, accompanied by Ravi Shankar's music, in *Pather Panchali*:

> My body heard this call and responded in the only way it knew how—viscerally. I felt a ripple in my mid-section, which rose through my chest and esophagus in a powerful contraction. I was not used to crying like this. I was not used to

> crying at all—it was as if I inhabited an emotional landscape so parched that I had no interior water table from which to draw. In the small Sahara of my heart, I had forgotten how to weep. Instead, I was convulsed, choking, snorting, and sobbing. (26)

Sprengnether captures, here and elsewhere, somatic language. She deftly develops, with a poet's sensibility, the contrast between her flowing tears and her desiccated state of mind. The passage subtly conjures up the image of childbirth, giving birth to a new life. Elsewhere she uses metaphors like "amputation" to elicit rejected emotions and, conversely, metaphors like a shimmering pool of water after a thunderstorm to evoke lifegiving wholeness. She demonstrates how denied emotions tunnel underground, returning with a vengeance. Weeping is a wordless drama that we ignore at our peril. *Crying at the Movies* remains a haunting cautionary tale, reminding us of the wisdom of tears. Tellingly, Sprengnether's father manufactured seismographs, delicate instruments for detecting the smallest oscillations of the earth. *Crying at the Movies* is itself an exquisite measure of the oscillations of mourning. We may not wail when we read *Crying at the Movies*, but we feel sad, a word that originally meant, as Sprengnether observes, "full" or "satisfied" (180). Given this early meaning, the sadness we feel at the end of her memoir betokens fullness and satisfaction.

Crying at the Movies elicited sharply contradictory responses from film reviewers. Richard Schickel, in a review published in the *Los Angeles Times*, praised the "alertness and disciplined nuance" of Sprengnether's responses, "her aching openness to the full range of unexpected possibilities a seriously intended film can offer." Suzanne Szucs, by contrast, faulted the memoir for giving the filmic characters "equal weight with her own real life." I can understand the reviewer's objection to personal criticism, but it is hard to fathom her belief that the memoir doesn't feel vulnerable enough: "her prose feels clinical and emotionless." Did Szucs and I read the same book? One cannot generalize about gender from only two reviews, but it's curious that the male reviewer was more sympathetic to the memoir than the female reviewer.

Memory is a process rather than a product, Sprengnether remarks in *Great River Road*, a touching meditation on later life. She learns one new disturbing detail about her father's death that she had not known while she was writing *Crying at the Movies*. During a conversation with her younger brother, she discovered that moments before their father's drowning, her older brother had boasted about how far he could swim. "And Dad told him to swim out to a stick that was floating by in the water" (25). According to her younger brother, their parents then began arguing who was at fault when their son found himself in trouble. The story, however, cannot be confirmed: neither her mother nor her older brother will talk about the drowning. Was her younger brother telling the truth? Or was he simply misremembering? There is no way to tell whether memory is accurate or treacherous. How could the father she idealized be so foolish for giving what turned out to be a disastrous command? The new information deepens Sprengnether's anger, which finally gives way to acceptance. "So he was human after all, not the god-like figure I had enshrined in my memory" (26).

Sprengnether observes early in *Great River Road* that trauma is characterized by endless repetition. In reliving her father's death, first in *Crying at the Movies* and then in *Great River Road*, she invokes Freud's repetition-compulsion principle in *Beyond the Pleasure Principle* (1920). She had anticipated a feeling of therapeutic relief from completing the books but not a new understanding of the past. Heightened self-awareness enabled her to see Freud in a new way. Writing an essay on Freud's early childhood traumas, she admits in *Great River Road* that her thesis owes much to her own experience with unresolved mourning. "I've been as evasive—even as ingenious—as Freud in my strategies of avoidance" (56).

Mourning Freud

Sprengnether's scholarly books are not disguised autobiography, but they contain the same themes that appear in her personal writings. There are only a few references to Freud in *Crying at the Movies*, but we can see how writing the memoir prepared her for *Mourning Freud*. Unresolved childhood mourning shaped Freud's life as fatefully and fitfully as it shaped Sprengnether's. The deliberate ambiguity in her title alerts us to its double focus. *Mourning Freud* explores Freud's experiences and theories of mourning along with the ways in which the post-Freudian age has lamented one of the giants in the history of ideas. Neither a Freud idealizer nor a Freud-basher, Sprengnether offers an intriguing discussion of a major area of psychoanalytic theory—a problem neglected by earlier psychoanalytic scholars.

Sprengnether begins her introduction, "Insight and Blindness," with an apt quote by the literary theorist Terry Eagleton: a "work's insights, as with all writing, are deeply related to its blindnesses: what it does not say, and how it does not say it, may be as important as what it articulates" (1). The introduction's title may also be an allusion to Paul de Man's *Blindness and Insight* (1971), a classic of deconstructive literary criticism. Sprengnether, well versed in psychoanalysis, deconstructionism, and feminism, brings to Freudian studies an uncommon knowledge of "high theory" as well as a capacity for close reading.

Part One of *Mourning Freud* focuses on biography and theory. Freud's life, Sprengnether suggests, is not consistent with the major theory he derived from his self-analysis: namely, the masculine model of the Oedipus complex. The first four years of Freud's life were filled with losses: the death of his younger brother Julius in early infancy; the departure of his first nanny, who was dismissed when she was caught stealing; and the disruption caused by the family's move twice in two years as a result of his father's business failures. These losses may have been compounded, Sprengnether plausibly conjectures, by the possibility that Freud's mother, Amalia, was depressed by Julius's death (along with the death, around the same time, of her brother, also named Julius) and by Freud's loss of her exclusive attention when she had six additional children in rapid succession.

Given these multiple early losses, how is it possible that Freud failed to mention the grief arising from early maternal loss? He curiously avoids any discussion of sorrow when theorizing in *Beyond the Pleasure Principle* his grandson Ernst's push-pull game of "fort/da," disappearance and return. Sprengnether wrote about this ritual of "gone" and "here again" in *The Spectral Mother* and *Great River Road*, but now she calls attention to a meaning that Freud misses. He theorizes his grandson's anger, denial, displacement, and compulsive repetitive behavior but not the sadness the boy almost certainly experienced. Understanding this sadness in her own life enables Sprengnether to intuit its presence in the lives of both Freud and his grandson.

Sprengnether points out that even after Ernst's mother (Freud's daughter Sophie) died suddenly in 1920 from the Spanish influenza, the analyst still refused to mention any grief that his grandson must have felt, as is evident in an astonishing footnote that appears in *Beyond the Pleasure Principle*. "When this child was five and three-quarters, his mother died. Now that she was really 'gone' ('o-o-o'), the little boy showed no signs of grief" (*SE*, vol. 18, 16, n. 1). Sprengnether characterizes Freud's next sentence as a "stunning *non sequitur*" (52): "It is true that in the interval a second child had been born and had roused him to violent jealousy" (16). In Sprengnether's view, Freud's interpretation of the fort/da ritual probably reveals more about his own efforts to deny grief than it does about his grandson's anguish.

Whereas Peter Homans (1989) and Mark Edmundsen (1990) regard Freud's creativity as arising from the mourning process, Sprengnether believes, along with Kathleen Woodward (1991), that Freud's inability to theorize his grief inhibited his creativity. "Challenging Freud's mastery of his own self-image in this way necessarily challenges the magisterial status of his theory." Some may be disturbed, she admits, by a deauthorization of Freud, but others "will feel compensated by its result: a less mythologized portrait of the man, a more open and questioning stance toward his work" (56).

Freud's major theory of mourning remains his 1917 essay "Mourning and Melancholia," the most influential twentieth-century statement on the subject. Sprengnether foregrounds both the strengths and weaknesses of this iconic work. She notes that although Freud's essay does not deal openly with maternal loss, it hovers in the background "as a kind of shadow text" (83), or, we might add, as a spectral mother. Sprengnether investigates Freud's statement near the conclusion of the essay, where he observes that "the conflict within the ego, which melancholia substitutes for the struggle over the object, must act like a painful wound which calls for an extraordinarily high anti-cathexis." Freud's next statement may be even more salient: "But here once again, it will be well to call a halt and to postpone any further discussion" (*SE*, vol. 14, 258).

Seizing on both the wound metaphor and Freud's abrupt conclusion, Sprengnether remarks that the effect of these closing comments is to "hold the wound metaphor in suspension, as if melancholia itself were an interminable illness" (84). What's most striking about the wound metaphor, which Freud had used in an 1895 letter to Wilhelm Fliess to describe melancholia, is its resemblance to his language about castration, a condition he attributes only to females. The threat of castration prevents a boy from acting on his desire for his mother, but the girl, according to Freud, already experiences castration through her awareness of phallic lack. Freud's theory of mourning allows him to escape from any recognition of his painful losses in early childhood.

Part Two, "Transitions," consists of three chapters: "Undoing Incest," "Freud as Memoirist," and "Literature and Psychoanalysis." Sprengnether begins "Undoing Incest" with an account of a revealing Freudian slip, recalling the chagrin she experienced when she met at a professional conference an editor of a book whose title—*Daughters and Fathers*—she accidentally inverted. "In placing fathers before daughters, I was contributing to the very phenomenon the book seeks to examine—the subordination and effacement of the daughter within Western family structures and traditions" (119). Later in the chapter she observes that Freud's attitude toward his youngest daughter, Anna, was possessive if not literally incestuous.

Sprengnether reads Freud's 1899 essay "Screen Memories" as a "trickster narrative" in that the person it describes, a university-educated man of thirty-eight whose slight phobia Freud was able to treat successfully, was the analyst himself. "Freud, in effect, writes a fictionalized account of his own inner musings in order to argue that memory itself is a writer of densely composed fictions" (150). The self-reflexiveness of Freud's essay anticipates current controversies over the reliability of memory (the "memory wars") in general, and life writing in particular. Sprengnether makes an observation that earlier scholars have noted, most in appreciation but some in criticism: Freud wrote like a literary writer. Indeed, the only major award that he received was the Goethe Prize for literature in 1930. But Sprengnether then makes a less obvious comment: "Freud, on the page, is the least coercive of theorists, allowing for doubt, conjecture, and even creative disagreement with him, which, in turn, invites new ideas and formulations" (180-1). Doubt and conjecture, we recall, characterized Sprengnether's attitude upon hearing the unsettling news about her parents' unseemly fight while her older brother was struggling to remain afloat. The best one can do is remain open to the truth, recalling Keats's Negative Capability: "that is, when a man is capable of being in uncertainties, Mysteries, doubts, without any irritable reaching after fact and reason" (261).

Ghosts into Ancestors

Sprengnether concludes *Mourning Freud* by suggesting that psychoanalysis can help us live with the dead by converting "Ghosts into Ancestors," the title of Part Three. Here she draws on Hans Loewald's distinction in "On the Therapeutic Action of Psycho-Analysis" (1960) between ghosts and ancestors: "Those who know ghosts tell us that they long to be released from their ghost-life and led to rest as ancestors" (29). Sprengnether suggests, in one of her most evocative sentences, that we contain the "ghost traces of those whom we love, lose, and mourn." She then raises a crucial question: "how do we communicate with ghosts in such a way as to transform them into ancestors?" (235). Those who have lost a beloved relative or friend know that there is no more urgent question than this one.

But a writer must be ready for this exorcism. In her essay "Ghost Writing: A Meditation on Literary Criticism as Narrative," appearing in *The Psychoanalytic Study of Literature* in 1985, Sprengnether remarks that the experience of psychotherapy has changed her understanding of literature. Reflecting back on some of her difficulties with writing when she was in graduate school, a time when she still believed in the "paradigm of objectivity," she realizes that she was not prepared to confront topics that might have undermined her fragile sense of self. She then shares with her readers a story told to her by her young daughter about a boy who had almost drowned. "One day at the beach a little boy she knew nearly drowned. By the time he was pulled out of the water, he had stopped breathing and had to be revived with mouth-to-mouth resuscitation" (43). This would have been an apt moment for Sprengnether to reveal her father's drowning—but she was not yet ready for this momentous disclosure.

Richard M. Waugaman concludes his sympathetic review of *Mourning Freud* published in *The Psychoanalytic Quarterly* by noting that Sprengnether's capacity for complexity "helps lead her readers away from the pitfalls of oversimplification and false dichotomies" (454). In another sympathetic review published in *American Imago*, Shelley Ann Cross observes that the ability to converse with ghosts recalls Bion's metaphor of the container. "The elements of melancholia," Cross writes, "are indigestible, like Bion's beta elements without a container with which to make meaning" (443). Regardless of whether we use Loewald's metaphor or Bion's, the challenge is to keep the dead alive, a question with which psychotherapists have long wrestled. As I remark in *Companionship in Grief* (2010), for years clinicians have accepted Freud's view of mourning, but there has been a sea change in their thinking:

> For example, in the first edition of *Grief Counseling and Grief Therapy* (1982), J. William Worden agrees with Freud and lists one of the "tasks of mourning" as "withdrawing emotional energy from the deceased and reinvesting it in another relationship." In the third edition (2002), however, Worden reverses himself and concludes that Freud was mistaken about the mourner's need to shatter the relational bond with the deceased. "We now know that people do not decathect from the dead but find ways to develop 'continuing bonds' with the deceased" (35). Worden now suggests, contrary to Freud, that one of the tasks of mourning "is to find a place for the deceased that will enable the mourner to be connected with the deceased but in a way that will not preclude him or her from getting on with life" (35). (*Companionship in Grief* 5)

Worden alludes to a new paradigm of mourning, called "continuing bonds," formulated in a 1996 volume edited by Klass, Silverman, and Nickman. Based on clinical and empirical research, they conclude that "survivors hold the deceased in loving memory for long periods, often forever, and that maintaining an inner representation of the deceased is normal rather than abnormal" (349). Sprengnether doesn't discuss the continuing bonds theory of mourning, but she would be sympathetic with the aim of keeping the dead alive while creating new life-sustaining relationships. Continuing bonds help us understand why we need to hold on to the memory of Freud while we continue to reevaluate and transform his theory in light of new clinical knowledge.

Sprengnether's self-analysis in *Crying at the Movies* and *Great River Road* emboldened her to analyze Freud's construction of psychoanalysis. Her two memoirs demonstrate that self-analysis is never complete. She did not have a hidden agenda when writing about Freud's mourning, but she put her own mourning to good use. Sprengnether's personal and scholarly writings attest to Daniel Rancour-Laferriere's central thesis in his edited volume *Self-Analysis in Literary Study* (1994): "self-analysis can be a boon to other-analysis, including psychoanalysis of literature. Literary analysis informed by self-analysis is in principle superior to literary analysis not so informed" (29). As Sprengnether declares in "Ghost Writing," literary interpretation is a "refracted form of autobiography" (45). Or as Bessel van der Kolk argues in *The Body Keeps the Score* (2014), citing the attachment theorist Beatrice Beebe, "most research is me-search" (111). Freud's psychoanalytic writings, Sprengnether reminds us, are memoiristic, containing often unacknowledged autobiographical material—like her own writings. Mourning loss, her own and Freud's, turns out to be transformative, enabling Madelon Sprengnether to integrate disparate memories and move forward in life.

Chapter 14

SOPHIE FREUD

LIVING IN THE SHADOW OF THE FREUD FAMILY

Living in the Shadow of the Freud Family (2007) is exceptional for many reasons. Written and edited by Sophie Freud, Sigmund Freud's granddaughter, the memoir provides a fascinating glimpse into her parents' disastrous marriage and the fraught legacy of bearing an iconic name. There are many biographies of Freud and several books written by disciples, rivals, and analysands, but *Living in the Shadow of the Freud Family* is unique in that it offers two separate accounts of the Freud family, the first written by his daughter-in-law, the second by his granddaughter.

Sophie Freud is a professor emerita of social work at Simmons College. She is not a psychoanalyst but rather a teacher of human development and psychological thought systems. She first wrote about her mother in an earlier book, *My Three Mothers and Other Passions* (1988). *Living in the Shadow of the Freud Family* serves, as Barry Silverstein points out in a glowing review, as a "prequel" to her earlier book (153). She annotates and expands her mother's autobiography, *Vignettes of My Life*, by including other voices and letters, such as her brother's memoir, her children's comments about their grandmother, and her own diary entries. There are few multivocal memoirs, and Sophie Freud presents us with clashing interpretations of reality that cannot always be resolved. Additionally, she narrates her own story about her life immediately before, during, and after the Second World War. "With my 81 years," she notes at the beginning, "I am already two years older than my mother was when she wrote her autobiography at the age of seventy-nine. She did so at my urging. She found it to be an exciting and absorbing task" (xv). So, too, was it an exciting and absorbing task for Sophie Freud to write her own book, conveying intense emotions that readers will themselves experience as they journey through this extraordinary double memoir.

Troubled from the Beginning

Ernestine ("Esti") Drucker, the daughter of rich and influential Viennese-Jewish parents, first met Martin Freud, the psychoanalyst's second child and oldest son, shortly before the Great War. She was immediately attracted to the handsome young man who soon became a dashing artillery officer. The Freud family, however, was suspicious of her. "It is possible that grandfather recognized at a glance that my mother, who was probably beautifully dressed, came from a wealthy family and would be a threat to the thrifty lifestyle practiced by the women in the Freud family" (42). Nor were Esti's own parents supportive of the marriage: her father did not want her to marry "another psychiatrist," one who "wrote pornographic books" (42). Esti began a long, passionate, one-sided correspondence with Martin when he was a prisoner of war in 1918. "My main occupation is to love you" (54), she confesses in a March 1919 letter. Four months later, she writes another missive betraying deep insecurity of which she seemed to be largely unaware. After claiming that she has "invincible self-confidence," she admits presciently that "Sometimes, on totally sad and bad days, I imagine that you no longer love me, then I take for comfort your old letters and read them again and again" (66).

Esti and Martin were officially engaged in September 1919, when his nine-month imprisonment in Italy ended, and they married in the same year, when she was twenty-three and he thirty. The marriage was troubled from the beginning, confirming the Freuds' worst fears about marital incompatibility. "Tante Mathilde [Sigmund Freud's oldest child] told me once," Sophie Freud remarks, "when she was already quite old, that my father had always been incapable of loving anyone, not his mother, nor his sisters, nor his wife, perhaps not even his children" (69). The contrast between Esti's early love letters to Martin and her later angry, embittered ones is jarring. Despite or perhaps because of Esti's overwhelming need to be loved and admired, the Freuds treated her poorly, and she never overcame her animosity. Martin started to gamble her money on the stock market, and she soon found herself impoverished. "The loss of this money," Sophie Freud writes, "which also involves loss of her financial independence, caused a lifelong bitterness" (73–4).

Esti reports in her autobiography that after her son (Anton) Walter's birth in 1921 and Sophie's in 1924, she decided "no longer to follow blindly some of Martin's unreasonable wishes and to start a more independent life" (81). She trained as a speech pathologist and lectured at the University of Vienna until Hitler's annexation of Austria resulted in her ouster in 1938. As the war clouds approaches, she recognized the Nazi danger and urged Anna Freud, the family's youngest child, that "Papa has to emigrate," to which her sister-in-law responded icily, "*Ein Professor Freud wander nicht aus*": "A professor Freud does not emigrate" (131).

After protracted negotiations, Sigmund Freud received seventeen life-saving exit visas, four of which went to Martin and his family. "I thus owe it to my grandfather to be among the few lucky ones to have escaped Vienna before the murderous persecution of its Jews" (137). Four of Freud's five elderly sisters were less fortunate; unable to leave Vienna, they, along with Esti's mother, Ida, were all murdered in concentration camps. Esti's marriage, strained before the war, now dissolved in all but name. After fleeing Vienna, the Freud family traveled to Paris; Martin and Walter, along with the rest of the Freuds, then moved to London, where they remained. Esti and Sophie left for Paris, where they lived for a year. The family was forever divided. In June 1940, as the German cannons could be heard outside Paris, mother and daughter began a harrowing bicycle journey to the South of

France, living from September 1940, to December 1941, in Nice, where Sophie began her diary. Then they departed to Casablanca, living there from January 1942, to October 1943, when they boarded a steamer for the United States.

Esti never realized the extent to which the Freuds despised her. Freud refers to her in a 1930 letter to his nephew as an "unreasonable, abnormal wife" (Molnar 1930). Nor did his attitude change. "She is not only maliciously meschugge [crazy] but also mad in the medical sense," Freud opined to his son Ernst in 1938 (*Living in the Shadow of the Freud Family* 187), a judgment shared by the rest of the family. Esti's refusal to grant her husband a divorce compelled him to adopt his London partner, Margaret, so that she bore his last name.

Living in the Shadow of the Freud Family reveals new information about the founder of psychoanalysis. The author challenges some of the assumptions made by Freud biographers, including the belief that Freud was traumatized in his childhood when his Catholic nursemaid was caught stealing and jailed. "My chest tightens every time I come upon the incarceration of that poor nursemaid in yet another Freud biography," Sophie Freud laments. "There is never any evidence that my grandfather, later in life, perhaps in his famous self-analysis, worried about the just treatment of that once-beloved nursemaid" (23). Nor did he worry about the Freud family housekeepers who, according to his granddaughter, were exploited. Freud was old and ill when she knew him, and she remembers him poignantly with his fingers in his mouth, always in pain from dozens of cancer surgeries and an unwieldly prosthetic device, which he called the "monster," required to separate his oral and nasal cavities.

Esti's description of the Freuds' strict discipline is memorable. "The Freuds had their noontime meal, the main meal in Vienna, at the stroke of one, and war or no war, you had to be there on time or not eat. This gave me an inkling of the kind of discipline that ruled the Freud family" (38). Dinner demanded the same inflexible regimen. "A few minutes before seven o'clock die Frau Professor said, 'Papa will be out any minute. Let's go to the dining room.' Sure enough, at the stroke of seven, the door opposite the end of the dining room opened, and out came the 'Professor' wrapped like a god of antiquity in a cloud of smoke" (42). The celestial psychoanalyst wrote a letter to Esti in early 1939 in which he observes that the lack of understanding between marital partners cannot be improved by a relative or friend's intervention, to which Sophie Freud observes wryly, "Freud, it seems, was hardly a pioneer of couple therapy" (182).

Sophie Freud remains ambivalent toward her grandfather, criticizing in her earlier publications many of his theories while acknowledging that she has been the beneficiary of his love and recognizable name. (Her attitude toward her regal grandfather is not unlike how the British feel toward the crown, a mixture of loyalty and affection tinged with mild irritation.) In "Grandfather Freud," one of the most moving chapters, she imagines writing a letter to him:

> Dearest grandfather, being your grandchild has stamped my life. You were a kind and protective presence in my young life, even if emotionally distant. My early identity as a princess helped me to remain steadfast during some difficult

years, shielded me from the self-destructive self-doubts that tormented my poor mother, spurred me on to start thinking for myself and raise my voice, and even gave me the courage to critique your theories, which, I know, you would not have forgiven me. (109)

To understand Sophie Freud's conflicting feelings toward psychoanalysis, we may turn to *My Three Mothers and Other Passions*, where she acknowledges her struggle against the double burden of her grandfather's legacy that imprisoned women's lives: the demand for conformity and obedience. Arriving in the United States in 1942, she attended Radcliffe College; her tuition was paid for by her grandfather's nephew Edward Bernays, who pioneered public relations. After earning a master's degree from Simmons College School of Social Work, she worked as a clinical social worker and supervisor in the field of child welfare. She received her PhD from the Florence Heller School for Social Welfare at Brandeis in 1970. Rumor had it, she admits, that the reason she was accepted into the doctoral program was in the hope of converting Freud's skeptical granddaughter. They succeeded, she adds ruefully, because she knew only the psychoanalytic approach.

Sophie Freud's counter-conversionary experience began when she read Erving Goffman's *Stigma* (1963). The book was life-transforming, enabling her to realize that the clinical writings she had read previously were untrue. "The books had lied to me. They had also lied about penis envy, the vaginal orgasm, female narcissism, menopause, motherhood, and about how to rear children and lead a good life. Later I started to write papers on many of these subjects, trying to sort out systematically the lies and the truths" (113).

Deepening Our Understanding of Psychology: The Worry Child

Sophie Freud has made a distinctive contribution to psychological theory, as the chapters in *My Three Mothers and Other Passions* demonstrate. She speaks with a clinical authority that commands respect even from those with a different theoretical orientation. Her scholarly and clinical articles, many of which were published under her married name, Sophie Freud Loewenstein, include the idea of a *Sorgenkind* (a German word that translates as "worry child"), a child over whom parents fret excessively. "I have never known a family without at least one *Sorgenkind*" (109). Ironically, she may have been inspired to use this word by her mother. In a March 23, 1919, letter, Esti calls Martin her "worry child" (*Living in the Shadow of the Freud Family* 57), mainly because he was a prisoner of war at the time. Sophie Freud calls her older daughter her own Sorgenkind.

Indeed, Andrea Freud Loewenstein's 1992 novel, *The Worry Girl: Stories from a Childhood*, demonstrates a fraught mother-daughter relationship. Despite the obligatory disclaimer at the beginning—"Although I have retained the Freud name in this book as an essential backdrop, it is a work of fiction"—the story captures Esti's Viennese voice and recreates the hostility she experienced when she encountered her future husband's parents. "I was too pretty for the family, this is what I heard Herr Professor say out from the corner of his mouth when my husband first brought me home" (12). The novel is consonant with everything we learn factually about Esti and Martin Freud in her mother's two books.

Apart from its biographical interest, *The Worry Girl* shows how the sins of the mothers are passed on intergenerationally. The evocative coming-of-age novel reveals how the young anxiety-ridden protagonist, Rachel, struggles to live up to the high expectations of a well-intentioned but demanding mother who cannot understand why her daughter is not at the top of her class. "And you," the mother reproaches her daughter, "you were a difficult child, you cried all the time, you demanded my constant attention. I believe that every family has, a Sorgenkind, a worry child, and it is often the first one. And you, you were my Sorgenkind" (21). The novel ends lyrically, with Rachel striking out on her and experiencing, for the first time, sexual love with another woman. Rachel may still be a worry child, but she has become her own person. Dedicated to her mother, *The Worry Girl* displays the same unsparing honesty that we see in Sophie Freud's own books.

Few subjects are off limits in *Living in the Shadow of the Freud Family*. Sophie Freud tells us, for example, about her mother's response upon learning that her granddaughter Andrea is a lesbian and consequently may not need the silver that Esti's grandchildren will inherit. "Mother made a grimace of horror, hissed, 'don't say such things,' and turned back to her silverware. 'Perhaps she would prefer a silver platter,' she said in her former voice'" (427).

Sophie Freud's study of 700 married women suggests that three-fifths had a "passion experience," defined as an intense and obsessive emotion for a love object, with their current or, if divorced, most recent husband. The remaining two-fifths of married women have not. She warns of the dangers of "overloving," where the love object becomes a narcissistic extension of oneself rather than a separate person. "Overloving involves possessiveness, anxious overprotection, and intense involvement" (178). She admits to overloving her clients at the beginning of her career.

Sophie Freud was never in psychoanalysis, but her two years in psychotherapy, which ended when her psychiatrist moved away, created an addictive dependency from which it took her an entire year to recover. "I resolved that this would be my last formal healing attempt. The dependency it has created was too frightening" (112). She emphasizes, far more than her grandfather or other psychoanalysts, that healing arises mainly from bearing witness to one's own suffering. Her own healing, she remarks, often occurs when she writes professional articles: her theoretical writings are thus highly personal documents. She recognizes that good teaching is usually therapeutic for teachers and students alike.

One of Sophie Freud's most provocative insights about her paternal family is that her grandfather not only knew about his son's womanizing but also encouraged it, consciously or not. She makes this observation in a chapter in *My Three Mothers and Other Passions* called "The Heirloom," in which she writes about herself in the third person. The "Daughter" encounters her famous aunt's "biographer," presumably Elisabeth Young-Bruehl.

The biographer was amazed how the Daughter's father had been able to collect so many beautiful women. The Daughter explained how her father's older sister had also told her that her father could not go down the street without women turning around. It was the Daughter's opinion that her chaste and ascetic grandfather had delegated the fulfillment of sexual pleasure to his oldest son. (295)

Sophie Freud supports this observation in *Living in the Shadow of the Freud Family* by quoting a letter her grandfather wrote to his son Ernst on May 14, 1938, the day Martin left Vienna for London via Paris: "But what will he do in England? He cannot live without women, and there he won't find the freedom he allowed himself here" (188). Paul Roazen supplies additional evidence in *Meeting Freud's Family* of Martin's playboy reputation. "Later in London, when Martin went to see a performance of *Romeo and Juliet*, Freud commented to a visitor that his son needed no further exposure to the role of Romeo, since he already was his own Romeo . . . certainly Freud's wife, who was present, would have picked up Freud's meaning" (162).

Martin Freud does not call himself a playboy in his 1959 book, *Sigmund Freud: Man and Father*, but one can read between the lines. Describing an attractive young woman around his own age who was devoted to the novels of Sir Walter Scott, as he himself was, Martin Freud imagines being the courageous and righteous knight Ivanhoe. "Soon we were deeply in love, holding hands whenever we could without being seen and exchanging letters of a highly sentimental kind" (150). In another passage, he boasts that while on leave during the First World War, he held in his arms an entirely unclothed Hedy Lamarr. The future film star, he adds, appreciating the irony, "was then two years old" (159). It must have been galling for Esti Freud to read her estranged husband's book. He mentions his wife a few times but never by her name. He refers with great pride to his son Walter, but not once does he refer to his daughter Sophie.

Despite his training as a lawyer and his work as the publisher of his father's books, Martin Freud was never successful professionally. Esti was. Notwithstanding her insecurity, vanity (she had two facelifts in old age as well as countless hormonal treatments, her daughter informs us, disapprovingly), and constant complaints, Esti Freud was endlessly resourceful and talented, working as a speech pathologist in three different countries, using three different languages. At the age of fifty-nine, she earned a PhD from the New School for Social Research. She lectured for the United Jewish Appeal and authored several articles published in leading medical journals.

Anna Freud

The chapters in *My Three Mothers and Other Passions* likely to be of the greatest interest to psychoanalytic readers involve the author's third mother, her Tante Anna. She had little relationship with Anna Freud until a visit to London in 1979, shortly after the death of Anna's lifelong living and working companion, Dorothy Burlingham. Two more London visits followed, resulting in a warm and trusting friendship between the two women.

Sophie Freud suggests in "The Legacy of Anna Freud" that her aunt's formulation of a new defense mechanism, "altruistic surrender," a repudiation of one's sexuality to care for another person, describes Anna Freud herself, her father's adored Antigone. Reading all eight volumes of Anna Freud's collected writings, Sophie praises her unique voice, originality, practicality, and observational powers. She remains convinced, though, that Anna Freud was imprisoned in her father's psychoanalytic metapsychology. This did not prevent the two women from becoming close: they met late in life when "theory" was less important than love. They had much in common, including never wearing cosmetics and both dressing in loose-fitting clothes. Anna Freud was angered by feminists who demonized her father, yet ironically, she led an unmistakably feminist life. Sophie Freud does not speculate, as others have, whether her aunt had a sexual relationship with Dorothy Burlingham. Nor is she interested in pointing out that Anna Freud's discussion of "beating fantasies" was based on her Oedipal feelings toward her father, who analyzed her.

Despite the geographical and emotional distance that separated the two women for most of their adult lives, Anna Freud remains Sophie Freud's ego ideal, the person she most admires. She captures her aunt's quiet humor, her restraint and modesty, her child-like delight in accepting gifts such as chocolates, and her love for knitting. The author presents a down-to-earth portrait of Anna Freud, a woman who, despite being semiparalyzed near the end of her life, allowed her niece the privilege of helping to take care of her. "Now you have found a daughter after all" (12), she tells her aunt during her last visit. It is a moment of poignant tenderness in *My Three Mothers and Other Passions*. She repeats the same statement later in the book, adding her aunt's response. "'Now you have found a daughter after all; are you glad?' I asked. 'Yes,' she smiled, 'very glad'" (82). Oddly enough, the American psychoanalyst Esther Menaker describes this exchange differently in her 1989 memoir *Appointment in Vienna*, underscoring Anna Freud's discomfort with expressions of love and admiration:

> I am reminded of a remark she made to a niece who cared for her in her final illness—a niece whose family had been estranged from the Freuds throughout most of her life and who longed to be accepted, especially by Anna. In the intimacy that arises between two people during a serious illness, when one of them is the physical and emotional caretaker of the other, profound feelings are stirred up. In this situation Anna's niece said to her, "*Tante* Anna, I think I am falling in love with you." "How inconvenient," was Anna's reply. (22)

Menaker doesn't cite how she learned about this remark nor why she omits Sophie Freud's name, but she can't help adding her belief that Anna Freud, who was Menaker's training analyst, found her own strong emotions toward her inconvenient. She idealized Anna Freud during the beginning of the two-year analysis, admiring her modesty, kindness, sincerity, and integrity, but over time Menaker concluded that they were not a good match, partly because of the analyst's suspicion of her passionate temperament. Sophie Freud, no less passionate, as can be seen from the title of her book, managed to win over her aunt's love. She mourned deeply Anna Freud's death, which occurred on October 7, 1982, at age eighty-six.

Biographers and autobiographers who write about living people confront the vexing problem of respecting the privacy of the living while also disclosing what may be wrenching and invasive truths. Two of Sophie Freud's children, her older daughter, Andrea Freud Loewenstein, and her son, George Loewenstein, both of whom are university professors, contributed to the book. Her middle child, Danya Jekel, who "detests to reveal private matters to the whole world" (*Living in the Shadow of the Freud Family* xx), did not. Not all relatives of a world-famous figure wish to be identified with a household name. When Sophie Freud gave a talk in 2008 at Carnegie Mellon University about her new book, George Loewenstein, a professor of economics and psychology at that institution, told Sally Kalson in an article in the *Pittsburgh Post-Gazette* that he had tried not to publicize his connection to the Freuds. "It's a trap, once you start exploiting it. My friends know, of course, but now the cat's out of the bag. I'm just glad it's not my last name." The name was not a trap to his mother, however. After she divorced her husband of forty years, Paul Loewenstein, in 1988, she took back her maiden name.

The name impressed one of her Radcliffe professors, the celebrated American poet Delmore Schwartz. Had he not gone out of his way to help her when she was struggling to learn English, she might have been a college dropout. Years later, Sophie Freud read his correspondence and noticed that he mentioned her name twice, observing that she turned out to be a "veritable butterball, full of assurance, and when the class read *The Turn of the Screw* and I asked Sophie what she thought, she said: 'A clear case of paranoia'" (320). Other Radcliffe professors, however, did not dazzle her. She had no use for a psychology professor who droned on endlessly. "When I mentioned my name the whole class (Radcliffe and Harvard) started to scream and the teacher said: 'Could you spell that please!'" (319).

Despite her name, Sophie Freud had no interest in being psychoanalyzed, as her "second mother," Tante Janne, Esti's youngest sister, recommended. Nor did she have an interest in becoming a psychoanalyst. Given her powerful mind and her many contributions to psychological theory, one can imagine Sophie Freud, had she followed her aunt's advice, becoming one of the "mothers of psychoanalysis," along with Helene Deutsch, Karen Horney, Anna Freud, and Melanie Klein.

In choosing which of her mother's and deceased brother's letters to include in *Living in the Shadow of the Freud Family*, Sophie Freud found it necessary to make difficult judgment calls. She was guided by a single editorial policy: she never omitted "unpleasant truths" (xx). Esti wrote two versions of the first ten pages of *Vignettes of My Life*. The first, which was dedicated to her granddaughter Andrea on the occasion of her eighteenth birthday, contains a sharp narrative voice, especially when she criticizes her own mother; the second is a blander, more censored version. Which version should an editor use? Andrea Freud Loewenstein, the director of the Master of Fine Arts program in creative writing at Goddard College in Vermont, praises her mother's decision to use the first version, but she was angry at Esti for attempting to sugarcoat the truth. "All this woman had was her accusatory rage, and it cries out from every paragraph of these 'uncensored' pages that screams again and again, 'You betrayed me!'" She could have stopped with this accusation, but she makes an additional criticism about her own mother, which Sophie Freud dutifully includes:

> One of the things we must think about in this book is how these patterns are passed on, even when the resolve is not to. My own mother did not make scenes, but she was the indubitable center of the household, the "diva" on whose love and approval both the children and my father depended, and which we all vied for, unable to turn to each other. She, in her own way was also "terrifying"; that is, I lived in fear of disappointing her and the knowledge that I constantly was. (12)

My guess is that few authors would have included this last comment, but it reveals not only unpleasant truths about Sophie Freud's relationship to her own children but also that truth and honesty are supreme virtues in storytelling. Everything is grist for the writer's mill.

In 1948 Esti wrote a highly flattering article, "Mrs. Sigmund Freud," which was published in *The Menorah Journal* in 1948 and reprinted in *The Jewish Spectator* in 1980. She praises her mother-in-law as the "best wife" possible for her heroic husband, concluding that she was "*par excellence* 'a grand woman.'" But when Esti sent a copy of the article to the eighty-six-year-old Martha Freud, the response was not what she expected, a stinging rebuke. "To view my modest person moved into the public eye is all too repugnant to me." One could have imagined Martha Freud responding differently, without harshly stating, "your description oppresses me and puts me to shame" (375). A blander, more censored version of the truth would not have conveyed, however, Martha Freud's displeasure. The reader understands her embarrassment while at the same time inferring Esti's mortification. Esti's epistolary idealization of her mother-in-law prompts Sophie Freud's de-idealization: she denounces the article as a "sanctimonious and deceitful fairy-tale repellent" (375). Some readers will find this criticism excessive. Unlike her mother, no one can accuse Sophie Freud of idealizing her forbears. *Living in the Shadow of the Freuds* belies her grandfather's assertion that biographers and autobiographers commit themselves to concealment, hypocrisy, and flattery.

Life Review

One of the values of writing a memoir is that it represents an opportunity for a life review, a process that involves the recollection, interpretation, and evaluation of positive and negative memories. As Gerben J. Westerhof observes, "Research from gerontological, cognitive and personality psychology has shown that life review is related to mental health and well-being." A life review may occur at any point in the life cycle, especially during periods of transformative change, but it's especially fitting in old age, and it may lead to a greater acceptance of the inevitability of death.

In researching the memoir, Sophie Freud came across documents that forced her to revise her understanding of her family. She never realized until rereading her mother's letters how haunted Esti was throughout her life by ubiquitous anxieties of every kind. She was stunned to find letters in her mother's estate in which Martin expressed concern for his daughter's well-being. Before discovering these letters, Sophie Freud had not known much about her father's life—including the year of his death, in 1968, at age seventy-nine. Now, however, after reading these new letters, she found herself regretting his absence from her life. He had not completely stopped thinking about her, as she once believed. In "The Heirloom," she writes about meeting her father's partner who reveals an ultimatum she gave to Martin early in their relationship:

> The mistress had told her with pride that her father had announced one day that he would not be home for dinner because one of his old flames was in town. She had told him not to look for her when he did come home. The Daughter's father had either loved his young mistress too much to let her go, or his adventures had become less essential to him. In any case, he had chosen to come home that evening ready to be taken care of in full comfort for the rest of his life. (*My Three Mothers and Other Passions* 295–6)

Writing about Martin Freud enabled his daughter to begin the protracted and painful task of mourning and reconciliation. She is too honest to say that she has completely forgiven him, but she has made the first step in overcoming lifelong anger.

By contrast, Esti does not seem to have learned much from the writing of *Vignettes of My Life*, partly because writing the memoir did not involve research into her past, and partly because unlike her daughter, she never appears psychologically sophisticated or introspective. Esti is certainly not psychoanalytically oriented, attuned to ambivalence. Nor does she understand why people dislike her. Paul Roazen, in his chapter "'The Black Sheep': Dr. Esti Freud," refers to her "capacity for self-criticism" (*Meeting Freud's Family* 141), but he doesn't give examples of this self-criticism in his discussion, nor is it apparent in Sophie Freud's books. According to Roazen, Esti expressed interest when she was still living in Vienna in becoming an analyst, but she was discouraged by Helene Deutsch, who was at the time head of the Training Institute. Esti never reveals this detail in her memoir. There are some factual errors in Roazen's discussion, as when he refers to Esti's divorce from Martin, which never happened. The accuracy of some of Roazen's other statements about the Freud family cannot be verified. "Esti discussed with Anna at the end of her life an instance of lesbianism within the family, and Anna's obvious disapproval at the news does count, I think, against there having been more than an intimate friendship between Anna and Dorothy Burlingham" (149).

If, as Roazen suggests, Anna Freud disapproved of lesbianism, one wonders whether this created a quandary for Sophie Freud over whether to include this information in her discussion of her daughter's sexual preference. Elisabeth Young-Bruehl reveals in *Subject to Biography* (1998) her disillusionment when she came across a letter Anna Freud wrote recommending against a homosexual applicant for psychoanalytic training:

"I know from past experience that it is no good for any kind of course, or any kind of institution, to permit people with sexual abnormalities." I hated this sentence—for myself, and for all homosexuals who have had to endure psychoanalytic intolerance and pathologization—and continued to hate it until, many months later, I found Anna Freud's unpublished clinical reflections on male homosexuality and began to understand what the sentence meant to her, how it protected her, how it represented her. She was, I discovered, willing to question herself, analyze herself, on this topic, and, slowly, to alter her view. (21–2)

In his memoir *Ernestine*—a name she loathed from childhood—Walter Freud echoes his paternal grandfather: "She was called T.M. meaning total meschugge as long as I remember in her Vienna days" (408). George Loewenstein observes that Esti brought out the worst in people. "She was, however, completely unaware of her role in this vicious cycle; to her the world seemed populated by rude, horrible people" (417). He believes that she was a victim of her own personality, concluding that she never became aware of her "character flaws."

Tellingly, Sophie Freud makes no attempt to "diagnose" these character flaws. There's no mention of her mother seeking clinical help, nor does her daughter suggest that this may have been helpful. In a review of Peter Kramer's *Listening to Prozac*, Sophie Freud calls herself, using the psychiatrist's term, leaning severely toward "pharmacological Calvinism" (427), and consequently, she never implies that her mother might have benefited from an antidepressant. Sophie Freud refuses to interpret her mother's problematic behavior in terms of the *Diagnostic and Statistical Manual of Mental Disorders* (DSM), a classificatory system for which she feels no enthusiasm. We are left to infer that Esti's many losses in her life—her family and homeland when she was forced to escape from Vienna, the loss of her husband and son, and the terror of poverty and abandonment—all contributed to her quarrelsome nature.

Writing as Exorcism

Living in the Shadow of the Freud Family helped Sophie Freud come to terms with her mother, who died in 1980 at age eighty-four. Reconciliation proved to be a lifelong struggle, mainly because, as she admits, with characteristic honesty, the lives of mother and daughter were so symbiotically connected, so fused, that the only way she could achieve independence and autonomy was by radically distancing herself from her, an act of self-preservation that was also filial neglect. She uses two metaphors to describe this estrangement: she developed a "stony heart" and felt emotionally "frozen." She makes no attempt to soften this betrayal, though readers are likely to respond with sympathy and understanding.

In her double role as editor and annotator of her mother's memoir, Sophie Freud conveys disturbing intergenerational patterns ignored by her grandfather in his own theoretical writings. She doesn't quote the philosopher Santayana, but she shows how those who don't remember the past are condemned to repeat it. Esti's tormented relationship with Martin foreshadows Sophie's equally tormented relationship with Esti. Sophie Freud shows the limits of her own empathy. She and her brother could not bear their mother's incessant complaints. "I am sure she never realized how upsetting I found her constant despairing telephone calls. She must have thought that we were not affected by her suffering" (364). There are moments in the book when the author's empathy fails her, as when she writes that her mother was "staging a nervous breakdown," soon after their arrival in Paris (173). Why "staged," one may ask? She never elaborates on why she thought her mother's breakdown was theatrical, not real. She calls herself a "negligent and unloving daughter," conceding that her mother "did not deserve my emotional abandonment of her" (389). She confesses that she sat next to her dying mother with an "icy and armored heart" (429). She quotes a 1954 letter when her mother states sadly that of all the many hurts she had endured in her life, her daughter's attitude "is perhaps the one that has affected me most deeply" (391). Ironically, Sophie Freud is the first to acknowledge that despite her many complaints about Esti, she is her mother's daughter in many ways, both good and bad.

Sophie Freud's relationship with her brother was also fraught. Their bond was broken several times by long periods of silence. Writing *Ernestine*, she observes, was Walter's gift to her. He was relentlessly critical of his mother in his memoir, and he made little attempt to understand or empathize with her life when she left him and the rest of the Freuds in 1938. He died in 2004 at the age of eighty-three. He was not alive when his sister's memoir was published, but she remains convinced that he would not have liked it—mainly because he didn't like *any* of her writings. Nevertheless, they were able to repair their relationship near the end of his life. She remarks that in marrying his wife, Annette, Walter, unlike their own mother or herself, "won the jackpot in the lottery of marriages" (384).

Living in the Shadow of the Freud Family is the only psychoanalytic memoir that offers multiple points of view of reality. Sometimes these different perspectives of people and events support each other, while at other times they do not. Whose point of view of Esti Freud do we trust: that of Sigmund Freud, Martin Freud, Walter Freud, or Sophie Freud? Esti often contradicts herself, as we all do, and she had many blind spots—again, as we all do. Her real relationship with her son, from whom she was estranged for twelve years, when they had no contact, was startlingly different from her fantasy relationship with him. All biographers and autobiographers confront the problem of determining whether memory is reliable or not. In the chapter "Room Full of Memories," Sophie Freud is surprised to discover that she and her brother recall in striking detail the same traumatic early childhood event, when their mother beat him for refusing to answer the question: "Who is the best mother in the world" to her satisfaction. This remains, she tells us, one of the few incontrovertible family truths upon which both brother and sister agree.

Other truths are provisional, nomadic, and contested. In the chapter "A Case of False Memory," Walter forgot about the scores of letters he received from his mother revealing her intense interest in his life. "You could not have forgotten all these things," Sophie Freud scolds him in an imaginary letter to her deceased brother (359). We also see conflicting evaluations of *Vignettes of My Life*. Sophie's son, George, pronounced it, bluntly, a "depressing document of a life nearly devoid of love." Walter Freud's opinion was "even less charitable"—a nice euphemism. The Freuds are a "very critical family," Sophie Freud remarks dryly. Yet, she would not have devoted years of time and effort to the project had she not believed in the value of her mother's words—and in her own.

Writing *My Three Mothers and Other Passions* and *Living in the Shadow of the Freud Family* enabled Sophie Freud to exorcise her paternal and maternal demons. In one of her most evocative statements in the former book, she observes that the "physical demonstration of intense emotions is inaccessible to me except through written words" (3). Psychological research, she reminds us, suggests that we should help old people remember their childhood. Her double memoir enacts the truth of this observation. Both mother and daughter learned a great deal about themselves, especially the latter, who as a result of researching the book gleaned, to her horror, that her maternal grandmother had not simply died of illness in a concentration camp, as Esti had been told, but was murdered at Auschwitz. The author's appreciation of her mother increased when she read *Vignettes of My Life*, which reveals her strength, courage, and resilience during arguably the darkest period of human history. Sophie Freud's book shows how writing allows her not only to bear witness and memorialize loss but also how to revise meaning when new information becomes available.

Authoring *Living in the Shadow of the Freud Family* had another unexpected benefit, helping Sophie Freud transition from a lifetime of work to retirement. "It gave meaning to my suddenly senseless life; it has become my closest friend in these somewhat solitary years" (xvi). The project became the "magic bastion Mother has bequeathed me to combat futility in my old age" (xxiv). I recall hearing Sophie Freud observe, when she spoke to my students in 2002, that books were her closest friends. She meant *reading* books, as she discusses in her 2004 article "The Reading Cure" published in a 2004 issue of *American Imago*. "Books are my best, my most faithful, my most reliable friends. People have to meet rather high standards to match my books in terms of being good company" (77). However much Sophie Freud loves reading books, I suspect that *writing* books was more satisfying. She spent eight years researching and writing the memoir, worrying that she would not be able to complete it: "it was a race between a piece of work and my aging brain" (xvi). Grit and determination allowed her to succeed.

Living in the Shadow of the Freud Family is an end-of-life memoir written by a mother and daughter in their twilight years. In the last paragraph of *Vignettes of My Life*, Esti remarks that she had tried to live according to Freud's "reality principle." She dedicates her book to her offspring and future descendants. She was in a coma shortly before her death, and her daughter now regrets not being with her at the end. We cannot predict our endings, but Sophie Freud vows, whenever death approaches, not to call out anyone's name in desperation, as her mother did. "Instead, I will turn my head to the wall and I will think of global warming, the rising oceans, the felling of forests for quick profits, the drilling of oil in beautiful wildlands, the plagues that will invade our countries, with an occasional atom bomb explosion" (436). If these are indeed Sophie Freud's final thoughts, she will have died in character, an advocate for social justice, world peace, and environmental protection.

Despite its depiction of a tortured mother-daughter, *Living in the Shadow of the Freud Family* is an act of filial love, like other end-of-life filial memoirs, such as David Rieff's *Swimming in a Sea of Death* (2008), about his mother, Susan Sontag, and Roland Barthes's *Mourning Diary* (2010). Writing is Sophie Freud's preferred method of working through convoluted thoughts and feelings. The "writing cure" becomes her most effective form of self-therapy. As with her grandfather and her mother, the latter of whom did not retire as a speech therapist until shortly before her death, Sophie Freud regards work as an antidote to psychic pain. Esti Freud might be displeased by the portrait of herself that appears in her daughter's book, but she would be comforted, I believe, by the fact that, for the first time, she has emerged from the shadow of the Freuds.

CONCLUSION

IRVIN D. YALOM AND MARILYN YALOM—
A MATTER OF DEATH AND LIFE

What makes a memoir psychoanalytic? Apart from the tautological answer that it is written by a psychoanalytic theorist, clinician, memoirist, or scholar, psychoanalytic memoirs reveal a high degree of *ambivalence*. After completing the present book, I did a search on "ambivalent" and "ambivalence" and discovered that, excluding the conclusion, where I suddenly became self-conscious about my use of the two words and tried to find synonyms (none of which is satisfactory), they appear forty-four times, far more often than in any of my previous books. Nor is this surprising. Psychoanalysis teaches us that fear and desire, love and hate, attraction and repulsion are inextricably related. We are, paradoxically, ambivalent about the concept itself, preferring to believe that our love (or hate) is pure. It's understandable that psychoanalytic memoirists are ambivalent about disclosing sexual or aggressive feelings that dwell in our unconscious selves—particularly since, as Freud observed wryly, psychoanalysis brings out the worst in people. How can a memoirist *not* feel ambivalent about painful and shameful self-disclosures?

I use the word *ambivalent* so often in my teaching that, more than half a century ago, when I first began teaching at Cornell as a graduate student, one of my students gave me a sign, elegantly handwritten in Gothic-style calligraphy, "Be Ambivalent Clearly." The white cardboard on which the words are written has turned yellow with age, but it holds a prominent position on the bookshelf in my university office, a reminder of the importance of living with sharply conflicting thoughts and emotions. During the pandemic, when I taught at home through Zoom, the sign was behind me, so that my students could see their ambivalent professor.

An amusing sidebar: Freud never knew how to pronounce "ambivalent," as H.D. observes in *Tribute to Freud*:

> When, on one occasion, I was endeavoring to explain a matter in which my mind tugged two ways, I said, "I suppose you would say it was a matter of ambivalence." And as he did not answer me, I said, "Or do you say am-*bi*-valence? I don't know whether it's pronounced ambi-*valence* or am-*bi*-valence." The Professor's arm shot forward as it did on those occasions when he wished to stress a finding or focus my attention to some point in hand; he said, in his curiously casual ironical manner, "Do you know, I myself have always wondered. I often wish that I could find someone to explain these matters to me." (87)

Am*bi*valence appears in all of the memoirs in my study: Sigmund Freud's relationship to biography and autobiography; the Wolf-Man's connection to psychoanalysis; Helene Deutsch's feelings about motherhood; Wilhelm Stekel's behavior toward Freud; Carl Jung's secret history of sexual trauma; Wilfred Bion's service during the Great War; Marion Milner's attitude toward the "angry parrot"; Masud Khan's friendship with the "old fox," D.W. Winnicott; Jeffrey Masson's memory of his past sexual adventures and misadventures; Robert Rodman's view of privacy; Louis Breger's attitude toward emotional over-control; Brenda Webster's years of lying on the couch; Madelon Sprengnether's experience crying at the movies; and Sophie Freud's account of the mother-daughter relationship. The memoirists' disclosure of these fraught subjects, associated with lifelong emotional scars, only intensified the ambivalence.

"Dealing with ambivalence is the crux of much of what goes on in psychotherapy," Daniel N. Watter, past president of the Society for Sex Therapy and Research, wrote me upon reading an early draft of this chapter. "I have often said that it is ambivalence, more than any other state, that propels people to enter treatment."

Nowhere is this ambivalence better seen than in *A Matter of Death and Life*, written by Irvin D. Yalom and Marilyn Yalom, published in 2021. It is both an end-of-life memoir and a spousal loss memoir. Yalom never imagined that he would feel compelled to write the book. He met his future wife, Marilyn Koenick, when he was only fourteen, and it was love at first sight for him (though not for her). Married for sixty-five years and rarely apart from her, he would have easily given up his life for her. But that would not have prevented her from dying. Yalom is an existential psychiatrist, not a psychoanalyst, and although he is a frequent critic of Freudian theory, his memoir is bound to interest anyone who wishes to learn more about the talking cure and the writing cure.

Full disclosure requires me to admit that Yalom has long been my favorite therapist-novelist. He is, next to Freud, the greatest writer of psychotherapy tales. In 2015, I began writing a book-length study of his many clinical textbooks, short story collections, and novels. In late 2016, I sent him an email asking him if he would be willing to read my completed manuscript, which I had not yet submitted for publication. "I'm bowled over by your letter," he wrote back immediately, and generously agreed to read the manuscript. He pointed out a few factual and interpretive errors and called attention to some of his publications that I had not yet read. He characteristically made no effort to respond to my few criticisms of his writings. When I told him that I planned to spend several days reading his unpublished writings and correspondence at the Yalom Archives at Stanford University, where he was a professor of psychiatry for thirty years, he invited my wife and me to his home in Palo Alto, where we spent a delightful evening. He was at the time completing a memoir that I briefly mention in my book *Writing the Talking Cure: Irvin D. Yalom and the Literature of Psychotherapy*, published in 2019. I wasn't exaggerating when I stated in my acknowledgments that writing a book on Yalom was the least expensive and most effective psychotherapy in my life. None of my books has given me greater pleasure to write. After completing my study of Yalom's writings, I felt bereft.

Critical of Psychoanalysis

Yalom has never been sympathetic to psychoanalysis. In *Every Day Gets a Little Closer* (1974), he advises his patient (and coauthor) Ginny Elkin not to be suspicious of her compassionate instincts. "I in effect told her to stop this Freudian reductionism and accept generosity or gentleness as positive and important truths about herself which stand by themselves and don't require further analysis" (20). Yalom thus dispenses with the Freudian defense mechanism of reaction formation, suggesting that kindness and cruelty are coequal. In *Existential Psychotherapy* (1980), Yalom argues that the idea of death had little appeal to Freud because it would not lead to eternal fame, as would his theory of castration. In Yalom's words, death was "old hat" to Freud, "Old Testament"; "it was not Freud's aim to join a long procession of thinkers stretching back to the beginning of time" (73). Yalom has criticized the idea of analytic neutrality, the belief in an omniscient analyst, the rigidity of orthodox analysts, the phallocentric nature of Freudian theory, and the exclusive emphasis on early childhood experience at the expense of the here and now. One of the best professional decisions Yalom made, he observes in *The Gift of Therapy* (2002), was *not* to become a psychoanalyst. Despite his criticisms of psychoanalysis, Yalom recognizes Freud's genius as a thinker and writer. In the chapter in *The Gift of Therapy* called "Freud Was Not Always Wrong," Yalom observes that psychoanalytic institutes may become the "last bastion, the repository of collected psychotherapy wisdom, in much the same way the church for centuries was the repository of philosophical wisdom" (221).

Yalom is candid about his long odyssey of personal therapy. In *The Gift of Therapy*, he remarks on his 750-hour, 5-times-a week therapy, during his psychiatric residency, with the Freudian analyst Olive Smith, and then a year-long psychoanalysis with the British analyst Charles Rycroft. Later he went into treatment with therapists from a wide variety of clinical approaches. Yalom has acknowledged, perhaps more than any other mental health professional, the intensity of his own death anxiety, and he has never been reluctant to disclose how being in therapy has helped him live with existential terror. From the beginning of his career, he has admitted to being a wounded healer, sharing his vulnerabilities with his patients and readers. These revelations have made him "human" and "authentic," words that characterize the man and his work.

Yalom has made a profound contribution to our understanding of psychotherapy. His "teaching stories"—*When Nietzsche Wept* (1993), *Lying on the Couch* (1997), *Love's Executioner and Other Tales of Psychotherapy* (2000), *The Schopenhauer Cure* (2006), and *The Spinoza Problem* (2012)—have sold millions of copies, been translated into thirty languages, and earned him worldwide fame. One senses from *Becoming Myself: A Psychiatrist's Memoir*, published in 2017, when he was a mid-octogenarian, that Yalom's distinguished writing career had come to a fitting conclusion: in Nietzsche's words, "What has become perfect, all that is ripe—wants to die."

That's why reading *A Matter of Death and Life* is a shock. Nothing prepared Yalom for his wife's death. In 2019, Marilyn Yalom was diagnosed with multiple myeloma, cancer of the plasma cells. As a result of her chemotherapy drug, she suffered a stroke; for a few minutes she lost the ability to speak. Hospitalized for two weeks, she announced to her husband when she returned home that she wanted to write a book with him documenting the coming months, which she knew would be perilous. They agreed to write alternating chapters, each from his or her own point of view. She continued to work on the book until two weeks before Thanksgiving, when she became too ill to write. She died on November 20, 2019, at age eighty-seven.

I'm a fast reader (and, alas, a faster forgetter), but I could read only a few pages of *A Matter of Death and Life* at a time. Husband and wife write with heartbreaking candor, crafting a book *in extremis*. "Ultimately, I have come to the understanding that one stays alive not only for oneself but for others," Marilyn declares (14), but her suffering grew so intense that after ten months she decided on physician-assisted suicide (or what her doctor calls physician-assisted dying), a decision that horrified her husband, who was not prepared to let her go.

His Muse

In a 2015 interview with Terence Clarke in the *Huffington Post*, Yalom stated that he fell in love with his future wife because they both loved to read literature. He elaborates on this in *A Matter of Death and Life*. Marilyn introduced him to the world's great literature and broadened his narrow view of the world. A literary critic and cultural historian, Marilyn Yalom later became an acclaimed writer herself, the author of groundbreaking books such as *A History of the Breast* (1997), *A History of the Wife* (2001), and *How the French Invented Love* (2012), which was short-listed for the Phi Betta Kappa Gauss Literary Award and for the American Library in Paris Book Award. She was decorated as an Officier des Palmes Académiques by the French government in 1991. A professor of French for many years at California State University, Hayward, she then became a senior scholar at the Clayman Institute for Gender Studies at Stanford. The Yaloms' marriage was closer than that of any of the other writers in my study; she is the only person who can be considered her spouse's lifelong muse.

For longtime readers of Yalom who associate his writings with exuberance and wit, his presence in *A Matter of Death and Life* is ghostly. As a result of a pacemaker and using a cane in the house and a walker outdoors because of impaired balance, his existence seems precarious. A near-fatal stroke occurred after recent knee surgery. Memory problems plague him. He's not afraid of dying, but he's terrified of losing his beloved wife. They are, in Marilyn's words, "two old people in the final dance of life" (42). Although rationality and clarity have been his lifelong values, Yalom is overwhelmed by irrational thoughts. Fiercely secular his entire adult life, he tries talking back to his dark self: twice on the same page he uses expressions that do not appear elsewhere in his writing: "Good Lord" and "By God" (115). Even his grammar becomes shaky, as when he tells us, in the chapter "Death Arrives," that Marilyn "lays down on the bed" (140).

Robert Rodman, we recall, was reluctant to share any information with his patients that his wife was dying. Yalom discloses this to his patients. Following his wife's death, he is overcome by numbness; the only times it disappears is when he is writing or seeing patients. When a patient who has read Marilyn Yalom's obituary expresses the fear that she is burdening him with her own problems, he thanks her and replies that he finds it helpful to help others, words that touch her deeply.

It's so horrifying for Yalom to imagine life without his wife that he has the fantasy of dying with her. This is what happens in Ovid's myth of Baucis and Philemon, two devoted lovers who cannot contemplate life apart from each other. "Since we have lived out harmonious years together," Baucis says, "let the same hour take the two of us, so that I never have to see my wife's grave, nor she have to bury me" (Book VIII). The two lovers are granted their wish by the gods to die simultaneously, transformed into trees entwined in each other's branches. John Bayley discusses Ovid's myth in *Elegy for Iris* (1999). As I point out in *The Art of Caregiving in Fiction, Film, and Memoir* (2021), a darker version of the story appears in Michael Haneke's 2012 film *Amour*. An elderly married couple, Anne and Georges Laurent, played by Emmanuelle Riva and Jean-Louis Trintignant, respectively, both of whom were octogenarians in real life, dramatizes the plight of caregiving. Paralyzed by a stroke, Anne demands to die. Georges, unable to witness her prolonged suffering, suffocates her in a graphic scene that is almost too terrible to watch. He then appears to take his own life.

As I have suggested in the chapters on the Wolf-Man and Brenda Webster, those who write about suicide often have personal reasons that may not become apparent until late in the writer's life. Marilyn Yalom was never suicidal, but her rational decision to choose physician-assisted suicide triggers her husband's suicidal thoughts. Suicide has been a central topic in Yalom's fictional and nonfictional writings. He recognizes that suicide would be a betrayal of his life's work, which involved helping suicidal patients through their own struggles. Nevertheless, Yalom concludes that he may be a suicide risk, an observation that allows him to understand for the first time the intensity of his suicidal patients' crises. He cites in *A Matter of Death and Life* Nietzsche's iconic dictum, "The thought of suicide is a great consolation: by means of it one gets through many a dark night" (10), a comment that appears in Yalom's earlier stories. In *Existential Psychotherapy* he recalls Beethoven's statement that the reason he didn't kill himself after losing his hearing was because of his music. In *Love's Executioner* Yalom persuades a character, Paul, to agree to a no-suicide contract despite knowing that such agreements are absurd: I won't treat you again if you kill yourself. Both Nietzsche and Josef Breuer suffer from suicidal ideation in *When Nietzsche Wept*. In *The Schopenhauer Cure*, Yalom dramatizes the lifelong impact of Heinrich Schopenhauer's suicide on his philosopher-son's life. "Every suicide leaves a wave of shock, guilt, and anger in the survivors, and Arthur experienced all these sentiments" (108). Philip Slate's father commits suicide, an act that leaves him unable to trust others and leads him into therapy with the novel's therapist, Julius Hertzfeld.

I remember reading somewhere that the suicidologist Edwin Shneidman was so despondent after his wife's death that he entered therapy late in life, worried that he might take his own life and sabotage his commitment to suicide prevention. We don't consider it ironic for an oncologist to develop cancer; why, then, should we become judgmental when mental health professionals become suicidal? Yalom's fear of committing suicide after his wife's death compelled him to reenter therapy, an admission that may help readers who find themselves in a similar situation.

A Portrait of the Therapist as a Younger Man

Julius Hertzfeld is among Yalom's most authorial characters—more autobiographical than the novelist realized at the time. Following his wife's death, Yalom finds himself consumed by a sexual obsession involving women he has known or seen recently. "I am flooded with both desire and shame. I wince at such disloyalty to Marilyn, buried only a few weeks ago" (169–70). I'm not aware of any other memoir written by a mental health professional that contains this confession, one with which I identify strongly. I recall the shame I felt when I began looking at women differently after learning of Barbara's terminal cancer diagnosis; I lacked the courage to include this unsettling detail in *Dying to Teach*.

Rereading *The Schopenhauer Cure*, written nearly two decades earlier, Yalom is stunned to discover that the sixty-six-year-old Julius experienced the same unwelcome sexual obsession:

> I married Miriam, my high school sweetheart, while I was in medical school and ten years ago she was killed in a car crash in Mexico. To tell the truth, I'm not sure I've ever recovered from the horror of that event but to my surprise my grief took a bizarre turn; I experienced a tremendous surge of sexual energy. (188)

Yalom's sexual obsession is not so much an example of life following art but rather an instance of a novelist in his sixties imagining a situation that would befall him in his late eighties. Yalom had forgotten about this detail in *The Schopenhauer Cure*, but his body remembered.

Yalom has always believed in the ancient Roman playwright Terence's observation—"I am human, and I think nothing human is alien to me"—but one can only begin to imagine the intensity of his ambivalence about certain self-disclosures, including the holes in his memory. He's ambivalent about disclosing the extent of his irrational thoughts and feelings. He cannot remember most of the details of his wife's funeral, an event that precipitated traumatic repression, a concept he credits to psychoanalysis. He feels a flash of irritation that she is dying first, which strikes him as an act of abandonment. He agrees with psychoanalysts about the impact of early childhood trauma, something he had underestimated. After Marilyn's death, he appreciates and resents his children's concern for his safety. He is still their father, but now he feels infantilized.

The power of denial stuns Yalom. He constantly talks to Marilyn after her death and believes that he must tell her everything about his life without her. Equally significant, for months he believes that an event seems "real" only if he shares it with her. He understands that his "magical thinking" is irrational, contradicting his long-held view that he must take full responsibility for determining reality. Nevertheless, he never expected magical thoughts. Yalom refers to (and slightly misquotes) the title of Joan Didion's *The Year of Magical Thinking* (2005), one of the best-known memoirs of spousal loss.

There are few therapists who admit that life experience has deepened their understanding of former patients, whom they would now treat differently. Rereading *Momma and the Meaning of Life* (1999), Yalom reflects on the longest story in the volume, "Seven Advanced Lessons in the Therapy of Grief," a case that now has a different meaning for him. Irene, a Stanford surgeon, has lost her husband to cancer, and she reluctantly enters therapy with Yalom, convinced he cannot help her because of his lack of personal experience with grief or bereavement. He rejects her argument—an oncologist can treat cancer without having had the disease—and succeeds in restoring her trust in building new relationships despite the inevitability of future loss. He now recognizes, however, the truth in her claim. He can't specify how he would now treat Irene differently, but he's convinced that his new understanding of spousal loss makes him a more effective therapist. Tellingly, with the exception of Louis Breger, whom Yalom resembles in several ways, no other memoirist in my study has written about changing therapeutic treatment as a result of new life experience. Nor has any psychotherapist, to my knowledge, written about the experience of rereading his or her own books, a novel form of life review. Forgetfulness can be a valuable asset, Yalom says ruefully, and then describes the pleasure and comfort of reading, as if for the first time, his stories, an example, to coin an awkward neologism, of autobibliotherapy.

Yalom's fifty-minute sessions with patients resemble intimate conversations with friends. He shares personal information with patients as long as it benefits the patients themselves. Reciprocity remains at the center of Yalom's vision of healing, where patient and therapist teach and learn from the other. He is not afraid to weep in *A Matter of Death and Life*, a phenomenon we have not seen elsewhere in his writings.

One of the most painful moments in Yalom's life was the decision to retire. Many people regard this decision as bitter-sweet, but Yalom was grief-stricken—and then wrote about it. The precise moment of decision came on July 4 when, returning to his office from a holiday fete with his family in a nearby park, he was unexpectedly greeted by a psychotherapist from Scotland, Emily. He had forgotten completely that he had scheduled a session with her. To make matters worse, he cannot remember his past sessions with her. "I'm invisible, I'm invisible," Emily wails. "Four times we've met and you don't know me" (37). He can only apologize, admit his mistake, and reassure her that his memory lapse has nothing to do with her. When she tells him that she, too, is worried about failing memory, particularly the difficulty recognizing faces, he replies, "Your condition, known as facial blindness or prosopagnosia, is *not* a precursor to Alzheimer's" (39), adding that one of his favorite writers, Oliver Sacks, suffered from the same problem. The chapter succeeds, aesthetically and psychologically, because it abounds in concrete details that show therapist and patient as fellow travelers, or, more accurately, fellow-sufferers. Yalom may not have the mental concentration to work with patients, but he has lost nothing as a writer.

A Lifeline

"We write to make sense of our existence, even as it sweeps us into the darkest zones of physical decline, and death," the Yaloms observe in the preface, the only time they speak in the same voice. "This book is meant, first and foremost, to help us navigate the end of life" (xiii). Their observation recalls Joan Didion's insight in *The White Album* (1979): "We tell ourselves stories in order to live" (11). Didion's husband, the novelist John Gregory Dunne, also understood the benefits of writing. "Clarity only comes," he writes in *Harp* (1989), "when pen is in hand, or at the typewriter or the word processor, clarity about what we feel and what we think, how we love and how we mourn; the words on the page constitute the benediction, the declaration, the confession of the emotionally inarticulate" (15–16). For these authors and others, writing becomes crucial for meaning making.

People often withdraw into themselves upon learning of their impending deaths. The Yaloms are an exception. Each writes and reads about the other's fears. Their collaborative writing project represents a unique form of family therapy. Writing becomes a way to express unspeakable truths. Yalom's joint writing project with his wife is an "elixir of life" (53) for the two of them, more for him than for her. To use a different metaphor, writing is his lifeline. No author is happier to write than Yalom; the high point of his career, he admits, was penning his novels. In a letter to Marilyn written 125 days after her death, he confesses that their collaborative project has kept him alive.

Irvin Yalom and Marilyn Yalom are master prose stylists, and their energetic prose belies their old age. Marilyn Yalom's writing, in particular, sparkles. Most writers, myself included, cannot write a simple declarative sentence without endless revision, yet she did not have the time to revise or edit her writing. In his psychoanalytic autobiography *Fragment of a Great Confession* (1949), Theodor Reik observes that books are written three times: the first time in memory and daydream; the second time in reality; and the third time when the author rereads the published book (215). But Marilyn had, at best, the benefit of only imagining the book in fantasy and daydream. How did she write so well without knowing the end of the story? How was she able to imagine a future for her husband of which she would not be a part? Dr. Johnson quipped that "when a man knows he is to be hanged in a fortnight, it concentrates his mind wonderfully." Perhaps, but the reality of imminent death prevents most people from mental concentration. How was Marilyn Yalom able to remain mentally focused?

What if Yalom can no longer write? The question is too anxiety-forming for him to raise. Writing has served the same lifegiving function for many of the memoirists in my study. Recall that Marion Milner continued to write on the last day of her life, when she was in her nineties. Attachment theorists affirm the importance of connection—and writing is a supreme example of writers' connection with their readers. "In a generation, perhaps two at best, no one will read my books or think of me," (56) Yalom laments. It is the only statement with which readers will disagree.

Part of the skill of writing is knowing what to include and exclude from a story—the art of playing silence. Marilyn Yalom insists that her impeding death is not "tragic" because she has led a long, fulfilling life. We don't see the last thirty-six hours of her life because they were, in her husband's words, horrific. Instead, he limits her final words to "No life. No more" (139), her answer to the palliative physician's question whether she is ready to swallow the drugs that will mercifully end her suffering.

A Matter of Death and Life will become an invaluable resource for therapists who help patients through their own bereavement experiences. Therapists may recommend that patients write about their own encounters with grief. Readers' comments on the Amazon website reveal their deep gratitude to the Yaloms, as we have seen in Stefania Magidson's tribute to Robert Rodman's *Not Dying*. The popularity of Yalom's writings does not reflect our "therapeutic self-help culture," as Sven Birkerts (whom I quoted in the introduction) complains, but rather our need for hope from memoirists who expose their own vulnerability. Marilyn Yalom cites several of the books she read about dying and death, including Sherwin Nuland's *How We Die: Reflections on Life's Final Chapter*. I read the same book when Barbara was dying, and what most helped me was Nuland's conclusion about believing in hope when rescue is impossible: "The greatest dignity to be found in death is the dignity of the life that preceded it. This is a form of hope we can all achieve, and it is the most abiding of all. Hope resides in the meaning of what our lives have been" (242). *A Matter of Death and Life* conveys that dignity and hope.

Yalom told his friends that *Becoming Myself* would be his last book—and then came *A Matter of Death and Life*. He is now writing another book of clinical tales. In short, he writes to live and lives to write—a ghostly writer who remains, to his readers' delight, haunted by stories. He is a latter-day Scheherazade, spinning stories to stay alive, using his knowledge of literature, psychotherapy, and philosophy to entrance his readers and, in the process, remain alive for another day.

"Two Eternities of Darkness"

Yalom ends *A Matter of Death and Life* by quoting the opening sentence from Nabokov's 1951 autobiography, *Speak, Memoir*: "The cradle rocks above an abyss, and common sense tells us that our existence is but a brief crack of light between two eternities of darkness" (222). The image poignantly conveys Yalom's belief that we have no existence or consciousness before or after life. Interestingly, Marilyn first uses the image in her chapter on hospice care, where she observes that Greek and Roman writers such as Seneca, Epictetus, and Marcus Aurelius each believed that individual existence is a "miniscule crack of light between two eternities of darkness, one before life and one afterwards" (122). Did her chapter inspire her husband to end *A Matter of Death and Life* with the same image? If so, it would be another example of Marilyn as her husband's muse in life and death.

It is a perfect conclusion, but there's an irony about quoting from Nabokov's autobiography of which Yalom might be unaware. Throughout all of his writings, Nabokov mocks Freud, whom he regards as the Viennese witch doctor. "I have ransacked my oldest dreams for keys and clues," he writes in the third paragraph of *Speak, Memory*, "and let me say at once that I reject completely the vulgar, shabby, fundamentally medieval world of Freud, with its crankish quest for sexual symbols (something like searching for Baconian acrostics in Shakespeare's works) and its bitter little embryos spying, from their natural nooks, upon the love life of their parents" (6). Nabokov may have rejected Freud, but in almost every foreword to the English-language edition of his novels, Nabokov gratuitously goes out of his way to deride Freud, suggesting the need to keep the psychoanalyst alive. The idea of Freud engendered Nabokov's mordant wit and imagination. In the end, as *A Matter of Death and Life* suggests, Freud, Nabokov, and Yalom are linked, all striving to defeat the treachery and unreliability of memory by telling the truth of their lives. In doing so, the writers remain alive to the reader long after death has extinguished their lives. Memoirs are, like photography, memento mori, a reminder of the inevitability of death, an effort to stop time so that the reader can understand writers when they are no longer alive. When Otto Rank gave an inscribed copy of *The Trauma of Birth* to Freud in 1923, the latter, accepting the book's dedication to him, remarked that Rank's productivity, as well as his own, was gratifying. Freud then quoted words by the ancient Roman lyric poet Horace—"*Non omnis moriar*": "Not all of me shall die" (*The Letters of Sigmund Freud & Otto Rank* 180). I suspect that all memoirists, psychoanalytic and otherwise, hope that their writings will preserve a part of themselves for posterity.

WORKS CITED

Altman, Neil. "Wilfred Bion: From World War I to Contemporary Psychoanalysis." *International Journal of Applied Psychoanalytic Studies* 13 (2016): 163–78.

American Psychiatric Association. *Diagnostic and Statistical Manual of Mental Disorders (DSM)*, 4th ed. Washington, DC, 1994.

Bair, Deirdre. *Jung: A Biography*. Boston: Little, Brown and Company, 2003.

Bakan, David. *Sigmund Freud and the Jewish Mystical Tradition*. Princeton, NJ: D. van Nostrand, 1958.

Balsam, Rosemary Marshall and Alan Balsam. *Becoming a Psychotherapist: A Clinical Primer*, 2nd ed. With contributions by Iza S. Erlich and Henry Grunebaum. Foreword by Roy Schafer. Chicago, IL: University of Chicago Press, 1984.

Banville, John. "Uncovering the Great Freudian Slip." *Irish Times*, November 14, 2009. https://www.irishtimes.com/culture/books/uncovering-the-great-freudian-slip, accessed August 15, 2020.

Barthes, Roland. *Mourning Diary: October 26, 1977–September 15, 1979*, translated by Richard Howard. New York: Hill & Wang, 2010.

Bayley, John. *Elegy for Iris*. New York: Picador, 1999.

Beidler, Peter G. "The Sources of the Stekel Quotation in Salinger's *The Catcher in the Rye*." *ANQ: A Quarterly Journal of Short Stories, Notes, and Reviews* 26 (2013): 71–5.

Berman, Jeffrey. *The Art of Caregiving in Fiction, Film, and Memoir*. New York: Bloomsbury Academic, 2021.

Berman, Jeffrey. *Companionship in Grief: Love and Loss in the Memoirs of C.S. Lewis, John Bayley, Donald Hall, Joan Didion, and Calvin Trillin*. Amherst: University of Massachusetts Press, 2010.

Berman, Jeffrey. *Dying in Character: Memoirs on the End of Life*. Amherst: University of Massachusetts Press, 2012.

Berman, Jeffrey. *Dying to Teach: A Memoir of Love, Loss, and Learning*. Albany, NY: State University of New York Press, 2007.

Berman, Jeffrey. *Joseph Conrad: Writing as Rescue*. New York: Astra Books, 1977.

Berman, Jeffrey. *Mad Muse: The Mental Illness Memoir in a Writer's Life and Work*. Bingley: Emerald, 2019.

Berman, Jeffrey. *Norman N. Holland: The Dean of American Psychoanalytic Literary Critics*. New York: Bloomsbury Academic, 2012.

Berman, Jeffrey. "'One's Effort to Find a Little Truth': Ethel Schwabacher's Artistic and Psychoanalytic Odyssey." *The Psychoanalytic Review* 78 (1991): 607–28.

Berman, Jeffrey. "Review of Brenda Webster. *After Auschwitz: A Love Story*." *Women's Studies* 43 (2014): 979–80.

Berman, Jeffrey. "Review of Brenda Webster. *The Last Good Freudian*." *San Francisco Chronicle*, May 7, 2000.

Berman, Jeffrey. "Review of Brenda Webster. *Vienna Triangle*." *San Francisco Chronicle*, January 13, 2009.

Berman, Jeffrey. "Review of Louis Breger. *Freud: Darkness in the Midst of Vision*." *American Journal of Psychotherapy* 55 (2001): 431–4.

Berman, Jeffrey. "Review of Madelon Sprengnether. *Mourning Freud.*" *Journal of the American Psychoanalytic Association* 67 (2019): 405–10.
Berman, Jeffrey. *The Talking Cure: Literary Representations of Psychoanalysis*. New York: New York University Press, 1985.
Berman, Jeffrey. *Writing the Talking Cure: Irvin D. Yalom and the Literature of Psychotherapy*. Albany, NY: State University of New York Press, 2018.
Berman, Jeffrey. *Writing Widowhood: The Landscapes of Bereavement*. Albany, NY: State University of New York Press, 2015.
Berman, Jeffrey and Paul W. Mosher. *Off the Tracks: Cautionary Tales about the Derailing of Mental Health Care*, 2 Vols. New York: International Psychoanalytic Books, 2019.
Bettelheim, Bruno. "Review of *The Autobiography of Wilhelm Stekel: The Life Story of a Pioneer Psychoanalyst.*" *American Journal of Sociology* 56 (1950): 287–8.
Bion, Wilfred *All My Sins Remembered: Another Part of a Life [together with] The Other Side of Genius: Family Letters*, edited by Francesca Bion. Abingdon: Fleetwood Press, 1985; rpt. London: Karnac, 1991.
Bion, Wilfred. *Attention and Interpretation*. London: Karnac, 1970; rpt. 2007.
Bion, Wilfred. *Clinical Seminars and Other Writings*. Abingdon: Fleetwood Press, 1987; rpt. London: Karnac, 1994.
Bion, Wilfred. *Cogitations*, edited by Francesca Bion. London: Karnac, 1992; new extended ed., 2005.
Bion, Wilfred. *Experiences in Groups and Other Papers*. New York: Basic Books, 1961.
Bion, Wilfred. *The Long Week-End 1897–1919: Part of a Life*, edited by Francesca Bion. Abingdon: Fleetwood Press, 1982; rpt. London: Routledge, 1991.
Bion, Wilfred. *A Memoir of the Future*, originally published in three separate volumes: *The Dream* (1975), *The Past Presented* (1977), and *The Dawn of Oblivion* (1979). A single-volume edition was published in London by Karnac in 1991.
Bion, Wilfred. *War Memoirs 1917-19*, edited by Francesca Bion. London: Karnac, 1997.
Birkerts, Sven. *The Art of Time in Memoir: Then, Again*. Saint Paul, MN: Graywolf Press, 2008.
Blanchot, Maurice. *The Writing of the Disaster*, translated by Ann Smock. Lincoln: University of Nebraska Press, 1995.
Bléandonu, Gérard. *Wilfred Bion: His Life and Works 1897–1979*, translated by Claire Pajaczkowska. Foreword by R. D. Hinshelwood. New York: The Guilford Press, 1994.
Bloom, Harold. "Freud, the Greatest Modern Writer." *New York Times Book Review*, March 23, 1986.
Bloom, Harold. *Omens of Millennium: The Gnosis of Angels, Dreams and Resurrection*. New York: Putnam, 1996.
Bloom, Harold. *The Western Canon: The Books and Schools of the Ages*. New York: Harcourt, 1994.
Blumenthal, Ralph. "Did Freud's Isolation Lead Him to Reverse Theory on Neurosis?" *New York Times*, August 25, 1981.
Blumenthal, Ralph. "Scholars Seek the Hidden Freud in Newly Emerging Letters." *New York Times*, August 18, 1981.
Bollas, Christopher. *Mayhem*. London: Free Association Books, 2006.
Bollas, Christopher. "Obituary: Masud Khan—Portrait of an Extraordinary Psychoanalytic Personality." *The Guardian*, June 26, 1987.
Borch-Jacobsen, Mikkel and Sonu Shamdasani. *The Freud Files: An Inquiry into the History of Psychoanalysis*. Cambridge: Cambridge University Press, 2012.

Boring, Edwin G. and Gardner Lindzey, eds. *A History of Psychology in Autobiography*, Vol. 5. New York: Appleton-Century-Crofts, 1967.
Bos, Jaap and Leendert Groenendijk. *The Self-Marginalization of Wilhelm Stekel: Freudian Circles Inside and Out*. New York: Springer, 2007.
Boynton, Robert S. "Till Press Do Us Part: The Trial of Janet Malcolm and Jeffrey Masson." *The Village Voice*, November 28, 1994.
Breger, Louis. *The Book of Barbara: Love and Grief: A Psychotherapist's Journey*. Pacific Palisades, CA: Sharq Press, 2015.
Breger, Louis. *Dostoevsky: The Author as Psychoanalyst*. New York: New York University Press, 1989; rpt. New Brunswick, NJ: Transaction Publishers, 2009.
Breger, Louis. *A Dream of Undying Fame: How Freud Betrayed His Mentor and Invented Psychoanalysis*. New York: Basic Books, 2009.
Breger, Louis. *Freud: Darkness in the Midst of Vision*. New York: Wiley, 2000.
Breger, Louis. *Freud's Unfinished Journey: Conventional and Critical Perspectives in Psychoanalytic Theory*. London: Routledge and Kegan Paul, 1981.
Breger, Louis. *Psychotherapy Lives Intersecting*. New Brunswick, NJ: Transaction Publishers, 2012.
Breuer, Josef and Sigmund Freud. *Studies on Hysteria*. 1885. *The Standard Edition of the Complete Psychological Works of Sigmund Freud*, translated and edited by James Strachey, Vol. 2. London: The Hogarth Press, 1975.
Briehl, Marie H. "Helene Deutsch: The Maturation of Woman." In *Psychoanalytic Pioneers*, edited by Franz Alexander, Samuel Eisenstein, and Martin Grotjahn, 282–98. New York: Basic Books, 1965.
Cain, Albert C. and Barbara C. Cain. "On Replacing a Child." *Journal of the American Academy of Child Psychiatry* 3 (1964): 443–56.
Caldwell, Leslie, ed. *Art, Creativity, Living*. London: Karnac, 2000.
Carotenuto, Aldo. *A Secret Symmetry: Sabina Spielrein Between Jung and Freud*, translated by Arno Pomerans, John Shepley, and Krishna Winston. Foreword by William McGuire. New York: Pantheon Books, 1982.
Carrere, Robert A. "Review of *Psychotherapy Lives Intersecting*." *Psychotherapy* 50 (2013): 593–4.
Celenza, Andrea. *Sexual Boundary Violations: Therapeutic, Supervisory, and Academic Contexts*. Lanham, MD: Jason Aronson, 2007.
Charles, Marilyn. "Marion Milner: *A Life of One's Own; An Experiment in Leisure; On Not Being Able to Paint; The Hands of the Living God: An Account of a Psychoanalytic Treatment; Eternity's Sunrise: A Way of Keeping a Diary*." *American Journal of Psychoanalysis* 72 (2012): 287–304.
Chodorow, Nancy J. *The Psychoanalytic Ear and the Sociological Eye: Toward an American Independent Tradition*. London: Routledge, 2020.
Clark, Ronald W. *Freud: The Man and the Cause*. New York: Random House, 1980.
Clarke, Terence. "Irvin D. Yalom: A Conversation." *Huffington Post*, May 7, 2015. https://www.huffingtonpost.com/terence-clarke/irvin.d.yalom-a-conversation, accessed July 19, 2016.
Couser, G. Thomas. *Memoir: An Introduction*. New York: Oxford University Press, 2011.
Crews, Frederick. *Freud: The Making of an Illusion*. New York: Metropolitan Books, 2017.
Cross, Shelley Ann. "Review of *Mourning Freud*." *American Imago* 76 (2019): 436–45.
Csikszentmihalyi, Mihaly. *Flow: The Psychology of Optimal Experience*. New York: HarperCollins, 1990.

Curtis, Rebecca, Cynthia Field, Ifat Knaan-Kostman, and Kelly Mannix. "What 75 Psychoanalysts Found Helpful and Hurtful in Their Own Analysis." *Psychoanalytic Psychology* 21 (2004): 153–202.
Davis, Douglas A. "Freud, Jung, and Psychoanalysis." In *The Cambridge Companion to Jung*, edited by Polly Young-Eisendrath and Terence Dawson. Cambridge: Cambridge University Press, 1997, 35–51.
De Man, Paul. *Blindness and Insight: Essays on the Rhetoric of Contemporary Criticism*, 2nd ed. Minneapolis: University of Minnesota Press, 1971.
Derrida, Jacques. "To Speculate—on 'Freud.'" In *A Derrida Reader: Between the Blinds*, edited by Peggy Kamuf. Hemel Hampstead: Harvester Wheatsheaf, 1991, 518–68.
Deutsch, Helene. *Confrontations with Myself: An Epilogue*. New York: Norton, 1973.
Deutsch, Helene. "Freud and His Pupils." *Psychoanalytic Quarterly* 9 (1940): 184–94.
Deutsch, Helene. *Neurosis and Character Types*. London: Hogarth Press, 1965.
Deutsch, Helene. *A Psychoanalytic Study of the Myth of Dionysus and Apollo: Two Variants of the Son-Mother Relationship*. New York: International Universities Press, 1967.
Deutsch, Helene. *The Psychology of Women*, 2 Vols. New York: Grune & Stratton, 1944–1945.
Deutsch, Helene. *Selected Problems of Adolescence*. New York: International Universities Press, 1967.
Deutsch, Helene. *The Therapeutic Process, the Self, and Female Psychology: Collected Psychoanalytic Papers*, edited, with an introduction by Paul Roazen., translated by Eric Mosbacher & Others. New Brunswick, NJ: Transaction Publishers, 1992.
Didion, Joan. *The White Album*. New York: Simon and Schuster, 1979.
Didion, Joan. *The Year of Magical Thinking*. New York: Knopf, 2005.
Dragstedt, Naomi Rader. "Creative Illusions: The Theoretical and Clinical Work of Marion Milner." *The Journal of Melanie Klein and Object Relations* 16 (1998): 425–536.
Dunne, Edward J. and Karen Dunne-Maxim. "Preface." In *Suicide and Its Aftermath*, edited by Edward J. Dunne, John L. McIntosh, and Karen Dunne-Maxim. New York: Norton, 1987.
Dunne, John Gregory. *Harp*. New York: Simon and Schuster, 1989.
Eagleton, Terry. *Literary Theory: An Introduction*. Minneapolis: University of Minnesota Press, 1983.
Edmundson, Mark. *Towards Reading Freud: Self-Creation in Milton, Wordsworth, Emerson, and Sigmund Freud*. Princeton, NJ: Princeton University Press, 1990.
Ehrlich, Robert. "Bion's Agony in The Long Week-End." *Journal of the American Psychoanalytic Association* 65 (2017): 639–64.
Eissler, K. R. *Victor Tausk's Suicide*. New York: International Universities Press, 1983.
Eliot, T. S. *After Strange Gods: A Primer of Modern Heresy*. New York: Harcourt, Brace, 1934.
Ellenberger, Henri F. *The Discovery of the Unconscious: The History and Evolution of Dynamic Psychiatry*. New York: Basic Books, 1970.
Ellmann, Maud. "Psychoanalysis and Autobiography." In *A History of English Autobiography*, edited by Adam Smith, 313–28. Cambridge: Cambridge University Press, 2016.
Elms, Alan C. *Uncovering Lives: The Uneasy Alliance of Biography and Psychology*. New York: Oxford University Press, 1994.
Emerson, Ralph Waldo. *Letters and Social Aims. Complete Works, Centenary Edition*, Vol. 8. Boston: Houghton Mifflin, 1904.

Epstein, Mark. *The Zen of Therapy: Uncovering a Hidden Kindness in Life*. New York: Penguin, 2022.
Erikson, Erik H. *Gandhi's Truth: On the Origins of Militant Nonviolence*. New York: Norton, 1969.
Erikson, Erik H. *Young Man Luther*. New York: Norton, 1958; rpt. 1962.
Fike, Matthew. "C. G. Jung's *Memories, Dreams, Reflections* as a Source for Doris Lessing's *Briefing for a Descent into Hell*." *Journal of Jungian Scholarly Studies* 11 (2016): 18–28.
Fitzgerald, F. Scott. *The Crack-Up*. New York: New Directions, 1945.
Flax, Michelle. "A Crisis in the Analyst's Life: Self-Containment, Symbolization, and the Holding Space." *The Psychoanalytic Quarterly* 80 (2011): 305–36.
Foley, Jack. "An Interview with Brenda Webster." *Women's Studies* 32 (2003): 657–64.
France, Peter. *Rousseau's Confessions*. Cambridge: Cambridge University Press, 1987.
Frank, Arthur W. *The Wounded Storyteller: Body, Illness, and Ethics*. Chicago, IL: University of Chicago Press, 1995.
Freud, Anna. "Beating Fantasies and Daydreams." *International Journal of Psychoanalysis* 4 (1923): 89–102.
Freud, Martin. *Sigmund Freud: Man and Father*. New York: The Vanguard Press, 1958.
Freud, Sigmund. "Address Delivered in the Goethe House at Frankfurt." 1930. *The Standard Edition of the Complete Psychological Works of Sigmund Freud*, translated and edited by James Strachey, Vol. 21. London: The Hogarth Press, 1961.
Freud, Sigmund. "Address to the Society of B'nai B'rith." 1946. *The Standard Edition of the Complete Psychological Works of Sigmund Freud*, translated and edited by James Strachey, Vol. 20. London: The Hogarth Press, 1959.
Freud, Sigmund. *An Autobiographical Study*. 1925. *The Standard Edition of the Complete Psychological Works of Sigmund Freud*, translated and edited by James Strachey, Vol. 20. London: The Hogarth Press, 1959.
Freud, Sigmund. "Analysis Terminable and Interminable." 1937. *The Standard Edition of the Complete Psychological Works of Sigmund Freud*, translated and edited by James Strachey, Vol. 23. London: The Hogarth Press, 1964.
Freud, Sigmund. *Beyond the Pleasure Principle*. 1920. *The Standard Edition of the Complete Psychological Works of Sigmund Freud*, translated and edited by James Strachey, Vol. 18. London: Hogarth Press, 1955.
Freud, Sigmund. "'A Child Is Being Beaten': A Contribution to the Study of the Origin of Sexual Perversions." 1919. *The Standard Edition of the Complete Psychological Works of Sigmund Freud*, translated and edited by James Strachey, Vol. 9. London: The Hogarth Press, 1959.
Freud, Sigmund. "'Civilized' Sexual Morality and Modern Nervous Illness." 1908. *The Standard Edition of the Complete Psychological Works of Sigmund Freud*, translated and edited by James Strachey, Vol. 9. London: The Hogarth Press, 1959.
Freud, Sigmund. *The Complete Letters of Sigmund Freud to Wilhelm Fliess, 1887–1904*, translated and edited by Jeffrey Moussaieff Masson. Cambridge, MA: Belknap Press of Harvard University Press, 1985.
Freud, Sigmund. "Contributions to a Discussion of Masturbation." 1912. *The Standard Edition of the Complete Psychological Works of Sigmund Freud*, translated and edited by James Strachey, Vol. 12. London: The Hogarth Press, 1958.
Freud, Sigmund. "Delusions and Dreams in Jensen's *Gradiva*." 1907. *The Standard Edition of the Complete Psychological Works of Sigmund Freud*, translated and edited by James Strachey, Vol. 9. London: The Hogarth Press, 1959.

Freud, Sigmund. "Dostoevsky and Parricide." 1928. *The Standard Edition of the Complete Psychological Works of Sigmund Freud*, translated and edited by James Strachey, Vol. 21. London: The Hogarth Press, 1961.

Freud, Sigmund. *Fragment of an Analysis of a Case of Hysteria*. 1905. *The Standard Edition of the Complete Psychological Works of Sigmund Freud*, translated and edited by James Strachey, Vol. 7. London: The Hogarth Press, 1953.

Freud, Sigmund. *From the History of an Infantile Neurosis*. 1918. *The Standard Edition of the Complete Psychological Works of Sigmund Freud*, translated and edited by James Strachey, Vol. 17. London: The Hogarth Press, 1955.

Freud, Sigmund. *The Interpretation of Dreams*. 1900. *The Standard Edition of the Complete Psychological Works of Sigmund Freud*, translated and edited by James Strachey, Vol. 4. London: The Hogarth Press, 1953.

Freud, Sigmund *Leonardo da Vinci and a Memory of His Childhood*. 1910. *The Standard Edition of the Complete Psychological Works of Sigmund Freud*, translated and edited by James Strachey, Vol. 11. London: The Hogarth Press, 1957.

Freud, Sigmund. *The Letters of Sigmund Freud*, selected and edited by Ernst L. Freud, translated by Tania and James Stern. New York: Basic Books, 1960.

Freud, Sigmund. *Moses and Monotheism*. 1939. *The Standard Edition of the Complete Psychological Works of Sigmund Freud*, translated and edited by James Strachey, Vol. 23. London: The Hogarth Press, 1964.

Freud, Sigmund. "Mourning and Melancholia." 1917. *The Standard Edition of the Complete Psychological Works of Sigmund Freud*, translated and edited by James Strachey, Vol. 14. London: The Hogarth Press, 1957.

Freud, Sigmund. *New Introductory Lectures on Psycho-Analysis*. 1933. *The Standard Edition of the Complete Psychological Works of Sigmund Freud*, translated and edited by James Strachey, Vol. 22. London: Hogarth Press, 1964.

Freud, Sigmund. "On Dreams." 1901. *The Standard Edition of the Complete Psychological Works of Sigmund Freud*, translated and edited by James Strachey, Vol. 5. London: Hogarth Press, 1953.

Freud, Sigmund. "On Narcissism: An Introduction." 1914. *The Standard Edition of the Complete Psychological Works of Sigmund Freud*, translated and edited by James Strachey, Vol. 14. London: The Hogarth Press, 1957.

Freud, Sigmund. "On the History of the Psycho-Analytic Movement." 1914. *The Standard Edition of the Complete Psychological Works of Sigmund Freud*, translated and edited by James Strachey, Vol. 14. London: The Hogarth Press, 1957.

Freud, Sigmund. *The Origins of Psychoanalysis: Letters to Wilhelm Fliess, Draft and Notes: 1887–1902*, edited by Marie Bonaparte, Anna Freud, and Ernst Kris, translated by Eric Mosbacher and James Strachey. Introductory Essay by Steven Marcus. Introduction by Ernst Freud. New York: Basic Books, 1954; rpt. 1977.

Freud, Sigmund. "Psychoanalysis: Freudian School." 1925. *The Standard Edition of the Complete Psychological Works of Sigmund Freud*, translated and edited by James Strachey, Vol. 20. London: Hogarth Press, 1959.

Freud, Sigmund. *The Psychopathology of Everyday Life*. 1901. *The Standard Edition of the Complete Psychological Works of Sigmund Freud*, translated and edited by James Strachey, Vol. 6. London: The Hogarth Press, 1960.

Freud, Sigmund. "Recommendations to Physicians Practising Psycho-Analysis." 1912. *The Standard Edition of the Complete Psychological Works of Sigmund Freud*, translated and edited by James Strachey. Vol.12. London: The Hogarth Press, 1961.

Freud, Sigmund. "Screen Memories." 1899. *The Standard Edition of the Complete Psychological Works of Sigmund Freud*, translated and edited by James Strachey, Vol. 3. London: The Hogarth Press, 1962.
Freud, Sigmund and Karl Abraham. *A Psycho-analytic Dialogue: The Letters of Sigmund Freud and Karl Abraham, 1907–1926*, edited by Bernard Marsh and Hilda C. Abraham. New York: Basic Books, 1965.
Freud, Sophie. *Living in the Shadow of the Freud Family*. Westport, CT: Prager, 2007.
Freud, Sophie. *My Three Mothers and Other Passions*. New York: New York University Press, 1988.
Freud, Sophie. "Passion as a Mental Health Hazard." In *The Evolving Female*, edited by C. Heckerman. New York: Human Sciences, 1980.
Freud, Sophie. "The Reading Cure: Books as Lifetime Companions." *American Imago* 61 (2004): 77–87.
Freud, Sophie. "Review of *Final Analysis*, *Against Therapy*, and *The Assault on Truth*." *Psychoanalytic Books* 2 (1991): 1–16.
Freud, Sophie. "Review of *Listening to Prozac*." *Psychoanalytic Books* 5 (1994): 427–36.
Fussell, Paul. *The Great War and Modern Memory*. Oxford: Oxford University Press 1975; rpt. 2013.
Gabbard, Glen O. and Eva P. Lester. *Boundaries and Boundary Violations in Psychoanalysis*. New York: Basic Books, 1995; 2nd ed. Arlington, VA: American Psychiatric Association Publishing, 2016.
Gay, Peter. *Freud: A Life for Our Time*. New York: Norton, 1988.
Gedo, John. *Portraits of the Artist: Psychoanalysis of Creativity and Its Vicissitudes*. Introduction by Peter Gay. New York: Guilford Press, 1983.
Gilbert, Sandra M. *Wrongful Death: A Memoir*. New York: Norton, 1995.
Gilbert, Sandra and Susan Gubar. "Ceremonies of the Alphabet: Female Grandmatologies and the Female Authorgraph." In *The Female Autograph: Theory and Practice of Autobiography from the Tenth to the Twentieth Century*, edited by Domna C. Stanton. Chicago, IL: University of Chicago Press, 1987, 21–48.
Gilman, Sander L. *The Case of Sigmund Freud: Medicine and Identity at the Fin de Siècle*. Baltimore, MD: Johns Hopkins University Press, 1993.
Gilman, Sander L. *Difference and Pathology: Stereotypes of Sexuality, Race, and Madness*. Ithaca, NY: Cornell University Press, 1985.
Gilman, Sander L. *Freud, Race and Gender*. Princeton, NJ: Princeton University Press, 1993.
Gilman, Sander L. *The Jew's Body*. New York: Routledge, 1991.
Givelber, Frances and Bennett Simon. "A Death in the Life of a Therapist and Its Impact on the Therapy." *Psychiatry* 44 (1981): 141–9.
Glover, Edward. *Freud or Jung*. London: George Allen & Unwin, 1950.
Godley, Boynton. "Saving Masud Khan." *London Review of Books* 23 (2001). https:/www/lrb.co.uk/the-paper/v-23/no4/wynne-godley/saving-masud-khan.
Goffman, Erving. *Stigma: Notes on the Management of Spoiled Identity*. Englewood Cliffs, NJ: Prentice-Hall, 1963.
Gordon, James S. "You Can't Always Get What You Want." *Washington Post*, November 18, 1990.
Green, André. *On Private Madness*. Madison, CT: International Universities Press, 1997.
Grosskurth, Phyllis. *Melanie Klein: Her World and Her Work*. New York: Knopf, 1986.
Grotstein, James. *A Beam of Intense Darkness: Wilfred Bion's Legacy to Psychoanalysis*. London: Karnac, 2007.

Grotstein, James. "Review of *Bion's Dream: A Reading of the Autobiographies*." *American Imago* 67 (2011): 463–9.
Grotjahn, Martin. "Review of *M. Masud R. Khan: The Long Wait and Other Psychoanalytic Narratives*." *American Journal of Psychotherapy* 45 (1991): 139–40.
Guarton, Gladys Branly. "Transgression and Reconciliation: A Psychoanalytic Reading of Masud Khan's Last Book." *Contemporary Psychoanalysis* 35 (1999): 301–10.
Hadler, Mona. "Ethel Schwabacher and the Paradise of the Real." In *Ethel Schwabacher: A Retrospective Exhibition*, edited by Greta Berman and Mona Hadler. New Brunswick, NJ: Rutgers University Press, 1983.
Hale, Nathan G., ed. *James Jackson Putnam and Psychoanalysis: Letters between Putnam and Sigmund Freud, Ernest Jones, William James, Sandor Ferenczi, and Morton Prince, 1877–1917*. Cambridge, MA: Harvard University Press, 1971.
Haneke, Michael, dir. *Amour*. 2012.
Hemingway, Ernest. *A Farewell to Arms*. New York: Scribner's, 1929
Herman, Judith Lewis. *Trauma and Recovery*. New York: Basic Books, 1992.
Hirschmüller, Albrecht. *The Life and Work of Josef Breuer: Physiology and Psychoanalysis*. New York: New York University Press, 1989.
Holland, Norman N. *Meeting Movies*. Madison, NJ: Fairleigh Dickinson University Press, 2006.
Holland, Norman N. *A Sharper Focus*. http:///asharperfocus.com/criticism.html.
Holland, Norman N. "The Story of a Psychoanalytic Critic." *American Imago* 56 (1999): 245–59.
Homans, Peter. *The Ability to Mourn: Disillusionment and the Social Origin of Psychoanalysis*. Chicago, IL: University of Chicago Press, 1989.
Homans, Peter. *Jung in Context: Modernity and the Making of a Psychology*. Chicago, IL: University of Chicago Press, 1979.
Hopkins, Linda. *False Self: The Life of Masud Khan*. New York: Other Press, 2006.
Horowitz, Mardi, Nancy Wilner, Charles Marmor, and Janice Krupnik. "Pathological Grief and the Activation of Latent Self-Images." *American Journal of Psychiatry* 137 (1980): 1157–62.
Ilahi, M. Nasir. "Review of *Winnicott: Life and Work*." *Journal of the American Psychoanalytic Association* 53 (2005): 311–16.
Jacobus, Mary. *Psychoanalysis and the Scene of Reading*. Oxford: Oxford University Press, 1999.
James, Henry. *The Turn of the Screw*, edited by Robert Kimbrough. 1898. New York: Norton Critical Edition, 1966.
James, William. "On a Certain Blindness in Human Beings." In *Talks to Teachers on Psychology: And to Students on Some of Life's Ideals*. Cambridge, MA: Harvard University Press, 1983.
Jones, Ernest. *Free Associations: Memories of a Psycho-Analyst*. New York: Basic Books, 1959.
Jones, Ernest. *The Life and Work of Sigmund Freud*, 3 Vols. New York: Basic Books, 1953–1957.
Jung, C. G. *Memories, Dreams, Reflections*. Recorded and edited by Aniela Jaffé, translated by Richard and Clara Winston. New York: Pantheon, 1963; rpt. New York: Vintage, 1989.
Jung, C. G. *In Memory of Sigmund Freud*. https://chmc-dubai.com/in-memory-of-sigmund-freud, accessed January 20, 2021.
Jung, C. G. *Two Essays on Analytical Psychology*, translated by R. F. C. Hull. Princeton, NJ: Princeton University Press, 1966; rpt. 1972.

Kahr, Brett. "F. Robert Rodman, 1934–2004." *American Imago* 61 (2004): 539–42.
Kalson, Sally. "In the Shadow of Freud: Granddaughter to Recall Her Escape with Her Mother from Nazis to U.S." *Pittsburgh Post-Gazette*, February 6, 2008.
Keats, John. *Selected Poems and Letters*. Cambridge, MA: Riverside Press, 1959.
Kernberg, Otto. *Borderline Conditions and Pathological Narcissism*. New York: Jason Aronson, 1975.
Khan, M. Masud R. *Alienations in Perversions*. London: Karnac, 1979; rpt.1980.
Khan, M. Masud R. *Hidden Selves: Between Theory and Practice in Psychoanalysis*. London: Hogarth Press, 1983.
Khan, M. Masud R. *The Long Wait and Other Psychoanalytic Narratives*. New York: Summit Books, 1988.
Khan, M. Masud R. *The Privacy of the Self*. London: Hogarth Press, 1974.
Kirsner, Douglas. *Unfree Associations: Inside Psychoanalytic Institutes*. Updated ed. Lanham, MD: Jason Aronson, 2009.
Klass, Dennis, Phyllis R. Silverman, and Steven L. Nickman. *Continuing Bonds: New Understandings of Grief*. Washington, DC: Taylor and Francis, 1996.
Kramer, Robert. *The Birth of Relationship Therapy: Carl Rogers Meets Otto Rank*. Giessen: Psychosozial-Verlag, 2019.
Kris, Ernst. *Psychoanalytic Explorations in Art*. New York: International Universities Press, 1952.
Laing, R. D. *The Divided Self*. London: Tavistock, 1959.
Larson, Thomas. *The Memoir and the Memoirist*. Athens, OH: Swallow Press/Ohio University Press, 2007.
Lasch, Christopher. *The Culture of Narcissism: American Life in an Age of Diminishing Expectations*. New York: Norton, 1979.
Lawrence, D. H. *The Letters of D. H. Lawrence*, Vol. 2, edited by George J. Zytaruk and James T. Boulton. Cambridge: Cambridge University Press, 1982.
Lehrman, Philip R. "Freud's Contributions to Science." *Harofe Haivri* 1 (1940): 161–76.
Lessing, Doris. *Briefing for a Descent into Hell*. 1971; rpt. New York: Bantam, 1977.
Lessing, Doris. *The Golden Notebook*. 1972; rpt. New York: Bantam, 1972.
Letley, Emma. *Marion Milner: The Life*. New York: Routledge, 2014.
Lieberman, E. James and Robert Kramer, eds. *The Letters of Sigmund Freud & Otto Rank: Inside Psychoanalysis*. Baltimore, MD: Johns Hopkins University Press, 2012.
Lindzey, Gardner and William M. Runyan, eds. *A History of Psychology in Autobiography*, Vol. 9. Washington, DC: American Psychological Association, 2007.
Lodge, David. *Deaf Sentence*. New York: Penguin, 2009.
Loewald, Hans. "On the Therapeutic Action of Psychoanalysis." *International Journal of Psychoanalysis* 41 (1960): 16–33.
Loewenstein, Andrea Freud. *Loathsome Jews and Engulfing Women: Metaphors of Projection in the Works of Wyndham Lewis, Charles Williams, and Graham Greene*. New York: New York University Press, 1993.
Loewenstein, Andrea Freud. *The Worry Girl: Stories from a Childhood*. London: Women's Press, 1993.
Loftus, Elizabeth and Kathleen Ketcham. *The Myth of Repressed Memory: False Memories and the Allegations of Sexual Abuse*. New York: St. Martin's Press, 1994.
Maeder, Thomas. *Children of Psychiatrists and Other Psychotherapists*. New York: HarperCollins, 1989.
Maenchen, Anna "On the Technique of Child Analysis in Relation to Stages of Development." *The Psychoanalytic Study of the Child* 25 (1970): 175–208.

Magidson, Stefania, in Dialogue with Carmen Firan. *Searching for the White Magician: Spiritual Psychology and the Manifestation of Destiny*. California: New Meridian, 2017.
Mahony, Patrick J. *Cries of the Wolf Man*. New York: International Universities Press, 1984.
Mahony, Patrick J. "Freud's Writing: His (W)rite of Passage and Its Reverberations." *Journal of the American Psychoanalytic Association* 50 (2002): 885–907.
Mailer, Susan. *In Another Place: With and Without My Father, Norman Mailer*. Northampton: House Press, 2019.
Makari, George. *Revolution in Mind: The Creation of Psychoanalysis*. New York: Harper Perennial, 2008.
Malcolm, Janet. *In the Freud Archives*. New York: Knopf, 1984.
Malcolm, Janet. *The Journalist and the Murderer*. New York: Vintage, 1990.
Malcolm, Janet. *Psychoanalysis: The Impossible Profession*. New York: Knopf, 1981; rpt. Vintage,1982.
Malcolm, Janet. "Review of *The Long Wait*." *New York Times*, April 9, 1989.
Mantel, Hilary. *Giving Up the Ghost*. 2003; rpt.: New York: Picador Modern Classics, 2017.
Marchand, Philip. "Final Analysis: Feuding." *Toronto Star*, April 24, 1993.
Marcus, Laura. *Auto/biographical Discourses: Criticism, Theory, Practice*. Manchester: Manchester University Press, 1994.
Marcus, Laura. *Autobiography: A Very Short Introduction*. Oxford: Oxford University Press, 2018.
Margolick, David. "Psychoanalyst Loses Libel Suit Against a *New Yorker* Reporter." *New York Times*, November 3, 1994.
Mason, Albert. "Bion and Binocular Vision." *International Journal of Psychoanalysis* 81 (2000): 983–9.
Masson, Jeffrey Moussaieff. *Against Therapy*. Foreword by Dorothy Rowe. New York: Atheneum, 1988; rpt. London: Fontana, 1990.
Masson, Jeffrey Moussaieff. *The Assault on Truth: Freud's Suppression of the Seduction Theory*. New York: Farrar, Straus and Giroux, 1984; rpt. with a new preface and afterword, Penguin, 1995.
Masson, Jeffrey Moussaieff. *A Dark Science: Women, Sexuality, and Psychiatry in the Nineteenth Century*, translated by Jeffrey Moussaieff Masson and Marianne Loring. New York: Farrar, Straus and Giroux, 1986.
Masson, Jeffrey Moussaieff. *Final Analysis: The Making and Unmaking of a Psychoanalyst*. Reading, MA: Addison-Wesley, 1990.
Masson, Jeffrey Moussaieff. *My Father's Guru: A Journey through Spirituality and Disillusion*. Reading, MA: Addison-Wesley, 1992.
Masson, Jeffrey Moussaieff. *Slipping into Paradise: Why I Live in New Zealand*. New York: Ballantine, 2004.
Masson, Jeffrey Moussaieff and Susan McCarthy. *When Elephants Weep: The Emotional Lives of Animals*. New York: Delta, 1995.
"Masson v. *New Yorker Magazine*, Inc., 501 U.S. 496 (1991)." https:/www.law.cornell.edu/supct/html/89-1799.ZO.html). cornell.edu. Retrieved October 17, 2020.
McCarthy, James B. "Disillusionment and Devaluation in Winnicott's Analysis of Masud Khan." *American Journal of Psychoanalysis* 63 (2003): 81–92.
McGuire, William, ed. *The Freud/Jung Letters: The Correspondence Between Sigmund Freud and C. G. Jung*, translated by Ralph Manheim and R. F. C. Hull. Princeton, NJ: Princeton University Press, 1974.

Meltzer, Donald. "The Evocation of Object Relations." *British Journal of Psychotherapy* 14 (1997): 60–7.
Menaker, Esther. *Appointment in Vienna: An American Psychoanalyst Recalls Her Student Days in Pre-War Austria*. New York: St. Martin's Press, 1989.
Meng, Heinrich and Ernst L. Freud, eds. *Psychoanalysis and Faith: The Letters of Sigmund Freud and Oskar Pfister*, translated by Eric Mosbacher. New York: Basic Books, 1963.
Merton, Robert. *Sociological Ambivalence and Other Essays*. New York: Free Press, 1976.
Meyers, Linda I. *The Tell*. Berkeley, CA: She Writes Press, 2018.
Milner, Marion. *Bothered by Alligators*. Introduction by Margaret Walters. Hove: Routledge, 2012.
Milner, Marion. *Eternity's Sunrise: A Way of Keeping a Diary*. London: Virago, 1987; rpt. With a New Introduction by Hugh Haughton. New York: Routledge, 2011.
Milner, Marion. *An Experiment in Leisure* [Joanna Field]. London: Chatto & Windus; 1937; rpt. With a New Introduction by Maud Ellmann. London: Routledge, 2011.
Milner, Marion. *The Hands of the Living God: An Account of a Psycho-analytic Treatment*. Foreword by D. W. Winnicott. New York: International Universities Press, 1969.
Milner, Marion. *The Human Problem in Schools: A Psychological Study Carried Out on Behalf of the Girls' Public Day School Trust*. London: Methuen, 1938.
Milner, Marion. *A Life of One's Own* [Joanna Field]. London: Chatto & Windus, 1934; rpt. Los Angeles: Tarcher, 1981.
Milner, Marion. *On Not Being Able to Paint* [Joanna Field]. London: Heinemann, 1950; 2nd ed., 1957. Foreword by Anna Freud; rpt. 1981.
Milner, Marion. *The Suppressed Madness of Sane Men: Forty-Four Years of Exploring Psychoanalysis*. London: Tavistock, 1987.
Misch, Georg. *A History of Autobiography in Antiquity*, translated by E. W. Dickes, 2 Vols. London: Routledge and Kegan Paul, 1950.
Molnar, Michael, trans. and annotator. *The Diary of Sigmund Freud, 1929–1939: A Record of the Final Decade*. New York: Scribner's, 1992.
Money, Jennifer. "Review of *The Last Good Freudian*." *Women's Studies* 32 (2003): 665–6.
Morley, Robert. *The Analysand's Tale*. London: Karnac, 2007.
Nabokov, Vladimir. *Lolita*. New York: Berkley Medallion Books, 1966.
Nabokov, Vladimir. *Speak, Memory*. In *The Portable Nabokov*, 3rd ed., edited by Page Stegner. New York: Viking, 1973.
Nietzsche, Friedrich. *Beyond Good and Evil*. In *The Philosophy of Nietzsche*. New York: Modern Library, 1954.
Nouwen, Henri J. M. *The Wounded Healer: Ministry in Contemporary Society*. New York: Doubleday, 1979.
Nuland, Sherwin. *How We Die: Reflections on Life's Final Chapter*. New York: Vintage, 1993.
Nussbaum, Martha C. "Dr. True Self." *The New Republic*, October 27, 2003.
Obholzer, Karin. *The Wolf-Man: Conversations with Freud's Patient—Sixty Years Later*, translated by Michael Shaw. London: Routledge & Kegan Paul, 1982.
Orcutt, Candace. "Masud Khan: The Outrageous Chapter 4." *The Psychoanalytic Review* 106 (2019): 489–508.
Ornstein, Paul. *Looking Back: Memoir of a Psychoanalyst*. With Helen Epstein. Lexington, MA: Plunkett Lake Press, 2015.
Ovid. *The Metamorphoses*, 2nd ed., translated by Anthony S. Kline. CreateSpace Independent Publishing Platform, 2014.

Paskauskas, R. Andrew, ed. *The Complete Correspondence of Sigmund Freud and Ernest Jones: 1908–1939*. Introduction by Riccardo Steiner. Cambridge, MA: Belknap Press of Harvard University Press, 1995.

Phillips, Adam. *Becoming Freud: The Making of a Psychoanalyst*. New Haven, CT: Yale University Press, 2014.

Phillips, Adam. *Darwin's Worms: On Life Stories and Death Stories*. New York: Basic Books, 1999.

Phillips, Adam. *Monogamy*. New York: Random House, 1996.

Phillips, Adam. *Side Effects*. New York: HarperCollins, 2006.

Phillips, Adam. *Winnicott*. Cambridge, MA: Harvard University Press, 1988.

Pickering, George. *Creative Malady: Illness in the Lives and Minds of Charles Darwin, Florence Nightingale, Mary Baker Eddy, Sigmund Freud, Marcel Proust, and Elizabeth Barrett Browning*. New York: Delta, 1974, rpt. 1976.

Plath, Sylvia. *The Bell Jar*. 1963; rpt. New York: Harper and Row, 1971.

Plath, Sylvia. *The Collected Poems*, edited by Ted Hughes. New York: Harper and Row, 1981.

Plath, Sylvia. *The Journals of Sylvia Plath*, edited by Frances McCullough. New York: Dial Press, 1982.

Plath, Sylvia. *Letters Home*, edited by Aurelia Schober Plath. New York: Harper and Row, 1975.

Raab, Kelley A. "Creativity and Transcendence in the Work of Marion Milner." *American Imago* 57 (2000): 185–214.

Rancour-Lafferiere, Daniel, ed. *Self-Analysis in Literary Study: Exploring Hidden Agendas*. New York: New York University Press, 1994.

Rangell, Leo. *My Life in Theory*, edited by Fred Busch. New York: Other Press, 2004.

Rank, Otto. "Active and Passive Therapy." 1935. In Rank, Otto. *A Psychology of Difference: The American Lectures*, edited by Robert Kramer. Foreword by Rollo May. Princeton, NJ: Princeton University Press, 1996.

Razinsky, Liran. "Psychoanalysis and Autobiography: Leiris, Freud and the Obstacle to Self-Knowledge." *Journal of Modern Literature* 44 (2020): 129–47.

Reik, Theodor. *Fragment of a Great Confession: A Psychoanalytic Autobiography*. New York: Farrar Strauss, 1949; rpt. New York: Citadel Press, 1965.

Remnick, David. "When He Was Good: A Life of Philip Roth." *The New Yorker*, March 29, 2021.

"Review of *The Last Good Freudian*." *Kirkus Reviews*, March 15, 2000. https://www.Kirkusreviews.com/book-reviews/brenda-webster-the-last-good-freudian, accessed August 25, 2020.

Rieff, David. *Swimming in a Sea of Death: A Son's Memoir*. New York: Simon & Schuster, 2008.

Riviere, Joan. "A Character Trait of Freud's." In *Psycho-Analysis and Contemporary Thought*, edited by John D. Sutherland. Introduction by Sylvia Payne, 145–9. London: The Hogarth Press, 1953.

Roazen, Paul. "An Author's Reexamination: Helene Deutsch: A Psychoanalyst's Life." *Psychoanalytic Psychology* 21 (2004): 622–32.

Roazen, Paul. *Brother Animal: The Story of Freud and Tausk*. New York: Knopf, 1969.

Roazen, Paul. *Freud and His Followers*. 1975. New York: New American Library, 1976.

Roazen, Paul. *Helene Deutsch: A Psychoanalyst's Life*. New York: Anchor Press/Doubleday, 1985.

Roazen, Paul. *The Historiography of Psychoanalysis*. New Brunswick, NJ: Transaction Publishers, 2001.

Roazen, Paul. *Meeting Freud's Family*. Amherst: University of Massachusetts Press, 1993.
Roazen, Paul. "Review of *The Long Wait*." *Psychoanalytic Books* 2 (1991): 19–25.
Rodman, Robert F. "Architecture and the True Self." *The Annual of Psychoanalysis* 33 (2005): 57–66.
Rodman, Robert F. *Keeping Hope Alive: On Becoming a Psychotherapist*. Foreword by Robert Coles. Cambridge: Harper & Row, 1986.
Rodman, Robert F. "Leo Rangell and the Integrity of Psychoanalysis." In *The Psychoanalytic Core: Essays in Honor of Leo Rangell, M.D.*, edited by Harold P. Blum, Edward M. Weinshel, and F. Robert Rodman, 15–43, Madison, CT: International Universities Press, 1989.
Rodman, Robert F. *Not Dying: A Psychoanalyst's Memoir of His Wife's Death*. New York: Random House, 1977.
Rodman, Robert F. *The Spontaneous Gesture: Selected Letters of D. W. Winnicott*. Cambridge, MA: Harvard University Press, 1987.
Rodman, Robert F. *Winnicott: Life and Work*. Cambridge, MA: Da Capo Press, 2003.
Rogers, Carl. "Autobiography." In *A History of Psychology in Autobiography*, edited by Edwin G. Boring and Gardner Lindzey, Vol. 5, 341–84. New York: Appleton-Century-Crofts, 1967.
Rose, Gilbert J. "Review of *The Suppressed Madness of Sane Men*." *Psychoanalytic Books* 2 (1991): 127–32.
Rubenstein, Roberta. *The Novelistic Vision of Doris Lessing: Breaking the Forms of Consciousness*. Urbana: University of Illinois Press, 1979.
Rudnytsky, Peter L. *Psychoanalytic Conversations: Interviews with Clinicians, Commentators, and Critics*. Hillsdale, NJ: The Analytic Press, 2000.
Rudnytsky, Peter L. *Reading Psychoanalysis: Freud, Rank, Ferenczi, Groddeck*. Ithaca, NY: Cornell University Press, 2002.
Sachs, Hanns. *Freud: Master and Friend*. Cambridge, MA: Harvard University Press, 1944; rpt. Books for Libraries Press, 1970.
Sacks, Michael. "Review of *Final Analysis*." *Journal of the American Psychoanalytic Association* 41 (1993): 306–9.
Sacks, Oliver. "Not Dying." *Web of Stories*, October 2, 2012.
Salinger, J. D. *The Catcher in the Rye*. New York: Little Brown, 1951; rpt. Bantam: 1963.
Samuels, Andrew. "Introduction: Jung and the Post-Freudians." In *The Cambridge Companion to Jung*, edited by Polly Young-Eisendrath and Terence Dawson, 1–13. Cambridge: Cambridge University Press, 1997.
Sandler, Paulo Cesar. "Bion's War Memoirs: A Psychoanalytical Commentary: Living Experiences and Learning from Them: Some Early Roots of Bion's Contributions to Psychoanalysis." In *Building on Bion: Roots*, edited by Robert M. Lipgar and Malcolm Pines, 59–84. London: Jessica Kingsley Publishers, 2003.
Sayers, Janet. "Intersubjective Winnicott." *American Imago* 61 (2004): 519–25.
Sayers, Janet. *Mothers of Psychoanalysis: Helene Deutsch, Karen Horney, Anna Freud, Melanie Klein*. New York: Norton, 1991.
Schachter, Joseph. "Psychotherapy: Lives Intersecting." *Contemporary Psychoanalysis* 48 (2012): 418–22.
Schickel, Richard. "Calling It as They See It." *Los Angeles Times*, April 14, 2002. https://www.latimes.com/archives/la-xpm-2002-apr-14-bk-schickel14-story.html, accessed August 30, 2020.
Schiffer, Irvine. *Charisma: A Psychoanalytic Look at Mass Society*. Toronto: University of Toronto Press, 1973.

Schiffer, Irvine. *The Trauma of Time: A Psychoanalytic Investigation*. New York: International Universities Press, 1978.
Schur, Max. *Freud: Living and Dying*. New York: International Universities Press, 1972.
Schwabacher, Ethel. *Arshile Gorky*. New York: Macmillan, 1957.
Schwabacher, Ethel. *Hungry for Light: The Journal of Ethel Schwabacher*, edited by Brenda S. Webster and Judith Emlyn Johnson. Bloomington, IN: Indiana University Press, 1993.
Schwartz, Murray M. "Psychoanalysis in My Life: An Intellectual Memoir." *American Imago* 75 (2018): 125–52.
Sedgwick, David. "Winnicott's Dream: Some Reflections on D. W. Winnicott and C. G. Jung." *Journal of Analytical Psychology* 53 (2008): 543–60.
Seelye, Katharine Q. "Janet Malcolm, Provocative Journalist with a Piercing Eye, Dies at 86." *New York Times*, June 17, 2021.
Selzman, Lisa Jennifer. "Review of *The Last Good Freudian*." *New York Times*, May 21, 2000.
Shapiro, Rhoda. "A Case Study: The Terminal Illness and Death of the Analyst's Mother—Its Effect on Her Treatment of a Severely Regressed Patient." *Modern Psychoanalysis* 10 (1985): 31–46.
Shengold, Leonard. "The Freud/Jung Letters." In *Freud and His Self-Analysis*, edited by Mark Kanzer and Jules Glenn, 187–201. New York: Jason Aronson, 1979.
Shengold, Leonard. *Is There Life without Mother?: Psychoanalysis, Biography, Creativity*. Hillsdale, NJ: The Analytic Press, 2000.
Shneidman, Edwin. "Foreword." In *Survivors of Suicide*, edited by Albert C. Cain. Springfield: Charles C. Thomas, 1972.
Silverstein, Barry. "Review of *Living in the Shadow of the Freud Family*." *American Imago* 65 (2008): 152–60.
Simon, Rich. "The Top 10 Most Influential Therapists of the Past Quarter-Century." *Psychotherapy Networker*, March/April 2007. https://www.psychotherapynetworker.org/magazine/article/661/the...
Slater, Lauren. *Lying: A Metaphorical Memoir*. New York: Random House, 2000.
Smith, Dinitia. "Love Is Strange: The Crusading Feminist and the Repentant Womanizer." *New York*, March 22, 1993.
Smith, Robert C. *The Wounded Jung: Effects of Jung's Relationships on His Life and Work*. Chicago, IL: Northwestern University Press, 1996.
Souter, K. M. "Some Origins of the Thought of W. R. Bion." *International Journal of Psychoanalysis* 90 (2009): 795–808.
Spence, Donald J. *Narrative Truth and Historical Truth: Meaning and Interpretation in Psychoanalysis*. New York: Norton, 1984.
Spiegel, Maura and Danielle Spencer. "Accounts of Self: Exploring Relationality Through Literature." In *The Principles and Practice of Narrative Medicine*, edited by Rita Charon, Sayantani Dasgupta, Nellie Hermann, Craig Irvine, Eric R. Marcus, Edgar Rivera Colon, Danielle Spencer, and Maura Spiegel, 15–36. New York: Oxford University Press, 2017.
Sprengnether, Madelon. *Crying at the Movies: A Film Memoir*. Saint Paul, MN: Graywolf Press, 2002.
Sprengnether, Madelon. "Enforcing Oedipus: Freud and Dora." In *The (M)other Tongue: Essays in Feminist Psychoanalytic Interpretation*, edited by Shirley Nelson Garner, Claire Kahane, and Madelon Sprengnether, 51–71. Ithaca, NY: Cornell University Press, 1985.

Sprengnether, Madelon. "Ghost Writing: A Meditation on Literary Criticism as Narrative." In *The Psychoanalytic Study of Literature*, edited by Joseph Reppen and Maurice Charney, 37–49. Hillsdale, NJ: The Analytic Press, 1985.

Sprengnether, Madelon. *Great River Road: Memoir and Memory*. Moorhead, MN: New Rivers Press, 2015.

Sprengnether, Madelon. *Mourning Freud*. New York: Bloomsbury Academic, 2018.

Sprengnether, Madelon. *Rivers, Stories, Houses, Dreams*. Drawings by C. D. O'Hare. St. Paul, MN: New Rivers Press, 1983.

Sprengnether, Madelon. *The Spectral Mother: Freud, Feminism, and Psychoanalysis*. Ithaca, NY: Cornell University Press, 1990.

Stekel, Wilhelm. *The Autobiography of Wilhelm Stekel: The Life Story of a Pioneer Psychoanalyst*, edited by Emil A. Gutheil, Introduction by Hilda Stekel. New York: Liveright, 1950.

Stekel, Wilhelm. *Impotence in the Male: The Psychic Disorders of Sexual Function in the Male*. Authorized English Version by Oswald H. Boltz, 2 Vols. New York: Liveright, 1927.

Stekel, Wilhelm. "On the History of the Analytical Movement." In *The Self-Marginalization of Wilhelm Stekel: Freudian Circles Inside and Out*, edited by Jaap Bos and Leendert Groenendijk, 131–62. New York: Springer, 2007.

Stekel, Wilhelm. *Psychoanalysis and Suggestion Therapy: Their Technique, Applications, Results, Limits, Dangers, and Excesses*, translated by James S. Van Teslaar. London: Kegan Paul, Trench, Trubner, 1923.

Sterba, Richard. *Reminiscences of a Viennese Psychoanalyst*. Detroit: Wayne State University Press, 1982.

Stevens, Anthony. *Jung: A Brief Insight*. New York: Sterling, 1994.

Storr, Anthony. *C. G. Jung*. New York: Viking, 1973.

Sulloway, Frank J. *Freud: Biologist of the Mind*. New York: Basic Books, 1979.

Szucs, Suzanne. "Book Review: *Crying at the Movies*." July 9, 2003. https://www.mnartists.org/article/book-review-crying-movies-madelon-sprengnether, accessed August 20, 2020.

Teusch, Rita K. "A Biographical Sketch of Felix Deutsch." *American Imago* 74 (2017): 519–24.

Thomas, D. M. *The White Hotel*. New York: Viking, 1981.

Twain, Mark. *The Mark Twain-Howells Lectures*, edited by Henry Nash Smith and William M. Gilson, 2 Vols. Cambridge, MA: Harvard University Press, 1960,

Valantin, Simone. "Berta Bornstein." *Encyclopedia.Com*. https://www.encyclopedia.com/psychology/dictionaries-thesauruses-pictures-and-press-releases/Bornstein-berta-1899-1971, accessed August 18, 2020.

Van der Kolk, Bessel A. *The Body Keeps the Score: Brain, Mind, and Body in the Healing of Trauma*. New York: Penguin, 2014.

Waugaman, Richard A. "Review of *Mourning Freud*." *The Psychoanalytic Review* 88 (2020): 447–54.

Webster, Brenda. *Auschwitz: A Love Story*. San Antonio, TX: Wings Press, 2014.

Webster, Brenda. *Blake's Prophetic Psychology*. Athens, GA: University of Georgia Press, 1983.

Webster, Brenda. "Helene Deutsch: A New Look." *Signs: Journal of Women in Culture and Society* 10 (1985): 553–71.

Webster, Brenda. *The Last Good Freudian*. New York: Holmes & Meier, 2000.

Webster, Brenda. *Paradise Farm*. Albany, NY: State University of New York Press, 1999.

Webster, Brenda. *Sins of the Mothers*. Dallas, TX: Baskerville Publishers, 1993.
Webster, Brenda. *Vienna Triangle*. San Antonio, TX: Wings Press, 2009.
Webster, Brenda. *Yeats: A Psychoanalytic Study*. Stanford, CA: Stanford University Press, 1973.
Westerhof, Gerben J. "Life Review and Life-Story Work." *The Encyclopedia of Adulthood and Aging*, June 19, 2015. https://doi.org/10.1002/9781118521373.wbeaa209.
Whitebook, Joel. *Freud: An Intellectual Biography*. Cambridge: Cambridge University Press, 2017.
Wilde, Oscar. *The Artist as Critic: Critical Writings of Oscar Wilde*, edited by Richard Ellmann. New York: Random House, 1969.
Williams, Meg Harris. *Bion's Dream: A Reading of the Autobiographies*. London: Karnac, 2010.
Wilson, Edmund. *The Wound and the Bow: Seven Studies in Literature*. New York: Oxford University Press, 1947; rpt. 1965.
Winnicott, D. W. "Critical Notice of *On Not Being Able to Paint*." *British Journal of Medical Psychology*. 1951; rpt. in *Art, Creativity, Living*, edited by Leslie Caldwell, 117–19. London: Karnac, 2000.
Winnicott, D. W. "D. W. W.'s Dream Related to Reviewing Jung." In *Psycho-Analytic Explorations*, edited by Clare Winnicott, Ray Shepherd, and Madeleine Davis, 228–30. Cambridge, MA: Harvard University Press, 1989.
Winnicott, D. W. "Review of *Memories, Dreams, Reflections*." *International Journal of Psycho-Analysis* 45 (1964): 450–55.
Winter, Alison. *Memory: Fragments of a Modern History*. Chicago, IL: University of Chicago Press, 2012.
Wittels, Fritz. *Freud and His Time*, translated by Louise Brink. New York: Grosset & Dunlap, 1931.
Wittels, Fritz. "Revision of a Biography." *The Psychoanalytic Review* 20 (1933): 361–74.
Wittels, Fritz. *Sigmund Freud: His Personality, His Teaching, and His School*, translated by Eden and Cedar Paul. London: Allen and Unwin, 1924.
The Wolf-Man. *The Wolf-Man by the Wolf-Man*, edited, with notes, an introduction, and chapters by Muriel Gardiner. New York: Basic Books, 1971.
Woodward, Kathleen. "Between Mourning and Melancholia: Roland Barthes's *Camera Lucinda*." In *Aging and Its Discontents: Freud and Other Fictions*, edited by Kathleen Woodward, 110–29. Bloomington, IN: Indiana University Press, 1991.
Woolf, Virginia. *A Room of One's Own*. San Diego, CA: Harcourt Brace Jovanovich, 1929.
Worden, J. William. *Grief Counseling and Grief Therapy: A Handbook for the Mental Health Practitioner*, 3rd ed. New York: Springer, 2002.
Wortis, Joseph. *Fragments of an Analysis with Freud*. New York: McGraw-Hill, 1975.
"Wounded Healer." *Wikipedia*. https://en.wikipedia.org/wiki/Wounded_healer, accessed January 13, 2021.
Wurmser, Léon. "Shame: The Veiled Companion of Narcissism." In *The Many Faces of Shame*, edited by Donald L. Nathanson, 64–92. New York: Guilford Press, 1987.
Yalom, Irvin D. *Becoming Myself: A Psychiatrist's Memoir*. New York: Basic Books, 2017.
Yalom, Irvin D. *Existential Psychotherapy*. New York: Basic Books, 1980.
Yalom, Irvin D. *The Gift of Therapy: An Open Letter to a New Generation of Therapists and Their Patients*. New York: HarperCollins, 2002.
Yalom, Irvin D. *Momma and the Meaning of Life: Tales of Psychotherapy*. New York: Basic Books, 1999.

Yalom, Irvin D. *The Schopenhauer Cure*. New York: Harper Perennial, 2006.
Yalom, Irvin D. *Staring at the Sun: Overcoming the Terror of Death*. San Francisco: Jossey-Bass, 2008.
Yalom, Irvin D. *The Theory and Practice of Group Psychotherapy*. New York: Basic Books, 1970. 4th ed., 1995; 5th ed., with Molyn Leszcz, 2005.
Yalom, Irvin D. and Ginny Elkin. *Every Day Gets a Little Closer: A Twice-Told Therapy*. New York: Basic Books, 1974.
Yalom, Irvin D. and Marilyn Yalom. *A Matter of Death and Life: Love, Loss, and What Matters in the End*. Palo Alto, CA: Redwood Press, 2021.
Yerushalmi, Yosef H. *Freud's Moses: Judaism Terminable and Interminable*. New Haven, CT: Yale University Press, 1993.
Young-Bruehl, Elisabeth. *Anna Freud: A Biography*. New York: Summit Books, 1988.
Young-Bruehl, Elisabeth. *Subject to Biography: Psychoanalysis, Feminism, and Writing Women's Lives*. Cambridge, MA: Harvard University Press, 1998.
Zinsser, William, ed. *Inventing the Truth: The Art and Craft of Memoir*. Revised and expanded ed. Boston: Houghton Mifflin, 1998.

INDEX

Abraham, Karl   45, 47, 87
Adler, Alfred   19, 20, 54, 59, 87, 88, 115
alpha and beta elements   96, 103
Altman, Neil   96
altruistic surrender   221
ambivalence   3, 5, 9, 14, 21, 31, 35–42,
    49, 51–2, 58, 60, 69, 73, 78, 87,
    101, 110, 163–4, 176, 181, 217,
    224, 229–30, 234
amor fati (love of fate)   72
anima and animus   73, 86, 90
anti-psychiatry movement   38, 146
anti-Semitism   12, 57, 135–40
archetype   72–4, 88, 91
attachment theory   181
Attenborough, Richard   205
Atwood, Margaret   8
Auden, W.H.   113

Bair, Deidre   80, 92
Balsam, Rosemary   106
Banville, John   180–1
Barthes, Roland   228
Bayley, John   172, 233
Beck, Aaron   3
Beckett, Samuel   95
Beers, Clifford   39
Beidler, Peter G.   70
Berman, Jeffrey
    The Art of Caregiving in Fiction, Film, and Memoir   233
    Companionship in Grief   172, 212
    Dying in Character   128
    Joseph Conrad: Writing as Rescue   112
    Mad Muse   4–5
    Norman N. Holland: The Dean of American Psychoanalytic Literary Critics   7
    The Talking Cure   28, 37, 191

Writing the Talking Cure: Irvin D. Yalom and the Literature of Psychotherapy   230
Writing Widowhood   172
Berman, Jeffrey and Paul W. Mosher
    Off the Tracks: Cautionary Tales about the Derailing of Mental Health Care   67, 147
Bernays, Minna   84
Bettelheim, Bruno   89
Beuscher, Ruth   206
bibliotherapy   36, 57, 235
binary thinking   5, 17, 27, 71, 93, 124
Bion, Wilfred   6, 95–107, 158, 212, 230
    All My Sins Remembered   95, 99, 103–6
    Attention and Interpretation   107
    Clinical Seminars and Other Writings   106
    Cogitations   98
    Experiences in Groups and Other Papers   96, 103
    The Long Week-End, 1897–1919   95, 98, 100, 103
    A Memoir of the Future   95, 98–100, 103–6
    War Memoirs, 1917–19   6, 95–107
Birken, Andrew   205
Birkerts, Sven   1, 237
Blackett, Patrick   115–16, 124
Blake, William   117
Blanchot, Maurice   161
Bleuler, Eugen   9, 60
Bloom, Harold   10, 22, 137
Blumenthal, Ralph   143
Blunden, Edmund   105
Bollas, Christopher   132, 140–1
Bonaparte, Marie   182
Borch-Jacobsen, Mikkel   12, 20
borderline personality disorder   183

Boring, Edwin   2
Bornstein, Berta   194–5
Bos, Jaap   65
boundary violations   30, 150
Bowlby, John   181
Boynton, Robert S.   139, 157–8
Breger, Louis   6, 14, 20, 57, 61, 79, 82, 83, 175–88, 230, 235
   The Book of Barbara   6, 186–7
   Dostoevsky: The Author as Psychoanalyst   176
   A Dream of Undying Fame   180, 187
   Freud: Darkness in the Midst of Vision   20, 177–8, 180, 186–7
   Freud's Unfinished Journey   180
   Psychotherapy Lives Intersecting   6, 175, 181–6
Breuer, Josef   9, 14–15, 20, 179, 180, 233
Briehl, Marie H.   42
Brunswick, Ruth Mack   5, 25, 28, 33–6, 39, 85

Cain, Albert C.   164
Caldwell, Leslie   127, 189
Cameron, D. Ewen   147
Campion, Jane   204
Carotenuto, Aldo   85–6
Carrere, Robert A.   185
castration fear   26, 29, 33, 35, 60–1, 115, 211, 231
Celenza, Andrea.   67
Cézanne, Paul   118
Charcot, Jean-Martin   58
Charles, Marilyn   128
Charon, Rita   91
Chodorow, Nancy C.   20
Clark, Ronald W.   11
Clarke, Terence   232
collective unconscious   74, 77, 91
complicated grief   51–2
Conrad, Joseph   8, 43, 110–12
"continuing bonds"   212–13
Couser, G. Thomas   5
"creative illness"   16, 92
Crews, Frederick   178, 197
Cross, Shelley Ann   212
Csikszentmihalyi, Mihaly   114
Curtis, Rebecca   183, 185

Da Vinci, Leonardo   16–18
Davis, Douglas A.   80
death instinct   63, 101
deconstruction   209
Delboeuf, Joseph   10
De Man, Paul   209
derealization   39
Derrida, Jacques   22
Deutsch, Felix   45–6, 48, 52, 149
Deutsch, Helene   5, 12, 41–52, 57, 190, 199–200, 222, 224, 230
   Confrontations with Myself   5, 41–52
   "Freud and His Pupils"   47
   Neurosis and Character Types   190
   A Psychoanalytic Study of the Myth of Dionysus and Apollo   12
   The Psychology of Women   41, 50
   Selected Problems of Adolescence   51
   The Therapeutic Process, the Self, and Female Psychology   48
   "A Two-Year-Old Boy's First Love Comes to Grief"   50–1
Deutsch, Martin   49–51
Diagnostic and Statistical Manual of Mental Disorders (DSM)   152, 225
Dickens, Charles   18, 43, 144
Didion, Joan   172, 204, 235, 236
"Don Juan complex"   65, 154
Dostoevsky, Fyodor   31, 35, 36, 168, 176–7, 182, 187
Dragstedt, Naomi Rader   127
Dryden, John   118
Dunne, Edward J.   193
Dunne, John Gregory   204

Eagleton, Terry   209
Edmundson, Mark   210
ego psychology   198
Ehrlich, Robert   105
Eissler, K.R.   143, 145, 148, 195–6
Eliot, George   88
Eliot, T.S.   117, 132, 138
Ellenberger, Henri F.   15–16, 60, 92, 93
Ellmann, Maud   7–8, 115
Elms, Alan C.   80–1
Emerson, Ralph Waldo   8
empathy   59, 103, 122, 153, 171, 180, 226
end-of-life memoir   128, 227–8, 230

Epstein, Mark   123
Erikson, Erik H.   4, 9, 132, 191

"father-hunger"   73, 84, 206
Ferenczi, Sándor   19, 20, 27, 39, 82, 85, 179
Fiedler, Leslie   138
Fike, Matthew   89
Fitzgerald, F. Scott   159, 164, 168
Flax, Michelle   167
Fliess, Wilhelm   13, 14, 16, 19, 79, 83–4, 144–5, 179, 210
flow experience   114, 187
Foley, Jack   197
folie à deux   33
Forster, E.M.   113
"fort/da" ritual   210
Fowles, John   97
France, Peter   55
Frank, Arthur W.   72
free association   27, 73, 113, 116, 148, 185, 202
free drawing   114, 119
free writing   113–14, 125
Freud, Anna   6, 25, 26, 41, 48–9, 85, 118, 132, 135–6, 138, 143–8, 196, 217, 220–2, 235
Freud, Ernestine ("Esti")   6, 215–20, 222–8
Freud, Martha   10, 11, 13, 179, 223
Freud, Martin   6, 84, 215–20, 224, 226
Freud, Sigmund
  "Address Delivered in the Goethe House at Frankfurt"   10
  "Address to the Society of B'nai B'rith"   19
  "Analysis Terminable and Interminable"   9, 190–1
  An Autobiographical Study   5, 9–23, 62, 72, 87
  Beyond the Pleasure Principle   101, 209–10
  "A Child Is Being Beaten"   61
  "'Civilized' Sexual Morality and Modern Nervous Illness"   60
  The Complete Letters of Sigmund Freud to Wilhelm Fliess, 1887– 1904   13, 14, 19, 144–5
  "Contributions to a Discussion of Masturbation"   60–1
  "Delusions and Dreams in Jensen's *Gradiva*"   22
  "Dostoevsky and Parricide"   176
  Fragment of an Analysis of a Case of Hysteria   4, 12, 21, 27, 147, 201, 236
  From the History of an Infantile Neurosis   25–9
  The Interpretation of Dreams   10–13, 18, 22, 39, 58, 60, 63, 179
  Leonardo da Vinci and a Memory of His Childhood   16–18
  Moses and Monotheism   145–6
  "Mourning and Melancholia"   163, 206, 210
  New Introductory Lectures on Psycho-Analysis   46, 92
  "On Dreams"   10
  "On Narcissism: An Introduction"   151
  "On the History of the Psycho-Analytic Movement"   14–16, 21, 68, 87, 180
  "Psychoanalysis: Freudian School"   88
  The Psychopathology of Everyday Life   15, 22
  "Screen Memories"   211
Freud, Sophie   6–7, 158, 192, 215–28, 230
  Living in the Shadow of the Freud Family   6, 215–28
  My Three Mothers and Other Passions   215, 218–21, 224, 227
  "Passion as a Mental Health Hazard"   192
Freud, Walter (Anton)   216, 220, 225–7
"Freudian slip"   45, 127, 148, 211
"fundamental rule" of psychoanalysis   185
Fussell, Paul   105

Gabbard, Glen O.   85
Gardiner, Muriel   25, 28, 29, 32, 34, 35, 37, 195, 197
Gay, Peter   15, 46, 53, 57, 61, 79, 82, 84, 177, 179
Gedo, John   90

Gifford, Sanford   46
Gilbert, Sandra M.   106, 125
Gilman, Sander L.   19, 140, 145, 180
Givelber, Frances   166–7
Glover, Edward   71
Godley, Boynton   139
Goethe, Johan Wolfgang von   8, 10, 23, 36, 72, 88, 211
Gordon, James S.   158
Gorky, Arshile   189
Green, André   123
Groddeck, Georg   11–12
Grosskurth, Phyllis   104
Grotjahn, Martin   140
Grotstein, James   95, 106
Guarton, Gladys Branly   140
Gubar, Susan   125
Gutheil, Emil A.   54, 56, 68

Hadler, Mona   190
Halberstadt, Sophie Freud   30
Hale, Nathan G.   20
Haneke, Michael   233
H.D. (Hilda Doolittle)   4
Hemingway, Ernest   97, 101
Herman, Judith Lewis   202
Hirschmüller, Albrecht   14
Holland, Norman N.   7, 202
Homans, Peter   80, 89, 210
homophobia   69, 136
homosexuality   56, 59, 79–80, 83, 225
Hopkins, Linda   132–40
Horney, Karen   41, 222
Horowitz, Mardi   52

identification with the aggressor   135
Ilahi, M. Nasir   170
incest   62, 77–8, 145, 205, 211
intellectualization   207

Jacobus, Mary   121
Jaffé, Aniela   71–2
James, Henry   18, 205
James, William   17
Jensen, Wilhelm   22, 47
Johnson, Samuel   107, 236
Jones, Ernest   5, 18, 20, 27, 30, 32, 33, 35, 53, 54, 57, 64, 67, 82–3, 163, 164, 177, 180

Joyce, James   7–8, 22, 73
Jung, C.G.   3, 5–6, 9, 17, 19–20, 27, 54, 62, 64, 71–93, 112, 115, 117, 121, 179
  Black Book and *Red Book*   89–90
  Memories, Dreams, Reflections   1, 71–93, 119, 133
  "In Memory of Sigmund Freud"   88
  Two Essays on Analytical Psychology   74, 121

Kahr, Brett   162
Kalson, Sally   222
Kardiner, A.   4, 59
Keats, John   106, 113, 114, 117
Kernberg, Otto   153
Khan, Masud R.   6, 127, 131–41, 148, 230
  Alienations in Perversions   132, 136
  Hidden Selves   132, 133, 136
  The Long Wait   6, 131–41, 143
  The Privacy of the Self   136
Kieslowski, Krszsztof   205
Kirsner, Douglas   143
Klass, Dennis   212–13
Klein, Melanie   41, 95, 101, 104, 106, 110, 113, 135, 136, 166, 170, 222
Kohut, Heinz   7, 153, 166
Koller, Carl   11
Kraepelin, Emil   26
Kramer, Robert   38
Kris, Ernst   191
Kris, Marianne   168, 190–1

Laing, R.D.   89, 146
Larson, Thomas   5
Lasch, Christopher   66
Lawrence, D.H.   8, 112, 121, 198
Lehrman, Philip R.   70
Lesser, Michael   204
Lessing, Doris   89–90
Letley, Emma   117–18, 126
Lewis, C.S.   172, 205
libido theory   50, 61, 84, 164
Lieberman, E. James   38
life review   105, 223–4, 235
Lindner, Robert   7
Lindzey, Gardner   2, 4
Lodge, David   32–3
Loewald, Hans   105, 211–12

Loewenstein, Andrea Freud   138, 218, 222–3
Loewenstein, George   222, 225
Loftus, Elizabeth   146
Ludwig, Otto   69–70

MacKinnon, Catherine A.   146, 156
Maeder, Thomas   51
Maenchen, Anna   196–7
magical thinking   204, 235
Magidson, Stefania   9, 161, 172–4
Mahony, Patrick J.   22
Mailer, Susan   7
Makari, George   62
Malcolm, Janet   18, 140, 144, 156–8
Mantel, Hilary   8, 69
Marchand, Philip   152, 155
Marcus, Laura   1, 5
Margolick, David   157
masochism   42, 55, 80, 166, 190
Mason, Albert   106
Masson, Jeffrey Moussaieff   6, 138, 143, 159, 195, 230
   Against Therapy   147, 158
   The Assault on Truth   138, 145–7, 156–9
   A Dark Science: Women, Sexuality, and Psychiatry in the Nineteenth Century   146
   Final Analysis   6, 143–58
   My Father's Guru   154–8
   Slipping into Paradise   158–9
   When Elephants Weep   159
masturbation   60–2, 65–6
McCarthy, James B.   134
McGuire, William   84, 86
Meltzer, Donald   106
"memory wars"   211
Menaker, Esther   7, 221–2
Meng, Heinrich   23
Merton, Robert   12
Meyers, Linda I.   7
Milner, Marion   6, 74, 109–29, 132, 135, 230, 236
   Bothered by Alligators   109–10, 115–16, 125–8
   Eternity's Sunrise   109, 111, 113, 120, 123–5

   An Experiment in Leisure   109, 114–17, 124
   The Hands of the Living God   109–10, 118, 120–3, 132
   The Human Problems in Schools   117–18, 124
   A Life of One's Own   109–16, 119, 122, 135
   On Not Being Able to Paint   6, 109, 117–21, 126–7, 132
   The Suppressed Madness of Sane Men   114, 128
Minuchin, Salvador   3
Misch, Georg   5
Molnar, Michael   17, 217
Money, Jennifer   198
Moore, Marianne   168
Morley, Robert   149

Nabokov, Vladimir   28, 237–8
narcissistic personality disorder   152–3
narrative medicine   91
negative capability   113–14, 211
nekyia   90
Nietzsche, Friedrich   8, 10, 11, 14, 18, 23, 66, 72, 126, 199, 231, 233
Nouwen, Henri J.M.   71–2
Nuland, Sherwin   237
Nussbaum, Martha C.   169

Obholzer, Karin   26, 28–9, 31, 33–40
object relations   96
Oedipus complex   21, 44, 59, 87, 145, 181, 201, 209
O'Flaherty, Wendy   157
omnipotence of thought   204
Orcutt, Candace   137
"originology"   191
Ornstein, Paul   7
"overloving"   219
Ovid   233

Paskauskas, R. Andrew   67
Paz, Octavio   168
"penis envy"   120, 145, 151, 196
Pfister, Oskar   23, 30
Phillips, Adam   21, 62, 132, 141, 176, 177, 179

Pickering, George   16, 92
Plath, Sylvia   18, 205–7
"*post-artem depression*"   37
postmodernism   35
posttraumatic stress disorder   79, 95
primal scene   26, 28–9, 33, 35, 149
projective identification   96, 113, 119, 135, 207
Proust, Marcel   22, 43
psychobiography   16–18

Raab, Kelley A.   128
Rancour-Laferriere, Daniel   213
Rangell, Leo   171
Rank, Otto   11, 19–20, 38–9, 172, 179, 238
Ray, Satyajit   203
Razinsky, Liran   8
"recovered memories" movement   146
Reik, Theodor   7, 8, 236
Remnick, David   17–18
repetition-compulsion principle   78–80, 100–2, 198, 209
"replacement child"   164
Richards, Val   128
Rieff, David   228
Rilke, Rainer Maria   120, 132, 158, 199
Riviere, Joan   167
Roazen, Paul   34–5, 41, 44–54, 61, 68, 69, 85, 89, 137, 192, 199, 220, 224, 225
Rodman, Robert C.   6, 127, 137, 141, 161–74, 187, 230, 233, 237
   "Architecture and the True Self"   171
   Keeping Hope Alive   162, 164, 169, 173
   Not Dying   6, 161–74, 237
   The Spontaneous Gesture: Selected Letters of D.W. Winnicott   161
   Winnicott   161–2, 166, 169–71, 173
Rogers, Carl   3–4, 38, 147
Rose, Gilbert J.   128–9
Rosen, John   147
Roth, Philip   17–18
Rousseau, Jean-Jacques   55, 66–7
Rubenstein, Roberta   89

Rudnytsky, Peter   11, 61–2, 85, 138
Rycroft, Charles   138, 231

Sachs, Hanns   13, 62
Sacks, Michael   158
Sacks, Oliver   172
sadism   36, 56, 80, 146, 166, 197
Salinger, J.D.   53, 69–70
Salomé, Lou-Andreas   199
Samuels, Andrew   80
Sandler, Paulo Cesar   96
Sayers, Janet   41
Schachter, Joseph   186
Schickel, Richard   208
Schiffer, Irvine   143, 148, 150–2, 154–6
Schopenhauer, Arthur   60, 231–4
Schur, Max   177
Schwabacher, Ethel   189–93
Schwartz, Delmore   222
Schwartz, Murray M   7
Sedgwick, David   91
"seduction theory"   27, 77, 138, 144, 145, 155, 195
Seelye, Katharine Q.   158
self-analysis   10, 22, 66, 85, 87, 90, 109, 114, 117, 119, 176, 178, 202, 209, 213, 217
Selzman, Lisa Jennifer   198
sexual abuse   27, 44, 78–80, 146
Shaffer, Peter   120
Shakespeare, William   22, 105, 106, 132, 188, 205, 206, 238
Shapiro, Rhoda   167
Shengold, Leonard   79, 83, 157
Shneidman, Edwin   34, 193, 194, 233
Silverstein, Barry   215
Simon, Rich   3
Slater, Laura   1
Smith, Dinitia   152
Smith, Robert C.   72–3
Sontag, Susan   228
Sorgenkind ("worry child")   218–19
Souter, K.M.   99
Spence, Donald J.   146
Spiegel, Maura   91
Spielrein, Sabina   85–6
spousal loss memoir   6–7, 161, 168, 170, 172, 230, 235

Sprengnether, Madelon 6, 201–13, 230
  Crying at the Movies 6, 200–9, 213, 230
  "Enforcing Oedipus: Freud and Dora" 201
  "Ghost Writing" 212–13
  Great River Road 206, 208–10, 213
  Mourning Freud 202, 209–12
  Rivers, Stories, Houses, Dreams 204
  The Spectral Mother 201–2, 210
Stekel, Wilhelm 5, 19, 20, 34, 53–70, 76, 230
  The Autobiography of Wilhelm Stekel 5, 53–70
  Impotence in the Male 56, 60, 65–9
  "On the History of the Analytical Movement" 68–9
  Psychoanalysis and Suggestion Therapy 70
Sterba, Richard 11, 69
Stevens, Anthony 72, 80
Stewart, Harold 127–8
Storr, Anthony 80
Strachey, James 15, 26, 61
Styron, William 90
sublimation 115
suicide 2, 13, 27, 33–9, 48, 54, 64, 68, 69, 78, 90, 112, 181, 183, 190–4, 199, 204, 206–7, 232–4
Sullivan, Harry Stack 184
Sulloway, Frank J. 15
Szasz, Thomas 38, 146
Szucs, Susanne 208

Talamo, Parthenope Bion 96, 99, 104
Tarkovsky, Andrei 204
Tausk, Victor 34, 48, 199
Terence 234
Teusch, Rita K. 46
therapeutic alliance 30, 122, 137, 196
therapist self-disclosure 2, 165–7, 185
Thomas, D.M. 82, 147
Thompson, Martina 128
Tolstoy, Leo 163
transference and countertransference 40, 64, 79, 86, 161, 173–4, 178, 186, 190
trickster narrative 211
Twain, Mark 18, 187

Valantin, Simone 194
Van der Kolk, Bessel A. 213
Virgil 12

Wagner, Richard 65, 89, 92
Walters, Margaret 125, 128
Watter, Daniel N. 230
Waugaman, Richard A. 212
Webster, Brenda 6, 42, 189–200, 230
  Auschwitz: A Love Story 194, 227
  Blake's Prophetic Psychology 198
  "Helene Deutsch: A New Look" 199
  The Last Good Freudian 6, 189, 193, 194, 197–8, 200
  Paradise Farm 189, 194, 197
  Sins of the Mothers 189, 193
  Vienna Triangle 199, 200
  Yeats: A Psychoanalytic Study 197
Weir, Peter 204
Westerhof, Gerben J. 223–4
Whitebook, Joel 81
Whitman, Walt 18, 23
wild analysis 56–7
Wilde, Oscar 8, 52, 132
Williams, Meg Harris 101
Wilson, Edmund 92
Winnicott, D.W. 62, 90–1, 110, 121, 123, 127, 128, 132–41, 161, 166, 169–70, 230
Winter, Alison 146
Wittels, Fritz 17, 58, 61, 63, 177
Wolff, Toni 73
Wolf-Man (Sergei Pankejeff) 5, 25–40
Woodward, Kathleen 210
Woolf, Virginia 8, 44, 110–11, 114, 125, 191, 194
Worden, J. William 212
Wortis, Joseph 4, 18, 54
"wounded healer" 71–2, 92, 166, 231
"writing/righting wrong" 106
Wurmser, Léon 101

Yalom, Irvin D. 3, 7, 14, 60, 166, 183, 230–8
  Becoming Myself 231, 237
  Every Day Gets a Little Closer 231
  Existential Psychotherapy 183, 231, 233
  The Gift of Therapy 231

Momma and the Meaning of Life 235
The Schopenhauer Cure 60, 231, 233, 234
Staring at the Sun 32
Yalom, Marilyn 230–8
Yerushalmi, Yosef H. 180

Young-Bruehl, Elisabeth 48, 144–5, 219, 225

Zinsser, William 1
Zweig, Arnold 17
Zweig, Stefan 17

www.ingramcontent.com/pod-product-compliance
Lightning Source LLC
Chambersburg PA
CBHW062124300426
44115CB00012BA/1807